The #MeToo Movement in Iran

Sex, Family and Culture in the Middle East Series

This innovative series explores the connections and influences impacting ideas about marriage, sexuality, and the family throughout history in the MENA region, and until the present day. Individual volumes consider the ancient, early Islamic, medieval, early modern, and contemporary periods to investigate how traditions and practices have evolved and interacted across time and countries.

Series Editors:

Janet Afary, Professor and Mellichamp Chair in Global Religion and Modernity, UC Santa Barbara

Claudia Yaghoobi, Roshan Institute Professor in Persian Studies and the director of the Center for the Middle East and Islamic Studies, The University of North Carolina at Chapel Hill

The #MeToo Movement in Iran

Reporting Sexual Violence and Harassment

Edited by
Claudia Yaghoobi

I.B. TAURIS
LONDON • NEW YORK • OXFORD • NEW DELHI • SYDNEY

I.B. TAURIS
Bloomsbury Publishing Plc
50 Bedford Square, London, WC1B 3DP, UK
1385 Broadway, New York, NY 10018, USA
29 Earlsfort Terrace, Dublin 2, Ireland

BLOOMSBURY, I.B. TAURIS and the I.B. Tauris logo are trademarks of Bloomsbury Publishing Plc

First published in Great Britain 2023
This paperback edition published in 2025

Copyright © Claudia Yaghoobi, 2023

Claudia Yaghoobi and contributors have asserted their right under the Copyright, Designs and Patents Act, 1988, to be identified as Authors of this work.

For legal purposes the Acknowledgments on p. ix constitute an extension of this copyright page.

Series design by Adriana Brioso
Cover image: Collage, Portraits, (1982–1987),
Sonia Balassanian, image courtesy of the artist

All rights reserved. No part of this publication may be reproduced or transmitted in any form or by any means, electronic or mechanical, including photocopying, recording, or any information storage or retrieval system, without prior permission in writing from the publishers.

Bloomsbury Publishing Plc does not have any control over, or responsibility for, any third-party websites referred to or in this book. All internet addresses given in this book were correct at the time of going to press. The author and publisher regret any inconvenience caused if addresses have changed or sites have ceased to exist, but can accept no responsibility for any such changes.

A catalogue record for this book is available from the British Library.

A catalog record for this book is available from the Library of Congress.

ISBN: HB: 978-0-7556-4725-5
PB: 978-0-7556-4729-3
ePDF: 978-0-7556-4726-2
eBook: 978-0-7556-4727-9

Series: Sex, Family and Culture in the Middle East

Typeset by Newgen KnowledgeWorks Pvt. Ltd., Chennai, India

To find out more about our authors and books visit www.bloomsbury.com and sign up for our newsletters.

For Jin, Jiyan, Azadi
For all the women and men who have been subjected to gender-based and/or sexual violence, sexual harassment, and rape
For Jina (Mahsa) Amini, Nika Shahkarami, Sarina Esmailzadeh, and many other women who fought and died for freedom
For Nika Shahkarami, a sixteen-year-old teenager who disappeared on September 20, 2022, during the protests in Iran following Jina Amini's death. Ten days later, the news of her death spread. Her death involved violence, torture, and possibly rape by the Islamic regime's security forces in detention
For Armita Abbasi, and all dissident women and men and queer people, who have been/are systemically being tortured and raped in Iran's prisons

Contents

Acknowledgments	ix
Note on Transliteration and Translation	x
Prologue: #MeToo Movement and Redefining the Private Sphere *Ziba Jalali Naini*	xi
Introduction: Bodies, Spaces, and Places *Claudia Yaghoobi*	1
1 Like a Wrapped Chocolate: The Islamic Republic's Politics of Hijab and the Normalization of Sexual Harassment *Esha Momeni*	11
2 The Iranian #MeToo and the Double Bind of Iranian Feminism: Between Religion, the Global Gender Struggle, and Liberal Feminism *Dilyana Mincheva and Niloofar Hooman*	23
3 Rhetorical Listening to the Iranian #MeToo Movement in Diaspora *Yalda N. Hamidi*	39
4 Structural and Material Considerations and the Nexus of Power and Sexuality in the Iranian #MeToo Movement *Mahdi Tourage*	53
5 Twitter Data Analysis on #MeTooIran *Yasamin Rezai and Mehdy Sedaghat Payam*	71
6 #Unveiling_the_Iranian_MeToo: Symptomatic Reading of Iranian MeToo through the Lens of Political Economy *Paria Rahimi*	89
7 Whose Voice Is Missing? MeToo Digital Storytelling on Instagram and the Politics of Inclusion *Golnar Gishnizjani*	107
8 Sexual Violence, MeToo, and Iranian Lesbians' Censored Voices *Mahdis Sadeghipouya*	123

9 The White-Collars' New Masculinities in #MeToo: How to
   Maintain Gendered Privileges?   135
   Somayeh Rostampour

10 *Hush! Girls Don't Scream* (2013) by Puran Derakhshandeh and the
   #MeToo Movement in Iran   149
   Maryam Zehtabi

Afterword: Patriarchalism, Male Abuse, and the Sources of the #MeToo
Movement in the Muslim Middle East   161
   Roger Friedland, Janet Afary, and Charlotte Hoppen

Notes   205
Bibliography   251
List of Contributors   281
Index   287

Acknowledgments

The idea for this book emerged out of my desire to support survivors of sexual assault and rape in the ways I could and with the capacities I had. When, in 2020, the courageous survivors came forward with their narratives of being subjected to such heinous sexual crimes, they were largely gaslit and their narratives invalidated by the accused who still dominated positions of power. To stand in solidarity with the survivors, I decided to invite contributors to write and document these narratives. Hence, I owe tremendous gratitude not only to the survivors for their courage in breaking their silence but also to all my colleagues in this volume, who, regardless of the taxing task of writing about sexual harassment and rape, welcomed my invitation. However, the work would not have been possible without the support and encouragement of many colleagues and friends who in one way or another helped me. For that, I am indebted to them. I would also like to thank the University of North Carolina, Chapel Hill, Institute for the Arts and Humanities Publication Support Grant, which allowed me to complete this book. Similarly, I offer my regards to the editorial board at IB Tauris, external reviewers, and administrative staff.

Note on Transliteration and Translation

For transliteration, we have tried to use the *International Journal of Middle East Studies* system (IJMES) for Persian. However, common or established pronunciation has guided how certain names and terms appear in the manuscript. Similarly, for direct quotations, the original transliteration has been used. Hence, readers might note some inconsistency. All translations, summaries, and paraphrasing of the Persian primary and secondary sources are the authors' unless otherwise stated.

Prologue

#MeToo Movement and Redefining the Private Sphere

Ziba Jalali Naini

The social movement called "MeToo" is the embodiment of a public protest against one of the age-old historical violences, typically against women, but also against children and men. In fact, it represents the voice of the victims of sexual harassment and abuse. In Iran, however, this time women (some men and queer folks too) have broken their silences and publicly revealed the widespread taboos against sexual harassment, which happens to all age ranges, in all places, and in various situations. The phrase "MeToo" is in fact the simplified version of the sentence that refers to all victims of sexual abuse and indicates solidarity, namely that "it has happened to me too and you are not alone." Despite the bravery in crossing the red lines of the strong traditional and cultural beliefs and their derivative clichés, sexual harassment narratives are extremely painful for the victims to recount, especially in terms of their psychological aspects. The victims take a significant step further by breaking their silence and recalling previous emotional trauma and pent-up anger, which could otherwise be interpreted or judged as complicity with the abuser. They break their silence while taking major steps toward identifying their shared pain in a larger society in order to act radically and fundamentally in addressing this issue. This in and of itself is regarded as a paradigm shift in Iranian women's rights movement, because it distorts the rigid border between private and public spheres and its outcomes. It also challenges the specifications derived from gender segregation and the discriminations based on the separation of these two spheres and their special values. This also refers to the traditional dual space of life andarūnī (internal)/bīrūnī (external), which represents the measures of an ideological gender segregation to preserve the virginity of girls and the integrity of the lineage of the husband's children. The best arrangement was for women to stay at home and in the private/secret space of the family.

Similar to most social movements, it is difficult to pinpoint the exact origins of the #MeToo movement. However, the inception of the movement in the West, in terms of historical and social changes in women's rights movements, can be traced back to two historical moments in 2006 and 2017. In 2006, Tarana Burke's mother encouraged her to start a social initiative to defend the poor and improve the lives of girls who were/had been exposed to sexual violence. Burke, an African American working-class woman from New York, was the victim of sexual abuse and rape both as a kid and as a teenager. She began the initiative to relieve her personal anguish, and the local community eventually welcomed it. This is how the "MeToo" movement was born in the first place.[1] The second moment was in October 2017, eleven years after Burke's initiative, when the "MeToo" hashtag began trending on social media via the confessions of the Hollywood actress, singer, and songwriter Alyssa Milano, accusing Harvey Weinstein, the famous producer and giant in Hollywood cinema, of sexual abuse. Immediately after this, similar allegations were made against Weinstein by over a hundred women, leading to his expulsion from his "empire" and his eventual bankruptcy.[2]

Since then, voices like Milano's, who had suppressed their rage for years, have surfaced and have served as a rallying cry for other societal forces to join the chorus, condemning sexual assault especially in the workplace. Many victims have bravely and boldly responded to this call, and the movement has dominated the Western world. For instance, the #MeToo was viewed 4.7 million times and revealed numerous cases of sexual abuse on social media in less than twenty-four hours at one point. In addition, this movement was not limited to the United States—thousands of individuals from Canada and Europe also joined this massive social movement. After this social media initiative led to official complaints against celebrities and senior executives, many well-known social and political figures denounced sexual abuse perpetrators. The issue that arose after all this commotion was whether this movement against sexual assault would be a temporary one or would turn into a mass movement of activism that would eventually lead to social change.

In 2020, through feminist websites and digital media, a similar movement emerged in Iran. Unprecedentedly, well-known people in the realm of art and academia were accused of sexual assault by victims who came forward with their stories. Without a doubt, in a society such as Iran, where people's relationships are based on value concepts such as honor (*nāmūs*), zeal (*gheirat*), and innocence (*ismat*), narrators of sexual harassment may still be exposed to cases of honor killings and life threats and pay a high price and experience severe consequences for coming forward. This is incomparable to societies where such taboos have already been broken. In Iran, victims of sexual harassment largely deal with the fundamental values of their families such as honor, chastity, and morality. Hence, most narrators began telling their stories of sexual assault using pseudonyms for both themselves and the perpetrators. In fact, it was social media users who identified the perpetrators based on the narrators' confessions and implicit indications. Some social media users expected the victims to reveal the perpetrators' names so that they could inspire the silenced victims to voice their experiences too.

In Iran, however, the movement was met with both support and criticism. The critics of the movement typically raise the question of the consequences of exposing rape—for them, the question is whether disclosing rape or sexual harassment will really stop the rapist, or is broadcasting their punishment in public a kind of propagating of improper behavior? On the other hand, the supporters of disclosing sexual harassment and the abusers' names argue that doing so is a sort of punishment for the abusers and a lesson for others, both in the private realm of family members and in the public sphere by their employers, bosses, and even academia.

Given these debates, exposing an inappropriate act, misconduct, or a sexual assault seems to be not only a correct and responsible thing to do but it also serves to restore the victim's human rights. As a result, a person who is aware of and committed to his rights should never remain silent in the face of such crimes. This responsibility however has cultural and legal consequences. In other words, in the absence of cultural and family awareness, as well as legal recourse, there is no appropriate response to the reactions following the disclosure of harassment. The victims are blamed for what has happened to them, which is often worse position than their initial silence. Given that victim blaming[3] is part of the dominant Iranian culture, the majority of the victims prefer to keep their mental and physical trauma hidden. But disclosing the stories of sexual abuse may ultimately help to decrease the number of cases exposed to violence and aggression in the future.

At the same time, according to the responses on social media, even if the aggressor denies his actions and responsibility, his greatest asset, which is his social capital, is irreversibly ruined. The danger lies in the fact that some of these aggressors might end up being discharged and declared as innocent by the court (if the case goes to the court); however, no matter what, they can hardly regain their former social image and reputation. Hence, it is advisable to review and verify all details before exposing both parties' names. Otherwise, some might be falsely accused and demand to rehabilitate and recover their social credibility. It must be acknowledged that breaking private and public boundaries requires the necessary cultural background and moral support to ensure that the community's security and credibility are not compromised.

Undoubtedly, in the MeToo movement, abusers and perpetrators are certainly reprimanded in the public and lose their social reputation. Therefore, there have been few critiques of the movement such as the "justice by the citizens," which refers to the fact that expelling the accused from the society prior to trial and proof of their guilt is one of the most dangerous approaches in these circumstances.[4] Or, as Jessica Butcher, a successful entrepreneur known as one of the fifty women who inspired digital technology in Europe in 2016, put it: "Has today's feminism begun to offend itself?" In addition, Butcher also claimed that the "MeToo" movement is used to "reinforce a discourse that always identifies women as vulnerable." According to her, approaches of this movement "are not in the interest of equality campaigns [and that] the MeToo not only damaged women's self-esteem, but also overnight tarnished the image of many innocent men."[5]

From a legal standpoint, proving a crime, like other legal and criminal litigation, is the first step toward achieving the victim's rights within the framework of the Islamic penal code. In addition, the victims must prove their claim in some way, while being forced to respond to relatives and the public about the reasons for the violence. In sexual harassment reports, if the victims who shared their experiences of the violence do not prove the abusive behavior, they will be at risk of criminal accusations.

In Iran's Islamic penal code, rape and sexual assault do not have a precise legal definition, and most sexual crimes originate from adultery. In fact, the crime of "rape" is not recognized and what exists is known as "forced adultery." The border between adultery—in which the parties of the relationship are found guilty—and rape—in which only the woman is found guilty—is narrow, and if the perpetrator cannot be proven, the victim herself becomes a criminal. Both adultery and forced adultery are types of illicit relations and are proven in the same way, but it is difficult to prove them, and the unproven charge of adultery (*qazf*) itself is considered a crime, which is punishable by eighty lashes. The overlap between the two is one of the reasons why victims do not go to the judicial authorities because victims who appeal to the law potentially expose themselves to being accused. However, adultery has been criminalized, and in order to prove adultery, the three elements of confession, testimony, and knowledge of the judge are considered. Of course, the element of confession is excluded in the matter of rape. The witness element is also very rare or impossible. Therefore, the only reliable element remains the knowledge of the judge.

The judge's knowledge is first determined based on the initial report of the police, and forensic medicine, then the plaintiff's claim, the defendant's evidence in the crime investigation sessions, the relationship between the accused and accuser, testimony of witnesses, and sent messages by the accused. According to Article 102 of the Code of Criminal Procedure, the investigation of crimes against chastity is prohibited unless the crime is visible or is accompanied by a complaint from a private plaintiff and the presentation of reasons. For this reason, victims of such crimes in many cases avoid filing complaints against the rapists; hence, the statistics of the reported crimes that the judicial authority compiles do not match with the actual number of the committed crimes.[6] But changes were made in 2014 by amending laws such as Note 2 of Article 224 of the Islamic Penal Code, which adopted that "whenever a person commits adultery with a woman who is not willing to commit adultery, while she is unconscious, asleep or drunk, his behavior will be considered as rape. In adultery by deceiving and fooling an underage girl or by kidnapping, threatening or intimidating a woman, even if it causes her to surrender, the above sentence is also valid."[7]

In addition, in the bill of the "Preservation of Dignity and Protection of Women against Violence," the definition of the concept of violence is more comprehensive and closer to international definitions. "Violence" is defined as "any behavior, whether act or omission that is committed against a woman due to her gender or vulnerable position or type of relationship, and causes harm or damage physically, mentally or to her personality, dignity or restriction or deprivation of rights and her legal freedoms."[8] Iranian government agencies accelerated the approval of this bill after the beginning of the wave of confessions under the "MeToo" movement, which may be an attempt to provide a proper and supportive situation for realization of the rights of the victims of sexual crimes. The role of NGOs and human rights organizations and the pursuit of independent lawyers, sociologists, and psychologists should not be overlooked in clarifying these social problems and providing up-to-date and comprehensive and practical legislation.

Globally, horrible acts of harassment and rape occur in various societies, and the victims of such violence keep their pain secret for a variety of reasons. As a result of processes such as preaching by relatives, or blaming victims of sexual harassment, normalizing and hiding sexual abuse, and a lack of community support, the victims largely suffer from depression, suicide tendency and attempts, reluctance to marry, and a variety of other physical and mental trauma. So, the question remains as to how harassment and rape can be publicly discussed and communicated in Iran and at what price? In the absence of specialized legal groups that support and work on rape victims, is it necessary to raise it at all? If not, the rapist will go unpunished and would continue to harass other victims; when society, intellectuals, and even families have also been considered accomplices, what should be done? Such questions have provoked a variety of responses in both Iran and the West. The courage of the narrators and the taboo-breaking dimensions of Iranian women's movements in such circumstances are significant and incomparable to what has been done in the West. Academics such as Zizek have critiqued the "MeToo" movement and harassed narrators in the West saying: "They want power and the sad fact is that one of the ways to achieve power in social connections in many Western nations, particularly in the United States, is to seem to be a victim. And now, if someone comes forth to refute this claim of victimization, he'll be blamed of abusing the victim and other things."[9] As mentioned earlier, any movement confronts numerous pressures and costs at its inception. But the movement's very positive achievements will be revealed and evaluated in the medium and long term. With the presence of proper penal laws in the society, suitable treatment system, along with family and supportive society, many traumas and injuries of rape will be compensated and treated for the victims of violence.

Women from the lowest classes of the society, from impoverished cultural and economic backgrounds, and those who frequently endure employment insecurity and lose their jobs are among the silent population of this movement. Even in Western societies, the lower classes of the society had limited role in this movement; however, to jump to conclusions about Iran's MeToo might be premature as the movement is still young and centered on well-known cultural and artistic figures and has not yet reached the lower socioeconomic classes. Actually, every thought and attitude should arise from a certain social stratum or class and local community. Depending on their authenticity, depth of social ties, and their common claims and demands, this attitude would develop among its members and soon spread to the whole society. Considering the movement as a class-based one is an ideological assumption that can only serve to undermine the movement. In addition, in Iran, any movement or protest that does not originate from within the society is often criticized as being superficial, imported, and temporary. However, we have to acknowledge that it is vital to rely on the widespread global transnational feminist movements. The potentials and the flaws, as well as the power, of every movement or protest may be also linked to that society's potentials and failures in embracing and understanding the problem and trying to reflect it to the responsible audience. The least impact such collective movements have is the reflection on the chronic and hidden problems of the society and the consequent empowerment and awareness of individual rights.

According to a senior consultant with a prominent company in standard assessment in Canada, the "MeToo" movement has expanded the discourse about appropriate workplace behavior. He continues, "We used to think it was in men's nature to act inappropriately, but now we know that this seemingly normal behavior is deemed a violation and has been condemned. This, in my opinion, is a wonderful thing." According to Kenneth Fredeen, "The frequency of sexual harassment complaints in organizations has increased, and this change has made the voices of the victims heard. All organizations have been asked to address this problem radically through warnings and, if necessary, dismissals. This is a turning point. Let's keep moving forward."[10]

Sexual harassment is part of a broader category of violence against women that has been confined to the private sphere and secrecy. Domestic violence, spousal abuse, and marital violence are examples of intimate partner violence (IPV), which is becoming a global social and public health crisis. Unsurprisingly, there is no single universally accepted definition or a conceptual framework for IPV that encompasses the phenomenon's complexity. Although some theoretical frameworks for studying IPV appear to have an advantage over others, their validity has yet to be verified. Due to the complex and multifaceted nature of IPV, a limited theoretical position may cloud our understanding of this phenomenon.[11] An example of IPV in Iran is stoning for adultery as one of the sharia rulings. According to Islamic tradition, "the testimony of four just persons who witnessed the crime with their own eyes" and "four times the confession of the accused apart from pressure and in a free atmosphere" are required to prove adultery.[12] Some academics such as Ayatollah Bayat Zanjani believe that "it comes out that the intention of Islam's sharia is not to easily prove the committing of adultery."[13] Despite the fact that certain Shiite authorities believe stoning is practically "impossible and highly improbable," the "judge's knowledge" is now one of the ways to impose a stoning sentence in Iran's Islamic penal code, which has been in effect since the 1979 Revolution. In recent years, several stoning judgments have been granted in Iran, according to human rights organizations, based on "judge's knowledge" or "forced confessions."[14]

As a result, in Iran, only in very rare cases a family will report a sexual assault of their daughter or the women of the family that happens within the family or elsewhere. For a better understanding of the dynamic between the private and the public, the following narrative illustrates an Iranian father's mindset. This experience is about a person who had a sabbatical study in Canada with his family, but he preferred to return earlier. His strange reason was that his ten-year-old daughter had gradually realized that she could get him arrested for mistreatment by dialing a simple police number, and that Canada was not like Iran, a country where he could easily punish his daughter severely. He might have told his daughter that this is her fate and that she had no right to complain! And he could punish her even more if she contacted the cops. That person returned to his paradise, where minor and major crimes/sins go unnoticed and its officials ignore the fact that even slight infractions can lead to grave crimes.[15]

The rise of the MeToo movement in Iran raised the question of whether Iran's existing legal framework and institutions are capable of dealing with such issues. What are the restrictive laws in Iranian society? What are the regulations for penalizing sexual harassment or the aggressor in society to avoid the occurrence and repetition of sexual assault? How are people reacting to this issue? What psychological, legal, and medical resources have been made available to women who have been abused in order to prevent the violence from continuing and to treat the injuries that have resulted from it? What are the criteria for distinguishing the private from the public sphere, as well as the requirements for each? Is it still the case in our legal system that the "private sphere" has contradictory meanings and rights in regard to old traditional beliefs and values?

One of the most influential impacts of the MeToo movement in Iran began last year with narratives in the field of art, journalism, and cinema, which started with an unprecedented series of controversial tweets. On March 23, 2022, an assistant director and programmer of Iranian cinema explained a series of events happening behind the scenes of a movie and claimed that she was subjected to harassment after several encounters between her and a famous actor by publishing twenty-two threads of tweets. This assistant director, whose narrative on Twitter was accompanied by widespread reactions, claimed that some of the film crew knew about this incident. This revelation was the beginning of the "IranMeToo" domino. Consequently, a group of women involved in cinema issued a statement protesting the violence against women in the field. After this statement, which had eight hundred signatures, a five-member women's committee including Haniye Tavasoli, Taraneh Alidoosti, Somayeh Mirshamsi, Ghazaleh Motamed, and Maral Jeyrani was formed by the majority vote in order to deal with sexual harassment and any violence in the film industry. Part of the statement reads:

> In the narratives that have been published about the painful experiences of women in Iranian cinema, all kinds of harassment comprising under the

umbrella of sexual violence have come up; including insults with sexual and gendered words, blackmailing the victims by depriving them the right to work and or be paid, sexual assault by threatening the victim's job security, unwanted physical contact, insistence and coercion to sexual acts, and finally physical violence and rape.[16]

This was the first time that such an accusation was made publicly against one of the well-known figures of cinema in Iran, and a large number of women in cinema as well as the society sympathized with and supported it.

Following this, the Association of Planners and Assistant Directors was the first association that reacted to this disclosure and supported the assistant director. The association also expressed its regret for the humiliating and immoral encounters and the creation of mental insecurities and even threats and physical attacks behind the scenes of the Iranian film industry and announced that this is not the first time that such incidents have happened. The Iranian Cinema Actors Association took a similar approach and condemned any violence, insults, and unethical behavior toward the actresses and issued a statement.

In the first meeting of the Cinema Organization's Council of Directors held this year, Mohammad Khazaei paid attention to the statement made by Iranian women cinematographers regarding the creation of an independent committee with an absolute majority of women to deal with complaints against sexual violence and ordered for special investigation and attention. He formed the Council of Professional Ethics in Cinema. This example of mobilization within the civil society, in spite of all the difficulties and criticisms, confirms the awareness of the public toward women's rights. And this is only the beginning. This is a sign of new awareness, deep understanding, and sensitivity of society as well as professional organizations and institutions toward women's rights, which is only the first step on the path toward a gender equal society.

Introduction: Bodies, Spaces, and Places

Claudia Yaghoobi

The word "rape" stamped repeatedly across her fractured face, overlayed with fingerprints, legal documents, and what seems like a page from a religious scripture, Sonia Balassanian's collage of the woman (the cover image of this volume) gazing at the onlooker haunts the viewers, inviting them to acknowledge the "unspeakable." She is the voice of the many unheard, silenced, invisible. She is the mirror held up for society to see as she is gazing at society simultaneously. In short, she demands to be seen, acknowledged, and validated while also raising awareness. She is the reason for this volume to come to life.

While the "MeToo" movement and the fight against sexual violence began unofficially a long time ago, it rose to prominence in the United States in 2017 and continues to do so globally even to this day. Initially, it aimed at raising awareness about sexual violence and harassment by exposing abusers. The goal of the movement was to get rid of all forms of gender violence, change policies, give people resources, and provide access to healing.[1] The movement in the United States began as a grassroots campaign ten years before it took off on social media in 2017 when users were asked to post their stories of sexual harassment and rape with the hashtag #MeToo. Since then, it has penetrated not only national but also global consciousness as increasing number of elite and powerful men are being accused of and charged with sexual harassment.

The Iranian #MeToo campaign took off on social media in August 2020, proliferating stories of rape, sexual abuse, and harassment. However, the number of individuals who have spoken out against harassment is still minuscule. Because of the political considerations inside Iran, there have only been few forums where the systemic nature of these injustices has been analyzed. These injustices are further complicated by the class status, nationality, immigration status, sexuality, gender identity, and disability of the victims, issues that require much greater attention. Although Iran's #MeToo is specific to the country, it has global as well as local significance. One area where Iran's #MeToo distinguishes itself from its

American counterpart is its interlocutors, who are ordinary Iranian women (I use "women" because the majority of narratives have come from individuals identifying as such) sharing their experiences of sexual harassment and assault within the public sphere of digital media regardless of the country's historical silencing of minoritized populations. Another outstanding difference is that the majority of men who have been accused so far are part of the progressive, educated, middle-class social strata, including artists, academics, and creative individuals with major social capital and status. These are men who claim to be feminists or advocates of women's rights giving women (the victims/survivors) a sense of false safety while abusing them and exposing them to sexual violence.

While Iran's MeToo has been a crucial form of resistance, to this date, no major work has considered how the Iranian MeToo movement might enrich our critical and pedagogical practices. Hence, this volume aims to begin a conversation about sexual assault and the voices that testify to it within academic discourses and activist spheres. Pioneering works on gender, sexuality, sexual harassment, and gendered violence that this volume benefits from, to name a few, include Zahra Tizro's *Domestic Violence in Iran* (2012), K. S. Batmanghelichi's *Revolutionary Bodies: Technologies of Gender, Sex, and Self in Contemporary Iran* (2020), Janet Afary's *Sexual Politics in Modern Iran* (2009), Afsaneh Najmabadi's *Women with Moustaches and Men without Beards* (2005), Homa Hoodfar's *The Women's Movement in Iran* (1999), and Mahnaz Afkhami's *Sisterhood Is Global* (1984).[2] However, research on the recent discourse around sexual harassment, rape, violence, and consent, among many other topics, and their impact on women, men, and nonbinary and queer individuals in contemporary Iran have been limited or exclusively within the journalistic domain. This edited volume fills that gap by bridging the existing historical, sociological, and ethnographic research with an analysis of the current discourse around sexual harassment and MeToo in the context of today's religious, cultural, literary, social media, digital/globalized world. As the first book of its kind focusing on Iran's MeToo, the volume stands in solidarity with the survivors and the work of activists and journalists that already exists.

Methodological Structure and Theoretical Approach

This volume focuses on the various methods that women, men, and nonbinary and queer individuals have used to bring about change within the context of Iranian feminism. The chapters not only contextualize this emergent movement within the history of Iranian women's feminist activism but also investigate the ways that the new generation of Iranian activists and those who have been subject to sexual violence demand justice by raising their voices and organizing, campaigning, and demonstrating both on digital media and on the streets. By doing so, they subvert the discourse considering them as mere victims; they claim their agency in narrating their stories of fight, flight, and otherwise. Acknowledging and redefining the survivors' agency in "doing whatever ... [they] deemed necessary at the time to survive the attack, whether that entailed fighting back or submitting to the rapist," as feminist theorist Carine M. Mardorossian argues, this volume intends to view women's "passivity itself ... [as] a defense mechanism," showing the victims/survivors that they are more than "their traumatic experiences, that they had the capacity to act and organize even as they were dealing with the psychic effects of rape or domestic violence."[3] Considering this agency in an intersectional context complicated by class status, religion, ethnicity, sexuality, gender identity, and disability, the contributors also attend to both promises and dangers, advantages and shortfalls of the nascent MeToo within the realm of digital media and the more traditional forms of activism in Iran.

Much of the theoretical discourse in the volume focuses on the feminist intersectional discussions, theories about subverting hegemonic discourses and power structures, and feminist geography relevant to public versus private spaces when discussing the public/private sphere of activism, campaigning, digital media activism, and filmmaking. The volume's focus on digital media activism and its consideration of class, gender, sexuality, religion, ethnicity, and disability matters, among others, make it stand out from other works done before and bring in nuanced perspectives.

One of the overarching arguments of the volume zooms in on the survivors' strategic mechanisms of raising awareness, voicing their experiences of harassment, demanding public acknowledgment for their place within public discourses historically denied to them, and fighting back against targeted violence and narratives aimed at excluding them from public spaces and conversations.[4] Over the past four decades (and historically) in Iran, gender segregation and subordination of the female body (and voice) has been on the agenda of not only the state but also the male-centered Iranian society. However, this volume demonstrates that while the female body has been the target of such disciplining and subordination, and subjected to violence, sexual assault, and rape, often because it has appeared in "the wrong place" (hypervisible in the public), Iranian women (and other sexually minoritized individuals) have utilized the same discourse about "proper places/spaces" and shifted their activism and resistance toward the paradoxical private/public sphere of the digital media protest, pushing back against the mainstream narratives and outing the perpetrators of sexual violence and rape on social media platforms.

Since sexual harassment and rape are forms of violence against bodies considered inferior such as women's bodies as well as racialized and sexualized bodies, it is important to discuss what "gender-based violence" signifies here. To examine violence in the sociocultural context of violent acts in order to interpret them holistically is also crucial to discussions of sexual violence. Defined by the United Nations as any act resulting in physical, psychological, emotional, or sexual harm to women, gender-based violence also includes verbal or economic abuse, sexual harassment, forced labor, child marriages, honor killings, and so many other forms of violence against women (and other minorities). Gender-based violence has been described as a tool for subordinating women and other gendered bodies, and with the juridical and social inequalities within societies, it will continue to serve as a legitimate form of domination not only for heterosexual men but also for states.[5] Violent acts have also been considered as a mechanism for expressing feelings and/or establishing various forms of gendered, class, and racial differentiations.[6]

However, as scholar of social change Zahra Tizro demonstrates in their book *Domestic Violence in Iran: Women, Marriage and Islam*, while gender-based violence is a global issue, the way that it presents itself in various cultures, it is important to investigate the intertwinement of local factors and roots of it too. Tizro argues that gender-based violence "is not the result of unaccountable or pathological behaviour, but of a learned, conscious and calculated behaviour originating from a social system of deep-rooted inequality and patriarchy. Unequal power relationships affect some individuals in such a way that they are encouraged to exercise their power over others and to intimidate or control them."[7] In the context of power dynamics and hierarchies, in many parts of the world, including in the Middle East, enforced sexuality within marriage is viewed as the husband's right and the wife's duty.[8] However, outside marriage, rape, which is infused with patriarchal meanings, is considered an offense, albeit against other men rather than the female survivor. It is seen as an attack on the honor of other men.[9] In addition, sexual harassment and rape are legitimated by the behavioral patterns of the victim—the public views the assault as a consequence of an inappropriate behavior or even form of dressing. As mentioned earlier, sexual violence has direct links with maintaining and exerting power and control over the victims. In most patriarchal societies, violence is utilized to reinforce societal hierarchy and order.

The subordination of the female body and other minoritized bodies (inferior bodies) has roots in patriarchal institutions and their practices, which privilege heterosexual men and male bodies. This privilege facilitates male exertion of power on these "inferior" bodies. For instance, in the context of marriage or heterosexual relationships, gendered servitude is an integral part of heterosexual social relations between men and women and often translates into physical and economic obligations and dependence for women.[10] Hence, central to patriarchal power structures is the securing of heterosexual male domination over other bodies, and "the forms and functions of male sexuality, such as rape, sexual harassment, physical assaults and so on, in the social control of women [and other minoritized bodies], represent the male attitude towards women as inferior members of society."[11] Now, this inferior body is required to remain within the space/place designated to it by patriarchal social order, transgression of which threatens male dominance and subverts heterosexual male-centered, hegemonic narratives about their place in society.

Bodies elicit questions about the space and place they occupy. Within patriarchal societies, women are identified with their body sphere while men have the privilege of disembodiment. In his concept called "hexis," Pierre Bourdieu has discussed the social significance of bodies and their physical placing in space through bodily posture, gestures, facial expressions, and speaking voice. The relationship between the social world and its inscription on bodies includes the ways that individuals and groups present their bodies to others, moving or making space for their bodies.[12] Bourdieu argues that "one's proper place" is clearly expressed through "the space one claims with one's body in physical space, through a bearing and gestures that are self-assured or reserved, expansive or constricted ('presence' or 'insignificance')."[13] According to Bourdieu, men are entitled to occupy more of the available space than women so they are "present" in space while women are "insignificant." Such arguments demonstrate the female body as a site for sociocultural, religious, and political inscriptions, understood as a sex object—an object of male desire in need of control. This however does not mean that women (nonbinary and queer individuals and other gendered and classed bodies) necessarily conform to the above expectations as they are able to disrupt and subvert the existing discourses.[14] For instance, feminist geographers such as Linda McDowell challenge such essentialist assumptions about women's "proper place" in society. As McDowell explains,

> Assumptions about the correct place for embodied women are drawn on to justify and to challenge systems of patriarchal domination in which women are

excluded from particular spatial arenas and restricted to others. In this sense to "know their place" has a literal as well as a metaphorical meaning for women, and sexed embodiment is deeply intertwined with geographical location.[15]

Relationships in societies are interdependent on spaces via mechanisms such as sex segregation or even dress code. For example, in the context of veiling, veiled bodies, and city spaces in Turkey, feminist geographer Banu Gökarıksel has also commented on the politics of dressing and spaces, and the resulting restrictions versus advantages they might have for different women. According Gökarıksel, mobility within public spaces results in the shaping of identities in relation to power: "through their mobility subjects are formed both by and in relation to power."[16]

Similarly in Iran, since the Islamic Revolution of 1979, women's and other minoritized bodies' presence in public places—considered "improper"—have gradually become more visible, which has created a serious concern for the state and the male-dominated society. According to Masserat Amir-Ebrahimi, "With their increasing presence in universities, various governmental administrations, public and private organizations, and NGOs, women gradually became active agents of social change, generating important challenges regarding the status and rights of women under Islamic law in the private (family) and the public spheres."[17] Amir-Ebrahimi views the spread of global culture via technology and the internet as some of the main reasons for this type of visibility within public spheres and the demand for justice and equal rights in public and private spaces. Examining one of the first online blogging platforms of Iran, she argues that Iranian women began "breaking the silence about their lives, conditions, frustrations, and desires ... [and started talking] openly about political, social, and cultural issues, but also about their personal lives, opinions, feelings, and aspirations for the first time ... The 'freedom' of expression in this new virtual world had a tremendous impact on women and young bloggers."[18]

While the relationship between mobility of the subjects and power structures have historically influenced Iranian women's rights activism, in contemporary Iran, the digital media and the internet have morphed into the spaces that bring the traditional activism and the digital one together, merging the local with the global. Because digital media exists simultaneously at the local, national, and global levels, survivors of sexual harassment and rape have been able to disseminate their narratives marked by dissent hashtags such as the #MeToo. Using social media platforms and the hashtag #MeToo, survivors and activists have begun fighting against such gender, sexual, and class-based violence by building a platform based on solidarity and abolishing all forms of oppression and discrimination.

Chapter Breakdown

The volume includes a prologue, this introduction, ten chapters, and an afterword. Contextualizing the historical framework of Iranian MeToo activism within the larger Iranian feminist movements as well as the historical background within the context of Middle East, the contributors address how the privileged position of men who have been outed as rapists helps them to aggregate social, political, sexual, and economic capital through various networking to delegitimize the narratives of the survivors and, in fact, use their testimonies to their benefit. While Iran's #MeToo challenges the political economy of a capitalist society that re-produces systems of oppression such as sexual assault, one way this privileged position is considered is Iran's class-based system within the power hierarchies that allow men from the upper class of society to exploit those from more oppressed social groups. Within this complex web of power and privilege, the question of consent is significant. After discussion of the various confluences of positions of power and privilege in silencing the voices of the survivors to the assaulters' benefit in accumulating socioeconomic, sexual, and political capital, the volume also covers the intersections of various systems of oppression specifically highlighting marginalized voices such as the experiences of lesbian and the lesbophobe attacks within the online digital world. In these chapters, the contributors highlight the power dynamics within digital feminist networks in Iran with its unique attributes due to political, social, and religious structures. Many of these feminist networks have been selective in their support of the survivors, which also speaks to the intersection of class and power leading to inclusion of some and exclusion of others from the feminist discourses and support. The volume ends with a chapter focusing on cultural productions, specifically cinematic works, through which some filmmakers have challenged normalizations of sexual harassment by offering alternative discourses that have arguably paved the way for #MeTooIran.

Ziba Jalali Naini's prologue, "#MeToo Movement and Redefining the Private Sphere," addresses the foundational concepts in understanding Iran's MeToo, its manipulations and misconstruing, the social, cultural, and legal discourses around MeToo in Iran, and the support as well as the criticism that the campaign has faced.

In Chapter 1, "Like a Wrapped Chocolate: The Islamic Republic's Politics of Hijab and the Normalization of Sexual Harassment," Esha Momeni investigates how the enforcement of hijab has contributed to the objectification of the female body as an element of hostile Iranian masculinity in postrevolutionary Iran. According to Momeni, the compulsory nature of this hijab enforcement by the state shifted the discourse away from piety and religious practice toward the male libido. Hijab became a tool shielding men from sexual temptation and blaming women for male sexual violence. Momeni argues that this shift has condoned male sexual aggression, establishing hostile masculinity and violence against women.

Focusing on the digital world of social media such as Twitter as well as Iranian news media, and legal discourses surrounding testimonies of survivors of sexual assault and the various reactionary waves to these narratives, in Chapter 2, "The Iranian #MeToo and the Double Bind of Iranian Feminism: Between Religion, the Global Gender Struggle, and Liberal Feminism," Dilyana Mincheva and Niloofar Hooman provide a nuanced account of the Iranian iteration of the #MeToo movement through close readings of publicly available Twitter testimonies of ordinary Iranian women and mediated reactions to these testimonies provided by clerics, feminists, and Iranian intellectuals, both domestic and diasporic.

Chapter 3, "Rhetorical Listening to Iranian #MeToo Movement in Diaspora, problematizes the reluctance of academic scholars in taking up research on the topic and encourages further study. In this chapter, Yalda N. Hamidi charts out the reasons for why gendered violence has become less than a favorite subject of study for Iranian academic feminists in the diaspora and proposes a methodological intervention for rapprochement and invites Iranian academic and transnational feminists to utilize some of their intellectual privileges to raise the voice of the Iranian #MeToo movement.

Highlighting the intersection of power and privilege in silencing the voices of the survivors of sexual harassment, Mahdi Tourage, in Chapter 4, "Structural and Material Considerations and the Nexus of Power and Sexuality in the Iranian #MeToo Movement," provides us with debates on the concept of consent. While it is generally acknowledged that mutual consent, preferably spelled out in a contract, is the best possible basis for material and ethical relations of exchange between humans, especially regarding coitus, this chapter questions its feasibility.

Yasamin Rezai and Mehdy Sedaghat Payam in Chapter 5, titled, "Twitter Data Analysis on #MeTooIran," examine the implications of the #MeToo movement on social media. In this social movement, native to the digital world and social media platforms, social media users publicize allegations of sex crimes, mostly toward people who benefit from certain social, class, racial, gender, or political power in relation to others, who mostly are identified to be on the marginalized side of power dynamics.

In Chapter 6, "#Unveiling_the_Iranian_MeToo: Symptomatic Reading of Iranian MeToo through the Lens of Political Economy," Paria Rahimi shows how the narratives of the MeToo movement can critique and challenge the political economy—the particular mode of production of the capitalist society that engenders different forms of oppression, including sexual assault.

In Chapter 7 "Whose Voice Is Missing? MeToo Digital Storytelling on Instagram and the Politics of Inclusion," Golnar Gishnizjani asks important questions such as "does everyone have an equal right and opportunity to participate in feminist online campaigns, particularly the #MeToo hashtag?" In doing so, this chapter examines the intersectional struggles of the #MeToo hashtag in Iran.

Mahdis Sadeghipouya in Chapter 8, "Sexual Violence, MeToo, and Iranian Lesbians' Censored Voices," turns our attention to the minority groups who have been excluded from the movement. This includes lesbians, who as both women and lesbians endure different experiences of sexual violence that sometimes target their sex, sometimes their sexuality, and sometimes both at the same time.

Somayeh Rostampour, in Chapter 9, "The White-Collars' New Masculinities in #MeToo: How to Maintain Gendered Privileges?," problematizes the questions regarding class and social status within the movement. While the #MeToo movement in Iran has remained limited largely to middle-class women, it has been able to challenge the "impunity of men" and implement some degree of "gender justice" in social media.

In Chapter 10, "*Hush! Girls Don't Scream* (2013) by Puran Derakhshandeh and the #MeToo Movement in Iran," Maryam Zehtabi considers the act of writing about one's private life as a statement of rebellion in a context that forcefully stifles any expressions of the self in individuals. Normalizing the act of speaking openly about sexual assault, however, did not start with the #MeToo movement. Zehtabi discusses how *Hush! Girls Don't Scream* by Puran Derakhshandeh paved the way for the outpouring of support for the #MeToo movement in Iran.

Roger Friedland, Janet Afary, and Charlotte Hoppen's afterword, titled "Patriarchalism, Male Abuse, and the Sources of the #MeToo Movement in the Muslim Middle East," is based on a survey the authors conducted in 2018, just after the #MeToo movement was bursting onto the scene in the Middle East. They surveyed tens of thousands of younger adults in Algeria, Egypt, Iran, Pakistan, Palestine, Tunisia, and Turkey about their experiences with molestation and sexual violence using Facebook banner ads. Analyzing the survey data, the afterword offers significant information about the kinds of men who are most likely to engage in public molestation and domestic violence.

The Limitations of This Volume

The varied interests and expertise of the authors of this volume contribute to a better understanding of sexual harassment, gender-based violence, and rape in contemporary Iranian society; however, no single volume can address all the possible issues on any topic, let alone topics as complex and interconnected as these. Most victims and survivors remain anonymous, and many have yet to come forward. While the number of scholars with the necessary skills in the study of gender and sexuality has increased over the course of the twentieth and twenty-first centuries, the available sources and tools for addressing sexual assault and rape are minimal due to sexual harassment and rape being a taboo-laden topic within Iranian culture. The chapters in this volume have attempted to provide insights into significant issues related to the broad and complex topics of rape, sexual harassment, sexual violence, among many others. In addressing key issues, some questions are answered while others are yet to be explored.

One question that has gotten significant attention in recent years is that of gender-based violence, particularly toward women. However, narratives about such violence targeted at the nonbinary and queer folks and men have largely been missing from the public domain. The chapters in this volume also focus primarily on women survivors with a few chapters focusing on lesbian individuals and class-based violence, leaving violence toward other minoritized communities largely unexplored. It is our hope that this volume will be the beginning of many discussions around the topic, which will also address the ones the current volume fails to cover.

1

Like a Wrapped Chocolate: The Islamic Republic's Politics of Hijab and the Normalization of Sexual Harassment

Esha Momeni

In the summer of 2020, the hashtag #MeToo became a trend on Iranian social media platforms. Many women came forward to share their stories of sexual harassment and assault with the public. However, because Iran lacked adequate social, legal, and political structures to aid the victims and defend their rights, this historic global movement hardly went beyond a campaign to raise awareness. Two weeks into the start of the campaign in early August 2020, journalist Neda Sanij captured the social and political implications of this moment in the following lines:

> Women's experiences of sexual harassment and rape [that became public with the #MeToo movement] startled many for several reasons: the high number of victims, their bravery in coming forward and telling their stories, victim blaming, and victim's feelings of vulnerability in the absence of a judicial system that could properly examine their stories and safeguard their citizenship rights.[1]

A year later, on a summer day in 2021, I attended a clubhouse meeting on the topic of women and the issue of sexual harassment in Tehran's public spaces. The organizers were proposing the removal of the billboards and advertisements that obscured the pedestrian bridges and created danger zones. The flow of the conversation came to a halt when the topic of hijab was brought up. A few men insisted that women's hijab was the key to their safety in public whereas women claimed that wearing their complete Islamic hijab did not protect them from harassment. The inability of the male participants to accept women's reality has been conditioned by the Islamic Republic's hijab advertisement that has constantly promised that hijab would bring security to women and girls. In fact,

Figure 1.1 Advertising the hijab as a security measure on billboards.

"Hijab is security" has been the state's primary motto and the central theme of its images (Figure 1.1).

Hijab has only given Iranian women security against the state violence in enforcing mandatory hijab. Under the Islamic Republic, the enforcement of the compulsory hijab has subjected Iranians to daily brutal structural violence. The killing of 22-year-old Zhina (Mahsa) Amini on September 16, 2022, while she was in the custody of the so-called morality police for improperly wearing her hijab marked a new low in state brutality. In addition, by identifying hijab as the key determinant of women's safety in public, the Iranian government absolves itself of its responsibility to protect half the population and provides protection for sexual predators.

There are no official national reports on interpersonal gender-based violence in Iran; however, studies on various demographics in smaller cities and official comments indicate that it is prevalent and on the rise. Based on a 2015 report published on domestic violence in Iran, 52.7 percent of married women have been subjected to emotional and verbal abuse and 37.8 percent to physical abuse. Reza Jafari, head of Social Emergencies, said: "Domestic violence against women in Iran saw a 20% rise from March 2017 to March 2018."[2] In November of 2018, Fatemeh Ghassempour, the president of the Research Center for Women and Family in Tehran, stated that 66 percent of Iranian women experience domestic abuse in their lifetime,[3] which is more than double the global average of one in every three women (30 percent). Perhaps the accurate rate is higher than that as many women do not report abuse due to cultural and social taboos.[4] The prevalence of violence against women is not confined within the private realm and has become a serious public health concern. In a 2016 survey of female students at the University of Mazandaran (a city north of Iran) about their experiences with street harassment, the authors found that out of 362 students, 97.4 percent experienced harassment, including verbal harassment, in the past year.[5]

The issue of sexual harassment and gender-based violence in Iran cannot be divorced from the state's hijab policies and discourse, making mandatory hijab an issue of the Iranian #MeToo movement. Surveying hijab policies–related cultural productions, and secondary studies on the topic, in this chapter, I investigate the Islamic Republic's discourse and advertisement on hijab and argue that they have contributed to the sexual harassment epidemic and overall violence against women as they objectify and devalue women's bodies. I contend that the state hijab propaganda shifted the focus of the hijab discourse away from piety and religious practice toward the male libido. Hijab is portrayed as a veil that shields men from sexual desire and temptation, thereby depicting Iranian men as sexually powerful and blaming women for male sexual violence. This essentialist discourse justifies and condones male sexual aggressiveness, therefore building a natural connection between masculinity and violence against women. Unrestricted access to female bodies has benefited Iranian men across the political spectrum. This shared male privilege, which is administered and defended by the authorities of the Islamic Republic of Iran, obstructs the structural political transformation required to guarantee civil and citizen rights.

Modernization: Heteronormativity, Citizens' Bodies, and the Visual Field of the Nation

Embedded within the structure of Western modern nation-state is heteronormativity: a set of cultural, legal, institutional, and interpersonal practices that uphold the belief that there are only two genders, that gender represents biological sex, and that only sexual desire between these "opposite" genders is natural or appropriate.[6] Gender theorist Afsaneh Najmabadi argues that heteronormativity in Iran is a cultural product of modernization processes. Starting in late nineteenth century, Iranians responded to the scrutinizing gaze of Europeans, who perceived homoeroticism and same-sex practices as backwards and perhaps unmanly.[7] As a result, males as objects of desire vanished from Qajar paintings.[8] In turn, paintings depicted women with bare breasts, visually establishing the gender binary. In a study of the relationship between visuality, power, domination, and control in Israeli-Palestinian conflict, Gil Hochberg argues, "How much one can see, what one can see, and in what way one can see or be seen are all outcomes of specific visual arrangements that are created and sustained through particular configurations of space and various processes of differentiations along national, ethnic, racial, religious, gender, and sexual lines."⁹ Hochberg identifies concealment and surveillance are two organizing principles that shape the visual arrangement. These principles were utilized in the early twentieth century to develop the concept of a modern heteronormative nation in Iran: homoerotic desire was concealed and the "heteronormalization of eros and sex" became scripted as a condition of "achieving modernity."¹⁰

Since the formation of the modern nation-state of Iran in early twentieth century, the image of the nation has been the major concern of the power and its engineering of the national identity. Iranian historian Mohamad Tavakoli-Targhi characterizes the field of vision and the process of meaning making in this era as "perspectival, competitive, and theatrical."¹¹ However, the regulation and controlling of the visuals of the public space by different regimes have been consistently structured around two main elements: heteronormativity and the Western male gaze. Citizens' bodies, particularly female bodies, have been at the center of this image's development.

In the early twentieth century, modernization's visual production, which emphasized heteronormativity through the propagation of heterosexual desire in cultural products, expanded to public spaces centered on citizens' bodies and attire. In 1928, Reza Shah passed the first dress code law ordering "all male Iranian subjects," except for clerics, to replace their traditional attire with Pahlavi hat and European suit.¹² In May 1935, Reza Shah instructed his ministers that Iranians must become Westernized, beginning with the wearing of chapeaux, European-style hats.¹³ In 1936, Reza Shah banned urban-dwelling women from donning the veil, naming the project "Women's Awakening," in which women were surveilled, prosecuted, and punished.¹⁴ Iranian historian Houchang Chehabi views the visual Europeanization of Iranians as an emanation of the rulers' desire to be included in the Western modern world, "showing the Europeans that one was worthy of their company in the society of nations, and what better way to prove this than to become physically like them?"¹⁵ If uniforms were to homogenize the population and create a unified nation, the European uniform was to seem appealing to the Western gaze.

The Male Gaze and the Objectification of the Female Body in the Making of Hegemonic Masculinity

Scholars have conveyed that the creation of nation-state has equally been the creation of hegemonic masculinity. This development was aided by objectifying the female body and making female citizens discursively accessible to the nation's male citizens. Cultivating male gaze was a component of the process of establishing heterosexuality and gender hierarchy enabled by Western photography technology. Laura Mulvey's male gaze theory highlights how the camera lens looks at the world and the female body though the viewpoint of a heterosexual man. In this view, women are represented as passive objects of male desire. Within this visual power relation that shapes and is shaped by gender norms, Mulvey states:

> Woman then, stands in the patriarchal culture as a signifier for the male other, bound by a symbolic order in which man can live out his phantasies and obsessions through linguistic command by imposing them in the silent image of woman still tied to her place as a bearer of meaning.[16]

The beginning of objectification of the Iranian female body, allowed by photography and then by cinema, followed the West's lead. Looking at locally produced pornographic photos, Ali Behdad argues that Iranian early photography in the Qajar era (late nineteenth century) "grafted" certain visual and literary tropes from Europe, including an objectifying male gaze.[17] As in nineteenth-century pornographic representations, Behdad notes in the case of a naked Persian woman, "the passive poses of women and their diffident and melancholic gaze in these locally produced images speak to the male expectation and fantasy of women as desirable objects to be looked at and possessed," a representation that has no roots in Iranian art predating the nineteenth century.[18]

In this era, the visual representations of the female body were tied to a discourse on pleasure.[19] Parallel to this erotic visual portrayal of the female body, a nationalist gendered narrative was evolving, following a global pattern in the development of the modern nation-state. Home and homeland were both discursively connected to female purity and maternal concepts while the nation itself was perceived as masculine, a community of brothers.[20] The relationship between the motherland and the masculine nation was dominated by the idea of honor (*nāmūs*) framed within the discourse of protection. Feminist scholar Minoo Moallem states that "while all members of society in the modern Iranian nation-state were expected to submit to normative respectability, gender notions assigned different roles to men as protectors and women as the protected."[21] Objectifying female bodies and gendering national identity were both necessary for the modern male militant citizen to emerge.

The objectification of the female body had a critical role in the development of the modern nation-state and its patriarchal foundation. Moallem explains how

Reza Shah's establishment of a centralized state was built on several principles, one of which was the restructuring of gender ideologies around hegemonic masculinity.[22] "Hegemonic masculinity," a term coined by R. W. Connell, refers to the highest-valued manifestation of masculinity that is produced in relation to subordinated masculinities and femininities. It is also described as the pattern of behavior and actions that enable men to maintain their domination over women. While hegemony is not synonymous with violence, it may be based on force.[23] Studying the formation of Pahlavi manhood and hegemonic masculinity, Wendy DeSouza argues that "the army police parliament, and growing bureaucracy promoted hegemonic masculinity: a socially enforced gender standard that 'emphasize[s] toughness stoicism acquisitiveness and self-reliance through violence.'"[24] In Iran, Reza Shah himself became a symbol for hegemonic masculinity as a strong uncompromising father figure. Although Reza Shah's masculinity was tied with violence, the violence was not necessarily directed toward women.

During the second Pahlavi reign (1941–79), new models of masculinity were formed, shaped by urbanization, Westernization, and industrialization.[25] The cultural productions of this era promoted stereotyped desired masculinities that were class-bound and conformed to contemporary Western ideals of masculinity that celebrated heroism, and warriorship, as well as a protector/guardianship of women, children, and the community. A new type of character, the tough guy, or *lūtī*, emerged as the primary masculine hero particularly in film industry. *Lūtī* embodied a traditional lower-class manhood that was physically powerful, courageous, morally upright, and down to earth, willing to protect the weak and fight the bully risking his life.[26]

Shahin Gerami argues that the revolution and the Islamic Republic established a social order that was hypermasculine.[27] During the 1979 Revolution and the rise of the Islamic political groups, a new form of masculinity arose that was dubbed revolutionary and Islamic. The protective masculinity disappeared, and the angry violent man took center stage with a new enemy: the modern Iranian woman. Gerami states that all revolutionary doctrines, from fundamentalists to Marxists, preached a strong pro-male tone and focused on the denigration of urban women. Urban women embodied and symbolized Pahlavi decadence for both groups. One typical phrase used to describe an object that was rotten on the inside but attractive on the surface was "it looks like Tehrani ladies."[28] The prototype of the "Tehrani woman" was a middle class, nontraditional, educated woman who celebrated her agency by being active in the public sphere. Since the inception of the Islamic state, this class of women has been its most prominent dissidents,[29] and the regime has been feverishly attempting to control them using violence, allocating budget, and founding new organizations.[30] However, the state's hijab campaign has had a detrimental influence on the lives of all Iranian women and girls regardless of their relationship with hijab.

The Islamic Republic's Hijab Discourse and Its Transformation

The Islamic Republic's implementation of the mandatory veil and gender segregation echoes late-nineteenth- and early-twentieth-century modernization efforts, in that they both organized the visual field by arranging gender expression symbols to achieve a certain national imagery. Similarly, Islamization of the nation and the public space was shaped by heteronormativity and the Western gaze, with an emphasis on the citizens' bodies and attire. If the goal of modernization policies was to produce citizens with a Western appearance, the Islamic Republic based its visual identity on rejecting Western style. State officials punished men for wearing the necktie, which was banned as it was believed to represent imperialism and Western culture. Men's hairstyles and hairstylists were continuously surveilled, and some models were banned to resist manifestations of Western culture.

Although Iranian male citizens have been subjected to the state regulatory politics of the public space, the female body took a special place in the visual creation of the Islamic nation. The hijab became a symbol of the Islamic Revolution and a distinct marker of its identity, and, as a result, the state made veiling mandatory on March 7, 1979.[31] Traditional Iranian women already observed hijab, so the mandatory rule exclusively targeted the so-called modern woman. The Iranian man's quest for power in the new world order was highlighted by the veiling of "all Iranian women" and making them inaccessible to the Western gaze. Mandatory hijab marked the postrevolutionary nation-state not only as Islamic but also as hypermasculine.[32]

Despite the state rhetoric, the Islamic Republic's sex-segregation policies, including mandatory hijab, were not an attempt to return to an Islamic past (Islamic revival) and the authentic gender relations of pre-Westernized era. In the traditional arrangement, gender segregation and practices of veiling were rather inscribed across sex (male and female) differences between men and women. Those distinctions were reflected in both public and private spheres of life. The Islamic Republic gradually redrew the lines based on sexuality, moving from the traditional principles of sex segregation to modern disciplinary technologies of power that used sexuality to access and discipline individual bodies.

A shift in the Islamic Republic's discourse of hijab took place from a focus on religious purity and chastity, concerned with social order, to one on sexuality and male desire. Before the revolution in the 1970s, the hijab, which throughout the Pahlavi era had turned into a symbol of oppression and a badge of backwardness, transformed into a symbol of defiance and a new Islamic identity for many women.[33] Following the revolution, Ayatollah Khomeini deemed the veil important for revolutionary women in order to differentiate them from corrupt (Westernized) women.[34] In gendered dynamics of revolutionary man and modern woman, the hijab's ultimate goal was seen to be the preservation of society's order and morality, with women and men held accountable—albeit unequally—for its maintenance. While women were forced to cover their bodies, men were advised to control their gaze. Ayatollah Motahari, whose thoughts in his 1968 book became the cornerstone of the Islamic Republic's official viewpoint on hijab, argued that it is not women's appearance that causes disorder in society but rather their "innate drive to display their beauty" that stimulates sexual desire in men who lack self-control.[35] He contended that the purpose of the hijab is to shield women from being regarded as sexual objects and from men's aggressive sexual behavior as well as to keep the social and moral order intact. In Motahari's view, shielding women's bodies was shielding the Islamic *Ummah* (society/community).[36]

The politics of hijab enforcement has been haunted by the gendered dynamics of revolutionary masculinity and the uncontainable contemporary woman. After mandating the hijab, wearing an improper hijab was viewed as a sign of a woman's moral depravity in the Islamic state's ideology that dominated all official ideological apparatuses.[37] Prior to the revolution, it was predominantly the urban modern woman who did not wear the hijab and opposed the postrevolutionary mandatory hijab. The same demonized female figure that personified and epitomized Pahlavi decadence for the revolutionary guerilla evolved into the postrevolutionary era's morally corrupt and sexually deviant bad-hijab woman (improperly veiled woman). As a result, the Islamic Republic's hijab discourse and policies centered on the bad-hijab woman. Placing the bad-hijab woman at the center of the hijab discourse and policies and connecting it to the figure of the demonized Pahlavi urban woman offers a different interpretation of the Islamic Republic's four-decade fixation on hijab enforcement, which also involves the revolutionary masculinity.

The Revolutionary Man's Masculinity and His Sexual Fantasies

The discourse of the bad-hijab woman revolves around the Islamic state's hegemonic masculinity, male sexual prowess, and desirability. The dominant rhetoric around this relationship changes from the piety of the Muslim woman to safeguarding the religious man from being aroused by the bad-hijab woman. In this discourse, male control over his intense sexual emotions is deemed impossible. This essentialist interpretation frees the revolutionary masculinity from being moral and serving as a guardian, which were characteristics of the Pahlavi-era hegemonic masculinity. Violence against the bad-hijab woman who is held responsible for the pious man's moral corruption is therefore not only justified but also asked for by her. The Islamic revolutionary man's fantasies of desirability by the oversexualized bad-hijab woman present themselves in the state's justification of women's ban from the stadiums. Women were banned from attending men's soccer matches in the immediate aftermath of the 1979 Revolution, a policy that was slowly extended to other sports.[38] The reasons specified for women's ban from the stadiums were that the male athletes' clothing (jerseys) and their partial nakedness might arouse women sexually.[39] This fantasy is also found in the cultural productions of *sigheh* marriages (temporary marriages) that center around discussions of female sexuality, hegemonic masculinity, and gender-based violence.

In her book on temporary wives, cultural studies scholar Claudia Yaghoobi examines the representation of women who enter temporary marriages, *sigheh*, in cultural production of the Islamic Republic. According to Yaghoobi, "Sigheh women occupy a crucial space in the social imagination of society and in particular men's fantasy world."[40] Yaghoobi analyzes two important movies, *Showkaran* (Hemlock 1998) and *Zendegi-ye Khosusi* (Private Life 2011), in this book. In both films, the male protagonists are devout revolutionary men with state ties who are married to traditional hijab-wearing religious women. While the majority of *sigheh* women who enter into temporary marriages are young and divorced and belong to lower socioeconomic backgrounds, in these two films, the *sigheh* wives are modernized, educated, financially independent women. For instance, in *Zendegi-ye Khosusi*, the female protagonist and *sigheh* wife, Parisa, smokes cigarettes, writes erotica, is divorced, lives alone, and has no hesitations about having a relationship with a man. She is adamantly opposed to institutions of religion and marriage, but after meeting the man, she seeks marriage and motherhood.[41] On the other hand, in *Showkaran*, the female protagonist Sima is a chief nurse at a hospital who freely interacts with *nā-mahram* (unrelated) males and mocks the male protagonist's religious beliefs.[42] Both women, however, readily accept the men's proposal to form a *sigheh* contract, which is primarily used to satisfy sexual desire, most frequently but not exclusively those of men, which is why Iran's middle-class, and urban population has viewed them as a form of sex work.[43] In light of the societal taboo against *sigheh* among middle-class modern women, the female characters in these films appear paradoxical. This contradiction satisfies the revolutionary Islamic man's fantasy and needs for two things: first, to be desired by the modern woman; and second, for the modern woman to undergo a profound metamorphosis into obedience. This phantasm underpins hijab policies and the characteristics of the Islamic hegemonic masculinity. Both films conclude with the female characters' deaths as a result of their decision to go public with their secret affairs. Sima dies in a car accident, and Parisa is shot and killed by the male protagonist. The female protagonist's body must be obliterated to conceal the male protagonist's moral depravity.[44] However, why does the Islamic practice of *sigheh* pose such a grave threat to the revolutionary man's life and reputation? Yaghoobi observes that both films present the female body as a battleground for contending ideologies in Iran.[45] These opposing ideologies are centered on two major clusters of polarities that have persisted throughout contemporary Iranian history: on the one hand, authenticity, tradition, and Islam; and on the other, modernity and Westernization.[46] Sima and Parisa, as modern Iranian women who embody the West for the revolutionary man, illustrate the man's helplessness to resist the changes of Westernization and his desire to appear appealing to the Western gaze. This absence of authority and control is detrimental to the revolutionary masculinity.

Zendegi-ye Khosusi concludes with the male protagonist conducting an imaginary discussion with Parisa after setting her body on fire. She inquires, "Do you regret it?" He responds, "Why regret?" It was entirely her own fault. She asks, "Don't you feel guilty?" He answers, "When the moment is right, individuals will overcome their sense of sin. The greater sin would have been allowing you to destroy my image and reputation." In this conversation, his image and reputation are inextricably linked to his masculinity, and what must be concealed by the death of Parisa is his incapacity to control himself and his desires, in other words, his questionable power. In this sense, the bad-hijab woman is a symbol of this failure and must be erased.

Conclusion

Not only does the Islamic state lack the political will to recognize and address sexual violence but it is also the primary perpetrator of gender-based violence. Although, as Moallem writes, unveiling and reveiling female bodies offered social agency for male citizen-soldiers and empowered local men, they took place in two distinct discourses, one of empowerment and awakening, the other of objectification, sexualization, and alienation.[47]

If Iranian elite men in the late nineteenth and early twentieth centuries responded to Europeans' male gaze that perceived them as "backwards and perhaps unmanly" by concealing homoeroticism and same-sex practices and dressing in European style, the mandatory hijab is an attempt in establishing a global narrative of a Shi'i hegemonic masculinity on the global stage. Hijab propaganda and politics have objectified and sexualized the female body on a daily basis, legitimizing and normalizing violence against them in an attempt to conceal the modern "Westernized" woman from the Western gaze, painting a powerful masculine image of the Islamic nation. Young women in Iran's second decade of the twenty-first century share aspects of the bad-hijab woman paradigm. The state's anti-bad-hijab discourse and utilization of violence in the public space to enforce hijab has normalized violence against women. Additionally, the state has extended its impunity for violence against women to its male citizens. Honor killings have been increasing in recent years, and each year, the nation is horrified by the tragic death of a handful of other young women. The Islamic man's sexual prowess is supported by persisting oppressive and inherently violent laws against women that assure men unrestricted access to sex, including keeping the female legal age of marriage low, and access to multiple temporary marriages and polygamy.[48] Iranian men's sexual needs and desires have been prioritized over women's citizen rights.

The death of Zhina (Mahsa) Amini has ignited an Iranian women-led movement demanding fundamental change and the overthrow of the Islamic Republic. The hijab, the symbol of masculine dominance in the Islamic Republic, has become the state's hanging rope. The photos of young ladies burning their scarves while dancing have replaced the angry revolutionary man as Iran's global image, bringing an end to the project of creating hostile masculinity.

2

The Iranian #MeToo and the Double Bind of Iranian Feminism: Between Religion, the Global Gender Struggle, and Liberal Feminism

Dilyana Mincheva and Niloofar Hooman

Introduction: The Familiarity and Locality of the Iranian #MeToo

The Iranian #MeToo movement is a particularly interesting case study for localized trajectories of feminism, which nonetheless articulate their struggles in a universalized and globalized jargon of equality, freedom, dignity, and human rights. Three significant particularities make the Iranian #MeToo movement distinct from its global and, specifically, Western counterparts: first, the development of the Iranian #MeToo within the restraints of a theological-legal state framework, which prescribes capital punishment for rape; second, the eruption of the Iranian #MeToo from within two, often ideologically opposed yet equally vibrant and convergent, on-the-ground versions of Iranian feminisms: liberal feminism, whose main concerns are universal human rights and freedoms, on the one hand, and Islamic feminism, whose project prioritizes "Islamic specificity," that is, liberation within the normativity and ethics of Islam, on the other; and third, the understanding that the stakes of #MeToo in Iran are comprehensible only if we take into account the fact that social media in this context are political tools for resistance first and foremost, a prerogative of the young, mobile, and networked generation of the Green Movement whose aspiration in the past thirteen years has been to project a reformed, liberalized, and democratized version of Iran, which reconciles the cultural and religious exclusivism of Shia Islam with universal human values. It is not surprising, therefore, that concerns over the boundaries and ownership of the female body—constituting the essence of the global #MeToo movement—are a dramatic arena in Iran for the interplay of existing and novel arguments around the idioms of locally specific trajectories of gender and social justice. At the same time, the Iranian #MeToo movement shares similarities with global trends, among them the realization of the commonalities in women's stories of oppression that inevitably generate imaginations for transnational solidarities against gender injustice, and the rising visibility of private individuals on social media whose meaningful interactions in the virtual space, across geographical borders and linguistic divides, create counter-publics of intimate and emotional bonds and thus expand the conversation of rights and freedoms outside of the claustrophobic confines of singular families, cultural-religious traditions, communities, or nations. In that last aspect, the Iranian #MeToo movement is an important contributor to a currently global feminist movement around the various faces and manifestations of patriarchal structures and misogyny and the strategies to confront them. It is important to emphasize immediately that a careful look at the Iranian #MeToo movement, through a lens that keeps in tenacious simultaneity its local and global dimensions and projections, accomplishes an important (to us as researchers) goal: it navigates reflexively between the various appropriations of the Iranian feminist subject as either "oppressed" by a retrograde religion and society (the classical orientalist proposition) or falsely liberated through a nativist anti-imperialism (which manifests itself in what is often considered unchangeable juridical-religious or cultural praxis). Our research shows that the reality of the Iranian women of the #MeToo movement is rather nuanced: oppression is neither narrated by women on Twitter as rooted in global geopolitical schemes nor described as a faceless systemic abstraction shorthanded as "the regime" or "the state." Yet, it is also evident, in the cacophony of testimonies, that both politics and the state are there too, particularly within the domain of Islamic legal frameworks, as they structure the private and public domains of a society, which comes to terms with the definitions, mediations, and consequences of feminist activism in the face of misogyny.

Methodology and Sources

Our assessment of the effects of the #MeToo movement in Iran is based on an in-depth discursive analysis of a wide variety of testimonies and interpretative frameworks that have been circulating in the Persian print and cyber public sphere since August 2020. We collected print, electronic, and public Twitter testimonies provided by activists, scholars, legal and media experts, and ordinary women and intersected the analysis of this rich material with insights derived from a deep, semi-structured conversation with Shima Ghooshe, a high-profile Iranian lawyer who has a career providing defense to domestic abuse and rape victims and who has been active recently in defending women who came forward with stories of abuse as part of the Iranian #MeToo. Ghooshe's insights were invaluable because she provided us with a reflection on the legal pressures that the movement initiated on the sharia-derived legal system, while also articulating the limitations of those pressures to bring about substantial legal reform. All collected evidence, which traversed the legal, the public, the scholarly, and the personal, revealed intersecting possibilities and dead ends, existing in complex simultaneity, faced by #MeToo-driven feminist activism in Iran. While the activists and scholarly voices engaged with the debates on the boundaries and specificities of the Iranian #MeToo were abundant, followed by a rising number of personal testimonies of ordinary women, who have been largely invisible in previous iterations of feminist organizing in Iran, it was striking for us to find that Islamic clerics and, specifically, conservative Iranian women whose prerogative has been the scriptural rereading of the Islamic dogmatic texts through a female-centered perspective, stayed silent on the effects of #MeToo in Iran. This, however, does not mean that religious discussion is absent from the movement; on the contrary, our argument suggests that contestation of religious dogmatism permeates the Iranian feminist discourse of the #MeToo era without a rejection of the cultural or spiritual dimensions of Islam. The différend between rights-based feminisms and the religious framework of feminist agency, indeed, was partially resolved when, in January 2021, the Islamic state announced its intention to adopt a bill that criminalized sexual harassment as well as any physical, emotional, or reputational violence inflicted on women.[1] While this bill does not reflect other important issues such as child marriage or marital rape, it is certainly celebrated as one of the important successes of Iranian feminism in the aftermath of the global #MeToo. It is important to note that even if epistemologically the arguments between "rights," derived from social and secular deliberation, and "religious agency," derived from metaphysical reasoning, continue to pull women in different directions, feminist solidarity in the face of #MeToo has proven capable of productively reducing some aspects of the ideological antagonisms. Other aspects of the religious-secular divide, however, continue to persist. They are most evident in the opinions mobilized in opposition to the proposed anti-harassment bill from 2021. In the last section, we address the demands for redefinition that the #MeToo movement presents for Islamic feminism.

We collected data[2] and conducted qualitative research for this chapter in the period between August 2020 and January 2022. The analysis shared here is part of an ongoing project that aims to map in a holistic and comprehensive way the epistemological, legal, and activist dimensions of feminism in Iran in light of the global #MeToo campaigns. The media sources that we analyze in this chapter include discussions unfolding in feminist journals such as the prestigious quarterly edition *Zanan Emrooz* and the national newspaper *Etemad*. These were read comparatively with reports issued by various feminist and women's rights organizations (Bidarzani, Harasswatch, and Iranian Women's Association). We monitored the #MeToo-related materials shared by the Iranian Student News Agency (ISNA), Borna News Agency, and IMNA News Agency, and followed, during the period of the study, the public Twitter testimonies in Farsi of twelve Iran-based accounts. Notably, we traced the scholarly opinions of public Iranian intellectuals on the effectiveness of #MeToo, among them Vali Morad, Morteza Pedarian, Maryam Sadat Hosseinifar, all of whom have shared nuanced positions in feminist and mainstream Iranian outlets. Additionally, we paid special attention to critique and argumentation provided by activist circles. Atena Kamel, Shima Vezvaei, Sahar Maranloo, Delaram Ali, Shahin Gholami, Minoo Heydari Kaydan, Niloofar Hamedi, Shiva Nazar Ahari, and Kambiz Norouzi are among the activists whose opinions on the accomplishments of the Iranian #MeToo meet and diverge. Finally, we placed Iran-based activism in relationship with diasporic developments of Iranian feminism in the contested work of Masih Alinejad, Roya Hakakian (based in North America), and Samaneh Savadi (based in the United Kingdom). The diasporic context of Iranian feminist activism has its own layer of complexity because it is positioned between advocacy for universal rights and freedoms embodied in the rule of presumably secular law (considered classic achievements of liberal feminism), and narratives of Islamophobia that aim to reduce the complexity of Islamic contexts to an assembly of orientalist cliches. It is particularly difficult for diasporic women to navigate the ungenerous terrains of the "native informant," the "self-hating Muslim," the "ex-Muslim," and the "Muslim woman with false consciousness" that are often partnered with accusations of power- and attention-seeking, coming from progressive circles in the West.[3] On the other hand, it is, indeed, difficult to resist the instrumentalization of testimonies of feminist suffering for the purposes of geopolitical dividends.[4]

#MeToo in the Words and Actions of Iranian Women: The Fight, the Hope, the Future

In the motley amalgam of interpretative frameworks provided by activists, legal experts, scholars, and feminists, it is easy to distinguish two opposing sentiments vis-à-vis the ability of the Iranian #MeToo to bring systemic challenge to patriarchy and misogyny and therefore to be a positive force in the lives of Iranian women. It seems that activists, scholars, and legal experts capable of providing feminist assessment are still wary of the fact that #MeToo visibility is a prerogative of a privileged class of Iranian women who have access to internet self-expression. This is clearly articulated by Atena Kamel in an article for *Zanan Emrooz* where she speaks of two main barriers in front of women to their widespread participation in the movement: one is the fact that activism on Instagram, Facebook, and Twitter requires possession of expensive technology, which is still out of reach for many rural and poor women; and second is the high familial, societal, and occupational costs that women need to sustain if they decide to come forward with testimonies of sexual harassment. Since sexual harassment is difficult to prove and even more difficult to punish, women who make their stories public risk further social marginalization and face ostracization from their communities.[5] Kamel's position is echoed by other activists who agree that gender inequalities and issues of sexual harassment are systemic problems in Iran, and they cannot be solved by individual gestures of courage. These systemic inequalities are built into the sociocultural structure and enforced, in the analysis of Sahar Maranloo,[6] by an Islamic penal code (specifically note 2 of Article 224), which is preoccupied with defining the conditions of adultery but is not oriented toward drafting a sex crime law or creating public conditions for women to pursue an open pathway of justice, devoid of shame, in cases of sexual harassment. Maranloo is particularly skeptical of the ability of media campaigns such as #MeToo to bring the needed legal changes that recognize and define sexual harassment, but she welcomes these campaigns as a form of resistance that can broaden public conversation.

Maranloo's legal skepticism is confirmed in the interview that we conducted with Shima Ghooshe, who represented a group of five women who accused Keyvan Emamverdi of sexual assault in a first-of-its-kind trial in Iran that opened in November 2021. Emamverdi, an archeology graduate from Tehran University, was subsequently accused of committing more than three hundred rapes over a period of ten years. Ghooshe has been deeply involved with issues of rape and sexual harassment throughout a long career of legal feminist activism. Yet Emamverdi's case was different, first, because of the very public nature of the trial and the gravity of the possible penalty (for 'corruption on Earth') and, second, because of Ghooshe's deep involvement with sexual assault victims who made their stories public, specifically prompted by the global #MeToo enthusiasm. She shared with us that for many years women who experienced rape or sexual assault have been publicly silent and the only relief that Ghooshe, as a lawyer, was able to provide them was simply listening to their stories. After Emamverdi's case, Ghooshe got involved in other cases where victims openly sought legal help and filed lawsuits against their abusers. Ghooshe is unequivocal in her positive assessment of the #MeToo movement as a feminist activity, which has facilitated the public conversation around sexual harassment and rape tremendously: a conversation that happens today not only in cyberspace but also, increasingly, in the actual public sphere, in courts, and inside the private homes of victims and perpetrators. Among other things, the complexity of the public conversation, prompted by #MeToo, comes not only from the gravity of the punishment (if rape is proven) but also from a layer of geopolitics that gets invested in it. In the past, feminist movements in Iran have frequently faced the accusation that they bring in Western, imperialist, and Zionist propaganda in the country.[7] It is no surprise then that Emamverdi's lawyer publicly accused Ghooshe of spreading Zionist influences in the country, suggesting that his client was a "victim" of a global, anti-Muslim, anti-Iranian campaign.[8]

Ghooshe's generally positive reception of the Iranian #MeToo is, however, counterbalanced by a warning that despite some advances, women at large find it very difficult to discuss matters of sexual assault with their families. For example, the women who sued Emamverdi had not shared their experiences with their families; those of them who lived outside of Tehran needed to find excuses for their frequent travels to the capital. Crucially, Ghooshe insists, women who are ready to face the legal system today and seek gender justice (in her practice) belong to various social, ethnic, religious, and economic groups, with the inclusion of minoritarian and marginalized Baha'i women alongside Muslim women of all classes. This observation goes against some of the accusations of urban-driven elitism in #MeToo that activists and scholars of feminism have raised. Ghooshe's observations are somewhat echoed by activist Shahin Gholami's analysis in a special collection of articles published in celebration of International Women's Day (March 8) in 2021.[9] Gholami outlines a long historical list of activities that feminist organizations have initiated in the past, including the forming of various collectives for prevention of domestic violence and protection of women's rights, and sexual harassment awareness campaigns, with limited public effect. She insists that it is only after the spontaneous, and deeply democratic, eruption of various testimonies in public that target abusers of all kinds—from ordinary people to celebrities and clerics[10]—that rape and harassment have become a political and public issue in Iran. Gholami defines the Iranian #MeToo movement as similar to the second wave of feminism with its fundamental emphasis on politicizing the issue of sexual harassment and the female's right to control her own body.

From a legal standpoint, it is important for Ghooshe to note that sexual assault and rape are considered an abuse of divine justice, not just a violation of man-made justice, according to the strict, Islamically derived, normative wrap of "corruption on Earth," that is, rape, and as such gets punished with the death sentence, leading to gross miscarriage of actual justice for the victims of sexual assault. This moral legal framework, mirroring developments in early Islam, is unable to fully capture social progress in the domain of sex crimes. In short, Ghooshe argues that the strictest punishment, provided as an ethical framework for safeguarding the pristine divine order, in effect, protects the perpetrators. She shares with us that many women had approached her with accusatory testimonies in the case of Emamverdi, but once informed that a sentence could lead to capital punishment, they withdrew their testimonies. Counterintuitive to what might seem right, Ghooshe is particularly disillusioned with the sentence against Emamverdi. The reason, on the one hand, is her own ethical opposition to capital punishment; significantly, on the other hand, it has to do with Emamverdi's case acting as a public PR for a legal system that refuses to change, and for the Islamic state and the way it handles cases of grave moral transgression such as rape, subsumed here under the category of adultery. The capital punishment, therefore, gets enacted as a response to a crime defined as "adultery" and only for the sake of making a public point about the strictness of Islamic law, which is applied under certain circumstances and only under very strict testimonial conditions.[11] The various nuances of sexual assault and harassment—which could range from the verbal to penetration with hands and sex toys, to unwanted hugging and kissing—are either not factored in at all by the law or are so lightly punished that they could hardly have any preventive public effect. Importantly, while public pieties such as the single sentence of one offender provide no systemic justice for women who live with very nuanced and multifaceted forms of harassment, they also actively cement the ethical Islamic veneer of the legal system and the state as incorruptible in the face of the gravest moral offense. What Ghooshe articulates, therefore, is a hard-to-break double bind between legal interpretations of divine-oriented social justice and gendered sociocultural patriarchy enabled to an extent as a result of these interpretations.

Ghooshe's legal observations find resonance in analytical interventions provided by women activists such as Minoo Heydari Kaydan, Niloofar Hamedi, and Shiva Nazar Ahari. Many testimonies that come their way get published on the sites of Bidarzani and the Iranian Women's Association, but they need to be anonymized due to the deep-seated cultural systems of honor, shame, and modesty in Iran. These activists document a widespread misogyny, which transpires in victim-blaming, expectations of silence in the face of abuse, or women losing jobs and the support of their families when they decide to go public with personal accounts of sexual harassment. The Iranian #MeToo movement, therefore, for these activists has its local specificity in not being able to facilitate a social display of the faces and names of all women who have experienced sexual traumas. Our own eighteen-month-long observation of twelve active Twitter accounts where stories of abuse have been shared publicly simultaneously confirms this specificity and questions it to an extent. While some of the stories shared on Twitter come from abstract and difficult-to-define agents such as blume_50, sara_mf20, spongeNob3, keepdancing, and principessa1848, others are quite specific in terms of names, dates, and places of abuse. For example, wobewgeichmich names the perpetrator of sexual abuse and provides vivid details about when and where the crime happened. Other women from our Twitter pool revealed the identities of relatives who abused them or specific memories of past family events where harassment happened. One of the Twitter users, for example, described a work assault by revealing the details and naming the perpetrator.[12] It seems that the most common Twitter position is the one of confirmation that a sexual crime has happened to the woman who tweets and solidarity with others who have gone through similar experiences. Certainly, all Twitter data needs to be read in light of other larger conversations in Iran, grounded by activist, feminist, and legal work. While the Twitter sphere is a space of spontaneous eruption of testimonial sharing, questions of access, anonymity, and algorithmic clustering come in the way of comprehensive interpretations. All stakeholders in this conversation, however, tend to agree that the absence of relevant statistics on sexual harassment conceal the magnitude of the problem and reduce the scattered accounts to anecdotal evidence.

It is not surprising, therefore, that the Iranian #MeToo also presents voices critical of the movement yet committed to its ideals. Lawyer and media activist Kambiz Norouzi considers the anonymity of the accusers as opposed to that of the perpetrators in many of the circulating testimonies as a liability for the movement and its ability to bring about social change.[13] First, Norouzi claims, if the final goal is the de-stigmatization of women who have experienced abuse, then it is up to them to be able to address their abusers full front, putting their names and faces with the accusatory charges. While there are social costs to be paid, this seems to Norouzi the most effective way of driving social conversations. Second, the anonymity of the accusers envelops the movement in conspiracy theories: the charges are reduced to personal revenge, immoral attempts at ruining reputations, or accusations that foreign, nonindigenous interests propel the movement. In short, when women refuse to go public with their testimonies, the systemic and widespread nature of these abuses gets lost. It is not a coincidence, therefore, that Iran does not have any official statistics that speak to the frequency or nature of sexual harassment and abuse inside the domestic and public spheres.

Ghooshe points our attention to the fact that many women who share their stories in some detail on Instagram or Twitter currently reside outside Iran. Samaneh Savadi, a vocal activist currently working in the United Kingdom, also interviewed by the Iranian Women Association, clearly articulates the tensions between individual agency and structure within the Iranian feminist movement. It is worth quoting Savadi's reflection at length since it carefully captures a crucial set of arguments and interpretative arrangements that we unpack in the final sections of the chapter:

> We are not talking about an abuser, and it is basically too superficial to talk about an abuser and an abused person. We are talking about a structure called the rape culture. We define the rape culture as a pyramid with the rape at the top, sexist jokes, teasing, men sitting wide open in a taxi, whistling at the bottom of the pyramid. A little higher is the boss putting his hand on the employee's shoulder, offering some indecent proposals; the victim denunciation; the victim encouragement to remain silent, and so on, all of which together form a culture. The rape culture tells a woman to cover herself. It says if you are not to blame and you do not want to, no one will hurt you. It says men are like that. Men are a set of erotic animals that are not able to control themselves, and now if they reach out, it is a male trait. That is the nature of the men, and it must be accepted. However, the victim is silent about one event at a time and is suddenly forced to remain silent in the face of rape, so the rape culture survives … I think Iranian #MeToo and the harassment narrative movements have again brought women closer together. It has highlighted the notion of feminist sisterhood and standing together. Women with different political and religious orientations

stood together, believed in each other's statements, tried to defend each other's rights against all political affairs, did not leave each other alone. It should be celebrated, and this unity should be valued. This unity will help us to progress. We took steps on this shaky piece of wood, but now we are holding hands, and this is a turning point for all of us and for the Iranian women's movement. We just found each other and learnt the way. We must not stop, we must continue.[14]

Savadi's analysis clearly uses terms of reference—such as 'rape culture' as part of a social system of abuse as well as feminist sisterhood and solidarity as a product of continuous and concerted struggle—that penetrated the global vocabularies of #MeToo.[15] According to her, the #MeToo and, generally, the Iranian feminist movement must inevitably bring about some of the changes that, through various waves and fights, Western liberal feminists have accomplished throughout the long durée of the nineteenth and twentieth centuries: the right (if not the full actualization) to bodily integrity and dignity, the criminalization of rape and sexual harassment, and the legal and rights-based expansion of notions of feminist freedom and choice in the domestic and professional worlds.[16] Savadi clearly states in the interview that, for her, such "lacks" are what fuel the Iranian feminist movement. Her description brims with distinct universal aspirations and clearly defined goals in terms of rights-based solutions, which link the Iranian #MeToo movement to what is often considered "universal" in otherwise divergent histories of feminist struggles. Unlike Ghooshe, who seems more interested in understanding the moral dimensions of abuse and punishment, and how they could be integrated into a dynamic sharia-based and Shia-driven system of Islamic family law, Savadi's emphasis is distinctly worldly and secular.

The Iranian #MeToo and the "Native Informant": Diasporic Dilemmas and Positionalities

It is not difficult to see the recommendations of Samaneh Savadi and the advocacy work of Masih Alinejad and Roya Hakakian as fitting within the derogatory rubric, developed by postcolonial critiques of feminism and Islamic feminism, of the "native informant." Savadi, Alinejad, and Hakakian are vocal and visible Iranian women, currently residing in the United Kingdom and United States, who have made careers out of denouncing the systemic, pious, and state-sponsored versions of misogyny in Iran. These women's voices appear in influential media outlets such as *Washington Post*,[17] *Foreign Policy*,[18] and *New York Review of Books*,[19] among others, and they are guest speakers in prestigious Ivy League campuses in America.²⁰ They have a solid presence on Twitter and YouTube; they talk to a wide range of women in Iran and in the diaspora, in both Farsi and English; and they perpetually search for ways to expand their activist message to institutions and organizations that could promote feminism as part of a human rights agenda in Iran.²¹ Suffice it to say here that Masih Alinejad has seven million followers on Instagram and over three hundred thousand followers on Twitter. She is the initiator of the incredibly contentious and popular campaigns #MyStealthyFreedom (which is also the name of a New York–based nonprofit organization aimed at promoting women's rights in Iran) and #LetUsTalk, both meant to fight compulsory hijab in Iran and to reveal various other forms of oppression, from honor-based violence to systemic misogyny supported by the Iranian state and the legal system. The icon of Iranian Islamic feminism, Ziba Mir Hosseini, for example, is particularly critical of activism of this caliber. In an article in 2011, she explained what a feminist struggle rooted in Islamic scripture might look like and how it diverges from the political agendas of "native informants" (such as Irshad Manji and Ayaan Hirsi Ali).²² Certainly, Hakakian and Alinejad are not Manji and Hirsi Ali, but nonetheless the comparison is hardly far-fetched. Similarly to Manji and Hirsi Ali, both Hakakian and Alinejad have been severely criticized by Western liberal elites, and by Islamic feminists, who say that they serve imperial, xenophobic, and Islamophobic agendas by speaking against the hijab and against forms of oppression sanctioned by religion.²³ The clearest manifestation of this liberal left-wing critique is possibly the recent polemic that Alinejad entered into on Twitter with Tim Mynett, the husband and PR manager of Congresswoman Ilhan Omar, with regards to the latter's proposal of an Islamophobia bill, meant to reduce hate crimes against Muslims in America.²⁴ The polemic was triggered by an opinion-based article opposing the bill that Alinejad published in the *Washington Post* in January 2022.²⁵ Concerns about marginalization of racialized groups based on culture or religion, about xenophobia and Islamophobia, are central to the left-wing agendas of Western democracies. At the same time, women who show solidarity with Alinejad point to the terrors of Islamism and the plight of women who live under theocracies profoundly uninterested in women's rights and well-being.²⁶

As "native informants," they are usually labeled as women who betray their religion by criticizing it publicly for the purposes of fame and political gain. Refusing to take a public stand against Islamophobia, these women prefer to focus on Islam, not simply as an abstract religion but as a complex religio-cultural systemic habitat where folkloric, scriptural, and authoritarian interpretations allow misogyny to reign supreme in women's lives. Our argument here is that the choice between "fighting" Islamophobia and "defending" Islamism is politically wrong, regardless of which side one wants to take, and it is also deeply dishonest in terms of feminist struggles and agendas in Iran. There are two main reasons for this: one addresses internal understandings of feminist justice articulated and sought within indigenous legal, societal, and cultural terms in Iran; the other addresses external dynamics and has to do with global discourses on Islamophobia as propelled by the women's question.

To clarify the internal stakes of this wrongful binary choice, we must emphasize that the accounts of misogyny in Iran that Alinejad and Hakakian provide for the anglophone media sphere are not, in fact, different from what many women who live, work, and write inside Iran share in Farsi for various Iranian outlets, activist, media, legal, and so on. All our data in Farsi, residing in the holistic intersection of multiple testimonies—from Twitter posts, to published interviews with activists, legal experts, and scholars—confirms that the diasporic activists are not imagining abuse to score sensational points for their own Western-based media activities. Indeed, public denunciations via #MeToo in Iran are still tentative, and many women prefer anonymity due to cultural and religious barriers that prevent them from going public with their testimonies. Women's silence, however, should not be taken as a sign that the strict morals embodied by the Islamic state work to prevent sexual abuse. This is exactly the image that the state ideology, wrapped in Islamic piety, wants to project. When women point to the complicity of state and piety as part of a large system that underpins their suffering, we need to pay attention, even if our positionality puts us in disagreement on some points. The women from our data do not make a macro-political argument about the industrial-military complex of the United States because they do not perceive their lives as entangled in these macro-political schemes on a daily basis. But they do perceive their lifeworlds as profoundly informed by the Islamic and legal praxis of the Iranian state.

To clarify the external stakes of the wrongful double bind between Islamism and Islamophobia, we should say that the labeling of women who approach Islam in a critical way as Islamophobic—particularly when they speak from the position of their own experiential embeddedness within the scriptural-religious-ritualistic praxis of Islam[27]—is not going to resolve Western forms of Islamophobia or anti-Muslim racism. If anything, putting these women outside of the legitimate scope of engagement with Islam serves only to deepen Islamophobia because it constructs Islam as the complete other of debate, that is, as incapable of generating impartial and reasoned positions. Ironically, this is the most Islamophobic position from which one might want to "defend" Islam. Ghooshe clearly states in the interview with us that feminism, which aims to change legislation in Iran, may often be labeled as anti-Islamic by conservative opponents, but it is not. She is clear that Shia forms of legality, unlike some of its Sunni counterparts, are open to historical change and progress. Religion does not have to be in the way of social progress and women's rights, Ghooshe argues. Yet it is now in Iran—through the public agents and bureaucrats who control and define all aspects of religious life, including jurisprudence; staying silent on that matter does not help women. The extreme politicization of critique against religiously sanctioned systems of misogyny forces experts to take sides and, as a result, prevents integrity in the analyses of testimonies of abuse, harassment, and violence. Feminism in such climate becomes hostage to larger macro-political agendas; the Iranian #MeToo risks getting lost in interpretations that either undermine the testimonies as false consciousness, personal revenge, confused desires for Western forms of liberation, and state conspiracies or sensationalize them for the sake of political division. Essentially, these bifurcations do not allow Iranian women to be heard on their own terms. While this pathological state of division through media-manipulated political communication is ubiquitous in a globally connected world, it is important to finally assess what that means for divergent feminist trajectories in Iran.

Conclusion: The Iranian #MeToo as Feminism on the Border

Divided political spheres are detrimental to projects of solidarity. Yet, an important feminist gain for women of all stripes in Iran, resulting from public pressures during the #MeToo campaigns, is the historic proposition of a bill against sexual harassment. The piece of legislation called Protection, Dignity, and Security of Women Against Violence is a text built on compromise where certain provisions are included such as penalties for violence and sexual misconduct, which ranges from sexual coercion to sexual messaging. Yet other important protections are missed, such as clear clauses against child marriage, honor-based violence, and marital rape.[28] Voices of conservatism, such as Zahra Ayatollahi, the head of the Women's Socio-cultural Council in the Supreme council of the Cultural Revolution, have been critical of the bill, interpreting it as a threat to Iranian family values and as a form of emasculation for the traditional patriarchal protectors of women in the face of their fathers, husbands, and sons.[29] Certainly,

Ayatollahi's ultraconservatism has been countered by the many progressive voices that we captured during our research and who made this legislation possible. Ayatollahi's critique, however, has been prevalent in Iranian society for many years; it harmonizes perfectly with the fears of Westernization and colonization disseminated by the Islamic state's propaganda machine. Importantly, these fears propel the development and cultural legitimacy of what is often considered an indigenous form of feminism, which in Western scholarship gets labeled as Islamic feminism. Mir Hosseini is perhaps the most visible proponent of this type of feminism, aimed at the destruction of patriarchy from within Islam's sacred texts and religious frameworks.[30] The main argument here is that the Qur'an and the Sunna (the collected narratives of the life and deeds of the Prophet Muhammad) contain all principles of social justice, equality, and equity for both men and women. The Qur'an gives humanity the trajectory toward justice, which does not translate in equal rights for men and women. Islamic feminism argues for "substantive equality" not "formal equality," in the words of Mir Hosseini.[31] This means, according to Hosseini, that Muslim women do not argue for legal treatments that recognize them as serving the same societal functions as men. Islamic feminism treats women as equal in dignity to men (not necessarily equal in rights), which allows them to have complementary social functions, based on which they could argue for equal opportunities in life and to fight for equitable life results. Hosseini situates Islamic feminism at the intersection of critique of Western modernity and critique of retrograde religious patriarchy. Her project is one of restoring the dimensions of progressive religion. Hosseini's most substantial argument is that, politically, feminist change in Iran is impossible without religious legitimation.[32]

Islamic feminism, of course, has developed into a full-fledged theoretical, theological, and epistemological position since the 1990s. It has multiple proponents and critiques, and a rocky intellectual trajectory.[33] It is important for us here to highlight that, within the Iranian context, two arguments of resistance toward Islamic feminism have emerged. They are also visible in the public operations of the #MeToo movement. First, Islamic feminism prioritizes religious identity over anything else. Since in Iran the official and noblest guardian of the Shia religious framework is the Islamic state, it is very difficult for Islamic feminists to escape a theological, epistemological, and legal alliance with the state. "Dignity," indeed, is the favorite word of both Islamic feminists and the legislators who drafted the revolutionary anti-sexual harassment bill, since "equal in dignity" is the Islamic response to the liberal proposition "equal in rights." As a vast and ambiguous territory, "equal in dignity" is difficult to define and as such serves the need for Islamically authentic legitimation of feminist legal changes. In the Iranian context, religion-based feminism, therefore, loses its critical cutting edge and becomes open to co-optations by state-sponsored ideologies. Islamic feminism here is not a resistance movement; it works within and often supports the status quo. The second argument against Islamic feminism, developed by scholars Leila Mouri and Kristin Soraya Batmanghelichi, is that, for all its aspirations of reflecting indigenous religious authenticity, it does not.[34] Islamic feminism for these Iranian scholars and activists is an entirely diasporic phenomenon: it originates in Western contexts as a theoretically hipster way of reconciling the minoritarian status of Muslim women in the West with demands for political visibility and status. If Islamic feminism has any meaning as a subversive force, it is in the Western academic contexts from which it originates and whose critical methodologies it adopts, as a corrective to imperialism, modernity, and neoliberalism. The high profile of Mir Hosseini in the Western academia, her training and professorial tenure in some of the most prestigious spaces of the Western academia, and her prolific writing in English are considered a liability when it comes to her ability to provide alternative to activisms inside Iran that have clearly defined goals and are wrapped in the language of universal human rights.

Finally, we showed that #MeToo in Iran is an arena where contentious arguments on feminism's meaning, epistemologies, possible futures, domestic and diasporic articulations clash and collaborate. Rather than addressing these encounters as a hopeless impasse, we suggest that they present a case for what Mincheva defines as "feminism on the border."[35] This is a type of feminism that refuses binary explanations and, rather, accepts the project of liberation as rooted in tensions linked to faith, belonging, and positionality. Importantly, border feminism as a productive and transformative encounter is impossible without care as a fundamental feminist practice. Care signals our ability as women and scholars to take the experiences of suffering and empowerment at face value and to approach them with scholarly integrity. This is, we think, the only approach that allows the Iranian #MeToo to be understood within its own local specificity while being part of global decolonial trends for feminist and gender justice.

3

Rhetorical Listening to the Iranian #MeToo Movement in Diaspora

Yalda N. Hamidi

Introduction

Since the beginning of 2020, social media has exploded with stories of Iranian #MeToo. Iranian women from different avenues of life came out with horrifying stories of their violated bodies, their jobs taken away by powerful men who abused them, and their reputations tarnished in their communities. Iranian women journalists have become pioneers in sharing stories of their abuse. Because of the legal barriers and political threats for victims of sexual violence within Iran, their stories have been picked up, shared, and enhanced by other Iranian cyberfeminist, activists, and journalists outside of the nation.[1] In this chapter, based on the already existing academic feminist scholarship in the field, I argue that lack of attention to sexual harassment and #MeToo is only a piece of a larger puzzle of the ways gender-based violence gets overlooked. However, it does not mean that Iranian academic feminists have ignored violence against women. On the contrary, violence against women has constantly been in the canon of Iranian diasporic and transnational feminism, except when it has come to the interpersonal level. This absence raises an essential and timely question for academic feminist scholarship, especially when one hears daily news of honor killings, domestic abuse, and sexual harassment inside Iran, and learns about the constant stories of resistance and collective action or, in less-hopeful cases, victim blaming, disappointment, and self-harm of the victims.

To categorize and provide a typology of Iranian transnational academic feminist scholarship, this chapter relies on Valentine Moghadam's four trends on transnational feminist networks.[2] I argue that Iranian academic feminists outside of Iran gathered under three branches of transnational feminism that address institutional, colonial, imperial, and neoliberal violence against women and opted out of a human rights–based feminism; the branch primarily focuses on interpersonal gender-based violence. Next, I stress the privilege of these academic feminists over voices of Iranian women who face the censorship of the Islamic state to highlight the significance of locating voices of Iranian women survivors and victims of interpersonal violence in making transnational solidarities.

Addressing Gendered and Sexual Violence in Iranian Feminism/s

A quick search for keywords such as "domestic violence," "rape," "sexual assault," and "violence against women" in English and Farsi academic databases related to studies on Iranian women's communities shows a vast difference in the level of attention paid to the topic inside Iran among Iranian sociologists, academic feminists, and women journalists versus their sisters in the diaspora. Against an abundance of literature on these topics in Farsi, the same key terms in English barely takes the research in a similar direction[3] and mostly offer different results, which focus more on violence imposed by governments against women and colonial/imperial violence against Iranians in economic and ideological terms. However, this data discrepancy around the topic of violence is not unique to Iranian-identifying researchers.

In the Global North, the feminist responses to the issues of gendered and domestic violence have not been consistent either. In "Feminist Strategies to End Violence against Women," Rebecca Jane Hall explains that mainstream

> feminist movements' advocacy for battered women in the 1970s and 1980s was dominated by white middle- and upper-class women and tended to focus on patriarchy as the root—and often the sole—cause of violence against women … The North American "battered women's movement," a second-wave feminist response to violence against women in the home, maybe contextualized within the feminist principle that 'the personal is political' and calls to make the private public.[4]

However, this scholarship has not been specifically responsive to instances of gendered violence among communities of women of color and on a global scale. For example, in rereading *Handmaid's Tale*,[5] Ruby Hamad reminds us that "the violence imposed on women's bodies in Atwood's dystopia has already been visited upon the bodies of black and Indigenous women many times over."[6] Different levels of access to privileges such as having a safe home, feeling safe with police and government forces in the public sphere, and protection against colonial and imperial violence play into a different articulation of gendered violence.

The intersectional realities of women's experiences of violence play into how scholars have addressed that issue within a specific community. Here, a brief review of the history of the emergence of Iranian local and transnational feminism/s can shed some light on the divergent ways of discussing violence on different sides of the international borders.

Iranian transnational feminism is the immediate fruit of Iranian women's feminism and patriotic womanhood and therefore carries some similar focal concerns. In a brief overview of the history of Iranian feminism, one can recognize a trajectory that begins with the Constitutional Revolution of 1906 and branches out to many different versions. Kumari Jayawardena argues that feminism in "Eastern" countries, Iran included, has been born only after the rise of anti-colonial nationalist movements, as secondary to nationalism.[7] In other words, a local version of nationalism resulted in the emergence of women's rights, only to promote the nation's modernization. Through a different historical investigation, Firoozeh Kashani-Sabet confirms Jayawardena's main argument in the Iran of the late nineteenth and early twentieth centuries and refers to "patriotic womanhood"[8] as the seed of Iranian women's activism. In this patriotic discourse, early activists argued for improvements in women's hygiene and education for the good of the larger nation. The same discourse was picked up by the first Pahlavi state and appropriated as "state feminism," also promoting women's education, hygiene, and employment to make a progressive nation. "A major watershed in the making of modern Iranian society was the bold and controversial attempt of Reza Shah Pahlavi (reigned 1925–41) to transform Iranian womanhood radically. The Women's Awakening of 1936–41 was a state feminism project that offered new opportunities in employment and education for some Iranian [women]."[9] During the 1960s and as a part of the Iranian leftist movement, Iranian leftist women formed their versions of feminism to advocate for gendered equality. What is immediately evident in reviewing the history of Iranian local and home-grown feminism/s is their primary engagement with the ideas of nationhood and government, and thus more attention is paid to the structural and institutional levels of violence against women.

With the 1979 Revolution, so many primarily middle-class and secular Iranian women academics and activists faced the dilemma of whether to leave

Iran or lose their jobs and feminist advocacies. Some of those who left Iran found jobs in academic spaces located in European and North-American universities, continued their studies on women's issues in Iran before and after the revolution, and joined transnational feminist movements and activisms. Additionally, the Islamic government has mobilized Muslim women who embraced its ideology and joined to support it. In the scholarship of the Iranian feminist diaspora, these women and their networking and movements have been labeled as "Islamic feminists." Resisting colonial and imperial dominance and collaborating with the Islamic state to raise women's education, employment, and Muslim women's rights inside Islamic families are some of the most critical issues for Islamic feminism.

Because of the scattered geographies of Iranian feminists and the diversity of the scholarship they produced, I rely on Valentine Moghadam's categorization of transnational feminist networks and movements to investigate how each of these groups examined issues of gendered violence. Moghadam explains, "Transnational feminist activism takes place on several levels (global, regional, local); addresses political, policy, and normative issues within global and local spaces; involves a variety of strategies (protests, petitions, conferences, coalition building); and mobilizes women from three or more countries around some priority issues."[10] Since Iranian academic women's scholarship examines feminism at different levels and shares the object of study with other contexts, I use the term "Iranian transnational feminism" to point to feminist scholarship about Iranian women, produced by Iranian academic women who left Iran after the 1979 Revolution.

Moghadam classifies four prominent trends in transnational feminist scholarship and networks as "those that target the neoliberal economic policy agenda; those that focus on the danger of fundamentalisms and insist on women's human rights, especially in the Muslim world; women's peace groups that target conflict, war, and empire; and networks engaging in feminist humanitarianism and international solidarity."[11] As I will explain in the next section of this chapter, Iranian feminists in the diaspora have concentrated their energy in addressing the role of the Iranian Islamic government and its fundamentalist gender policies, highlighting the issues of war and empire, and finally criticizing the neoliberal economies and globalization of the female labor market. However, in reviewing their literature, one can barely find studies that center the Iranian women's human rights issues, particularly the version that focuses on addressing interpersonal violence, including sexual harassment, and engages most effectively with the #MeToo movement.

Typology of Iranian Diasporic and Transnational Feminism

Human Rights–Based Iranian Transnational Feminism

The idea of human rights goes back to thirteenth-century philosophy, and was taken more seriously during the twentieth century, especially after the Second World War. Against its appealing logic, considering human beings as the same and equal in the Universal Declaration of Human Rights (UDHR) left women marginalized because the idea of "sameness" resulted in male experience becoming the standard. To address this shortcoming, the UN Commission on the Status of Women (CSW) pressed for the Convention on the Elimination of All Forms of Discrimination against Women (CEDAW), was adopted by the UN General Assembly on December 18, 1979, and entered into force on September 3, 1981. Among other goals, CEDAW deconstructs the cultural and religious justifications of violence against women.[12] This brief history explains why CEDAW has become a basis for human rights–based feminism, as one of the prominent trends in transnational feminist networking and activism.

In *Feminist and Human Rights Struggles in Peru: Decolonizing Transnational Justice* (2015), Pascha Bueno-Hansen emphasizes the healthy and functional marriage of feminism and human rights movements to fight back against armed conflict and its consequences of the disappearance of family members, torture, and sexual assault in Latin America. Specifically, in the case of Peru, feminists and human rights activists challenged the thin line between consent and coercion in the sexual relationship between civilian women and armed forces. Both Bueno-Hansen and Moghadam highlight that human rights–based feminist rhetoric has been picked up and utilized to respond to state violence, war, conflict, and their effects on women's lives. Human rights–based feminism has been used by many Bangladeshi, Indian, and Pakistani feminists to address topics from acid violence to rape and honor killings, and even genocide of the Rohingyas of the Rakhine state Myanmar by the non-Muslim government in their societies. Additionally, in *Between Feminism and Islam: Human Rights and Sharia Law in Morocco*,[13] the author elaborates on how Muslim people advocating for women's rights move back and forth on the faded lines between women's rights and their religious beliefs frequently.

Even though it seems natural for women's rights to be considered human rights, and while the notion of sisterhood makes it even more meaningful to imagine collaborations between feminist and human rights movements,[14] one can find a significant controversy in the feminist literature over adopting human rights as a frame for articulating women's situation. Inderpal Grewal is among the most prominent feminists who oppose combining the two. She argues that "it is only on the level of universalized constructions of 'women' as a category and the generalized invocations of oppression by 'global feminisms' 'American' practitioners that such discourses of rights become powerful [On the contrary, Grewal argues that] policy and action require addressing localized and transnational specificities that created gendered inequalities."[15] Hall seconds Grewal's argument by acknowledging the possibility of cultural appropriation around the international human rights frame. She writes:

> International human rights, as a normative framework and political tool for addressing violence against women, falls on the fault line between progression and regression. International human rights instruments have provided important and effective tools for transnational feminist organizing against violence, but this framework has also been co-opted as a legislative veil that obscures "business-as-usual" international policy and practice and in a twisted irony has also been appropriated by imperial powers to justify large scale violence.[16]

Dana Olwan elaborates on the dangers of such cultural appropriation, specifically when it comes to understanding immigrant Muslim communities. In "Gendered Violence, Cultural Otherness, and Honour Crimes in Canadian National Logics," Olwan clarifies how "the honour crime has been linked to recent waves of migration and culturally specific notions of honour. [It has been] imagined as a foreign and imported phenomenon brought to Canada by immigrants who fail to assimilate to national and 'western' ideals of gender equality."[17] In what she calls "Pinkwashing the Honour Crime,"[18] the author tracks the manufacturing of Islamophobia against the immigrant Muslim community inside Canada and a large Muslim community in Pakistan and identifies both as geographies of violence.

Not surprisingly, a group of Iranian transnational feminists who are concerned about the role of colonial and imperial violence adopt the same logic. For example, Sima Shakhsari addresses how the bodies of the Iranian homosexuals were appropriated after 9/11 by the discourses of the War on Terror to identify Iran as homophobic land and the Iranian homosexual as an ultimate victim in need of saving by Western media and activism.[19] This approach seems justified because of the dominance of the imperial power and the media's role in the misrepresentation, criminalization, and appropriation of the brown, Middle Eastern, Muslim, and Iranian bodies.

Even though it is impossible to disagree with the complexity of the human rights discourse and acknowledge some of the irreversible damages caused by the appropriation of human rights–based feminism in justifications of war and invasions against Muslim communities, one cannot ignore the shallow participation of Iranian transnational feminists in advocating for their sisters in gender-based violence issues of honor killing, sexual assault, domestic violence, and more. This is especially true when the Islamic state constantly relies on appropriating cultural and religious rhetoric to justify harm, blame the victims, and preclude the request for social justice for survivors. Maryamossadat Torabi highlights the role of the Islamic government in confining the citizen's access to the internet, which curtailed the #MeToo movement conscious-raising in the virtual public sphere.[20] On a different note, an Iranian woman testifying against a man who abused her might "quickly turn into a criminal if she can't prove rape," said Shadi Sadr, Iranian lawyer and human rights advocate based in London. Sadr explains, "When she [the victim of sexual assault] testifies that there was sex, she is testifying against herself as well."[21] In this context, Sadr points to the criminalization of women's bodies having a sexual relationship outside wedlock under Sharia law[22] and especially the stoning sentence for married women who have had/been forced into sex with someone other than their husbands.

Anti-fundamentalist Iranian Transnational Feminism

The critical engagements of feminists with religious institutions and their implications for women's lives have constantly been one of the dominant themes of transnational feminism over the history of feminist movements.

> During the twentieth century, there was the resurgence of religious conservative movements and their conspicuous influence on the gender agenda in global and national policy spaces. The alliance of the Catholic establishment represented by the Vatican with the Sunni establishment (Al-Azhar) and the Shia establishment (the Ulama of Iran), at the UN International Conference on Population and Development (ICPD) (Cairo, 1994), and at the UN Fourth World Conference on Women (Beijing 1995) was very much manifest in the synchronization of their agendas with respect to which elements of the gender agenda they should oppose and block.[23]

Among the subthemes that emerged in this genre of transnational feminist scholarship and occupied the canon are critiques of the religious insistence "on regulating relationships of the private domain, including sexuality, biological and social reproduction, marriage, gender roles and definitions of what constitutes a 'proper' family."[24]

However, the work of transnational Iranian feminists, in confrontation with the Islamic state, shows another layer of this story. In "Gender and Revolutionary Transformation: Iranian 1979 and East-Central Europe 1989,"[25] Moghadam attempts to explore the gendered relationships and consequences of revolutions for women, specifically focusing on the Iranian Revolution of 1979. Her analysis explains why the Islamic Revolution of 1979 has become the dominant signifier that many Iranian feminists have explored in the study of Iranian feminism and women's issues years after it happened. Not surprisingly, the two primary works that discuss gender-based and domestic violence are located within this category. Nevertheless, one can find different subthemes in this genre:

The first and probably the dominant narrative in anti-fundamentalist feminism/s is calling out the role of the Islamic state in oppressing women and taking their rights away. An early work, "Khomeini's Teachings and Their Implications for Women," by Haleh Afshar provides evidence for this subtheme. Afshar recognizes two problems caused by the Islamic Revolution for Iranian women: "One is the Quranic text which relegates women to the sphere of domesticity and gives them status below men. The second is the imposition of a particular clergy's interpretation which denies women even those rights accorded to them by the Quran such as economic independence and religious freedom."[26] Later in "Women, State, and Ideology in Iran," Afshar reiterates her argument for the role of the Islamic Revolution in repressing Iranian women in a broader scope, from the inside domestic sphere to employment, education, controlling sexualities, and women's ethic columns written in the newspapers. She concludes that the Islamic state and its ideology have resulted in women emerging as second-class citizens with fewer rights and more restriction on their private and public lives.[27] Similarly, Moghissi[28] recognizes how the Islamic state's developmentalist policies in Iran have opened possibilities for women, on the one hand, and its re-Islamization policies have enhanced the patriarchal ruling of women's lives and bodies, on the other. In chapter 4 of her book, subtitled "The Judicial System in Iran and Its Role in Relation to Domestic Violence against Women," Zahra Tizro analyzes the jurisprudential discourse and comes up with the justifications for domestic violence against women in Iran, as well as clergies' implications of those rulings in Islamic sharia family courts.[29]

In a slightly different subtheme, examining the sociological effects of the Islamic state on women's lives, and through a series of highly significant pieces of scholarship in Iranian Women's Studies,[30] Parvin Paidar (whose earlier writings are under the pen name of Nahid Yeganeh) investigates the role of three discourses of Iranian nationalism, the revolutionary discourse, and

Islamization in the social construction of Iranian womanhood in the twentieth century. Paidar's work is essential as she diverges from the single cause fallacy in studying Iranian women's lives and experiences and opens the door for more complicated scholarship on this matter to come. Janet Afary's research on *Sexual Politics of Modern Iran*,[31] before and after the 1979 Revolution, follows Paidar's multidimensional approach. Afary looks at Iranian history from the premodern era to years after the revolution and elaborates on the cultural, historical, and religious makeup of the social construction of gender. Then, in "The Sexual Economy of the Islamic Republic," she focuses explicitly on the postrevolutionary gender regime that appeared in Iran after the revolution and concludes

> that the policies of the Islamist government cannot easily be categorized as unpuritanical or moralistic. Rather, we can argue that various factions within the state actively deployed a new sexual economy for the population. Sometimes, the Islamist state privileged patriarchal interpretations of gender norms over more modern ones. At other times, it adopted modern projects such as family planning alongside a discourse that presented them as practices rooted in traditional Islam. In all cases, the state used modern institutions to disseminate and enforce these practices.[32]

In investigating the emergence of domestic violence against women's bodies, specifically in temporary marriages, Claudia Yaghoobi follows a similar logic. She identifies women's bodies as the site of an embodiment of the discriminatory gender roles as domestic violence against women by their male partners.[33] What is interesting in her work is the differentiation she makes between private family spaces in permanent versus temporary marriages and the power dynamic that makes the bodies of women in temporary marriages even more vulnerable. Then, she looks at the intersection of government policies in the Pahlavi era and under the postrevolutionary Islamic government and discusses how social and historical elements played into the unfolding of violence in any of these settings.

In "Feminism in an Islamic Republic: Years of Hardship, Years of Growth,"[34] Afsaneh Najmabadi summarizes the difficulties Iranian women have faced after the 1979 Revolution, from losing their employment status to being demoted into an unequal and secondary legal position regarding family jurisprudence. However, she takes a turn to document how Iranian women have navigated these rules and moved their way through negotiation, small victories, and significant losses. She writes, "The dominant method of reformist interpretations on women's issues has been to use more woman-friendly sources from an already existing set of authoritative exegetical texts."[35] What Najmabadi mentions above becomes the seed of Iranian Islamic feminism, also the third subtheme emerging in transnational anti-fundamentalist feminism. This activism explores new avenues for the relationship between women and Islam and attempts to create breathing spaces for women in the Shi'i jurisprudence.

From a similar, but not identical, standpoint, Ziba Mir-Hosseini engages with the relationship between women and religion by differentiating between various ways that Islamic clergies and even political parties close to them react to the women's question in Iran. In *Islam and Gender: The Religious Debate in Contemporary Iran*,[36] Mir-Hosseini categorizes traditionalist, neo-traditionalist, and modernist clergies and elaborates on how each group comes up with unique ways to articulate women's jurisprudence. Later, in the article "The Conservative: Reformist Conflict over Women's Rights in Iran," Mir-Hosseini elaborates on different responses from conservative and reformist politicians in approaching women's rights in Islam, and clarifies their implications for Iranian women in terms of public policies.[37] Finally, in "Islamic Feminism and Its Discontents: Toward a Resolution of the Debate,"[38] Moghadam identifies the existence and scholarship of Islamic feminism as one of the most controversial topics among Iranian feminists. After elaborating on the primary arguments, the author recognizes two camps of scholars as advocates and enemies of Islamic feminism. Unsurprisingly, Moghadam locates Najmabadi, Mir-Hosseini, and Nayereh Tohidi in the first groups and recognizes the work of Haideh Moghissi and Hamed Shahidian as the representatives of the second.

Anti-imperialist Iranian Transnational Feminism

The second group of transnational feminist movements and networks were formed against the wars and conflicts that endangered women's lives. "Late twentieth-century globalization was accompanied by a new wave of conflicts in Afghanistan, Bosnia, and Central Africa involving serious human rights violations against women."[39] Moghadam names organizations such as Code Pink and WIPLF, and later women's groups in Afghanistan, Iraq, and Bosnia, as examples of the networks that appeared in response. Most of the transnational feminist networks she mentions in this chapter do not have Iranian roots or any connections with Iranian transnational feminism. However, because of the focus of some branches of Iranian transnational feminism on the topics of the global war against female and queer bodies, the role of colonization and gaze in the construction of such bodies and gendering the citizens, and more importantly the anti-imperialist approach in scholarship, I place them in this group of transnational feminist networks.

As one of the leading scholars of the field of Iranian women's, gender, and sexuality studies in America, in "Mapping Transformations of Sex, Gender, and Sexuality in Modern Iran,"[40] Afsaneh Najmabadi highlights the importance of cultural interactions with Europe. Specifically, she focuses on European men's travel to Iran and Iranian elite men's trips to Europe. She locates the process of modernization at the heart of gendering Iranian citizens and the construction of ideas of beauty, love, and the erotic as by-products of the European gaze over Iranian subjects and internalization of the regimes of power and knowledge in this procedure.[41] Najmabadi uses the same theoretical approach in explaining the emergence of Iranian same-sex desires and transsexualities throughout the history.[42]

Minoo Moallem is the next Iranian postcolonial and postmodern feminist studies scholar whose research addresses issues of fundamentalism, war, and violence in unique ways. In "The Textualization of Violence in a Global World: Gendered Citizenship and Discourses of Protection,"[43] Moallem directly explains her concerns about the kind of violence that results from the social construction of the modern citizen in nationalist discourses, and the consequences of protective measures such discourses bring to the lives of others. She applies this frame of knowledge in theorizing the gendered and sexed Iranian bodies[44] and stretches this theoretical standpoint to talk about the bodies of immigrant Iranians and other Middle Eastern subjects who have been represented through orientalist discourses. In *Between Warrior Brother and Veiled Sister: Islamic Fundamentalism and Politics of Patriarchy in Iran*,[45] Moallem looks at the intersection of modernization and Islamic fundamentalism in Iran and their influences on Iranian women's lives. She is close to Najmabadi in highlighting the role of the "Western gaze," as a dominant element in such history, and calling out different levels of epistemic and discursive violence that target them. Finally, in writing a collective piece, "Transnational Feminist: Practices against War,"[46] Moallem and her cowriters revisit the American invasion of Afghanistan and call out how these imperial practices have constantly resulted in racialized, religion-based, and gendered violence against Afghan women.

Sima Shakhsari is the next scholar who focuses on the "War on Terror" and the politics of queerness for Iranian diasporic communities. In "Weblogistan Goes to War: Representational Practices, Gendered Soldiers and Neoliberal Entrepreneurship in Diaspora," they "argue that Weblogistan is implicated in discourses of militarism and neoliberalism that interpellate the representable

Iranian blogger as a gendered neoliberal homo oeconomicus. The production of knowledge about Iran in transnational encounters between the media think-tanks, policy institutions, and the Iranian diasporic self-entrepreneurs relies on gendered civilizational discourses that are inherently tied to the war on terror."[47] Later in "From Homoerotics of Exile to Homopolitics of Diaspora: Cyberspace, the War on Terror, and the Hypervisible Iranian Queer," Shakhsari argues that

> during the post-September 11 "war on terror," the Iranian homosexual became transferred from the position of the abject to the representable subject in transnational political realms. This shift involves Iranian opposition groups, transnational media, the "gay international" (in the words of Joseph A. Massad), and some Iranian diasporic queers who willingly insert themselves into national imaginations of the opposition in diasporic reterritorializations.[48]

As their primary line of argumentation, Shakhsari remains focused on the role of imperialism, the neoliberal war on terror agenda, and the consumption of the Iranian diasporic gay community in their later work.[49]

Anti-neoliberalist Iranian Transnational Feminism

In a series of articles and studies,[50] Roksana Bahramitash argues for the role of the Islamist government in Iran in increasing female employment since the 1990s. In making the case, Bahramitash elaborates on the rise of Islamism in the Middle East during the 1970s and its backlash in traditional and religious families restricting their female members' access to education and the labor market. On the contrary, in countries such as Iran and Indonesia, these families trusted religious regulations of the public sphere enough to allow their wives and daughters to leave domestic spaces, go to schools and universities, and find jobs. Moghadam takes a more complicated approach in studying the role of neoliberal policies in women's employment in Iran. In "Patriarchy in Transition: Women and the Changing Family in the Middle East,"[51] she highlights the importance of enduring patriarchy in the region and its intersection with Islamic states' support of jurisprudential family law. Her further comparative studies show that Iranian and Jordanian Islamic states have designed the development trajectories to keep them as close as possible to women's employment alongside neoliberal economic policies.[52] Finally, Moghadam argues that Iranian women workers have been hidden from history[53] and attempts to bring their voices back to scholarship through the lens of feminist political economy.

Taking a Step Back, Moving Forward

The rise of stories coming from victims of sexual abuse, the grassroots advocacy of activists such as Tarana Burke,[54] and the explosion of #MeToo on social media since 2017 have made it impossible for any feminist, academic or otherwise, not to take a stand on the issue. Since January 2020, Iranian women have joined this transnational activism to reclaim their violated bodies and seek justice. Unfortunately, the Iranian legal system lacks basic principles to assist these women and hear their voices. Iranian legal scholars, lawyers, feminists, and journalists have pointed out that saying #MeToo, or confessing to sexual violence perpetrated by a perpetrator, acts against the victims. It can provide evidence for courts to issue harsh sentences, ranging from lashing for single women to the death penalty for married women. In such a situation, the Iranian activists, non/academic feminists, and journalists outside Iran can play a critical role in echoing the voices of the victims and holding the government accountable for delivering justice to survivors, or at least protecting victims from more repressions and retaliations.

Therefore, this chapter looked into the academic feminist scholarship produced post the 1979 Revolution outside Iran to examine the potentials of this corpus of work to address gender-based violence, especially sexual harassment and abuse. Even though Iranian transnational feminists have addressed this topic at macro levels and called out fundamentalist, neo/colonial, imperial, and neoliberal macroaggressions against Iranian women, the content analysis of their scholarship reveals a gap in addressing interpersonal gender-based violence. This scholarly shortcoming could result from various reasons from a hesitation to call out the violence of brown men (who are already the targets of racialized criminalization discourses), to a fear of taking the spotlight away from those macroaggressions mentioned earlier, to even the personal choices academics make for their research based on individual and institutional preferences. Regardless, this void is a symptom of a critical flaw in Iranian transnational feminism and needs to be adequately addressed.

Specifically, I highlight this problem as a social justice issue and rely on rhetorical listening techniques to point out the structural barriers in listening to Iranian #MeToo voices. Krista Ratcliffe defines "rhetorical listening" as "a trope for interpretive inventions and more particularly as a code of cross-cultural conduct … Rhetorical listening signifies a stance of openness that a person may choose to assume in relation to any person, text, or culture."[55]

It has four steps: "promoting the understanding of self and other, proceeding within accountability logic, locating identifications across commonalities and differences, and analyzing claims as well as cultural logics within which these claims function."[56] Even though Ratcliffe primarily uses rhetorical listening to highlight the implicit whiteness in the texts, the method can shed some light on the absence of voices of #MeToo survivors in the genre of Iranian transnational academic feminism.

The first step, "promoting the understanding of self and other," can help locate the privilege and loss of academic feminists and survivors. This relationship is complicated and multidimensional as survivors come from different levels of privilege in their communities, and academic feminists can relate to various intersectional identities. However, one undeniable element in this relationship is the academic feminists' access to English-speaking platforms and the support they receive from their institutional affiliations. This transitions smoothly to "proceeding within accountability logic," as the second principle of rhetorical listening, which makes academic feminism accountable for incorporating the stories and voices of #MeToo survivors. "Locating identifications across commonalities and differences" opens the space to address different levels of intertwined macro- and microaggressions that Iranian-identifying bodies face in their lives inside and outside Iranian borders. While both groups suffer from histories of colonization, neoliberal oppression, and the current realities of economic sanctions, the situations are not identical. For example, Iranian women inside Iran must deal with the mandatory ruling of their bodies by the Islamic state, while Iranians outside find themselves vulnerable in occupying an identity of "limited whiteness" and the racial profiling[57] of their communities. It changes the priority of each group in resisting macro- or micro-levels of violence. Finally, the last step of rhetorical listening, "analyzing claims as well as cultural logics within which these claims function," would encourage scholars of the Iranian diaspora to analyze and represent gender-based violence and sexual abuse inside Iran in its specific context, without overlooking macroaggressions against communities of color in a different context. Again, Rebecca Dingo[58] brings examples of how certain feminist causes have been in circulation transnationally, and every time they appeared as a distinct problem that requires specific ways of addressing.

4

Structural and Material Considerations and the Nexus of Power and Sexuality in the Iranian #MeToo Movement

Mahdi Tourage

It is generally acknowledged that mutual consent, spelled out in a written contract, is the best possible basis for ethical relations of exchange between humans, especially regarding sexuality. In this contractual model, sexual relations are envisioned as symmetrical private relations of give and take, use and being used, entered into by relatively equal partners based on freely given mutual consent. However, sex involves entire structures of power such as patriarchy, class, race, cisnormativity, compulsory heterosexuality, and ableism. In this chapter, I will discuss an often overlooked aspect of the debate: the ways in which sexual relations are structured by the systems of patriarchal power that categorically privilege men. Instead of focusing on individuals or on the details of sexual assault cases, my focus will be on theoretical tools that allow us to interrogate patriarchal operations of power through which sexual relations are positioned as privatized, contractual, and consent-based, and the legal system as the fair arbiter of grievances by female victims of sexual assault.[1]

Taking a cue from French philosopher Jean Claude Milner's philosophical reflections on the #MeToo movement,[2] I will question the symmetry of heterosexual relations through the Marxist theory of labor and highlight the shortcomings of the consent-based contractual model of sexuality. In Milner's Marxist model of analysis (and earlier radical feminists of 1960s), weakness and strength are not merely descriptive but structural. It is the weakness of women already built into the structure of power relations that renders all contracts asymmetrical and unequal. Even when a woman (or a worker in Marxist analysis) is materially strong and freely gives her consent, the contract inevitably results in domination and exploitation. In this context, a woman's material advantage (e.g., being richer, more influential, even being physically stronger than a man) is irrelevant when her inferior position in the structure of power relations causes her consent to be of little consequence. I will conclude that the irreducible structural asymmetry of power between male perpetrators and their accusers renders these men guilty, whether they are acquitted of all charges or no charges are brought against them at all. Therefore, consent is an inadequate category for addressing sexual assault and rape cases, and arguing for improvement in women's material conditions (such as wage or pay parity or women in leadership positions) only partially addresses the causes of the problem rooted in structural arrangements of power. It is hoped that insights from considerations of the structural and material differences in sexual relations will open up ways of evaluating other forms of human relations of proximity such as marriage, which is also rooted in a structural asymmetry of power. Therefore, I will also discuss the issues of ownership and consent in Islamic legal discourse.

Needless to say, sexual violence does not discriminate; all people, no matter how they identify, be it as cisgender males and females, nonbinary individuals, or members of the LGBTQ2ST communities, can be both victims and/or perpetrators of sexual violence and rape. However, for the purpose of this chapter, I will focus specifically on sexual violence perpetrated by cis-heterosexual males. In addition, I will bypass other important considerations, such as race, age, bodily abilities, and many other differences, that are wielded as instruments of power and domination.[3]

Sexual Assault and Rape Accusations

In cases of alleged accusations of sexual assault and rape against men who are in the public eye, many comments on social media note that these sexual encounters do not warrant legal sanction or public judgment. These arguments are rooted in the logic that what takes place in a private space between two consenting adults is no one's business. However, "privacy" and "consent" are not magical words that could somehow absolve a violent sexual perpetrator.

In general, citizens in Western countries tend to have faith in their legal system to sort out contradictory claims in sexual assault cases. However, it is often the victims of sexual assault who are re-traumatized in what feminist legal scholars have termed "judicial rape."[4] The situation is worse in the legal context of Iran where women complainants are considered to be the instigators by default and afraid of being shamed or to "lose their reputation."[5] They could also be convicted for false accusations. In Iran, a female victim of rape risks being killed by her own father for dishonoring the family.⁶ Although statistics for Iran are hard to come by,⁷ in the United States it is estimated that two out of three sexual assaults are not reported to the police. Out of 1,000 sexual assaults, only 310 are reported to the police, 50 lead to arrest, 28 lead to felony conviction, and 25 perpetrators are incarcerated; this means that "out of every 1,000 sexual assaults, 975 perpetrators will walk free."⁸ It is worth noting that Iran's legal system does have some provisions for dealing with *āzār jinsī-i kalāmī* (verbal sexual assault) and *āzār jinsī bi ghair az tajāvuz* (sexual assault other than rape), yet it does not have a definition of "sexual assault."⁹ In addition, *zināy-i bi ʿunf* (rape) is defined as forced penal penetration—forced penetration of vagina with hand or other objects does not constitute rape.¹⁰ Nevertheless, rape as it is defined in Iran is taken seriously and classified as an "unforgivable" offense with a fixed mandatory sentence (*hadd*) of death, which, in practice, deters many victims from reporting and pursuing their cases in court as they are against capital punishment.¹¹ Once proven, the crime of rape cannot be forgiven by the victim.¹² According to the *Iran Human Rights Report*, 4.5 percent of state executions (12 out of 267) in 2020 were for rape charges.¹³

Consent

There is no one single comprehensive way to conceptualize consent in sexual encounters. Despite the most salient criteria for legitimizing sexual encounters, consent is a contested, often misunderstood concept, plagued by definitional problems: "If we have learned one thing from the #MeToo campaign ... it is that we as a society do not have a clear, uncontested idea of what sexual consent looks like, and that we do not all universally and equally value it."¹⁴ Keeping boundaries and definitions of foundational terms such as consent, modesty, honor, and rape as vague as possible allows for the perpetuation of "rape culture." A useful definition of rape culture is provided by Milena Popova in her recently published *Sexual Consent*: "Rape culture is the collection of ideas, practices, and structures in our society that make it easy for perpetrators to commit sexual violence and make it hard for victims to speak out or get justice."¹⁵ Yet Popova sees a "radical potential" for consent in complex operations of power in which it is entangled.¹⁶ She goes on to examine these entanglements and offer insights into the conditions necessary for the consent to be truly, freely, and meaningfully given.

Even though consent is often considered to be useful in sexual assault cases (because it is believed to be "an existing and reasonably well-known concept"[17]), relying on even the most comprehensive form of consent is problematic. Consent can justify all manners and levels of violence, even violence against one's own self. As C. K. Egbert writes, we would be wrong to assume "that people will simply not consent to something 'harmful;' women have 'consented' to death when abortion could easily save their lives."[18] Sexual consent can be further problematized as what in contemporary feminist philosophy is referred to as "adaptive preference." Adaptive preference is "self-depriving desire people form under unjust conditions," where they are simultaneously active agents choosing what they perceive to be in their own best interest "*and* participants in their own deprivation."[19] Adaptive preference takes into account the complexity of situations where consent, autonomy, and agency are complicated by other adaptive strategies.

Current studies of consent show four broad approaches: "the radical feminist approach, the 'no means no' and 'yes means yes' conceptions of consent, and recent developments that can be broadly summed up under the heading of 'sex-critical.'"[20] The "no means no" campaign of the 1980s and 1990s helped negotiate legal definitions of rape and raised awareness about unwanted sexual contact between people already known to each other, and shifted the responsibility to be attentive to women's expression of nonconsent to men. It also assumed personal agency of parties involved in consent negotiations.

The subsequent "yes means yes" conception of consent attempted to remedy the shortcoming of "no means no" that tied definition of consent to the utterance of "no" and focused on women's choice to refuse sex if they wish to do so. Both "yes means yes" and "no means no" reaffirmed women's agency and freedom as "neoliberal subjects," which meant shifting responsibility on women for their own actions in consent negotiations.[21] In response to previous approaches, the "sex critical" approach emphasizes cultural forces and pays attention to the nuanced issues of power, inquiring into the conditions under which women can "*freely* say 'no' to sex, as those are also the conditions under which our 'yes' becomes truly meaningful."[22]

Radical feminists, on the other hand, argue that the patriarchal system cannot be reformed because it is deeply rooted in power, control, and domination. Rather, the patriarchy's legal and political structures as well as its social and cultural institutions (such as the heteronormative family and organized religion) must be "ripped out root and branch."[23] Overwhelming amount of research and data indicate that the patriarchal family has never been a safe place for women and children.[24] The Marxist feminists seriously doubt the possibility of women's freedom in a patriarchal class-based capitalist society. Relying on the ideas of Karl Marx they emphasize a class-based analysis rather than gender-based analysis to explain women's oppression.[25] Recent publications indicate that radical Marxist feminist traditions, where sex, violence, intercourse, and rape are viewed as intimately intertwined with class power structures, are considered to be outdated tools of analysis. For example, Popova notes that this strand of inquiry belongs to the 1960s with its peak reached in the mid-1980s and later morphing into discourses that emphasize power as a multilayered complex web of entanglements.[26] Additionally, categorizing all sexual intercourse between men and women as "rape," regardless of its contractual-consensual basis, does not sit well with many intellectual traditions, for example, with "sex-positive" feminism.[27] However, taking a cue from a recent talk by Milner and in light of the debates prompted by #MeToo movement, it is beneficial to revisit Marx's basic problematization of consent in labor relations and implications of it for current debates on sexual violence.

Marxist Analysis of Labor Contract and Private Property

In his article "Reflections on the Me Too Movement and Its Philosophy," Milner argues that the significance of the #MeToo movement far exceeds its affective reverberations—it concerns all relations of power. The #MeToo movement is, in his assessment, a symptom of operations of power. For example, Milner argues that Harvey Weinstein's case, which opened up this movement, showed what women experientially or intuitively knew to be true: sexual abuse, assault, violence, and rape are not exceptions to the rules; they are rules. The normative aspect of them are indicated by the term "too," writes Milner, "a mechanism of indefinite addition," not just in the film industry, Hollywood, and in the United States but in all domains, in all places.[28] In other words, the #MeToo movement showed the pervasiveness of the patriarchal organizations of power put forth as the inevitable "natural" force structuring all aspects of our lives but most relevant to the goals of this chapter, structuring sexual relations and sexual violations. Patriarchy is at the core of a whole constellation of power relations: "Patriarchy, capitalism, racism, ableism, cis- and heteronormativity, and compulsory sexuality—and the people who benefit from these systems—all rely on a culture that obscures and dismisses boundary violations, that uses sexuality to construct some of us as less or more human than others, that blames and re-traumatizes the victims of sexual violence while enabling perpetrators."[29] The phrase "capitalist patriarchy" is useful for emphasizing the intimate connection between patriarchy and capitalism, "the mutually reinforcing dialectical relationship between capitalist class structure and hierarchical sexual structuring."[30] Just as capitalism is viewed as "the only viable political and economic system" outside of which no coherent alternative is imaginable,[31] patriarchy too is presented as the only viable system with no imaginable coherent alternative. It is this intimate connection between patriarchy and capitalism that makes Marx's critique of the latter an apt conceptual tool for interrogating the former.

One of the most salient features of Marx's critique of capitalism is his interrogation of the labor contract. In his *Capital*, he argues that under capitalism labor contract appears to be based on freedom and equality, therefore symmetrical. The buyer and seller of a commodity (e.g., labor power) are "free agents," "constrained only by their own free will" to enter into a contractual agreement that gives "legal expression to their common will."[32] The workers are not slaves but legal entities with free will. They may be *materially* strong, that is, they can refuse to enter into a contract and have the freedom to choose to sell their labor to another employer. Those who control the "means of production" cannot be faulted under such freely agreed upon contractual agreement of employment. However, Marx argues that the contract does more than delineating the term of commodity exchange. The contract is an agreement that establishes a relationship of subordination and generates the capitalist's authority.[33] Therefore the labor contract can never be symmetrical because the capitalist class owns and controls the means of production and enjoys surplus value produced by exploitation of the workers' labor. In other words, the always already *structurally* stronger capitalist class is the true beneficiary of the capitalist structure of exchange. The workers remain structurally weak even if they *materially* benefit from their contract. Because of this structural weakness, Marx argues, workers are the exploited weaker class even if they freely consent to a contract and agree on specific compensation for their labor. More importantly, the problem with the employment contract is not simply forced labor or exploitation of workers resulting from terms of its recompense but that it maintains the capitalist as master and everyone else as slaves.[34] This ownership-based structural advantage organizes social relations in ways that always privileges owners of the capital. Hence, the consensual contract is not a guarantor of symmetry of power between stronger and weaker in human relations; rather it actually perpetuates the structural weakness of the weaker party.

How is a Marxist analysis of labor contract related to sexual violence against women? To begin with, Catherine MacKinnon's words bear repeating here: "Sexuality is to feminism what work is to Marxism, that which is most one's own, yet most taken away."[35] As Milner and before him radical feminists have argued, the extent of capitalist structural control and material domination exerted by contractual arrangements of power is mirrored in the patriarchal economy of exchange governing heterosexual relations. Milner writes: "In the labor contract, the workers may seem to give their free consent; their structural weakness, however, remains the determining factor for their acceptance. The same is true of the so-called sexual contract."[36] Just as changes in their material condition are beneficial for workers, positive monetary gains can reduce material disparity in patriarchal sexual relations. For example, increasing the minimum wage, job security, and job stability can reduce the rate of intimate partner violence.[37] Even minimal increase in sales tax or the cost of alcohol could decrease rate of intimate partner violence; raising the price of an ounce of pure alcohol by 1 percent has been shown to decrease intimate partner violent rates by as much as 5 percent.[38] But the point of a Marxist intervention argued here is that material changes, like raising minimum wage, increasing sales tax on alcohol or limiting its availability, reliance on law enforcement and criminalization of gendered-based violence advocated by "carceral feminism,"[39] or even an enthusiastic ongoing consent advocated by the "yes means yes" campaign only address the symptoms of the problem, the root causes of which can only be addressed by structural changes.

Private property is another structural feature of patriarchy that adds to men's control of women's sexuality and reproductive system.[40] What facilitates the relations of domination and exploitation of workers, Marx argues, is private property, "the power possessed by private individuals in the means of production which allows them to dispose as they will of the workers' labor-power."[41] Marx holds that for the capitalist class, women are also treated like property and used for the transmission of private property.[42] Following Frederick Engels (but critiquing him for his essentializations, such as attributing women's historical economic disadvantages to their physical weakness), Simone de Beauvoir writes that the emergence of the patriarchal family is founded upon private property and man's proprietary right to own women and slaves for their labor and their reproductive capacity.[43] This is not different than many aspects of human relations of proximity (such as marriage), which are rooted in the possession of property and laws governing them. Popova writes: "Discussions of sexual violence and consent are frequently dominated by legalistic approaches, which in many Western jurisdictions have their roots in property law rather than the very messy, human lived experience of sexuality."[44] It is no surprise that in the

Western legal discourse rape is an offense against one's right to limit others' use of one's body as a property.[45]

Islamic Legal Discourse on Marriage and Property Laws

Islamic legal discourse (which shapes contemporary legal discourse in Muslim-majority countries such as Iran) too is rooted in property laws.[46] Zahra Tizro notes: "The orthodox jurisprudence is an overwhelmingly powerful force in shaping the minds and lives of ordinary people in the Islamic countries, particularly in Iran, as the mainstream discourse."[47] According to the Islamic law, an adult male of sound mind can contract a marriage, but most jurists, for example, the late Ayatollah Khomeini of Iran, require the father or a male guardian's permission for marriage of an adult virgin girl. Only if she has been previously married does she gain the full right to consent and to control her own property.[48] In any case, consent of the bride or her male guardian is a necessary component of the marriage contract. However, once she has given her consent to marry, her husband no longer needs consent for sexual activity. Tizro observes,

> Violence against women in traditional Islamic discourse is institutionalised through the marriage contract and its auxiliary institutions, norms and beliefs, which span all dimensions of women's lives from birth to death and from the private realm of the family to wider public life at community level and society at large, through strict control and surveillance exercised on the lives of virgin girls and married women in families and communities, and at a social level.[49]

In Iran, the marriage contract ties men and women into duties that are spelled out in the law governed by the orthodox jurisprudence. After consummation of the marriage, the wife has the right to the maintenance of the household, to hire a servant, or to receive payment for housework. In exchange for these, the husband has the right to be the manager of the family, to demand obedience from his wife, to discipline (hit) her in case of disobedience, to decide on the place of her residence, and to control her activities outside the house. These are in addition to his right to polygyny and unilateral divorce.[50]

An indispensable component of marriage that must be noted in the contract and agreed upon by both sides is the *mahr* (*mihrīyih* in Farsi), a financial or symbolic dower or "bride money" paid by the groom to the bride with important ramifications for defining the nature of their relationship. It is significant that *mahr* is paid to the bride and not to her father or guardian, which means as a contracting agent she has the right to own property, no doubt a progressive feature of Islamic marriage in seventh-century Arabia. Yet *mahr* turns out to be a "major source of problems in marriage and causing much suffering in both men and women, but especially in women."[51] Tizro provides many cases of such suffering in Iran, to which we can add divorce cases among Muslims in North America where *mahr* is perhaps the most litigated issue.[52] What is relevant to the goals of this chapter is that the exchange of *mahr* establishes the man's right of ownership over the woman's sexuality; it is a compensation paid by the husband as " 'the vulva's price,' *thaman al-bud'a*."[53] For Muslim jurists, female sexuality is a type of "property or commodity," and free women are considered to be "both person and property."[54] A free woman maintains ownership over her own body, except the exclusive right to her sexual organ is transferred to her husband after marriage in exchange (financial or symbolic) for a dower.[55]

The ownership of a woman's sexuality, first by her father or a male guardian and then transferred to her husband, has far-reaching implications for the control and surveillance of women's bodies and behavior in what Tizro calls "*effat-gheirat* discourse." *Effat* (chastity, also transliterated: *iffat*) includes a whole series of implicit cultural codes of behavior reflecting the exclusive rights of men to women's sexuality. *Gheirat* (also transliterated: gheyrat sexual jealousy) is men's passionate and aggressive defense of their exclusive rights to women's sexual faculties. Women are expected to internalize and observe these codes; otherwise they are punished by the codes of *gheirat*.[56] It is no surprise that the foulest insults in Persian (and other patriarchal cultures) directed at a man are about sexual violence against women related to him (his mother, sister, aunt, or wife). Commodification of women's sexuality is also the basis for constructing and policing codes of virginity and regulating women's bodies (through compulsory veiling, for example). The code of virginity, enforced through men's guardianship of women, ensures that "subjective concepts, such as chastity and modesty find objective and measurable realisation."[57]

Men's ownership of women's sexuality and regulation of the meaning of virginity are even extended beyond this world to include the sexual delights of paradise promised to the believers in the Qur'an. In their efforts to control the means of production of meaning of female sexuality, normative commentaries explain that the fate of righteous Muslim women who enter paradise will be associated with their earthly husbands. Male believers, on the other hand, will enjoy "marriage" with the *ḥūrīs*, the "wide-eyed damsels" promised them in the Qur'an (44:54; 52:20; 56:22), which describes these virginal maidens as having "swelling breasts" (78:33) and "still not deflowered, neither by man nor jinn" (55:74).[58]

According to Islamic jurisprudence, a female slave[59] was considered to be her owner's property. No contract or consent was necessary for sexual relation with a female slave by her male master. Islamic marriage is conceptualized along the same lines and is rooted in the institution of slavery. In fact, for classical Muslim jurists wives and slaves are "parallel legal categories."[60] Not surprisingly, Muslim jurists, who conceptualized female sexuality as a "tradable commodity," rendered rape as an infringement on someone else's property rights.[61] In this property-based approach, rape is not an affront to deity, and the volition or subjectivity of the female victim of rape is not granted recognition or legal significance. Hina Azam writes: "Indeed, the amount of the indemnity was frequently unaffected by whether or not she had consented or been coerced"; the female was "simply the carrier of a sexual capacity that actually belonged to the nearest male." A female victim of rape did not normally receive compensation for "sexual misuse."[62] Therefore, even though Muslim jurists distinguish between forced and consensual sex, in Islamic jurisprudence "marital rape is an oxymoron"; rape is in fact "a property crime that by definition cannot be committed by the husband."[63] Similarly, Iran's legal system has no provisions for recognition of rape within the structure of marriage.[64] This is due to the transactional nature of the marriage contract where "submission in matters of sexual nature" is required.[65] This is historically consistent with other patriarchal structures of power, for example, in English and Welsh law, where "historically marital rape was not considered an offence."[66] It should be noted that men's ownership of female sexuality also supports the so-called honor killings. Many Muslim scholars and religious leaders point out that Islam does not authorize such killings,[67] yet a father (or grandfather) is exempt from capital punishment for killing his own offspring—a legal provision that is instituted in Iran's criminal code with serious ramifications for women and sexual minorities.[68]

Capitalist Labor Relations and Patriarchal Sexual Relations

To understand the parallel workings of structures of power conditioning capitalist labor relations and patriarchal sexual relations, we can point to the similarities between the exploitation of workers and violence against women under capitalism and patriarchy, respectively. In the capitalist economy, the exploitation of workers' labor is inevitable for maintenance of all other systemic forms of exploitation. In "capitalist patriarchy," sexual violence against women (and all that is considered "feminine") is added to the imperative of exploitation, where women are no more than means of (re)production or instruments of labor.⁶⁹ We are reminded by Ann Cahill that "the crime of rape is not only assumed, but necessary for the perpetuation of other, more subtle forms of gender inequality."⁷⁰ It is in this context that the horrors of patriarchal rape culture and the contribution of feminist thinkers to Marxist theory of exploitation become apparent. Feminist thinkers added the missing cultural pieces to Marx's material-based conditions as the primary force that animates history. For Marx, exploitation of labor-power is "the first birthright of capital"; it is what gives rise to surplus value: "The rate of surplus value is therefore an exact expression for the degree of exploitation of labour-power by capital, or of the labourer by the capitalist."⁷¹ In patriarchy, the fundamental birthright of men is sex, something they have to have. Entire patriarchal social conventions and legal structures support "the idea that men are naturally more sexually aggressive and entitled to free sexual access to women, even without their consent."⁷² This violent misconception exonerates men and underlies the myth that anyone who is raped must have "asked for it."⁷³ Consider the requisite assumptions perpetuated by the rape-supportive patriarchal structures that to be "genuine," rape must be an extraordinary event and physically violent; perpetrated by extraordinary violent monsters, not boyfriends, husbands, or respectable members of clergy or society; a woman must not be wearing revealing clothing, drinking too much, walking alone at night, being perceived to lead the perpetrator on, making eye contact; she must put up the utmost resistance and register no pleasure, must report the incident immediately, must sustain physical injuries and emotional trauma, but must not be too hysterical reporting it.⁷⁴

Sexual violence and exertion of power, domination, and control are essential to the working of patriarchy. Some apologetic Muslim writers put forward the essentializing myth of "male's higher sex-drive" as justification for institutionalizing the veil and polygyny.⁷⁵ Similarly, the myth of "sex is indispensable to men's being" justifies male-on-male sexual violence in prisons. It also justifies production of militarized hypermasculinities. For example, American General George Patton is quoted as saying of his troops: "If they don't fuck, they don't fight."⁷⁶ Rape is patriarchy's fundamental rite of passage, "the ultimate expression of a patriarchal order," as Cahill puts it.⁷⁷ A woman is always mindful of this threat, even when she is materially advantaged, for example, is highly educated, independently wealthy, or physically strong.

Sexualized exertion of power and control structurally instituted in patriarchy is of course not limited to women. More importantly (and more relevant to the topic of this chapter), actual or threat of sexual harm is the most salient patriarchal weapon deployed against all that is marked as feminine. Sexual violence against structurally disempowered women is replicated with nonhuman animals. Both women and nonhuman animals have historically been considered less intelligent, primitive, and therefore objectified and sexually violated (e.g., consider forced impregnation—"rape"—of cows in dairy industry); both have been exploited for their reproductive capacity while being legally defined as the property of men.[78] As Carol Adams has shown, patriarchy has a vested interest in binding masculinity with meat eating and sexualization and violation of women's and animals' bodies.[79] It is worth noting that in the context of Islamic ethics, Kecia Ali has shown that concerns with gender justice cannot be at the expense of ignoring "the intertwined nature of meat-eating and female subjection."[80] Along the same lines, killing, harming, or threatening pets and nonhuman animals (killing domesticated animals in farming and wild animals by hunting) has historically been a way for men to establish and maintain power and control over women.[81] Men terrorize women "by threatening a beloved child, cat, or parakeet."[82] Killing nonhuman animals to establish or maintain power and control over women is the marital advice passed on in a well-known Persian expression that can be translated as: "The cat must be killed at the door of the bridal chamber."[83]

It is important to decouple rape from the view that men's sex drive is primarily a biologically driven impulse. Rape is an act of power that is structurally supported by social contract.[84] Even certain nonsexual gestures and ordinary cultural practices, such as eye contact or "wearing a short skirt, or accepting a drink from a man, are seen to generate a contract on the part of women to have sex—specifically, penile-vaginal intercourse—with a man."[85] It is significant that a large portion of women who speak of their own experiences of sexual harassment, assault, and rape choose to remain anonymous. This is due to one of the structural disadvantages that these women face; for example, under Iran's laws, they can be persecuted for wrongful accusations.[86]

In patriarchal rape cultures, the mere presence of a woman in public space (public spaces are always gendered as masculine) constitutes a contract where a man can sexually harass or assault her. Even public revolutionary spaces are not free from harassment and assault—many cases of rapes and sexual assaults were reported during the Occupy Movement.[87] During the 2013 demonstrations in Cairo's Tahrir Square, 169 women were sexually assaulted or raped in the span of four days of protests culminating in Mohamed Morsi's departure; 8 of those occurred the night of Morsi's forced departure.[88] Furthermore, women are assaulted as a result of a public event even if they are not present in public. For example, a 2014 study by Lancaster University found that women's report of abuse to police increased by 26 percent when England's national team won, 38 percent when they lost.[89] In her autoethnographic article, Fae Chubin (pseudonym) writes about her experiences of sexual harassment and sexual assault growing up in Iran. When she was in her twenties (in 2006) her "plan" to minimize her chances of being sexually molested included: "not to look around, walk kind of fast, show this intense sour look while you frown a little, making everyone know you are not the type of woman they can joke around with."[90] However, this plan did not keep her safe as she was sexually assaulted in broad daylight in the streets of North Tehran, which she describes in her article.

It is interesting to note that men's unwanted public sexual advances toward other men is often met with socially and legally justifiable violent response in what was known as "homosexual panic,"[91] or more recently LGBTQ "panic."[92] We should also note that men too can be sexually assaulted by women. However, differences in their positionality in the structures of power distinguish sexual assault of men by women. First of all, women's sexual aggressions toward men are not backed by a pervasive institutional structure.[93] Additionally, men often insinuate some pleasure at the idea of being sexually objectified. The objectification of men by women falls short of the criteria for treating someone as an object. For example, conspicuously absent are the female "ownership" of male victim, which makes him violable in the first place and denies him autonomy and subjectivity.[94] Finally, sexual advances and objectification of men by women increase men's institutional power. A good scriptural example of this can be found in the quranic narrative of young Joseph (the biblical figure whose life story forms the only sustained narrative in the Qur'an) whose social and religious significance is multiplied as a result of being seduced by his master's wife, Zulaikha (not named in the text).[95]

The asymmetrical nature of sexual objectification is evident in the part of the story where Joseph is objectified by high-society women of Egypt as he is made to enter into their banquet hall. In the story, the women of Egypt, who are given a fruit and knife, cut their own hands at the sight of Joseph's beauty (Qur'an 12:31). The gesture of cutting their own hands at the sight of Joseph is interpreted as menstruation (a sign of bodily deficiency and unclean nature) by later Muslim exegetes.[96] When Zulaikha's husband discovers the affair, he says: "Indeed your guile is enormous" (Qur'an 12:28). Most Muslim exegetes presumed these words of Zulaikha's husband, uttered in anger and addressed to his wife (or women of Egypt at the time), is a categorical denunciation of all women. The text of the Qur'an notes that during sexual encounter between Joseph and Zulaikha, Joseph advanced toward her (*hamma biha*), but he stopped short of sexual intercourse when "he saw the proof of his Lord" (Qur'an 12:24). Muslim commentaries explain the extent of Joseph's desire toward Zulaikha as the unfastening of the belt of his trousers; loosening his or her garments; sitting between Zulaikha's legs; or dropping his pants to his buttocks; "[sitting] with her as a man sits with his wife."[97] Yet, it is Joseph who emerges as the epitome of prophetic sinlessness, and all women are universally and categorically indicted as cunning temptresses causing social chaos and dangerous to social stability, necessitating their subjugation. Catherine MacKinnon's words could have been written to describe the dynamics of this situation: "Women have been the nature, the matter, the acted upon to be subdued by the acting subject seeking to embody himself in the social world."[98]

Structural Vulnerability and Sexual Relations

In sexual relations determined by patriarchal relations of power, consent is not a private transaction between two equal individuals based on a mutually beneficial contract. Consent is entangled in social structures and complex cultural forces and relations of power.[99] Therefore, considering the structural imbalance of power conceptualizing sex as a private act between two consenting adults is highly problematic. In this context, one of the functions of patriarchal family based in marriage is to control the ever-present threat of female sexuality by subordinating it to men's property rights, to which we can add governments' and states' interest in the control of female reproductive rights. Claudia Yaghoobi writes: "The view that female sexuality is a threat also illustrates how intertwining the personal and political has politicized the female body and sexuality."[100] It is not a coincidence that the workplace and the household are "typically figured as private space[s], the product[s] of a series of individual contracts rather than a social structure, the province of human need and sphere of individual choice rather than a site for the exercise of political power."[101] Binding marriage relations to the private space of the household, or sex to one's own private concern in the privacy of one's bedroom (like binding labor relations to the private space of workplace), is the basis of patriarchal terminologies of power that assert male dominance, such as "a man's home is his castle," or framing intimate partner violence as "*domestic* violence." Patriarchy has a vested interest in maintaining marriage as a property-based institution in which men control the terms of relationship (e.g., ownership and control of women's sexuality and their movement, men's unilateral right to divorce, and custody of the "produced" offspring). Such a relationship is essentially exploitative no matter how freely and consensually it is formed. These exploitative gender roles are maintained even in less formal sexual relations such as dating, sex work, or, in the case of Iran, *sigheh* (temporary marriage) sanctioned by Iran's legal system. Temporary marriage, which has a set date of expiry, where some degree of sexual freedom is given to women and not all its cases are detrimental to women's interests as shown by Yaghoobi, still revolves around the autonomy of men and passivity of women and is presented by the clergy as a solution "for bringing order back to a corrupt society."[102]

All relationships between one gender or class where weaknesses of one and strengths of another are structurally constituted must be suspect regardless of the weaker party's freedom to enter into a contract, or give their ongoing consent, or the presence of any harm. Articulating this point, Milner writes: It is irrelevant to check whether a particular woman is more powerful, more influential, richer, or even physically stronger than the man. These are descriptive features; they are of no consequence when compared with the structural fact that woman as such is the weaker party.[103] To Milner's argument, we can add that having social or political power is also irrelevant to a man's default position of structural superiority. For example, according to the standard Roman Catholic sacramental theology, no woman, not even Mary the Mother of God, can be ordained as a priest, but any baptized Catholic male can potentially receive the sacrament of ordination.[104] Men who are accused of alleged sexual misconduct argue that they are not attached to any political or economic power position themselves within the binary of having or not having power while overlooking the contextual, relational, multilayered reality of power. The most liberated, liberating, anti-patriarchal man is still awarded structural benefits and accumulates "patriarchal dividend"[105] regardless of his position in the hierarchy of power. It is worth noting here that the trans exclusionary radical feminists' (TERF) rhetoric against trans women (people born and raised male but identifying as female) is partially about trans women experiences of gender (or lack thereof) in the structure of patriarchal power.[106]

Similar to workers in a capitalist economy, women are positioned to be the exploited class because of their structural weakness and regardless of their material capabilities. A telling example is found in a voyeuristic documentary *Dah* (Ten) by the internationally acclaimed Iranian director Abbas Kiarostami.[107] In one scene, we are privy to an unscripted discussion between a married female driver who picks up a sex worker in the streets of Tehran. Answering the female driver's question about what compels her to "sell" her body in exchange for money, the sex worker, in her own streetwise vernacular, is heard telling the married woman: you too are selling yourself for a price, the difference between you and me is that "you [married women] are the wholesalers, we [sex workers] are the retailers."[108] In other words, the sex worker is pointing out common structural disadvantages that bind her and the "respectable" married woman against the varying material and agential capacities that differentiate them. In effect, she makes the shrewd observation that for women life is a Faustian bargain with patriarchy, the same way that it is for workers with capitalism. Linking the commodification of women's "sexual and reproductive capacities," for example, in "prostitution, surrogate motherhood, and even marriage contracts," Martha Nussbaum writes: "All of us, with the exception of the independently wealthy and the unemployed, take money for the use of our body."[109] Here we should add a material disadvantage in the form of additional gendered tax known as the "pink tax" imposed on all women for purchasing goods that are substantially similar to the ones acquired by men at lower prices.[110] Studies have shown that on average women's products cost 7 percent more than similar products for men, a figure that goes much higher when paying for identical services (27 percent more) and possibly even higher when adding the gender wage gap and variations in women's class, race, and bodily abilities.[111]

Concluding Remarks

The Marxist-feminist approach presented here is useful for thinking about sexual relations under patriarchal structures of power, even though in its sweeping generalizations it can deny women's agential capacity to enter any sexual contract. After all, adult women are capable of making choices that are in their own best interests. To refute the validity of all patriarchal sexual contracts denies women's subjectivity, agency, and choices that are meaningful to them. Nevertheless, this approach is useful in interrogating patriarchal means of control and domination, especially where imbalance of power relations is generated by propriety rights and consent-based contractual models. More importantly, this approach is relevant to the cases of accusations of sexual assaults, especially by men in positions of power.

Reducing the problem of sexual harm and exploitation of women to legal considerations, debating their victim's agency and material capabilities, and the presence or absence of consent distract from the structures of patriarchal power that enable and eventually exonerate them. It is almost certain (statistically at least, as noted earlier) that men allegedly accused of sexual abuse will evade conviction in criminal justice system should charges be brought against them. Considering their position within the structural context of patriarchal relations of power, they are already guilty of sexual impropriety.

Feminist scholars and activists have already offered remedies for "peeling back the layers" of rape culture that are upheld by the capitalist patriarchal structures of power. Popova sums these up as: believing the survivors and supporting them, legislative changes such as change in the legal definition of rape, avoiding victim retraumatization, and improving the collection and processing of forensic evidence. She also recommends considering the cultural and economic position of the victims and teaching children and young adults about bodily autonomy and consent.[112] The "consent-centric" definition of rape and subordination of sexual relations to property rights contribute to the rape culture. Therefore, it is important not to think of sexual relations simply as a private matter and a voluntary choice or to see the social contract as a model of equitable exchange. In structural terms, we must think about sexual relations in the greater political context of patriarchal power and control over means of production (production of knowledge or species, the means of generating and maintaining power).

Education, raising the consciousness of men, and legal reforms are worthwhile strategies for undermining rape culture, but none of these prevent the sexual assault of women. Rather, the lesson to take away from the sexual assault of women is that our self-awareness, gender-sensitivity, claims of being feminists or allies do not immune us against control, domination, and harming women. Hence, even with the best of intentions a slogan like "Not All Men" is inherently violent in its triumphalist denialism. Similarly, demanding change in the structures of power (where women are afforded greater control over their choices and be less vulnerable to exploitation) could also amount to nothing more than grand posturing and virtue signaling by men.

Nevertheless, the situation is not hopeless. Many feminist thinkers have shown us that we (here I mean men) are not hopeless prisoners of patriarchy. For example, bell hooks reminds us that we do not have to remain wedded to patriarchy: we can claim our rights to life and love through transformative changes, practice and model healthy relational skills, reject patriarchy's promise of power and domination, build "communities of resistance" to affirm what is "positive and potentially positive in male being," and build "a feminist men's movement that would proclaim the rights of men to emotional awareness."[113] We have learned to be harmful and violent, we can unlearn it. If we "were natural-born killers, hardwired by biology and destiny to take life, then there would be no need for patriarchal socialization to turn [us] into killers."[114] Patriarchy is the name of the disease that we are afflicted with; it "is the single most life-threatening social disease assaulting the male body and spirit in our nation."[115] To fight this disease, we can start by telling the truth about what happened to us in our patriarchal families where we learned that silence means survival. We must betray patriarchy and its code of silence and secrecy. To paraphrase Marx's famous quip, we have nothing to lose except our patriarchal chains.

5

Twitter Data Analysis on #MeTooIran

Yasamin Rezai and Mehdy Sedaghat Payam

#MeToo was initially born online to encourage women to speak out about sexual assault. Condemning sexual abuse and harassment, in this movement, social media users publicize allegations of sex crimes, mostly toward people who benefit from certain social, class, racial, gender, or political power in relation to those marginalized within the power dynamics.

#MeTooIran or #من-هم among Persian-speaking users on Twitter or other social media platforms is also relatively young. This chapter will trace the foreground and online discussions and roots of this online movement in Iran as the mentioned hashtags and the terminology appeared in August 2020 for the first time on the Persian-speaking Twitter sphere. This fast-growing Iranian social media movement needs the urgent attention of cultural critics and scholars who work in the fields of new media, computational sociology, and humanities. In this chapter, we gather and collect tweets containing #MeTooIran by employing the Tweepy library in Python. By analyzing the scrapped tweets, we found a contextual pattern for creating themed categories. This gives us and many other scholars a better statistical picture of the reality of topic distribution, the users' approach to this activism, and the predominantly used vocabulary about sexual assault by Iranian users.

Reviewing the literature on how the MeToo movement with computational method and Twitter data analysis has been studied in different regions and by other scholars, we chose and adapted a specific methodology for this chapter. Since the #MeToo movement is regarded as a social media movement, this study adopts a computational approach to the tweets related to this movement in Iran. We examined various hashtags that were used in tweets related to the MeToo movement. For this chapter, we specifically investigated whether a contextual pattern existed within tweets and whether they could be classified. Additionally, this data analysis, alongside the literature review, led us to the discovery of the movement's starting point.

In the larger context, the chapter sheds light on cultural aspects of feminism in Iran through discussions on Twitter about sexual assault; it also explores some existing questions and develops new ones. We hope to raise questions such as why and how the online platforms are hosting this movement and the available data on the matter, how they contribute to the vocabulary of feminism and sexual assault, and how they have helped activists and citizens from minority and historically silenced backgrounds to discuss sexual abuse and power dynamics.

The Outset of #MeToo in Iran: Possible Scenarios

In spite of the fact that Iranians have used social media for many sociopolitical purposes over the past decade, there is no social movement as virtual as the #MeToo movement in Iran. Unlike other social movements in Iran that began with physical gatherings in nonvirtual locations, the #MeToo movement took place entirely on the internet. As the #MeToo was launched and expanded merely on social media, it significantly changed the vocabulary of social media users about sexual assault. Although it did not have the opportunity to spread to mainstream media inside the country or be manifested in real-life settings, its impact on social media users' arguments and vocabulary was immediately apparent, particularly when users encountered narratives of sexual assault on social media platforms such as Instagram, Twitter, and Clubhouse. Even though its influence is clear today, it may be hard to recall when and how this movement began or what incidents sparked such a social media movement.

There are many conflicting discussions and assumptions about the outset of the #MeToo movement in Iran. The first interaction between Iranian officials and #MeToo on social media occurred in October 2018, when Iran's Supreme Leader, Ali Khamenei, shared a video on his official English-language Twitter account using the hashtag. The two-minute video consisted of a montage of clips: women from "western countries" such as the United States discuss their experiences with sexual abuse, especially at work, followed by clips of Khamenei speaking about Islamic solutions to resolve and prevent sexual assaults.[1] By offering the hijab as a suitable solution to prevent sexual assault, the video ends with a quote from him on March 8, 2018: "Hijab gives women freedom and identity." He reportedly suggested that the oppression imposed by patriarchal Western civilization on women has led to countless cases of sexual assault in such countries. He inculpates these countries for not referring to and applying Islam's perspective, which according to him is imposing hijab on women, and accuses them of preventing the world from hearing Islam's proposal as a true solution to a better society. Many Twitter users responded to such a suggestion by questioning Iran's rape rate, despite the compulsory hijab being a rule. Even though some sources have described this as the beginning of the MeToo movement in Iran, the movement did not spread or take root within the broader social media community at this stage. More specifically, Twitter users engaged in conversations as a reaction to Khamenei's tweet that mentioned the MeToo movement. In fact, Khamenei's tweet prompted discussions on the dysfunctional relationship between hijab and sexual assault. These conversations did, however, bring the discussion about the #MeToo movement, which was new at that time, to the attention of Iranian users.

In *Performing #MeToo: How Not to Look Away*, Judith Rudakoff believes that the movement started in Iran with Khamenei's tweet mentioning #MeToo along with the use of #MosqueMeToo, in the "Glossary of Primer on International #MeToo movement."[2] However, it is more accurate to pinpoint the origin of the movement to the sexual assault and child molestation perpetrated in 2018 by Mohammad Toussi, known as Saeed Toussi, a well-known Qur'an reciter and schoolteacher admired by Ali Khamenei. Several of his former students and their families reported allegations of sexual molestation and rape against him in 2017.[3] These students were all underaged and male-identifying. Right after this incident, Twitter users spread tweets, primarily from anonymous accounts and male-identifying users, condemning Toussi and Islamic extremists who are endorsed by the supreme leader. They offered their many personal narratives of their experience of child sexual abuse and sexual assault, especially in Iran's schools that are mostly single-sex, and within the Iranian educational system, with the hashtag MeToo in its English format and Toussi's name in Persian. This is to say that the MeToo movement in which narratives can be found on social media, labeled with the hashtag at large, originated with Toussi's case. The very first use of this hashtag in Iran was in its initial English spelling and alphabet, #MeToo, and on a relatively large scale by male users condemning children's sexual abuse at schools or in religious settings. As personal narratives of childhood sexual abuse spread on Twitter, other social media users in Iran joined the movement and followed suit, attempting to gain visibility on international platforms and in English-speaking communities. Interestingly, the first narrators were predominantly male and had experienced sexual assault at some point during their childhood, in schools, or during religious activities in schools.

However, Faranak Amidi (also known as Feranak Amidi), a multimedia journalist and women's affairs reporter for BBC World Service, believes that before Toussi's case, the hashtag was adopted by Iranian social media users when the Harvey Weinstein story broke; another version of the hashtag, called #MosqueMeToo, was also used to raise awareness about sexual harassment at Islamic holy sites and the annual Hajj pilgrimage.[4] As the MeToo movement climaxed among Muslim women in the Arab world, Iranian social media caught glimpses of the movement, but the hashtag and context of #MosqueMeToo were not prominently used or were nowhere to be found in Iran.[5] Even though some Iranians, especially the ones in the diaspora who identified as Muslims, used #MosqueMeToo on Twitter in some cases, it was more widely used by Muslim-identifying women around the world rather than by Iranians specifically. In these narratives under the mentioned hashtag, sexual assault happened specifically in mosques or during Islamic religious ceremonies. The hashtag was not widely used by Iranian women since not all Iranian women actively practice Islam or use it as an indication of their identity. This can be due either to the fact that attending mosques was not an essential part of these women's daily lives or to the fact that sexual assaults did not occur as frequently in mosques as in other urban settings. Having said that, though #MosqueMeToo may have indirectly paved the way for the emergence of the MeToo movement in Iran, it was not the genesis of the movement.

#MeTooIran alongside #MeToo and its new form, translated in Persian, #مه_من, went viral after a small multimedia news channel released a video interviewing female journalists on National Journalist's Day in Iran in August 2020. This documentary shared online portrayed a group of women journalists speaking out about their experiences of sexual assault at the workplace. Shortly after, a university student and survivor of sexual assault used Instagram to name her abuser. Mentioning "K.E.," a former art student of the University of Tehran initially named by his initials, launched a viral movement: more women with real names or anonymous accounts came forward to share their stories on Instagram and Twitter, many of them also naming "K.E." The online movement went beyond the borders of social media and led to a police investigation and the revelation that Keyvan Emamverdi had raped three hundred women and more than forty rape videos were found at his house.[6] This is how the MeToo movement in Iran was born and acknowledged by the public and activists.

Another hashtag, #از_سربازی_بگو, translated as "tell me about military service," trended in 2020-1 under which shocking narratives about rape and rape culture in the military were spread. Born under the umbrella of #MeTooIran and condemning compulsory military service for men in Iran, the narrators tweeted and spread their narratives using anonymous accounts due to the social pressure in Iran. Rape and sexual assault narratives by men who were sexually abused in single-sex schools during their childhood and adolescence also spread at the same time but soon subsided.

#MeTooIran and the Case of the Musician Mohsen Namjoo

A month after Keyvan Emamverdi's case in September 2020, Mohsen Namjoo, a New York–based Iranian superstar dubbed the Bob Dylan of Iran, faced multiple allegations of sexual misconduct. After rumors spread on Twitter in the summer of 2020, he released a video message denying the allegations. His accusers protested further; however, the superstar appeared in a Persian New Year's music show on MBC Persia in March 2021. Female artists in the music industry and survivors of sexual misconduct by Namjoo harshly condemned this Persian TV channel abroad and Arash Sobhani, the show's producer, for giving a platform to Namjoo despite the unresolved allegations against him. They believed this act expressed support for a person accused of sexual misconduct and ignored the women who spoke out against him. Instagram and Twitter exploded with hot debates around this case. Another voice-sharing social platform, Clubhouse, hosted many of these discussions. The significant difference was that conversations were led by a group of activists this time. Mina Khani, Shaghayegh Norouzi, and Shadi Amin were some Iranian diaspora women and LGBTQ rights activists leading the discussions. It was one of the first instances of dynamic conversations between the fans of Namjoo and feminists on social media. The main topics were the historical marginalization of women and other minoritized communities in Iran, the common culture of victim blaming manifested within the vocabulary of social media users, the misogynist tone of debates, and biases coming from a hegemonic system of patriarchy.

The cases of Aydin Aghdashloo, a notorious Iranian painter, and Namjoo were both significant as none of them were politicians or publicly affiliated with extremist Islamic groups as Toussi was. Although Aghdashloo had a case similar to that of Namjoo and his story appeared in the *New York Times*, Namjoo's case was one of the most talked-about topics of #MeToo in Iran.[7] It gained momentum among the public and activists, brought the Iranian diaspora and Iranians inside the country into one-on-one debates, and found its way to mainstream media of Persian channels abroad, such as BBC Persian and Iran International. It is noteworthy to mention it was one of the first cases where, in the beginning, all parties involved were of the Iranian diaspora: the artist himself, who lives in exile after being banned in Iran, the women who accused him of sexual misconduct, the activists involved, and the TV channel that fueled the debates by inviting him to a New Year's show.

The Iranian national state TV and local news media stations inside the country were never involved or discussed in this case. Therefore, social media turned to be the only space in which Iranians in the country and in the diaspora came together to discuss the culture of sexual assault and verbal harassment. This was a true example of a social media movement created and used not only by women but also by the marginalized members of the invisible community of LGBTQ in Iran. They broke their silence about the hardships of living in Iran, being sexually assaulted, and being unable to take the case to court or reveal it to their families because of the illegal and socially unaccepted nature of homosexuality and the complex situation of transgender people in Iran.

Literature Review

#MeToo Movement and Digital Feminist Research across Social Media Platforms

In exploring literature review and published research works on the #MeToo movement, Quan-Haase et al. conducted a synthesis review by employing a replicable approach. They noticed that while #MeToo is a global movement, the omission of any reference to geography or a lack of geographic diversity suggests a narrow focus on scholarship based in the Global North. Therefore, they suggested that the movement needs to be studied as tied to particular spaces, bounded geographies, and social contexts (e.g., cultural, religious).[8] In a similar vein, Xiong et al. suggest that future research should address cultural differences in using the hashtag across different countries.[9] Similarly, Lang broadly suggests that scholarship should continue to pay attention to feminist hashtag activism.[10]

Quan-Haase et al. observed a limited number of studies on #MeToo in which the movement has been analyzed as hashtag activism, that is, 22 in total. The majority of resources—988 items—recognized #MeToo as a significant social movement but failed to analyze participation, either online or offline, in the movement itself. All 22 papers discuss "methods used": 11 employ a critical lens to the study, 8 use quantitative analysis, 2 use mixed methods, and 1 uses qualitative methods. According to their work, there is a need for qualitative studies that directly engage individuals who participated in the movement. Quan-Haase et al. categorized the themes of the explored articles in various groups such as backlash, sexual violence, suggestions, intersectionality, geography, affordances and participation, and nonparticipation.[11]

In light of their recommendations and the numerous studies conducted on #MeToo in English-speaking Twitter environments, the study of this newly born social media movement in Iran is of significance. Considering Iran's unique cultural, sociopolitical, and religious status, this movement and its counterpart on English-speaking accounts share many similarities but also fundamental differences that urge for adopting various multidisciplinary perspectives. It is therefore the purpose of this chapter to contribute to filling this gap.

#MeToo Twitter Data Analysis Methodologies

In a study on the #MeToo movement, hashtag activism, and message frames, Xiong, et al. used semantic network analysis, thematic analysis, and correlation test to study how Social Movement Organizations (SMOs) use words and hashtags to participate in the #MeToo movement through Twitter. By employing semantic network analysis, they explored the words and linguistic structure used in the movement.[12] Semantic network analysis allows researchers to understand the most frequently mentioned symbols,[13] identify the dynamics of conversations in social networks,[14] and reveal the structure of texts by measuring co-occurrences of words.[15] By using thematic analysis to explore the emerging pattern among hashtags in the #MeToo movement, Xiong et al. found frames included in social movement organizations. The relationship between the number of hashtags and the frequency of retweets has also been explored by authors using a correlation test.[16]

It is noteworthy to mention that in Hashtag activism and message frames among social movement organizations, the researchers have created a selective list of SMOs as the first step. The goals of every involved SMO, their history, and their policies have been explored.[17] In their data collection procedure, Xiong et al. have only considered the Twitter handles of the selected SMOs. Then they removed all stop words and prepared a corpus of content words and measured the word frequencies. Correlational themes within used hashtags were then found and classified into different groups.[18]

In this chapter, however, the search was not executed by the Twitter handles of SMOs. A list of SMOs is rather difficult to prepare without official support from the authorities since #MeToo is a young movement in Iran. The existence of relevant SMOs in Iran is something to question: very few feminist organizations are legally active in Iran, and most of them are ideologically supervised by the Islamic Republic of Iran. Although some women's rights activists led this movement on social media at some points, there were no established or known SMOs officially involved. We discovered one account with the handle @me_too_iran on Twitter and @me_too_iran_movement on Instagram, launched in August 2020. As given in the bio, the accounts assert that it "echoes your voice in the fight against sexual violence: we are the voice of your narratives and provide a lawyer or psychologist to the victims if needed." The hashtag used by this account is #MeTooIran.

Xiong et al.'s findings indicate that in the #MeToo movement, there is a shift in point of action from organizational movements to cocreators in advocating for social change.[19] They believe that far fewer academic studies have explored how SMOs cocreate meanings with the public through the use of hashtags, and by applying this perspective to the #MeToo movement, they explored the words and meanings cocreated by both SMOs and public frame relevant issues within the movement on Twitter among English-speaking discourses around #MeToo.[20] In this study, we look at how cocreators, individual activists, and social media users (aka "the public") participate in and discuss the sexual harassment in Iran and gradually progress the discussions from collective action to a probably connective one.

Another study that analyzed tweets through a computational study was conducted by Sepideh Modrek and Bozhidar Chakalov. In "The #MeToo Movement in the United States: Text Analysis of Early Twitter Conversations," Modrek and Chakalov focus on first-person posts that reveal sexual assault and abuse of the victims, particularly at an early age. Since they study English tweets, they have limited their time span to one week in October 2017. Finally, they have used machine learning methods to classify and summarize their results.[21]

The Political and Social Atmosphere of Twitter in Iran

Hossein Kermani and Marzieh Adham investigated the structure of networked publics and their sharing practices in Persian Twitter during Iran's

2018 presidential election. Based on networked gatekeeping and framing theories results revealed that Twitter provided a space for Iranians to discuss general topics. However, this space is not necessarily used by voiceless and marginalized groups; the users are not limited to discussing controversial issues. A growing body of conservative crowdsourced elites emerged to defend the regime's ideology. Moreover, the dominant networked frames were shaped around routine subjects during election time. Thus, Twitter was not a platform for only seeking liberal demands. It was, to some extent, used to serve the regime's political interests. Furthermore, while many ordinary users rose to prominence, mainstream media continued to act as influential players.[22]

Methodology and Data Analysis

For our study, we combined computational analysis with textual analysis. With the help of computational methods, we collected and analyzed data, while textual analysis allowed us to study the data more deeply, from a different perspective. Both approaches provided diverse perspectives on how to explore tweets. By combining these two methods, we were able to work with a large number of tweets and read each one individually to gain a deeper understanding of our data. As a result, the focus is on two main research questions that offer a comprehensive perspective into the data about MeToo Iran:

> RQ1: What are the words and meanings created by the public in the discourse of feminism during the #MeTooIran movement?
> RQ2: How do hashtags in the Iranian MeToo movement appear contextually?

Methodology: Scraping #MeTooIran

More than one hashtag is associated with the #MeToo movement in Iran. This movement is still relatively new at the time of this study, as evidenced by the inconsistency in hashtagging. It also represents the lack of SMOs involved and how the formation of this digital movement is based on individual accounts with no strong social media strategies. This inconsistency complicated the procedure of scraping data. We targeted various forms of this hashtag and other relevant ones as there was not one main umbrella hashtag, and many have been developed since the movement began as seen below.

چرا_گزارش_ندادم (why I didn't report)
می_تو (me_too)
خشونت_جنسی (sexual violence)
قربانی_نکوهی (victim blaming)
قربانی_نکوهی_نکنیم (no to victim blaming)
من_هم_سکوت_نمیکنم (I won't stay silent either)
تجاوز (rape)
نام_متجاوز_را_بگو (say out your rapist's name)
من_هم_سکوت_نخواهم_کرد (I am not going to stay silent either)
زنان_میتو (women of metoo)
چرا_گزارش_نکردم (why I didn't report)
باجگیری_جنسی (sexual blackmail)
روایت_آزار (harassment narrative)
علیه_فرهنگ_تجاوز (against the rape culture)

This research aimed to analyze tweets from hashtags with the most relevant results. From all these keywords and hashtags, #MeTooIran provided us with the maximum number of relevant results. This hashtag was mainly and strategically used by the @me_too_iran Twitter account, the MeToo movement page covering the relevant content from and about Iran, run by Shaghayegh Norouzi, an Iranian actress and women's rights activist The hashtag was first retweeted by Norouzi on August 24, 2020. This account was originally created on August 14, 2020.

In the first tweet of me_too_Iran_movement account, Shaghayegh Norouzi says:

می_تو_مومنت_ایران رسما# همزمان با موج جدید افشاگری‌ها علیه آزار جنسی و تجاوز، صفحه باج_گیری_#تجاوز، و#آزار_جنسی،# فعالیت خود را در توییتر و در راستای همبستگی زنان علیه جنسی شروع کرد.

#من_هم#سکوت_نمیکنیم#

Translation: Along with the new wave of disclosures against sexual assault and rape, the page of me_too_movement_Iran has officially started its activity on Twitter to show its solidarity with women against #sexaul_assault, #rape, and #sexual_blackmail.

She later retweets this in her personal account. In our analysis, @me_too_iran is the only account consistently posting narratives about sexual assault and retweeting news about the movement. Although not officially registered as an

SMO, this account seems to be the main source on Instagram and Twitter to post relevant materials on the MeToo movement in Iran. From August 24, 2020, to February 22, 2022, a total of 1,780 tweets have been posted. Over half of these tweets (926 to be exact) were original tweets, and the rest were retweets, sharing the discussed tweets without adding any content.

The first step in scraping tweets with hashtag #MeTooIran from Twitter was to open a developer account and then upgrade our access level to "academic" so that tweets older than seven days were able to be scraped. A Python code was then written.[23] In this code, we used Tweepy, which is "an easy-to-use Python library for accessing the Twitter API." The output of this code was a CSV (comma separated values) file with several columns, including the date of creation, the tweet text, the screen name, the name, the date the account was created, and the URL (for original tweets only). Afterwards, we removed duplicates and Latin characters from tweet texts and reviewed the tweet texts individually to determine if any patterns could be found.

Categories: Contextual Themes and Patterns

In their 2019 essay, Mordek and Chakalov claim that the English tweets they extracted from Twitter fall into four categories: support, ambiguous revelation, detailed revelation, and others, "i.e., either negative comments, unrelated content, or riding off the hashtag."[24] However, the patterns discovered in tweets in the Persian language, in this case, were slightly different from Mordek and Chakalov's findings. A remarkable number of tweets of instructive content, educating the reader about women's rights and sexual harassment, have also been found. Moreover, the number of negative comments, mainly including victim blaming content, was noticeably high, and so we decided to assign a single category to them.

We acknowledge that many other ways of categorizing the data and discovered tweets are possible, and here we suggest categories after going through the tweets containing the various forms of #MeTooIran as the following patterns appeared. The categories are broad, and the main aim was for them not to overlap. It is, however, important to highlight that these tweets led us to subjective creation of these categories as if this pattern emerged among them.

1. **Support:** Any content that amplifies the voice of survivors and their narratives of sexual assault or stands in solidarity in various ways such as

expressing frustration, emotional support, or sympathy by re-hashtagging, or any content in which the user takes the side of the reported narratives have been counted in this category. Many tweets have been widely assigned to this category if any signs of "supporting" the movements, victims, or narratives have been detected. Tweets with educational purposes, discussing the topic, or narrating/reporting sexual assault are not included in this group.

2. **Victim blaming:** Any kind of victim blaming or teasing, ridiculing their narratives or the content around sexual assault, or expressing strong disbelief in the narratives are included in this category. Many tweets were around the discussion of whether a narrative holds true. Many were also posing questions about how these narratives, especially from anonymous accounts, have been fact-checked. These were not assigned to this category and were transferred to the "uncategorized."
Example: [User account removed] همه قبل از اثبات جرم بیگناهن
Translation: Everyone is innocent until they are found guilty.

3. **Educational:** Any educational content such as writing about historical roots of patriarchy, feminism, dynamics of power and its relationship with sexual assault, the law and legal aspects of reporting a sex crime in Iran or abroad are considered educational and instructive to the public and Twitter users. Many of these were tweeted by the @me_too_iran account. Many relevant hashtags as byproducts of these tweets have been formed and later broadly used by Twitter users. Some of them are
#نه_یعنی_نه! (No means no.)
#چرا_گزارش_ندادم (Why I did not report it.)
#نام_متجاوز_را_بگو (Name your rapist)

4. **Narrative:** Any content, including direct or indirect report or narrative of a sex crime, sexual assault, or harassment.

5. **Uncategorized:** Anything that did not belong to the aforementioned mentioned categories.

As shown here, of 870 tweets, the most significant portion, 247 of them or 28.4 percent of all the tweets, were categorized to express support for the movement according to the definitions and explanations given earlier. A total of 217 tweets were labeled as "uncategorized." The third most significant portion includes the educational or instructive tweets about the movement and sexual assault in general and Iran. A total of 138 tweets were assigned to the category of "narratives," meaning speaking out and reporting a sex or harassment crime,

Table 5.1 Total number of tweets from August 2020 to February 2022

Category	1. Support	2. Victim blaming	3. Educational	4. Narratives	5. Uncategorized	Total
Number	247	99	169	138	217	870

and 99 were labeled as "victim blaming" according to what this label consisted of and how it was defined.

In Table 5.1, uncategorized tweets have been left out and 653 tweets that were assigned to the first four categories have been visualized. With 21.1 percent of sexual assault narratives, there are around 40 percent supportive tweets and about 26 percent instructive tweets. Furthermore, 15.2 percent of tweets consisted of victim-blaming content and were in opposition to the 40 percent of support.

We should note that the scraped tweets were labeled by hashtag #MeTooIran. They consist of all tweets as well as shared ones or the ones tweeted under the hashtag #MeTooIran. The corpus of our study also includes conversations responding to these tweets. It was not difficult to predict that support would prevail over opposition, as the purpose of such social media movements and users' engagement was to encourage public discussion in a supportive manner. We consider the victim-blaming ratio to be relatively high on this front. Moreover, tweets containing educational content represent the second dominant category, expressing the effective initiation of the movement by attempting to raise public awareness around the issue.

Although victim blaming makes up the smallest percentage of tweets, it is still a significant proportion, and some of the arguments by users who promote this attitude are extremely offensive (Figure 5.1). These comments ranged from ignoring the issue to expressing strict opposition to what this hashtag has been trying to promote. Most of the tweets in this category were with the content of condemning the movement, women's rights activists, and feminist movements. A number of the tweets assigned to this category demonstrated a lack of knowledge in understanding what sexual consent is. Some of them also failed to accurately comprehend and therefore address sexual assault and utilized "bad behavior" or similar phrases to describe such acts. Others believed that no sexual assault report must be credible without exact proof or evidence by targeting the morality of such act ("My conscience wouldn't approve that I blame real people" "وجدان من می گه که اتهام های بی اساس به اشخاص حقیقی رو نپذیرم"). Some of them used swear words to blame victims, and some even went as far as blaming feminists in general. In one of these posts, the MeToo movement was

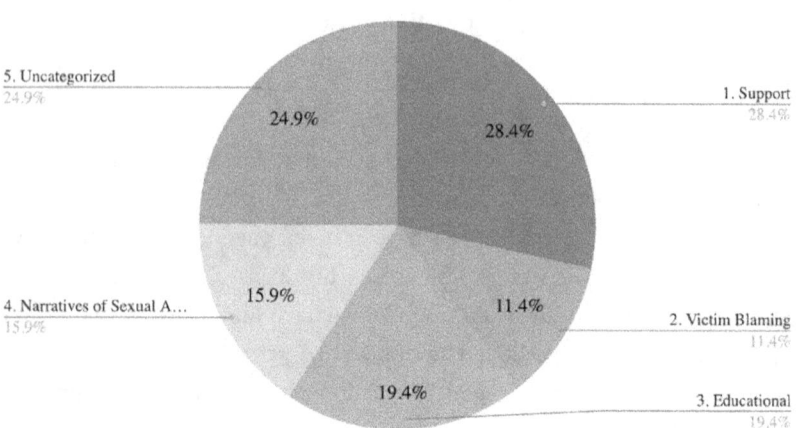

Figure 5.1 Pie chart for the overall number of tweets.

compared to a marital court, and another expressed surprise that sexual conduct between husband and wife without the wife's consent can be considered rape. At least on Twitter within this conversation, many of those who held this position persisted in maintaining their original stance, even after other Twitter users explained the concept of consent to them. The tweets below explain how victim blaming has long been a part of the culture and vocabulary while talking about sexual assault:

چیزی که جریان #من_هم بطور ویژه عریان کردمردانگی سمی غالب فرهنگ تجاوز ماست که به مردان این قدرت را میدهدکه آلتهای سرگردانی باشند درخیابان ومحل کار ودانشگاه وخانه!فرهنگ تجاوزی که زن ها را برای آلت سرگردان بودن مردهاسرزنش میکند!تقصیر توبودکه تجاوز شدی!

Translation: What #MeToo specially laid bare was the toxic masculinity of the rape culture which allows men to have wandering sex organs on the street, workplace, university and home. The rape culture that blames women for the wandering sex organs of the men! It was your fault that you were raped!

In response to the RQ2, Figure 5.2 shows a contextual pattern of the scrapped tweets associated with #MeTooIran after removing the uncategorized tweets.

Most Frequent Terms

This time after cleaning the corpus, we kept the stopwords in it and used the "stylo" package, developed by Maciej Eder et al. in R, to find the most frequent

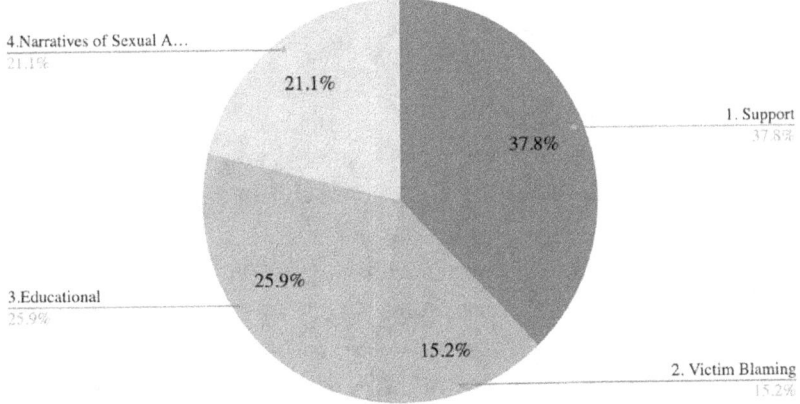

Figure 5.2 Pie chart of tweets excluding the uncategorized tweets.

words in the entire corpus of tweets. This package analyzes the text and creates frequency tables for the most frequent or repeated words regardless of whether they are "content words," that is, words that have meaningful content that is beneficial to the understanding of the text, or "structure words," words that add no specific meaning to the text and are mostly of grammatical application, such as prepositions.[25] The result demonstrated the top twenty words in the body of scraped tweets.

و (and)
به (to)
که (that)
از (from)
در (in)
این (this)
تجاوز (assault)
هم (too)
من (me)
جنسی (sexual)
با (with)
می (me)
رو (conversational form of را, a direct object identifier)
روایت (narrative)

را (direct object identifier)
آزار (assault/harassment)
های (plural identifier)
تو (too)
است (is)
شما (you)

In most other texts, the top twenty most repeated words are mainly structure words. These words, mostly being prepositions and linking expressions, do not contribute to the meaning of a sentence such as the first six words in the list. Due to the brevity of tweets (one tweet contains no more than 280 characters), and the importance of the topic, the words روایت, جنسی, هم, من, تجاوز, and آزار (meaning rape, too, me, sexual, narrative, and assault/harassment, respectively—the topmost frequent words in the MeToo movement of Iran) are found to be in the top twenty most frequent words. This reflects the importance of these words used in digital movement and proves the fact that such a movement against sexual assault does exist in the Iranian context on social media and uses similar vocabulary as its counterpart, #MeToo.

We also used the stylo package in R to count the top repeated words among tweets from the fourth category, sexual narratives, to find the most frequent words. This package offers a table with frequencies for the works that are processed through it. This table is based on the percentage of a word in a text and offers a broader insight into the text. Then, we divided these words into smaller categories to see how similar/different they were from the words that Modrek and Chakalov had found in their work.

In response to RQ1, the most common content words here were as follows: روایت (narrative), 2.5 percent; جنسی (sexual), 1.75 percent; تجاوز (rape), 1.58 percent; آزار (harassment), 1.58 percent; سکوت (silence), 0.5 percent; and تعرض (assault), 0.5 percent. The word "silence" was found to be the most repeated content word after predicted topic-relevant words such as "rape," "harassment," "sexual," "narrative," and "assault." There are many possible reasons or potential interpretations that make talking about an alleged sex crime complex in a real-life setting in Iran or among Iranians, including cultural and sociopolitical issues or the power dynamics involved in the assault. It seems that social media and this movement specifically have been a platform for these narratives to emerge and stand out, by real names or anonymously. Yet, the word "silence," whether it is endured or broken, appears to be the most repeated word in the narratives.

Conclusion

There are many hashtags that do not contain the term "MeToo" or من هم; however, they conceptually belong to the movement. This lack of consistent terminology in the period of the study has made the study of the MeToo movement quite complicated. The hashtag #MeTooIran, which was actively assigned to narratives of sexual assault by Norouzi's account, contributed to the collection and labeling of the tweets for our study. We acknowledge that these tweets were subjectively selected and labeled under this hashtag by the mentioned account and did not encompass all the tweets relevant to this movement on Twitter. There were other hashtags, such as #از_سربازی_بگو, translated to "tell me about your military service," and #چرا_گزارش_ندادم, translated to "why I did not report," that encouraged various groups of people to talk about sexual assault that was not part of our study.

The explored pattern in contextual themes of tweets with #MeTooIran, which are mostly in the Persian language, demonstrates that Twitter has been relatively hostile to this movement and survivor narratives of sexual assault in Iran. The subjective creation of categories among 870 tweets between August 2020 and February 2022 that were labeled by #MeTooIran resulted in the emergence of four thematized groups: supportive, victim blaming, educational, and narratives of sexual assault. Among these tweets, 217 were labeled as uncategorized, which means they did not belong to any of the previously mentioned classifications.

A prominent category of these tweets was educational and instructive content for the public about how to speak about sexual assault and for the survivors about how to report them. Topics such as the history of marginalized groups, especially women, and their historical vulnerability in patriarchal systems with limited access to legal resources for sex crime have been covered. The concept of consent in a sexual relationship and the suggested vocabulary for talking about sex crime and sexual harassment have been provided by individual activists and mostly the Twitter account of @Me_too_Iran. A remarkable proportion of tweets contained victim blaming and expressed strong opposition against this feminist wave and social activism.

The word "silence" has been found to be the most repeated word among the tweets from the category of narratives and reports of sexual assaults, which can mean most of the survivors have mentioned or pointed out this concept in some way in their narrative. In text analysis, a list of occupations mentioned in the narratives has been found, which sheds light on the industries and working atmospheres most repeated while narrating a sexual assault. These jobs are writer (0.175 percent), physician (0.14 percent), psychologist (0.14 percent), editor (0.14 percent), manager (0.1 percent), and CEO (0.1 percent).

Suggested Topics for Further Research

We had delimited our research into one single hashtag, mainly used by @me_too_iran to label the relevant content on Twitter as this hashtag offered the most relevant results. This term's Persian-translated form did not provide as much relevant data as it has been used for various other topics among Persian-language tweets.

Additionally, our research shows that the MeToo movement began in Iran, and the data analysis covers tweets from August 2020 through February 2022. By applying our methodology, future research may be able to be more specific about the selected periods or examined time spans, for example, by selecting different cases and researching different results in accordance with their research questions.

Although the theoretical section of this chapter deals with pinpointing the precise starting point of this movement in Iran, there are still many contrasting views about when and how the movement started off on social media. By going through the cases, similar methodologies can better prove the starting point of the movement on Twitter.

The role of SMOs can be further explored. Questions that can be further examined include if the @me_too_iran Twitter page can be counted as an SMO and whether this activism has been collectively or connectively moving forward. The role of any SMO, its existence, and relationship with individuals and/or mainstreaming channels can be further explored.

Our data, including the uncategorized tweets, around 25 percent of all tweets, are available. It is suggested that these tweets be explored and studied further, and other patterns of framing themes might be suggested and found.

6

#Unveiling_the_Iranian_MeToo: Symptomatic Reading of Iranian MeToo through the Lens of Political Economy

Paria Rahimi

The hashtag #MeToo was appropriated initially by the sexual assault survivor Tarana Burke. She used the phrase on Myspace to empower women and queer individuals who were sexually harassed and abused in the workplace.[1] In the following years, the tactic was adopted by other figures, including prominent celebrities, to make public allegations against sexual perpetrators. Since 2006, the #MeToo[2] has embarked on its journey and traversed different platforms and borders.[3] Despite the fact that it was generally welcomed by intellectuals, academics, and activists, the #MeToo has been criticized by a number of Marxist thinkers and Marxist feminists. Although the majority of them consider some emancipatory potentials and liberatory possibilities in this feminist practice, they also see some shortcomings. They find the #MeToo a powerful spark that has not gone far enough. They also argue that the #MeToo has been perverted to meet bourgeois feminism's needs.[4] In this chapter, I chart out these criticisms in three different but intertwined categories.

One of the criticisms leveled is that even though the #MeToo had been founded in 2006, it started trending only when it involved high-profile Hollywood celebrities. In the beginning, the campaign was launched by marginalized women who have experienced sexual harassment in the workplace, and for years the media were reluctant to cover it. In addition, even if the media took the issue up later on, the unrelenting sexual harassment of low-paid women in the service industries was still of no great interest to them. Women's experiences of sexual harassment in the agriculture sector and domestic service have not been heard and voiced by mainstream media.[5] Marxist thinkers criticize the #MeToo as a movement that excludes the voice of those who are doubly oppressed at the intersection of gender, race, and class. Employing an intersectional lens, they claim that people marginalized by different systems of power are at a greater risk of sexual assault and harassment. Similarly, Tarana Burke, the founder of the #MeToo campaign, critically has questioned the progression of the movement, asking, "Those most vulnerable to workplace abuse—working-class people and especially women and queers of colour, migrants, and domestic and sex workers—are among those #MeToo 'left behind.' How did we get here? And who does this shift serve?"[6]

Another criticism of capitalism by Silvia Federici in a talk delivered regarding the #MeToo considers men as oppressed and exploited in the patriarchal and capitalist society as well. The fact that male workers, the predominant portion of the wage labor force, must obey the frequent commands and endure the constant dominance of their exploiting bosses causes them frustration and powerlessness. This indignity in the workplace is mirrored in the same mechanism at home. The male proletarian exploits his wife as his inferior with control over her body, sexuality, and labor. This cycle reproduces the imbalanced power dynamics that is generated by capitalism in the first place. Therefore, the problem is not merely the powerful men who are condemned by the #MeToo, Federici argues. The problem is capitalism that must be overthrown. For doing so, the #MeToo can be assumed just as a step in this process that must be followed by radical changes in the material conditions of the workplace.[7] Similar to Federici, Slavoj Žižek has stated:

> We should be very careful and also critical about #MeToo. #MeToo is no longer what it was. It does not touch the real social problems, poverty, daily exploitation, and so on. And that's, for me, generally the problem with political correctness. It deals with polite forms of talking, acting and so on. It doesn't approach the true economic roots of this crisis.[8]

Other critics criticized #MeToo by addressing the individualistic nature of the practice. They also believe that #MeToo simplistically challenges the individual's actions rather than social relations of power. Calling out the assailants, #MeToo calls for new bosses rather than changing the misogynistic system. The approach leaves the unequal power dynamics unquestioned and the systemic violence of the workplace intact. Figuratively speaking, Rosalind Gill and Shani Orgad criticize #MeToo for focusing on "monsters" (e.g., Harvey Weinstein) instead of on the "monstrous capitalist, patriarchal and sexist system" (the meta-system of capitalism in general and the capitalist film industry in this particular context).[9]

In this chapter, coming from the same tradition, I comradely respond to Marxists' criticisms centered on #MeToo. I posit that Iranian #MeToo has challenged the political economy radically since patriarchy and capitalism are complicit in sexual harassment. I suggest #MeToo is a feminist practice, and every feminist issue is a question of the political economy per se. In some cases, the interconnection is not established clearly; however, in all of them, the connection can be discovered by considering the mediating variables. To do so, I draw upon examples from Iranian #MeToo that vividly spotlight the intersection and coalition of patriarchy and capitalism.

The History of Iranian #MeToo

When #MeToo gained global reach in 2017, Iranian women had already been battling sexual violence in a digital campaign called "Prohibition of Domestic Violence" for a year. In this digital campaign, women from different cities and social classes published their narratives about their experiences of violence and sexual harassment anonymously.[10] Following widespread allegations against many notable Hollywood figures in 2017, many Iranian women sent their sexual harassment and rape narrations to an Instagram influencer, Hourieh Rahimi. Protecting confidentiality and using the hashtag #MeToo, the influencer published these narratives in several Instagram stories.[11] #MeToo was used by a handful of artists and journalists in the same year as well, yet it did not trend virally. The second current of Iranian #MeToo dates back to August 2020, when arrays of Twitter users accused Keyvan Emamverdi of serial rapes. The hashtag has been used since then to condemn one hundred famous Iranian people, including artists, university professors, athletes, writers, and diplomats, among others.[12]

Methodology and Method: Symptomatic Reading

Deploying Althusser's hermeneutical method—symptomatic reading—I study some examples from Iranian #MeToo and single out Keyvan Emamverdi's case to which the bulk of the chapter is dedicated. While so far the application of symptomatic reading has been restricted to philosophical or literary works, I experiment with it in the study of social problems. Here, I aim to show that social order as a symbolic order is a text and can be studied by symptomatic reading or other methods that have been traditionally used for the analysis of written texts.

Putting forward the hypothesis of "meaningful action as a text," Ricoeur opens up phenomenology's doors to social sciences. He provides one site for social and political philosophers to make use of linguistic theories.[13] Given that they can be the object of scientific knowledge and explanation, similarly, Althusser considers social phenomena, like natural phenomena, to be ontologically real.[14] He studies and explains his objects by the application of his method—symptomatic reading.

Louis Althusser coined "symptomatic reading" to describe his method for reading Karl Marx's works. He believes symptomatic reading is the very method by which Marx himself read the classical economists. Althusser suggests that the best way to read *Capital* is reading it line by line, word by word, and "to the letter." He also invites Marx's readers to read "the German original" precisely, at least those parts in which "key concepts come to the surface."[15] Contrasting the German original with the French translation (Roy's, which was compared, (re)translated, and rewritten by Marx himself), Althusser compares connotations and word implications in both languages and shows how this (symptomatic) reading enables us to conceive Marxism more comprehensively and accurately.

Althusser's hermeneutical is rooted in Heideggerian phenomenology. To explain and clarify phenomenology, Heidegger benefits from the same metaphor. To him, that symptoms are indicators of a disease that is existent but invisible resembles the fact that the phenomenon is peculiar to and symbolic of a noumenon. Namely, noumenon addresses itself by its symptoms.[16] The method also stems from Freudian dream interpretation. The symptomatic reading is neither a transparent and objective reading of a text nor an innocent reading to grasp the preferred meaning and manifest content thoroughly. Instead, using psychoanalytical terms, Althusser defines it as a "guilty reading." The reader reads the text, double reads, inscribes, translates literally, and ultimately rewrites it in a new way that divulges the latent meanings.[17] This reading reveals the theoretical unconscious of the text through traces, contradictions, symbols, and gaps lagged in the time: not very different from how a psychoanalyst unfolds the unconscious by tracing dreams and slips.[18]

The act of discovering the revealing "traces" by the guilty reader proves resonant with Derridean deconstruction too. Like a "parasite," Derrida's deconstruction seeks to discover a gap in the structure to dismantle and then rearticulate it,[19] while, being a structuralist, Althusser prefers to advance the structure.[20] Symptomatic reading is always a method to scrutinize, deepen, and expand the text. It adds a supplementary to the text and lets the object/thing manifest itself by its phenomenon while it is in its being. Deconstruction, on the contrary, seeks to overthrow the system to build a new formation. Dwelling in the gaps and voids, deconstruction playfully challenges the structure/text/order in its quest for a new establishment—a post-structure. Contrariwise, symptomatic reading does not aim to undo or unweave but attempts to complete and progress the text/order.

In response to the criticisms of #MeToo, I "go back" to the Iranian #MeToo and find the answer within it. I allow the #MeToo to be "revealed" by itself. Is there any answer already inscribed in this event? Any answer that was offered in advance to a question that had not been asked at the time? I discover traces, unconscious contradictions, slips, and paradoxes; I read the #MeToo deeply. I "reread" it guiltily. I translate its acts into words literally and rewrite its unsaid replies to the never-posed question (of political economy). I interpret the #MeToo and read it symptomatically. I unveil #MeToo's guilty actors and acts in a three-act play.

First Act: Mr. Somebody

There are many types of sexual harassment, and the #MeToo narratives only address one specific type, characterized and identified by the reputed rapists who enjoy different privileges. In particular, in Iranian #MeToo narratives, the majority of the narratives focus on male rapists who have assaulted female victims, with the exception of a few, which highlights the cases of the nonbinary and gender queer folks as well. In all these narratives, the rapists benefit from symbolic capital; even if they are famous figures, they still have superior social or economic status. A perfect example of these uneven power relations and capital ownership is Mohsen Namjoo, a famous Iranian singer who has been accused of sexual assault and harassment by a number of female artists, including Luna Shad, Panida, Faravaz, Mahi, and many others.

In August 2020, Panida, an Iranian female singer, in an Instagram live broadcast, claimed that she had been assaulted by Namjoo. On April 14, 2021, in a clubhouse room with one thousand participants, Panida, in tears, retold her story, this time in more detail, adding her conversation with Namjoo: "One night he again sent a message," she said, "asking me to have dinner with him. I didn't answer. The day after, while we were filming, he abused and insulted me. 'You are a "nobody," and somebody ought to shut your mouth,' he revealingly said. 'You thought I wouldn't hear about what you've been saying.'"[21]

In a seventeen-minute audio recording leaked in April 2021, Namjoo said: "*Ironically*, after all these sexual harassment allegations, my works have been streamed more on Spotify. It's funny. My Instagram stats became better too. Another instance is the painting master (he refers to Aydin Aghdashloo); after all of the allegations accusing him of sexual rape, he sold his painting for the highest price." In another revealing flash/slip, Namjoo encapsulates his points by drawing on the famous motto: "*Every publicity is good publicity.*"[22]

In Panida's narrative, Namjoo has played the power relations card and his share of symbolic capital both to misconduct sexually and silence the assaulted singer afterwards. Similarly, in the leaked recording, the musician showcases the same relationality among different forms of capitals. What to him is the ironic and funny translation of fame to monetary profit is the backbone of Pierre Bourdieu's theory of capital.

Fully developed and comprehensive, Pierre Bourdieu's contribution to sociology is a theoretical cosmos. Bourdieu is impacted by a handful of figures; among them are Karl Marx and Max Webber, who exerted a powerful influence on him. Although he has borrowed vast arrays of terms and concepts from others, his scholarship is progressive and creative. Like Marx, Bourdieu understands society as relational and embraces the prime elements of the "conflict theory." From Marx's economist theories, he draws out the idea of capital; and from Weber, he borrows the symbolic while elaborating both in his distinctive way. The synthetic reading of Bourdieu gives rise to a number of capitals, including but not limited to the classical economic one. For Bourdieu, capital extends "to all the goods, material and symbolic, without distinction, that present themselves as rare and worthy of being sought after in a particular social formation."[23] However, Bourdieu refers to a dozen "capitals," the four fundamentals of which are economic, social, cultural, and symbolic.[24] Before bringing symbolic capital to light, a central concept to my argument, I would like to shed light on some other Bordieuan terms that will aid us in the understanding of symbolic capital.

Being reluctant to apply the Marxist terms "superstructure" and "infrastructure," Bourdieu uses the word "field," which can be defined as historical, nonhomogeneous social-spatial settings in which agents are engaged and their social positions are located.[25] The position is the aftermath of the agent's interaction with the specific rules of the field, habitus, and agent's capital. Each field is hierarchical and underpinned by a particular form of capital.[26] To Bourdieu, society is a structured hierarchy of relatively autonomous fields. Being Marxist and structuralist, Bourdieu considers society stratified and class-divided; howbeit, he marks a distance from Marx when he posits this stratification as autonomous.[27]

In "The Forms of Capital," Bourdieu contends that "it is, in fact, impossible to account for the structure and functioning of the social world unless one reintroduces *capital in all its forms* and not solely in the one form recognized by economic theory" (emphasis added).[28] What are "all forms of capital"? Further, he claims that interest cannot be produced without producing its negative counterpart. For him, this counterpart is what the economy, in a restricted sense, reckons as disinterestedness. Disinterested forms of exchange ensure the transubstantiation whereby the economic capital can present itself in the immaterial form of cultural and social capital and vice versa. Simply put, monetary profit cannot be maximized without cultural practices and artistic products.

Since the term "economic capital" is somewhat clear, and Bourdieu applies it fairly in the same way as that of the traditional Marxists, I instead outline his other types of capital: "Cultural capital" is the most elaborated kind of capital in Bourdieu's works. He explicates that cultural capital itself can have three forms. It can be in the embodied state, in the long-lasting dispositions of the mind and body. It can be in the objectified state, like pictures, books, musical instruments, and so on. Or it can be in the institutionalized state and reified as academic qualifications. The acquisition of more cultural capital hinges on spending more time and financial prosperity than artistic or educational aptitude. Thus, to prolong children's education beyond the necessary to reproduce the labor force, for instance, the family must hold sufficient economic capital. Similarly, cultural capital is convertible into economic capital in certain conditions.[29] On the other hand, "social capital" is defined as all durable actual/potential social networks, affiliations to institutions, memberships in groups, attendance to a prestigious university that entitles an agent to credit (in all its meanings). The amount of social capital one may enjoy depends on the volume of the economic, cultural, and symbolic capital they possess. Inversely, one's social capital (encompassing social obligations and connections, or a title of nobility) is convertible into economic capital.[30] "Symbolic capital" is one of those moments that Bourdieu reads Marx critically (and guiltily) in order to add something to economist Marxism. In *Outline of a Theory for Practice*, Bourdieu criticizes Marx for neglecting the symbolic facet at the expense of his preoccupation with economic capital.[31] He reads the book *Capital* symptomatically when he translates and rewrites Marx's axiom "capital breeds capital" to develop his multifaceted capital theory.[32] Bourdieu claims that the interplay between different forms of capital shows how capital goes to capital. For him, the most powerful conversion to be made is symbolic capital.[33]

Second Act: The Painting Master

As Mohsen Namjoo perfectly showed, the endless conversion of capitals is vividly illuminated in the case of Aydin Aghdashloo. Aghdashloo, known as the "Harvey Weinstein of Iran" and certainly one of the most acclaimed Iranian artists, has been accused of sexual abuse over thirty years by thirteen women, one of whom was underage at the time. Describing Aghdashloo as a formidable figure who straddles art and politics, an investigative article published by the *New York Times* highlights many robust ties and connections between Aghdashloo and his family with the government and religious officials.[34] A couple of months after dozens of Aghdashloo's former students and colleagues spoke out and shared their #MeToo narrations,[35] an artwork by the painting master was auctioned in Tehran. The painting must have been exhibited and sold to help the master reclaim his symbolic capital. Not only was the painting sold but it recorded the thirteenth Tehran Auction's highest-sold work at 125 billion rials ($553,478).[36]

In *Language and Symbolic Power*, Bourdieu defines symbolic capital as "simply the internalized or incorporated form of capital of whatever kind."[37] In another work, he describes it as "the form that the various species of capital assume when they are perceived and recognized as legitimate."[38] Symbolic capital is the double process of accumulation of other forms of capital. When an agent's economic, social, or cultural capital is recognized and perceived publicly as legitimate, the individual owns a prestigious standing, a good reputation, and renown in society— namely symbolic capital. Figuratively speaking, one way to think of symbolic capital is to consider it as a Sisyphean circulation. Bourdieu himself analogizes the conversion of capitals to that of energy and uses a geometrical metaphor, a double half rotation, to map the transformation of material capital into symbolic capital. All three forms of capital are ingrained in economic capital, and all of them can potentially transubstantiate to symbolic capital. Following the same logic, symbolic capital functions as monetary credit and can always be converted back into economic capital. Thus, symbolic capital is readily another moment of economic capital. According to Bourdieu, "Symbolic capital, a transformed and thereby disguised form of physical 'economic' capital, produces its proper effect inasmuch, and only inasmuch, as it conceals the fact that it originates in 'material' forms of capital which are also, in the last analysis, the source of its effects."[39] Hence, symbolic capital is not a fundamental or original and basic state of capital. It is merely a transfiguration of other kinds of capital. Using David Swartz's words, symbolic capital is "denied capital."[40] Loïc Wacquant, student, translator, and collaborator of Bourdieu, understands symbolic capital as one of the most complex ideas and the cornerstone of Bourdieu's system. In agreement with Swartz, he states that "symbolic capital designates the effects of any form of capital when people do not perceive them as such."[41] Being immaterial, symbolic capital is misrecognized economic capital. To put it differently, symbolic capital is not genuinely the fourth form, a different state of capital, but rather it is the legitimized and (mis)recognized form of capital. In a nutshell, Bourdieu's theory of practice shows that society is structured relationally, and all forms of capital are interlocked. Bourdieu highlights how different fields within society are connected and that the state must be considered a meta-field. He claims that capital can be more diverse than the overt form of fiscal capital; however, "in the last analysis," all other species are rooted in economic capital.

In the case of Aydin Aghdashloo, the artwork must have been sold at twelve billion rials, with a tenfold increase[42] to convert the economic capital into symbolic capital and reposition the painter to the field—the more expensive, the more valuable. Intensifying all speculations about the government being behind the auction scene, Alireza Sami Azar, in an interview, said the buyer of Aghdashloo's work is not a private but a legal person whose name should not be disclosed.[43] The government has invested in the painter hoping the investment will be paid off with more interest as soon as the master is back in the cultural and artistic field with his threatened honor and legitimacy reclaimed and his lost symbolic capital regained.

Third Act: The Exceptional Case of Keyvan Emamverdi

In August 2020, a great number of Twitter users started to reveal different aspects of the life of a man who later turned into the most famous rapist in Iranian history in the past fifty years. The accounts of the raped or assaulted women differ in details, but one thing remains common: they all say that a man invited them to his house, anesthetized them using sleeping pills in alcoholic drinks, and raped them. Some of the victims have explained how they were invited to go on tours or to social gatherings with him. Others have expressed how he pretended to be an intellectual who seemed like a glib talker. As women began voicing their experiences of assault, threatened by their narratives, Emamverdi resorted to harassing and blackmailing them using various anonymous accounts on social media. These revelations created an emotional ambiance and led the public to suggest different punishments for him, from hanging to dismemberment. Finally, Hussein Rahimi, the head of the Police Department in Tehran, announced that Emamverdi had been arrested and that women could now come forward and file their complaints officially, ensuring their anonymity. At the time, the news media proliferated with information about Emamverdi as an alumnus of the University of Tehran, archeology major, and the owner of a bookstore near Enghelab Square. The investigation revealed that Emamverdi had raped more than three hundred individuals in the span of a decade. The authorities uncovered videotapes of the incidents in his house. Emamverdi, however, admitted to only fifty of these rape cases, out of which only thirty have filed complaints against him. Of course, later the number was changed from three hundred to less than three hundred by the police, and Emamverdi himself, it is believed, had confessed to one of his victims that he had raped and assaulted over two hundred individuals. He claimed his sexual misconduct derived from his sadistic personality disorder, which turned out to be a lie. He also claimed that much of it was due to the thrill and adrenaline rush he derived from the act. To this day, he refuses to accept the charges brought upon him by the women. The survivors' lawyer, Shima Ghooshe, has stated that although there are only a handful of plaintiffs, there are many Twitter users who have posted screenshots of their conversations about his invitations and assaults. Some of the survivors even filed complaints on the phone from abroad. Due to cultural constraints, many of his accusers chose not to come forward and file complaints legally.

On September 26, 2021, Ghooshe announced on her Twitter account that his first court session has been canceled without prior notice.[44] Overall, the hearing in the case was put on hold for three times out of five, always for spurious reasons. The third time, on June 8, 2022, the lawyer tweeted, "It's the same scenario: the judge is on leave, the nerves and spirits of the plaintiffs are shattered, and the victims' psychological situation is treated with disdain."[45] Clearly, Emamverdi's case was a complicated one due to the great number of plaintiffs. However, on July 9, 2022, he was ultimately sentenced based on Article 286 of Islamic Law, which considers an individual a "corruptor upon the earth" (*mufsid-i fil 'arz*) and deserving of death, if said individual spreads vice and corruption.[46]

Out of the hundred figures accused of sexual rape, sexual assault, and harassment, Emamverdi is the only person who never had fame and symbolic capital before #MeToo outed him. Interestingly, he is also the only person who has been prosecuted legally and condemned juridically. This paradox and exception of Iranian #MeToo is the moment that symptomatic reading needs to delve into to bring truth to the fore and unveil it publicly. In many other cases of #MeToo, plaintiffs contacted the police, filed complaints, and demanded a trial;

however, none of the perpetrators were sued. This raises many questions: why does the Islamic Republic's juridical apparatus solely sue Emamverdi while there are so many others with similar allegations but more fame? Why are they not investigated? Why have all the documents been reckoned as insufficient, juridically invalid, and legally invaluable in the majority of rape cases? Why are the perpetrators not fired from their jobs and paid positions? The answer rests on the already inscribed contradiction of the #MeToo, on the unveiled paradox.

Let us go back to Bourdieu: as he points out capital underlies domination; however, the intervening role of capital is covert and subtle. Different procedures of capital conversion conceal the relation of economic capital with dependency and dominance.[47] The double accumulation and transformation of symbolic capital dissimulate its materialist and interested instinct. Being represented as disinterested and autonomous from the economic field, symbolic capital has been conceived as a legitimate disposition associated with honor and meritocracy. Therefore, the best way to safeguard and reproduce economic capital is by disguising it by the mask of symbolic capital—the form of capital that is mutually agreed upon, honored, and cannot be questioned.[48]

The symbolic capital of an agent is either endowed by an authority (state and/or its apparatuses) or legitimized and recognized publicly according to habitus (what is again the symbolized and internalized power relations).[49] This vicious cycle perpetuates the ongoing structures through a hidden process that obscures actual power relations and the unequal distribution of interests and privileges. When an individual who possesses symbolic capital uses it to control the less privileged one, they exercise symbolic violence, given that #MeToo perpetrators have exerted their power and dominance employing their symbolic capital. Economic capital lays the basis for symbolic capital, and symbolic capital lays the groundwork for symbolic power, which for Bourdieu is a world-making power.[50]

Emamverdi was an unknown bookseller and tour guide with a mediocre portion of cultural capital generated from his education in archeology at the University of Tehran. As a petit-bourgeois, he also enjoyed a modest share of economic capital. Having graduated from the University of Tehran (an academy with the highest amount of symbolic capital in the Iranian scholastic field) and working in a bookstore on Enghelab Street (the most cultural district of Tehran crowded by intellectuals, artists, and academics), he has a moderate degree of social capital too.

Emamverdi's place in the middle of all these hierarchies is an indicator of his general position as a member of the middle class in Iran's society. His occupation as a small-scale merchant, in a bookstore, has nothing to do with the state economy as it is not hinged upon it. Emamverdi's existence is of no significance to the system; in fact, it is more likely that the Islamic Republic benefits from his prosecution. Emamverdi's economic capital is insufficient for maximizing the monetary profit in the market. Moreover, his share of other capital species is too minimal to let him play a pivotal role in any field and yield immaterial capital. Hence, neither his economic capital nor his social or cultural capitals are legitimated and recognized publicly, and none can be translated into symbolic capital. Consequently, he does not possess sizeable credit that tethers him to the infrastructure. Emamverdi's arrest can probably raise the government's symbolic capital: the Islamic republic prosecuted a serial rapist to opportunistically reinforce its so-called skyscraping but illusionary tower of democracy. Although Emamverdi has had sufficient capital to encroach and exercise symbolic violence, his income from the retail store and his socioeconomic place cannot accommodate him in the tower.

The #MeToo narratives accuse reputed figures of sexual harassment and tie them with counter-values instead of honor and prestige. Thereby, in this activist practice, the symbolic capitals of the accused are questioned and doubted. The #MeToo revelations not only disclose rapists' names and their predatory behavior but also reveal the exploiting nature of capital of each kind. Questioning honor and legitimacy of harassers and rapists, #MeToo also questions all mechanisms and relations by which the capital is endowed. It retroactively reveals various field relations and undoes the transfigurations of different capitals; ultimately and potentially, #MeToo can help dismantle the system—the hierarchical meta-field.

The exceptional case of Keyvan Emamverdi as the paradox of #MeToo shows us that capital merely quests for maximization of profit. Hence, even among criminals, the one who is less privileged and is impotent of "breeding capital" is excluded and removed from the field. This paradox unmasks symbolic capital and uncovers the #MeToo showing that what is behind the veil is economic capital.

Hitherto, situating my argument on one of the paradoxes, I read #MeToo symptomatically. Now, I deploy symptomatic reading to analyze the text written by the paradox itself. In the same way that an archivist follows the traces to revive a lost material presence or reinscribes history to conjure up the returning specters of the past.[51] During the excavation, I came across a text message (SMS) sent by Emamverdi to one of the women he attempted to deceive. I read it line by line, word by word, and to the letter to bring the unconscious of the writer/actor/agent/rapist to the surface. I divulge the latent meanings of Emamverdi's text. I force him to answer/confess to what he (and #MeToo) had not asked at the time:

> Isn't it really ridiculous? You can write the most nonsensical poems; you can produce the worst translations and offer them to the readers. You can regurgitate the most clichéd ideas which have been expressed in a hundred different ways before you; you can take the most stupid positions regarding different issues; and at the same time, you can put on airs and act as if you were a very important person!
>
> You can do one of these things or all of them; you just need a few relations. A little fraternization, being a friend of this one or that one, just a little, not more! We speak of our relations; we speak for our relations; we speak from within our relations. We speak in order to extend our relations. We impose our relations upon the external world. We produce truth out of our relations; we make history through our relations. Don't we commit crimes through our relations?
>
> Which of us is brave enough, has the courage, has the neutrality, to talk about someone whom they "hate," to talk about someone with whom they have no relations? To write of someone with whom they have no relations "anymore"? To discover someone with whom they do not give-and-take? To introduce someone who is not a friend of theirs? To document someone whom they do not see?
>
> Which of us thinks that "significant silence" is an art? Which of us is ready to "share" something they "as a rule shouldn't" share? Which of us likes a work just for its own sake and doesn't pay attention to the name of the writer or the creator of the work? Or does the name of the author of the work change the pleasure we take in the work into indifference or hatred?[52]

Like Bourdieu, he understands the social fabric as relational and interwoven. Emamverdi believes that agents can be famous and proud poets, translators, speakers, thinkers while untalented, unqualified, and nonsensical. Cultural, intellectual, and artistic aptitudes are not prerequisites, as long as agents have relations. He uses the word "relation," which somehow may imply social networks, communications, and relationships (sometimes it has undertones of two of them, sometimes all of them) in accordance with the context. Translating the text into a Bordieuan language, Emamverdi sees social capital at the root of the distinction and recognition of an agent as a famous cultural figure. Bourdieu similarly claims "the volume of social capital possessed by a given agent depends on the size of the network of connections he can effectively mobilize."[53] Writing on cultural capital, he negates all essentialist, liberal, or commonsensical notions and views that consider an academic achievement or a cultural production sprung from natural and intrinsic talents of gifted individuals. To him, cultural capital is nothing but the transubstantiated face of economic capital. As noted above, like the Borromean rings, these three basic forms of capital are interlocked. Ultimately, the more an agent had the chance to mobilize connections and social networks, the more likely their capital would be recognized and appreciated symbolically (what reified in prestige and renown).

From the line "we speak of our relations" on, he no longer uses "relations" as merely social bonds, family kinship, or professional networks but rather power relations. He considers these relations as speculative into which we are absorbed inextricably. Our relations structure our social being while they are also structured by our social being. In his opinion, social agents objectify the speculative relations and attempt to realize them, (f)actualize them. Emamverdi's views on society align with the relational method of Marxists who understand social fractions related dialectically.

Let us read Emamverdi's text message with Bourdieu's concepts in mind. The idea of omnipresent social power relations, which are both virtual and actual, resonates with a comprehensive "theory of practice" that discusses how the underlying structures of the system are cemented with the symbolic presence of cultural capital, internalized by agents as a result of education, habitus set by symbolic violence, power nexus of economic field, and more importantly the relationship among different states of capital. Relations can be insubstantial like symbolic capital or be in the material form of economic capital. Power relations structure each field hierarchically, and the specific state of the capital of each field governs the power relations and perpetuates the hierarchy upon which society is structured, stratified, and class-divided.

In a very revealing moment, like a Freudian slip, the guilty agent confesses—relations, in all their latent and manifest meanings, power relations, social networks, symbolic capital, and their relationships with the primary capital species, clear the path for the privileged to commit crimes, rape, harass, assault, and exploit. The last two paragraphs of Emamverdi's text message prove how radically the Iranian #MeToo has fought back. The #MeToo activists are those—in reply to Emamverdi's text—who are brave enough, have the courage, have the neutrality to talk about perpetrators whom they "hate" and with whom they have no relations "anymore." The #MeToo praxis is anti-capitalist (anti-social capitalist, anti-cultural capitalist, anti-symbolic capitalist, and, ultimately, anti-economic capitalist). As the #MeToo digital (and archivist) activists "document" misuser/abuser criminals with whom they do not give-and-take, this introduces the rapists and assaulters with whom they do have a "conflict of interests."

Reading Emamverdi's text message "to the letter" helps us find symptoms in letters and even sometimes in punctuations. In this text message, the quotation marks are traces and symptoms that must be followed and read deeply. Emamverdi stresses "hate," the very word that is used in several tweets of his victims. The raped have used the same word to express their hatred toward him. Considerably, he uses a hyphen to link different parts of the word "take and give." The word in the original Persian text also has two parts and is often written with a space between the parts and is less likely to be written using a hyphen. It is worth mentioning that he has inserted space for the other compound verbs and adjectives; hence, using hyphens is not the stylistic of his writing. Inserting hyphen, he symbolically (and/or unconsciously) stresses the reciprocal logic of exchange. Thus, to answer his question: the #MeToo activists are those who have ruptured the connections and disrupted the mutual exchange. To him, "significant silence" is a conservative act rather than a valuable art; more pointedly, if people are silent, the logic of capital enforces them to be. Breaking their silence, they are no longer conservative actors; and their voices are rebelling against the logic of capital. #MeToo encourages women to share what, according to Islamic Republic's laws, is something they "as a rule shouldn't" share. Again, like the English language, the Persian equivalent of the word "share" is an economic term that can be applied in the context of social media, synonymous with the word "publish." Sharing their narratives publicly, the #MeToo activists share their economic profits publicly and freely too. All of them (even those who are no longer living in Iran) know that their narratives about relationships outside of wedlock would probably have some sociopolitical and judicial consequences that directly impact their social and economic amenities.

Another slip or prophetic flash is embedded in the last two questions of Emamverdi's text message. Why did Emamverdi not articulate his question like this: "Which of us likes a work just for its own sake and does not pay attention to the name of the writer or the creator of the work?" "Or does the name of the author of the work change the pleasure we take in the work?" "Don't readers of a book or viewers of an artwork usually overvalue and overrate that work impacted by names and propaganda?" The symbolic capital of a reputed publication, or an acknowledged movie director, or a prize-winning novelist influences critics' and readers' judgment and evaluations, mostly disregarding the work's own merits. His final questions are only valid about exceptional and rare cases in which the author has lost their honor, or their prestige is threatened —like #MeToo cases.

The symptomatic reading of the Iranian #MeToo shows that not only does #MeToo challenge the misogynist relations among social agents and the patriarchal structure of society but it also sheds light on how different forms of capital are in the service of patriarchy to exploit women and their bodies. The exceptional case of Emamverdi showcases that capitalism and patriarchy build a coalition to position women at the bottom of hierarchies. Disclosing a rape or revealing the name of a rapist, even by a bourgeois woman, is necessarily an anti-capitalist activist exercise of power as it challenges the skewed power relations.

The Last Curtain

Sexual harassment is not plainly just a strong and insatiable sexual drive. In each rape case, there are sexual desires, rapist(s), victims, and different enactments of power (such as threat, physical force, coercion, violence, and so on). While, in most rapes, the rapists abuse their victims by enacting physical force, the #MeToo narratives brightly illuminate the fact that force in a sexual assault is not just a physical power of a male body that submits to sexual will but can be about the complex and unequal power relations too.

Many Marxists and Marxist feminists criticized the incapability of #MeToo to challenge the system radically. Some of them criticize #MeToo for being bourgeois, apolitical, and in the service of liberal feminists. They accuse this feminist backlash of being class-blind to the oppression that women from the lower classes struggle with. Applying Pierre Bourdieu's theoretical concepts, in this chapter, I tried to respond to these criticisms, arguing that in this kind of rape outed by #MeToo, which is privileged by symbolic capital, the rapists have forced their victims into sexual activity with no need to exercise physical power. In all the cases except that of Emamverdi, the path has been paved, and the scene has been set for the sexual assault by the masked instance of economic capital that serves both capitalism and patriarchy, to wit, symbolic capital. The singularity of Emamverdi's case as the only rapist in the Iranian #MeToo who never enjoyed symbolic capital before the accusations and as the only case sued by Iran's government sheds light on the systematic nature of sexual rape and harassment. The system removes the individual perpetrator whose arrest does not disadvantage the state, the one who does not provide any profits for the state, and, has not had mutual economic/symbolic relationships with the infrastructure; *he, therefore, is incapable of maximizing the state's profit.* Allegedly, the Iranian #MeToo does not claim any economic demand, as it merely aims at outing famous figures whose prestige and reputation are honored and perceived publicly therefore, is incapable of maximizing the state's profit and interests. Yet considering the fact that perpetrators' reputation and honor are endowed and legitimized as symbolic capital by the state and its apparatuses and are momentarily convertible to economic capital illuminates that not only is #MeToo a critique of patriarchy but it is also a (feminist) critique of (symbolic) capital(ism).

7

Whose Voice Is Missing? MeToo Digital Storytelling on Instagram and the Politics of Inclusion

Golnar Gishnizjani

Introduction

In August 2020, three years after the wake of the global MeToo movement and sexual abuse allegations against high-profile figures and ordinary people, Iranians flooded social media with their own version of #MeToo. Iranian society did not engage in the ripple effect of #MeToo's global conversation; this might be a consequence of the Covid-19 pandemic, during which a lack of face-to-face communication and social interaction motivated women to share formerly private whispers publicly. It was a time for Iranian women to make a sharp, sudden, and loud sound or, as Sara Ahmed calls it, shape a "feminist snap" moment as "a series of accumulated gestures that connect women over time and space."[1] At the breaking point of #MeToo, women joined together in the digital space to call out sexual harassment. Even though social media provides opportunities for a wider range of women from different backgrounds, it is still not an equitable space for everyone to voice their painful truths. With this in mind, my inquiry in this chapter centers around whose voices become visible and who remains on the margins.

It may seem that Iran's #MeToo was a snappy moment that suddenly and unexpectedly broke the wall of silence and pushed back against some sociocultural boundaries. However, it should be noted that #MeToo, as a digital form of contestation, builds upon the legacy of Iranian women's historical activism. Because social media was the emergent space of #MeToo, it is vital to address the fact that since 2001, online spaces that allow Iranians to interact with each other and shape digital communities, such as Weblogistan, have been used extensively for political participation. Women's engagement with different forms of digital contestation turned a corner after the 2009 Iranian presidential election, the subsequent state crackdown, and widespread arrest of students, dissidents, and human rights activists, and the dismissal of university professors.[2] After the election, the forced exile of many prominent feminist activists and journalists intensified the role of the online sphere in practicing social and political liberation.[3] In addition, advances in internet technologies and the expansion of social media in Iran enabled women inside the country to use this new sphere actively to subvert dominant narratives.[4] The intersection of these trajectories made it possible for diaspora Iranians and feminist groups abroad to become involved in domestic issues; likewise, it enabled ordinary women in Iran to engage with online campaigns or hashtags concerning women's issues. Campaigns such as "My Stealthy Freedom" and the "Girls of Enghelab (Revolution) Street" are controversial examples that present women's efforts to establish collective actions.[5] Such campaigns exacerbated debates around "indigenous" or "authentic" and "diasporan" or "inauthentic" feminism in Iranian social media.[6] Questioning the limited understanding of those living in the diaspora about the fragile situation of women in Iran and criticizing the potentials and impacts of digital deliberation led to undervaluing different kinds of digital activism. This includes storytelling, which I suggest is the central performance strategy of Iran's #MeToo contributors on Instagram. Furthermore, #MeToo does not simply fit into the dichotomy of indigenous and diaspora contestations since the initiators, contributors, activists, and feminist groups that have actively pursued the issue of sexual harassment reside both outside and inside Iran. Regardless of the location and place of living, Iran's #MeToo participants built a form of digital storytelling by telling their personal experiences of sexual harassment.

Media scholar Nick Couldry defines "digital storytelling" as "the whole range of personal stories now being told in potentially public form using digital media resources."[7] Personal stories and fragments of daily life usually in the digital sphere are told by "ordinary people"; Sonja Vivienne calls these individuals "everyday activists."[8] Such stories are heavily personalized and developed based on the logic of visibility.[9] Accordingly, contributors to Iran's #MeToo can be understood as everyday activists sharing private moments with the public. These everyday activists are not strategic or organized and do not have specific leaders, but they disclose aspects of their personal experiences in a mundane environment that is sporadic yet collective.[10] What sets Iran's MeToo apart from other forms of digital storytelling is that digital personal stories became visible on Instagram through the accounts of feminist groups instead of through personal networks. Even though personal stories spread without much organization, the origination of feminist groups on Instagram as the main conduit for disclosing individual experiences has somehow placed these groups into leadership positions, which empowers them to decide which stories and experiences are worth highlighting.

Given the potential to challenge the structural disparity that women face on a daily basis, digital storytelling is the subject of much debate. From one perspective, digital storytelling is interpreted as "popular feminism" that emphasizes self-empowerment and neglects collective struggles.[11] Inspired by this concept, I argue that social media's visibility and virality affordances can be used to satisfy collective and activist needs. My approach questions the entrenched distinction between superficial and meaningful activism. Through references to Bidarzani,[12] Harasswath,[13] and me_too_movement_iran[14] feminist groups on Instagram, the following section explains how the #MeToo storytelling nexus is framed and mediated by the vernacular practices of the users and by challenging dominant perceptions of popular feminism on Instagram. To offer a more nuanced explanation of the limitations and shortcomings of digital storytelling, I shed light on the present and absent voices.

Methods and the Study Cases

This chapter draws on close observation and discursive textual analysis to explore the voices, issues, and participants who have formed Iran's #MeToo on Instagram. To accomplish this, in August 2020, I began following the MeToo hashtag to track related posts and create a list of Instagram accounts that were actively engaging with the hashtag at the time. This list included individuals who labeled themselves as activists, feminists, and feminist groups. Ultimately, I selected Bidarzani, Harasswath, and me_too_movement_iran as case studies since these accounts regularly shared exposed cases and generated a great deal of discussion. Depending on their causes, the selected cases' objectives and activities varied; however, opposition to sexual violence was and remains the common interest of these feminist accounts. The range of posts about sexual violence in general and #MeToo was diverse in the selected case, yet, I focused only on content about individual experiences of sexual abuse. Overall, 114 feed posts and 123 Instagram Story highlights were collected from August 2020 to December 2021. To help contextualize the examined posts, particularly those with a large number of comments, I also considered investigating comments.

My analysis primarily focuses on how #MeToo as a type of digital storytelling has emerged and evolved through users' vernacular practices and how the structure and format of storytelling are affected by the characteristics and algorithmic structures of the online platform. To capture the features of stories, what voices have (not) been revealed, and what details have (not) been shared, some issues were examined in the material; for example, in what way do the contributors characterize themselves? Are their posts primarily focused on sharing personal experiences, or do they challenge the prevailing sociocultural structures and power hierarchy? I carried out a keyword search for words that were used as identity markers, including terms and expressions that indicated ethnicity, socioeconomic status, urbanite/nonurbanite, gender and sexual identity, and bodily characteristics. These keywords were used to assess the inclusivity/exclusivity of shared stories.

To protect the contributors' safety, I removed all identifying information. I have quoted small excerpts from captions and comments without any direct or indirect identifiers to maintain anonymity.[15] In addition, I have translated the quotations from Persian into English to reduce the possibility of searching and accessing posts; I have also informed the administrators of the selected accounts about their inclusion in this research. As a qualitative study with a small sample size, this research does not claim to provide a complete portrayal of Iran's MeToo movement. Nonetheless, the data offer a vignette of digital feminism in a non-Western context.

Toward Connective Storytelling: Pushing the Edges of Instagram's Aesthetics and Boundaries

As feminism becomes more digitized and aestheticized, Instagram has developed into a critical space for "media-friendly and happy feminism that is accessible to a broad public."[16] The aesthetics of Instagram feminism is predominantly characterized by pink, girly, polished, weaponized images that highlight the symbol of normative femininity with empowering slogans.[17] Aligned with the algorithmic feedback loops, users who endorse imagined platform affordances gain more visibility.[18] Considering these key features, the practices of the three selected cases were found to clash with Instagram's aesthetic norms and rationale. These accounts are not photographic or person-centered; by contrast, they deploy affordances to post text-based interventions. Shades of purple and orange juxtaposed with black create the dominant tone of Bidarzani and Me_too_movement_iran respectively, representing the women's movement and an end to violence against women's campaigns. Posts from these accounts that share experiences of sexual abuse are recognizable due to the use of specific iconic images and phrases such as "those who broke the silence." Harasswatch also shares the contributors' experiences through customized illustrations or visual collages. For instance, in a narrative of sexual harassment by landlords, we see a woman trying to build a shelter by drawing simple lines while multiple eyes gaze at her out of the darkness. The reason for not utilizing various types of imagery and features on Instagram could be partly attributed to the seriousness of sexual harassment, which is inherently incompatible with happy and glittery Instagram images and will face an adverse reaction if used.

In addition to the aesthetics of these accounts, the metric culture of social media and the number of followers are indicators of popularity. Because these accounts have a relatively small number of followers, they cannot be categorized as popular accounts.[19] Moreover, besides administrators' perceptions about what and how things work on the platform, along with other metrics of culture criteria, the numbers of likes and comments indicate how meaningful the accounts are to followers. The account me_too_movement_iran exemplifies this matter. Since its feed contains posts that address personal experiences, it generates heated discussion, and thus, receives considerable engagement which consequently lead to higher profile visibility. Another strategy for visibility and connectivity is using extended captions, including minor and major details, to tell the stories vividly. Algorithmically, this practice is essential because Instagram considers the amount of time spent on a post crucial, and the algorithm promotes the post more when the engagement rate is higher.[20] Hence, the platform structure and administrators' awareness of how to receive more engagement led to the prevalence of long captions. Lengthy captions enable users to recollect their experiences of sexual abuse and share them in the comments section. Commentators initiate sub-discussion by replying to each other. They create a space for all followers and other users to feel that they are a part of a widespread phenomenon. This user-generated technical function links those who would not otherwise want to share their experiences explicitly or who do not typically have the chance to voice their stories through online feminist groups.

Even though sharing stories with details raises engagement and provides an opportunity for others to extend the piece by telling their personal experiences, the way of using such captions can cause reluctance to follow the continuation of the story. When Instagram character restrictions hinder writing long and completed captions, administrators use comments to complete the stories.

Even though Instagram has let users pin three comments to the top of the feed posts since July 2020, the study cases did not regularly utilize this feature to organize their comments. Alternatively, me_too_movement_iran started using Instagram slideshows after the early stages of #MeToo making the narratives homogenous and easy to follow. Instagram slideshows became a ubiquitous practice of deliberation in digital activism after the resurgence of the Black Lives Matter movement.[21] With the surge in aesthetic Instagram slideshows, the visual details of slides have also been modified on the me_too_movement_iran account. This modification includes changing the color of the first slides, which functions as the cover image, from orange to black, adding photos of the accused, and putting trigger warnings[22] on the posts. Revealing the names of the accused was another practice that ignited debates on this page. The other two accounts used abbreviations or kept the names of the accused confidential, which led to skeptical voices raising questions about the motivation of the groups by sharing unverifiable stories.

Hashtagging is another practice used to increase connectivity and visibility. The Persian version of #MeToo (#من_هم) is the most prevalent hashtag in the sample size, sometimes accompanied by the English version. Again, the me_too_movement_iran account deployed hashtags more constantly than the other accounts by adding the MeToo (#من_هم) hashtag to the narratives of harassment. Moreover, converting the names of those accused of sexual harassment into hashtags in captions and repeating them boosted post reach. Despite hashtags having a structural role on Instagram in terms of facilitating searches and annotation, the "platform vernaculars"[23] face issues around hashtagging that make the profiles less appealing.[24] Unlike Twitter as a discursive platform, Instagram does not prioritize hashtags as a central mode of argument, and users also do not encounter hashtags while scrolling their feeds.[25] Accordingly, activism on Instagram needs other technological strategies based on its affordances and limitations.

Instagram Stories is one of the common strategies to increase content circulation, though Instagram boundaries, such as the lack of regram functionality, impact the activism sphere by restricting content visibility.[26] Instagram Stories is a built-in tool that partially compensates for this shortcoming and improves the circulation of posts across the platform. The selected accounts relied on this feature to reshare their exclusive posts and introduce others' posts. Additionally, account administrators of the pages and other feminist activists regram posts via their own stories. This process forms an ephemeral chain with similar nodes that might be aesthetically different but demonstrates a type of virtual togetherness between separated accounts with common interests. Intermittent repetition of a post in a short period heightens visibility and creates new connections between users. The small sample size permitted the recognition of users who actively commented on and replied to others. By checking the profiles of such accounts (public ones), I found that they were not necessarily followers of the pages with which they engaged; rather, they followed one or more pages involved in shaping an iterative string of stories. Thus, interactions within and through online feminist groups are constructed based on existing relationships, as well as a nonreciprocal network structure.

All the practices concerning visibility and connectivity can be understood through the logic of "templatability." Even though Leaver et al. (2020) claim that templatability "diminishes the feeling of agency and sense of being able to meaningfully communicate or contribute to change,"[27] I suggest that it offers alternative pathways for some users to make contributions to digital activism within their sociocultural contexts. Although examining the aims of contributors for participating in the #MeToo discussion is beyond the scope of this chapter, it is worth noting that the perceptions of digital storytellers about change are varied. Perhaps making institutional and political changes or receiving justice through the judicial system is not a demand that can be fulfilled in the near future for survivors of sexual abuse in Iran, although they might have other intentions and motivations. As Vivienne discusses, digital storytelling might be therapeutic for some, while others tell stories to change intimate publics (including family, close friends, and acquaintances online and offline), allies, and specific unknown targeted (when a specific unknown audience is addressed for their influence and the duty of care) and, ultimately, the unknown masses.[28]

Anonymous Shared Stories: A Site of Voicing Dissent and Receiving Recognition

More than a technical feature and user policy, anonymity is the central characteristic of Iran's #MeToo on Instagram. The #MeToo movement, which is predominantly US-centric, is represented by figures like Alyssa Milano and Dana Loesch. In contrast, except for a handful of cases, Iran's #MeToo comprises of a collection of anonymous stories from ordinary women who have mostly been exposed to predator influential figures such as artists, scholars, and psychologists with respectable public images. Results of previous studies show that the desire for anonymity is partly due to the fear of a backlash in the form of "trolling, victim blaming, and other types of retribution or retaliation online."[29] Additionally, it has been illustrated that discussing sexual harassment and participating in #MeToo is viewed as immodest.[30] Therefore, it can be claimed that the presence of sexual taboos and societal pressure regarding such matters in conservative societies like Iran can potentially diminish the level of involvement in movements like #MeToo.

In Iran, the entanglement of several disciplinary discourses, including patriarchy, religious beliefs, and cultural customs, prevents women and others who experience sexual harassment from disclosing their stories publicly. This issue is reflected in #whydidInotreport (#چرا_گزارش_ندادم), one of several hashtags that were created shortly after the #MeToo debate began. For example, in one of the posts me_too_movement_iran account shared with this hashtag, it was mentioned, "I have a traditional family; I got the privilege to go to music and singing classes upon my insistence." The hidden truth in this short story is that the teller has been sexually harassed in music class but stayed silent since speaking out resulted in more limitations, including not being allowed to participate in music class and being blamed by the family for inappropriate behaviors. In these cases, #MeToo is interlinked with other conversations, such as the cost of reporting, its sociocultural stigma, and punishments. It may seem that setting up pseudonymous accounts that do not require or even request real names on platforms such as Instagram is an effective option to protect the victims' privacy. However, these pseudonymous stories raised questions and doubts about their authenticity, specifically in the climate of Iranian blame culture, where women are forced to wear the hijab to protect themselves, their family's honor, and society's chastity, as well as behave cautiously in public.

In such situations, online feminist groups provide a so-called safe space for unfolding anonymous stories and keeping individuals away from potential dangers. Contributors are still involved in a "parrhesiastic" act in the sense of truth-telling, not just for their benefit but as a duty to help others[31] and to open themselves up to criticism, judgment, and blame.[32] As Michel Foucault explains, "Parrhesia is a verbal activity in which a speaker expresses his [sic] personal relationship to truth, and risks his life because he recognizes truth-telling as a duty to improve or help other people."[33] However, mediated participation eases repercussions, and the conduits of sharing stories boost credibility. In one rare case of a disputed post where the survivor's identity was mentioned with her will and consent, in response to one of the comments that questioned the veracity of the story and sincerity of the teller, the narrator replied, "My narration was shared after three months of verification. I wanted to post it on my page, but for fear of people like you, I decided to do it through a channel that considers filters to make my narration believable." This shows that online feminist groups might be the spaces for those who may find disclosing their experiences on their personal accounts difficult, risky, or unbelievable.

The possibility of telling anonymous stories cannot be relinquished since it facilitates an Iranian version of a "speaking out narrative" about sexual violence to be rendered on Instagram as a platform that is not explicitly created for narrative-oriented experiences.[34] Nonetheless, Instagram enables the generation of a "shared story as a retelling, produced by many tellers across the iterative textual segment, which promotes shared attitude between its tellers."[35] Ruth Page categorizes shared stories as types of small stories characterized by their weak and unstructured narrativity, the capacity to engage with a large crowd, and the ability to go viral.[36] Accordingly, Iran's #MeToo Instagram narratives can be interpreted as a form of shared stories with their own narrative features. Much like the global conversations, in the beginning, #MeToo went viral on Persian Twitter; however, when the discussions spread to other platforms, the role of hashtags as a "storytelling device" changed.[37] Alyssa Milano's first spark of #MeToo on Twitter was not a request for narrative responses but for sharing whether others had also been harassed or assaulted.[38] Conversely, Iran's #MeToo on Instagram aimed to encourage individuals to share their experiences of sexual assault, which resulted in shorthand for more structured narratives. Therefore, on Instagram, the hashtag MeToo serves as an umbrella term to collect shared stories.

The fragmented stories of #MeToo are neither coherent narratives nor eventful instants. Through embracing a common attitude, the storytellers begin their narratives by taking readers back to the time of the incident to outline the situation and the context of the relationship with the accused. The survivors attempt to provide a background for their experiences by delving into their past. In addition, the storytellers address different positionality between themselves and their abusers. Although the relationship is expressed in the context of individual experiences, the repetition of the same structure in others' stories reflects the power hierarchy. Shared stories can be episodical when several individuals target one figure. The first story plays a crucial role in encouraging others and shaping the narrative structure. A case of harassment by an Iranian British anthropologist offers an example of this pattern. Bidarzani has shared the following episodic story: the opening narrative started with this sentence: "I was a young and jobless student; ... I didn't have good living conditions at home; my dad was restrictive ... I thought finding a job would be my salvation." Then, the teller describes the assault and mentions the predator's social status. With the replication of this pattern in the rest of the stories, contributors highlighted how the power mechanism of the patriarchal system institutionalized rape and silence cultures. By putting all these episodes together, multiple storytellers constructed a co-tellership, relying upon the gradual process of disclosing.

When #MeToo went viral, the instantaneity of the hashtag was notable on different platforms; however, the speed and intensity of sharing personal experiences did not go in the same direction. While the virality of the hashtag was temporal, circumspect, and gradual, the disclosure of personal experiences as a storytelling practice remained consistent. As a cultural script, #MeToo shaped the narrative, but it was restructured and co-constructed on Instagram. Due to the storytelling structure on Instagram, shared stories highlight some invisible aspects of life entangled with sexual harassment and abuse, including the double bind Iranian women may face. Iranian women are either expected to perform gendered piety or be sexually open and risk being labeled unworthy bodies.[39] For instance, in the dominant discourse of Iran, virginity is interpreted as a sacred thing, and women are forced to preserve it for the sake of family and societal honor.[40] However, in the rape culture, specifically when men are self-proclaimed as modern and progressive, virginity becomes a tool for manipulation and coercion. In such situations, women's resistance to unwanted physical contact, harassment, or rape is a pretext to control and keep them silent. In their stories, women said that abusers used pejorative sentences, such as "Are you really a feminist? You can't even decide for your body"; "What's the matter? Virginity? Come on … you can fix it"; "You are old-fashioned and rustic."

Shared stories are also a place for narrating perceived and experienced emotions at the time of the incidents, during a period of silence, and then during disclosure. Like other digitized narratives of sexual violence examined, a range of emotions from pain, fear, anger, outrage, and hate are discussed in the shared stories.[41] Although these emotive expressions display how women might perceive themselves as weak and deceived at the time of incidents, they also show that disclosing their experiences helps and encourages them to face those emotions. As a result, many storytellers note that they want their painful truths to be recognized: "I read others' experiences and dared to write about mine. I was worried it would be dangerous all these years, but now I want my voice to be heard." The stories of ordinary women who add their voices to #MeToo highlight the therapeutic feature of digital storytelling and its potential for allowing support and empathy. As one of the contributors said, "Maybe my silence breaking helps to heal my old wound, save others, and revive the discourse of social responsibility about sexual violence." The type of storytelling shaped within and through online feminist groups provides a platform for contributors to legitimize their pain. They connect with others through their painful bodily and emotional experiences and gain the power to question hegemonic expectations. However, digital storytelling as a type of narrative phenomenon is not neutral and can potentially promote a selective version of events and empathy.

Shared Stories of the Subalterns in the Dark Matter of #MeToo

Theoretically, the ordinary and anonymous women who add their personal stories to Iran's #MeToo belong to the subaltern populations. Subalterns are the groups who exist socially, politically, and geographically outside the hegemonic power structure, and the dominant public hijack their interests and needs.[42] From this perspective, members of the subaltern population do not have the same positionality as the dominant groups in the public sphere. There is a relational aspect, which means that one's relative position as privileged or underprivileged depends on the distinct context in which one is situated.[43] As Kimberlé Crenshaw indicates, "No one exists outside of the matrix of power."[44] Therefore, even within the group of disadvantaged anonymous storytellers, some contributors have more privilege and others less. It is worth mentioning that accessibility, affordability, and digital literacy are hurdles to Iranian women's participation in digital forms of feminist activism that make digital technology, by its nature, more exclusive. In Iran, such struggles intersect with other cultural norms and boundaries, such as class status, ethnicity, and being geographically far from the center of power, all of which affect people's meaningful participation in digital activism.

In the aforementioned case studies, my analysis of the identity markers that individuals employed to position themselves within power relations during the early stages of #MeToo reveals a lack of reflection on identity. In most shared stories, the storyteller's identity was not mentioned, though some signifiers designated that the narratives belonged to educated and urban women. For example, when storytellers disclosed being sexually harassed by a teacher or actor with a respected public image, or when allegations were made against a film critic and director, there were no identity markers to hint at the identity of the accused. Shared stories around such reputable figures are among the most debated and gained more visibility and attention. For instance, by disclosing the culture of sexual harassment at an educational institution, some contributors highlighted that they moved from the provinces to Tehran (from peripheral areas to the center) to pursue their education. In such stories, those women were in a vulnerable position at the time of the assault because of a lack of social, cultural, and economic capital, but later their relational privileges allowed them to voice their experiences. It is important to acknowledge that while the #MeToo participants in Iran may be classified as subaltern individuals, it does not imply that they are all structurally underprivileged in the same manner.

Due to the complexity of class stratification, it is hard to determine whether most storytellers are upper-middle-class women. Although there are shared stories about sexual harassment in the workplace, these narratives cannot be interpreted as the only signifiers of economic status and wealth. Furthermore, social status provides individuals with different levels of social and cultural capital. In this respect, journalists, baristas, and secretaries whose voices are part of Iran's #MeToo do not have the same power level. In the sample obtained for the study, a post about women vendors in the Tehran metro is one of the few that addresses how class status and marginalization, not in a geographical sense but in the sense of how being outside the hegemonic power system, compounds women's vulnerability to sexual exploitation. A 44-year-old woman vendor explained:

> Vendors are not humans, and you are more miserable when you are a woman. The government doesn't do anything but make things worse. After years of street vending, I chose the metro to be safer. The more easily the guards can see you, the more likely you will be harassed.

Such women are unlikely to use social media to share their stories of sexual abuse. A short description of their experiences came out because a member of the Harasswatch group took an interest, talked to women vendors, and shared their stories. Their precarious working conditions and government surveillance mean that these women cannot afford to report sexual abuse, and even if they raise the issue, they face negligence and disbelief.[45] The workplace is not the only hazardous environment for women who suffer from multiple types of oppression. They are also more prone to domestic violence, including marital rape, a subject that #MeToo's co-tellership has not yet broached. The research dataset underestimates the importance of marital rape and domestic violence despite Iran's #MeToo stories being first shared during the Covid-19 lockdown, and studies have shown an increase in domestic violence during the pandemic.[46] Contributors have addressed sexual violence within the family environment and in relationships, except for marital rape. However, most of these experiences map the issue out onto patriarchal institutions within society, weakening other discriminatory practices and factors.

As these examples show, the agenda of Iran's #MeToo is akin to the global version of women's experiences of sexual abuse, which excludes those who do not identify as women.[47] For example, there is a lack of discussion around the power imbalance in terms of queer folks, and Iran's #MeToo primarily emphasizes the voices of heterosexual women in heteronormative relationships. When the stories do not offer readers slight hints about the features of the contributors, they might intensify the notion that stereotypical women's experiences are more believable, since it is assumed that those who do not fit within the social norms (e.g., fat, disabled, or trans bodies) cannot be the target of sexual violence because they are "unvictimizable."[48] Here, the role of online feminist groups as mediators is critical in providing an environment in which it is possible for individuals to depict their intersectional identities. The administrative role in disseminating the stories can be channeled in such a way that individuals feel safer mentioning indirect identity markers and making their stories more personalized within an overall schema. Therefore, among the shared stories highlighting experiences of heterosexual women, there are a few stories of women whose lives are tied to other systems of oppression in addition to patriarchy. A shared story of Afghan women farmers on the outskirts of Tehran with 11 comments and 673 likes (these numbers are from the time of research and data collection) is one of the rare few that brings to light the complex entanglement of immigrant women's lives:

> Almost half of the Afghan women who reside on the outskirts of Tehran do not have an identity card, do not have enough literacy and skills to get a job, and farming is one of their few options. They work in the middle of nowhere, so the possibility of being harassed is high. Doing individual work in groups is an innovative way for these women to be less exposed to sexual harassment. Because of this, they mostly had to go to the bathroom as a group.

Like other vulnerable migrants, Afghan women in Iran might be reluctant to speak out about their exposure to sexual harassment because of the threat of deportation. They are also aware of injustices and inequities with Iran's judicial system, cultural disbelief, and intimidation, and hence they do not find the courage to report their sexual harassment experiences.[49] This painful story about the truth of Afghan women's lives has been revealed not because the contributor logged into Instagram to tell the story but because the feminist group reshared a previously published report in an online magazine.[50] Even though it indicates the importance of collective work that minimizes the cost and punishment of storytelling for individuals who do not have enough capital, the low engagement rate illustrates that they did not intensify the debate. In the same vein, Instagram Story highlights have not become a factor in the larger narrative since Instagram Stories do not facilitate public discussion and travel across the platform easily without linking to any feed post.

As a result, some personal experiences remain on the network's outer edge despite containing descriptions of intense pain, perhaps because, for dominant groups, they did not evoke similar experiences. In these cases, it might be the case that recalling personal memories and traumas did not result in joint pain that compelled others to react.[51] In other words, some stories exist in the "dark matter" of the network; they exist and have influence, but we can only see them by following their fragmented traces that are not connected to the greater network. Naomi Barnes proposes the notion of "trace publics" to define "small indications of publicness found in the 'dark matter' of the social network"; these indications are not connected to the greater network and exist off the grid.[52] In fact, the traces of digital stories about marginalized groups do not disappear but remain in the "dark matter" until something triggers public discussion with the result that the existing shared stories become visible. The stories of women facing multiple forms of oppression may not gain traction when initially shared, but they have the potential to become viral with the help of a catalyst. This underscores the significance of featuring a diverse array of stories within the storytelling network.

Merely listening to the loud voices may give the impression that certain groups of women have taken over Iran's #MeToo storytelling. However, by focusing on the off-center traces, we can find indicators that some marginalized groups have voiced their experiences, albeit to a limited degree of visibility. Therefore, disregarding these voices does not imply they are absent. However, irruption from the "dark matter" and linking to the network is not simply a user-based change that relies upon their practices and motivations; it occurs through and within the algorithmic structure, which is not static, perpetual, and easy for users to track.[53] In this regard, algorithmic activities and content moderation can reproduce inequity in digital activism.

Conclusion

While digital feminist activism on platforms such as Instagram is known for its aesthetic and individualistic nature, in this chapter, I highlighted how it could also provide new terrains for digital storytelling and everyday activism. By the time Iran's #MeToo reached Instagram, survivors of sexual abuse were not using their personal networks to share information and mobilize other activists; instead, online feminist groups set the stage for them to tell what counts as "parrhesia." After examining the stories posted about sexual harassment and abuse, I propose that storytelling within and through online feminist groups can connect individuals' painful experiences to each other and pave the way for practicing collectivity. Digital storytelling and digital activism eased the emergence of Iran's #MeToo and generated comprehensive public discussions; however, the control of contributors over their own stories is a debatable issue.

Iran's #MeToo comprises an assemblage of shared stories whose narrators do not have ownership over their stories. What appears on the screen are descriptions of painful truths experienced by anonymous individuals who are not in a position to control the publication process of their stories, either visually or narratively. The three case studies in this chapter adopted specific practices to disseminate the experiences of individuals. Thus, while the focus point of the shared stories is sexual harassment, feminists' practices for disclosure are differentiated. This gives administrators the power to make decisions about the storytelling's performative aspects and to highlight the voices. For example, they choose whether to share personal stories as Instagram feed posts or Instagram Stories that directly impact visibility, circulation, and attention to stories. Together with algorithmic bias and feedback loops, administrators' decisions can boost some voices while limiting the circulation of others across the platform. Even though Iran's #MeToo has no leaders, and no person became the symbol of it, the administrators' power in orienting the storytelling process might also affect the legitimacy of Iran's #MeToo as a bottom-up movement.

However, being an administrator is not just a matter of controlling the storytelling. It is also about keeping the process ongoing, sharing compelling stories, and growing the care community. Due to this, the skeptical tones of the reactions have changed slightly, and the diversity of voices has increased. After the initial stages of #MeToo, during which the voices of the more marginalized people were undermined, sexual violence has been viewed beyond a gendered phenomenon in some shared stories. Until now, the voices of the multiple marginalized survivors of sexual violence have remained less heard. Nonetheless, such small stories indicate the role of feminist groups in mitigating the cost of storytelling, as well as their endeavors to reach vulnerable survivors who cannot afford to speak out. However, it does not signify that Iran's #MeToo is an inclusive form of online feminist activism.

As discussed, the sexual violence women confront in marginal areas and precarious working conditions, and stories of queer folks and women in non-normative bodies remain in the "dark matter." Indeed, the women with more power and privileges predominantly frame and patrol the shared stories. Although it is reasonable to question the potential of digital storytelling in creating a collective snappy moment, I suggest that its multifaceted functions and impacts in the context of Iran need to be considered. It cannot be assured that these groups will produce enduring effects or have the capacity to generate opportunities to bring to light hidden narratives from the "dark matter." Nevertheless, they have the potential to act as agents of change at the micro level. Researchers and activists should also recognize marginalized voices when scrutinizing and challenging Iran's #MeToo. It is also crucial to understand the changes and the evolution of #MeToo as a digitally networked phenomenon depending on the users' practices and decision-making as well as technology and platform development.

8

Sexual Violence, MeToo, and Iranian Lesbians' Censored Voices

Mahdis Sadeghipouya

Our speaking out will irritate some people, get us called bitchy or hypersensitive and disrupt some dinner parties. And then our speaking out will permit other women to speak, until laws are changed, and lives are saved, and the world is altered forever.

—Audre Lorde

This chapter, as the title suggests, focuses on the censored voices of lesbians in discussions of sexual violence. Lesbians' stories are easily ignored under a barrage of stereotypes and phobias and are condemned not to be heard. Iranian women's rights movements and Iranian MeToo mobilization are no exception. As we have seen, not only have Iranian lesbian feminists experienced frequent lesbophobic exclusion but they have also been the target of intense lesbophobic violence in a few cases raised around the issue of sexual violence recently. In this context, it seems necessary to understand the reasons for the formation of such an exclusion at the heart of women's mobilizations, to either transform them into more inclusive mobilizations or transform the lesbian "non-mobilization"[1] into an organized one to empower it to speak about its own experiences of this kind of violence.

In this regard, I propose two major considerations in this chapter: first, for lesbian survivors of sexual violence, the main question that comes to mind is why are lesbians who are socially viewed as "women"*[2] excluded from discussions and even activism on the topic? Second, through lesbian exclusion from women*'s mobilizations, why are Iranian lesbians excluded from Iranian women's mobilization and alienated as "outsiders"[3] by their insider "sisters"? In other words, how did they become the "sister outsider"[4] in "multiple sites of related oppressions"?[5]

It should be noted that this chapter's analysis is based on my discussions, individually or collectively, with a small group of lesbian feminist activists in my activism and friendship networks. They all related their exposure to lesbophobic remarks amid MeToo mobilization on their social media platforms or offline discussions. I solicited their input in the hope of giving them voice. This chapter is therefore informed by my discussions with these lesbian activists who agreed to be directly quoted and to whom I am deeply grateful. All these activists identify as lesbians and women and/or "socially considered and so, threatened as a woman," as in our societies, "sex is a fundamental division that burdens all societies to an unrecognized degree."[6] They were all born and grew up in different cities of Iran: some of them still live there while others have left. I have however anonymized their identity for their security and of course for the ethical concerns of this chapter.

What I seek to do in this chapter is to present an analytical and a narrative point of view on the topic as a member of Iranian women's rights movement for over fifteen years and as a lesbian activist, born and raised in Tehran. Hence, I acknowledge that my analysis is what can be called auto-centrist and tied to my identity and class position. I have tried to stay away from (re)producing any kind of discriminatory gaze because of my position. This chapter is an effort to answer one main question: how can lesbian voices be silenced or censored in social movements such as in the Iranian MeToo movement?

Lesbians and Double Experience of Violence and Exclusion

Working on key concepts of sexual violence[7] and lesbophobic exclusion from any discussions on the topic, two major themes emerge: the first one is lesbians' exclusion from any considerations as potential victims or survivors of sexual violence, as well as noninclusion of lesbians as "non-legitimate" to talk about sexual violence; and the second one is the exclusion of lesbians from mobilizations and activities. Thus, Iranian lesbians are considered as the Iranian "lavenders"[8] of the feminist mobilizations, for reasons such as the lesbophobia present in these mobilizations, the "security problems," and so on.

In general, lesbians are doubly ignored in discussions of sexual violence: first, as women* who are likely to experience it within a misogynistic, patriarchal, and sexist sociopolitical system; and second, as legitimate women who benefit from the right and the opportunity to speak out and (re)act against this kind of violence. Focusing on lesbians' experiences of sexual violence, the main question here is: "Does it make a difference for survivors and perpetrators of sexual violence what the sexual orientation of the survivor is?" "What are the main reasons for excluding lesbian women as survivors of sexual violence, if it is not just the act of sexual violence that counts and not the person who has lived it but their appearance, their body, their age, their clothes, their sexual orientation, and so on?" and "What is unique about the LGBTIQA+ people that studies show queer survivors face 'an additional layer of judgment and stigma following the violence'?"[9]

Considering the second point, excluding lesbians from debates about sexual violence, thus, rejecting them from activism and campaigns, has caused Iranian lesbians to suffer from lesbophobic exclusion in the larger society and, additionally, face lesbophobic experiences. To put it in simple terms, due to their sexual orientation, they have been targeted and exposed to humiliation and discrimination. This illustrates how lesbians are doubly excluded from discussions about sexual violence: once as survivors who have experienced it, and then when they break their silence and try to mobilize.

A Short Story of Emergence of a MeToo Mobilization in Iran

The Iranian MeToo activism was born in the summer of 2020. Since then, Iranian civil society has exercised a fairly progressive mobilization in its recent history: various types of content, including volumes of academic papers and journalistic articles, book volumes, numerous TV and radio interviews, online discussions through different social media platforms, podcast episodes, and translations were produced on this campaign, which in and of itself is major progress if we consider the lack of legal and governmental supports. The firestorm of anger among Iranian women who have always faced many difficulties in speaking out about their experiences of sexual violence has swept through cyberspace via narrating and sharing their experiences, which encouraged others to share their own experiences as well. There are two important dates regarding this campaign: August 27, 2020, and April 17, 2021. The first concerns the revelation of an alleged experience of sexual violence via a Twitter account that accused an Iranian musician as the perpetrator.[10] Between the two dates, much happened, including a video message by the accused on April 16, 2021, in which he sought to apologize.[11] The video provoked many positive and negative reactions as well as many questions; some considered it a step forward in the Iranian MeToo movement, and many made it another controversial issue, especially because of its "authoritarian" tone, as well as the "lack of apologetic principles." Not much later, an audio file that led to severe criticism of him was leaked in which the accused appears to be speaking against the survivors within "a group of friends," as he later claimed. Apart from his comments about sexual violence, the survivors, as well as musician women who had campaigned against him, what is my concern here is his alleged lesbophobic comments about an unnamed lesbian. Here is a part of his comments:

> It is possible that she [a lesbian feminist who talked publicly about this affair] is not even a lesbian, but the only way she can get attention is to say she is a lesbian. Because she knows that if she says she is straight … there are things given by God, and her attractiveness is so below average that nothing can compensate for it.[12]

As mentioned earlier, this is just one of many highly controversial remarks by the accused in this seventeen-minute audio file, and to this day, it is one of the least discussed topics. The words and language used here such as "it is possible that she is not even a lesbian," "the only way she can get attention is to say she is a lesbian," and "her attractiveness is so below average that nothing has compensated for it" are the very signs of lesbophobia as one of the deepest and most intrusive forms of misogyny, the "side-order"[13] of it, which values lesbian women in a lesser position than the heterosexual ones, and at the same time valorizes her with the patriarchal criteria like that one of (God-given) "beauty." These lesbophobic remarks are the least discussed, because historically and systematically lesbian women have always been excluded from any discussions of sexual violence, from any mobilization against it, and, unfortunately, from feminist struggles as well. Although as of November 2022 the accused musician has never explained his comments in the published audio file, nor those regarding the lesbian feminist, and has even deleted his apology video from his Instagram page, this case has paved the way for a better understanding of the depth of misogyny, in the form of lesbophobia, when it comes to discussions of sexual violence.

Iranian "Lavender Menace": From "Women Are Not Born Women" to "Lesbians Are Not Women"

Simply put, the heading of this section belongs originally to one of the articles of Natacha Chetcuti-Osorovitz, in which she "aims to discuss the concept of becoming woman" and analyzes "how gender categorization is constructed in a heteronormative social system." Analyzing both de Beauvoir's and Wittig's works, she recalls "the general assumption about sex differentiation, and question[s] the way it is used in studies on gender, homosexuality and heterosexuality."[14] Iranian lesbians are the "lavender menace"[15] of feminists, who have historically believed in the lesbian question as a "nonpriority." Feminist movements believe that lesbians can even cause "security problems" for the mobilization and nascent women's activist associations and collectives in Iran, because of the criminalization of sexual relationships between two people of the same sex in the Islamic Penal Code. Iranian LGBTIQA+ people have always suffered from not benefiting from an organized mobilization because of these restrictions. American lesbians of the second-wave feminism who have benefited from the privilege of organized movements also suffered equally from the "sexist attitudes among the predominantly male membership"[16] in their LGBTIQA+ mobilization. Clearly, in a legal system where same-sex relationship is defined as a crime, and admitting to being lesbian, gay, bisexual, and pansexual can prove the crime, organized and open LGB[17] activism makes no sense.

Consequently, it seems necessary to explain such exclusions of lesbians from discussions of sexual violence, as well as from activism against it, especially when it comes to contexts in which sexuality is subject to criminalization by the state, like the Iranian one. Lesbian feminist activists should explain to the Iranian women's movements, and more generally to the civil society, that "lesbians are not women,"[18] in the words of the French lesbian feminist Monique Wittig, has a different meaning from not being considered as woman* by the society and its different mechanisms, so that they will not be a target of the society's violent misogynistic and lesbophobic treatments and attitudes. They should also insist on Simone de Beauvoir's famous statement that "one is not born, but rather becomes a woman," and so, all humans, considered socially as women*, can also experience sexual violence in various forms. Thus, lesbians who are socially considered as women* by others and/or themselves experience sexual violence like other women but are excluded from any discussions of the topic.

Lesbian People and the Experience of Sexual violence: From Punishment to Exclusion

The experience of sexual violence by Iranian lesbians and their exclusion in the feminist struggles are the main topics of debate here, not in the ordinary roles of survivors or victims of sexual violence but as outsiders[19] who may be survivors of sexual violence just like other people in their daily lives.

In this way, in such a system, lesbians become the target of ingrained misogyny and lesbophobic reactions from the accused rapists, as well as by their insider sisters who are, consciously or unconsciously, aligned with others to not consider lesbians worthy enough to speak out on the mobilization or at all on the sexual violence. Therefore, following Sojourner Truth (1799–1883), the American abolitionist and women's rights activist excluded from the white and middle-class feminist mobilizations, who gave her famous speech on May 29, 1851, where she questioned, "Ain't I a woman?," we can ask ourselves, "Ain't lesbians women* too?" If the answer is yes, why and how can their voices be silenced and censored?[20]

There have always been myths about sexual violence of all kinds that still exist and make it difficult to talk about topics such as "sexual crime is only committed by strangers," "if there is no rape, it is hard to call it sexual violence," "what happens between partners can hardly be called sexual violence," "sexual crime is usually committed by a man against a woman," "staring, ogling, suggestive looks, sexual 'jokes,' comments, harassment, etc. are not examples of sexual crime, and even sexually, it's not that bad, it's just a joke," and so on. These are just a few examples of the stereotypes we have always heard. While in recent years, and especially after the emergence of the MeToo activism around the world, the topic of sexual violence has been discussed in many diverse platforms and in depth, it is still clear that many myths about it remain to be deconstructed. What is very important to know is that lesbophobia can itself be a reason, a motivation for sexual violence.

Although Tarana Burke, the founder of the MeToo in the United States, describes its goal as "to get rid of all forms of gender violence," there are still members of minoritized[21] groups and communities who have experienced this kind of violence and are excluded from the mobilization everywhere. One such marginalized group is lesbians. Sexual violence can be directed against lesbian bodies, viewed as "female" bodies, as well as against their self-identification as lesbians. The former does not appear to be very different from the violence perpetrated against all others identifying as women*, but the latter is against their identity.

While the discussion of how people's gender identity and sexual orientation can lead to the experience of sexual violence is one with multiple and complex dimensions, to offer a better understanding of this experience and make it more touchable, I solicited the opinions and experiences of some lesbian activists active in feminist movements in Iran and the Iranian MeToo in different ways.[22] The main question I asked was: "As a lesbian, have you experienced sexual violence of any kind, and how do you think your sexual orientation impacted that experience?"

> I have experienced sexual violence in my life. My daily life, like many other women, has been filled with this experience, on the street, or even I have experienced it at home. In my family ... I'm not sure if being a lesbian, changes anything important, because we live a hidden lesbian life, right? Although I'm not sure that if we lived a public lesbian life, abusive men would leave us alone! I suppose in that case, their sexual violence could also have a punitive aspect! Like punishing the women who don't sleep with them! (Sanaz, 2021)

> Being a lesbian doesn't change anything in my opinion, but coming out as a lesbian, changes everything about the experience of sexual violence. I say that because I was married to a man before. Like many other women who feel something but under pressure ignore it anyway, I was also unaware of it, I mean my lesbianism, and I was married to a man who was my classmate at university. One day, I met a college classmate with whom I had small love experiences years ago, I mean teenage love when we were twelve years old. We continued to see each other and very soon we were back to the feeling we had with each other, a very hot love ... Yes, we fell in love again ... I told my husband about it. He didn't take it seriously, that was by itself a lesbophobic reaction, but he was a little shocked. I continued to talk about this love, my identification as a lesbian and my desire to end this marriage. I couldn't go on. That was the beginning of the problem. He didn't talk but started sexually harassing me. He thought the problem was sex and that with "good" sex, as he said, I would get my feelings back for him ... the last one was officially rape ... and I left him and this house forever, even though he continues to threaten me and has informed my family about my private life as a lesbian. (Firouzeh, 2021)

> My worst experience with sexual violence, verbally, was when I was 22 and lived in Babulsar [a northern city of Iran]. I met a male phycologist in Tehran, who thought I could be "cured" as lesbian. He talked a little bit about having sex with men as a "proven cure" for lesbians ... It was already annoying, but I continued to have my sessions with him, even though it didn't last long. It was at the beginning of the second session that he started to completely get into it and explain to me the experience of having intercourse with a penis, with all those disgusting words, and his mean mode. I left there forever! (Elaheh, 2021)

> As a lesbian, I never came out in Iran. I've worked in a bookstore for a few years, and I have a non-binary gender expression, as you can see. My boss was a cisgender heterosexual man who knew that I am a lesbian. He seemed a very

"open" person ... even if I was always scared of him because he was not a very polite person and made jokes about very sensitive issues. One day he asked me if I was "lez" or not. I didn't answer, of course, but he insisted and asked me, "I mean, are you the one who fucks her or the other way around?" And he laughed loudly. That was certainly sexual assault for me as a lesbian and non-binary. It's not just about actions. (Minou, 2021)

Sexual violence as lesbophobic punishment by perpetrators, as lesbophobic "treatment" even by doctors of all specialties, and as jokes and humor are the usual experiences of lesbians. Lesbian identity can play an important role in the experience of sexual violence. This experience can be seen as a particular type of violence aimed at punishing "deviant female" bodies that do not put themselves at the service of patriarchal systems: neither for the sexual pleasure of its men nor for reproduction purposes desired by the misogynistic nation-states.[23]

The punitive sexual violence against lesbian bodies can be considered a deeper and more complicated form of sexual violence because of the amalgamation of being a lesbian and being (considered as) woman*; that is why the lesbian issue is a multidimensional question that does not only focus on these various identities (chosen or imposed) but also raises the question of how lesbians suffer from discrimination and violence. This once again reveals the need and necessity of challenging the binary-based and one-dimensional sociopolitical perspectives while discussing sexual violence, and studying the lesbian question through multidimensional lenses of (political) sociology, to address the suppression of lesbians understudied in the arena of these binaries. Although the multidimensional aspects of sexual violence against Iranian lesbians makes it an important issue to address in the feminist mobilization, hidden lesbophobia, along with many other reasons such as fear of coming out as a lesbian in a legal context where same-sex sexual relationships are criminalized, also speaks about the fact that lesbian women* experience one of the most violent types of sexual violence, especially when it has a punitive aspect that targets their lesbian identity.

In this regard, neither the large-scale international MeToo feminist mobilization nor its recent Iranian version has been an exception. From the very first moments of the campaign, stories of lesbian sexual violence have not been heard properly, and once again the topic of sexual violence has been reduced to its heteronormative aspects that is supposed to be committed by a cisgender heterosexual male as the perpetual oppressor, toward a cisgender heterosexual female as the perpetual victim/survivor.

Iranian women*'s movements, and more importantly, Iranian women* activists and nonactivists have reached a new stage after finding the courage to talk about their experiences of sexual violence, without being ashamed of it, especially if the perpetrator is a well-known person. Moreover, exposing the experience of violence, committed by well-known men, such as famous artists, researchers, academics, journalists, to the public who follow the movement was one of the important features of MeToo. In this newly born mobilization, the lesbian experience of sexual violence deserves more attention. Criminalization of same-sex relationships, lack of organized support or activist groups by/for lesbians who experience sexual violence, the presence of lesbophobia in Iranian feminist mobilization, not being counted as legitimate women to share their experiences of sexual violence, the rooted and strong dualistic stereotypes that surround any discussions on sexual violence, and last, but not least, the lack of judicial and legal support against violence for sexually minoritized groups are some of the reasons why lesbians are excluded from discussions of sexual violence, and even from feminist activism against it. This exclusion within Iranian women's rights movements is one of two effective elements of the vicious cycle in which violence against lesbians is systematically disregarded, as well as the resulting exclusion. This exclusion in turn silences lesbian experiences of sexual violence.

"Sister Outsider"[24]: Lesbian Feminists and Feminist Struggles

As mentioned earlier, the Iranian LGBTIAQ+ activism has never been recognized as a movement, for various reasons, nor has that of the Iranian lesbians. It can be called a "non-movement," as Asef Bayat, an Iranian American theorist, calls activities and mobilizations that are not necessarily organized by a leadership core, or necessarily collective, but that have their impact on the collective life of a community.[25] In the absence of organized activism, lesbians have been unseen. They are the outsiders of Iranian women*, oppressed historically for being the "second sex,"[26] as well as of their mobilizations due to their "deviance" from an imposed "normal,"[27] allowed, and stereotyped womanhood in society.

This deviance as a "process in which individuals can engage (or not engage),"[28] for lesbians, becomes the main reason for their exclusion without giving them the opportunity to build a union based on this so-called deviant identity. Due to this exclusion, and in the absence of organized activism among themselves, Iranian lesbians find no way to talk about their experience of sexual violence, and in the process of being marginalized by society, these women* become outsiders everywhere, and this vicious circle continues to exist. As Jess Ison admits, the imposed absence of LGBTIQA+ community in the MeToo debates, particularly in intimate relationships, makes this rejection more stable and durable:

> The #MeToo campaign has given victims/survivors of sexual assault a space to speak and is challenging engrained misogyny. However, queer communities have largely been absent from the mobilization, despite increasing recognition that lesbian, gay, bisexual, transgender, queer, intersex and asexual (LGBTQIA) communities experience similar levels of relationship violence as heterosexuals.[29]

Considering the use of identity, especially identities "traversed by struggles,"[30] Shane Phelan in *Identity Politics: Lesbian Feminism and the Limits of Community*,[31] and Elizabeth Spelman in *Inessential Woman: Problems of Exclusion in Feminist Thought*,[32] respectively, show the importance of building collective within feminist mobilizations for lesbians. As Joshua Gamson writes, "Building collective identities requires not simply pointing out commonalities, but also marking off who we are not."[33] For lesbians, to mark off this identity, and who they are or are not, is not only about differences with heterosexual majority of women* but also about differences considered as deviance and therefore rejected by this majority.

Here are what my lesbian activist interlocuters shared about the exclusion of lesbians within feminist mobilizations and struggles in Iran:

> As an Iranian lesbian who has been active in the feminist mobilization for over a decade, I have always hidden who I am. Although I have never personally experienced lesbophobic violence or remarks within the mobilization, I have never seen this mobilization ready to accept lesbians and non-lesbians alike. I've always had a sort of hesitancy to tell my comrades that I am a lesbian. You know… we live in such a lesbophobic system and society that it becomes impossible to trust yourself and others to tell them the reality. (Sanaz, 2021)

> I remember once telling a feminist comrade in a collective that I identified as a lesbian. She didn't say anything, she looked at me and said "You have to keep it a secret. I'm not sure your personal life has any place in our activities. It is about non-priorities." But it wasn't just my "personal life." It was the root and the reason for my suffering as a woman. (Firouzeh, 2021)

> My experience of lesbophobia with Iranian feminists was very difficult. In one meeting, I just talked about minority women. Like lesbians and trans women. You may not believe that many comrades stopped me from talking about these minorities and reminded me that talking about these women could cause us

safety issues and that "we are not looking for problems!" There I realized that we are alone. (Elaheh, 2021)

For some time now, I have decided not to be active in the so-called women's movement in Iran. We are not rowing in the same boat. It is important for me to be myself as a lesbian. It's political, and not just about my bed! As a lesbian woman, I am doubly discriminated against in this society: once as a woman who has fewer rights than men, and once as a lesbian who is completely ignored, and whose existence is criminalized. If I can't fight for all that in this mobilization, I'd rather to fight alone or with lesbians. (Minou, 2021)

Historically, feminist movements around the world have by and large excluded different groups so Iran is not an exception. From Betty Freidan and her "lavender menace," an insulting term for lesbians in the 1960s, and the formation of lesbian activist groups such as the radical "Lavender menace" in the 1970s, to the Iranian feminist mobilizations that did not offer the same opportunity to all women* to fight for their rights, lesbians have always tried to find their place in the larger women's rights movements.

Hush! Lesbians Do Not Scream: Conclusion

Lesbians' exclusion occurs at different levels and in various ways: exclusion from being considered as the bearers of any form of sexual violence experiences, from any debate on this issue, and, finally, from any kinds of activism against this kind of violence. Although in this chapter I did not offer a particular case study, my analysis was based on the sexual case of the popular Iranian musician as well as his lesbophobic remarks in the leaked audio file. This can be a starting point for us to look further into the issue from a historical and system(at)ic perspective.

On the one hand, lesbian women*—whether they wish to be identified as such, or it has been imposed on them—experience censorship, silencing, and exclusion as survivors in all discussions on the topic of sexual violence. Sexual violence can be lesbophobic too for many reasons. On the other hand, lesbian feminist activists face lesbophobia targeted toward their lesbian sexuality within feminist movements. This means that they are targeted not only by the lesbophobic comments and behaviors of others, as "enemies," but also by their nonlesbian activist "sisters" within feminist mobilizations. Lesbians are always told to keep quiet, simply because they do not meet the expectations of cisgender and heteronormative systems, and therefore are not legitimate to speak out about sexual violence. This famous duo of "heterosexual and homosexual," in the words of Diana Fuss, has been constructed on the pillars of another conventional opposition: "the couple 'inside' and 'outside.'"³⁴ The exclusion of lesbians from conversations around MeToo, as well as from larger activisms about sexual violence, has roots in the same duality in which lesbians are othered, therefore excluded. Iranian lesbians, too, have been excluded from Iranian women*'s mobilizations for various reasons, and it is more likely that as lesbian women* they suffer from a deeper exclusion than nonlesbian women* do.

Most significantly, Iranian lesbians have not only faced lesbophobic exclusion from their nonlesbian counterparts in contemporary women's movements in Iran but also always lived a clandestine activist life and been present behind the scenes, for their safety as well as for the safety of the movement and their feminist sisters. As a result, they have never been able to speak about their identities as lesbians, but instead have always been forced to live under a disguise. The silence imposed on Iranian lesbian activists within the larger feminist movements endangers lesbian existence. It seems that they are confronted with the attitude that the American women's mobilization of the 1960s faced: to consider lesbianism as a sexual issue rather than a political one "which is still the case in societies governed by neoliberal states".³⁵ It is also dangerous for the safety of lesbian activists who have always been present, albeit closeted, in feminist movements in Iran.

Hence, if we are not willing to write a statement like "The Woman Identified Woman"³⁶ by the American lesbian feminists, and to say that the lesbian issue is fundamental to feminist mobilizations, we must at least try to show that the lesbian issue has always been a political one in Iran. Lesbians have been included nowhere but have been fighters everywhere.

The White-Collars' New Masculinities in #MeToo: How to Maintain Gendered Privileges?

Somayeh Rostampour

Introduction

The #MeToo campaign in Iran has tackled the "male impunity" for sexual violence and courageously transgressed the gender norms that are deeply rooted in Iranian society. By raising the question of gender violence in the public sphere, the survivors and feminist activists have been able to articulate the social experiences that were hitherto "personalized," repressed, and rendered invisible. While the campaign has remained largely limited to middle-class women, it has indeed challenged the existing patriarchal order and achieved some degree of "gender justice" by virtue of telling their stories on social media. The Iranian feminists have often analyzed the #MeToo narratives from the perspective of survivors, focusing on the existential, psychological, and social experiences of women. Yet, little attention has been paid to the alleged perpetrators' subjectivity, that is, their behavior and attitude toward gendered social relations. To have a more comprehensive picture of the #MeToo campaign, I suggest that we should also approach this campaign through the prism of the alleged perpetrators and take into account the sociological mechanisms through which the violence against women is produced and reproduced intersubjectively.[1]

It is important to note that this campaign has also provided new possibilities for men themselves to undo their patriarchal habits and thus being "educated" about feminist principles on gender harassment and sexual violence. Instead, most of the men who were involved in the Iranian #MeToo, including the ones accused, reinforced in practice the masculinist attitudes and fought tooth and nail to defend their "gender privilege." Analyzing this defensive position as the symptom of the vulnerability and the weakening of patriarchal masculinity, this chapter will try, first, to comprehend *why* and *how* the men in Iran, protecting their gendered interests, have adopted the "male backlash" stance against the egalitarian-feminist changes proposed by #MeToo. The hypothesis is that their indignant resistance to change is closely tied to their privileged social status and gender superiority. Second, by focusing on the middle-class educated men, introduced here as "white-collar," this contribution aims to examine the legitimizing forms of masculinism that essentially justify gendered violence as a response to various challenges posed by #MeToo. A wide range of alleged white-collar perpetrators' reactions to #MeToo has been analyzed, including their hostile backlash and their seemingly enthusiastic but ultimately empty support. Third, the present chapter claims that the old or traditional forms of masculinity—such as religious commitment, rigid personal probity and marital loyalty, and harsh homophobia—are replaced by the less explicit modes of masculinity that are secularized, hedonist, cultivated, and more flexible. We are thus witnessing the emergence of new forms of patriarchy that are capable of reproducing themselves under a legitimized configuration and through the social agents that have "acceptable" appearance and appropriate social status.

Theoretically, this chapter draws on the feminist and sociological fields of "masculinity studies" and "critical studies of men." In particular, Raewyn W. Connell's concept of "hegemonic masculinity" is employed here in order to illustrate men's social power in gendered hierarchies.[2] As for the fieldwork, this study uses three different resources: the survivors' narratives published on social media, mostly in Twitter (public accounts) and feminist websites (in Persian); the alleged perpetrators' statements (written and audiovisual) on the #MeToo movement; and the insightful, online discussions I had about the validity of narratives with one feminist group and a few activists who are both based in Iran and actively involved in the movement (in August and September 2021).[3] Due to confidentiality reasons, together with the sensitivity of the topic from a security and social-political point of view, the names of the aforementioned group and feminists as well as the content of the discussion cannot be revealed. Given that the heterosexual men have been the allegedly main perpetrators of violence in Iranian #MeToo, I focus here only on these men's violence against women. Nonetheless, I am well aware that #MeToo has prompted public attention to nonheterosexual stories and the harassment of men, which is primarily carried out by other men.

Masculinity as Male Privilege: A Brief Literature Survey

The #MeToo narratives have not only challenged male superiority but also unveiled the social structures that inhibit social change in gendered relations. Stressing on "men's resistance to change," various scholars have shown that men lose some of their male privileges and social power over women during the process of moving toward gender equality.[4] The critical thrust of this literature lies in expounding how men backlash against #MeToo in order to maintain their privileges. There is a strong connection between the preserving of these privileges and the exercise of gendered violence, which manifests itself in different forms of masculinities.[5] The interrelation between male privileges, gendered violence, and masculinity is best provided by the theoretical frame of masculinity studies.[6] The category of masculinity, far from being "biological," has to do with the historically constructed gendered privileges derived from the power relations and hierarchies between the genders. Connell particularly insists on "hegemonic masculinity" understood as "the most widely recognized way of being a man, the dominant form of masculinity and a configuration of practices that embodies, organizes, legitimates, and perpetuates male domination in the gender order as a whole."[7] According to her, hegemonic masculinity is not identified with violence but rather can be *accompanied* by the use of violence.[8] Yet, despite the richness and development of such a theoretical framework, the category of masculinity is barely discussed in the historical-sociological scholarship on the Middle East.[9] Iran's #MeToo has precisely brought into light the question of masculinity and violence, thus providing the intellectual possibility for the Iranian feminists to fill the gap that exists in this literature. The specific form of hegemonic masculinity that is identified and made visible in Iranian #MeToo does not seem to be a historical rupture with, but a continuation of, the forms of masculinity previously experienced as integral to modern Iranian history.[10] The latter studies demonstrate that patriarchal traditions remain significant among Iranian men in the construction of dominant masculinities both before the 1979 Revolution in its "Westernized" version[11] and in the postrevolutionary era in the form of "theological masculinity."[12]

#MeToo Call for Changes and Men's Indignant Resistance

Alison Bailey describes the concept of "privilege" as "a set of advantages systematically conferred to individuals, enjoy by virtue of their membership in dominant groups with access to resources and institutional power."[13] In the case of gendered privilege, this includes having authority over women, getting respect and services from them but without the social obligation to reciprocate, monetary benefits, institutional power, and control over one's life, as well as their quasi-monopoly over important positions in work, politics, or social media. There is a general tendency among the dominant classes and social groups to not recognize their rule over the dominant as a form of privilege and social power.[14] They often justify and understand their dominant social position in ways that have no relation to their privileges, as if the latter is derived from something other than the existing social structures of domination and oppression.

Like all other dominant groups who are not aware of their privileges, men assume that their "accomplishments" result from their "innate superiority."[15] In this context, and as an integral part of the hierarchical social relations, masculinity plays a significant role as it seeks to "protect" men's privileges and supremacy. As Connell observes, "The privileges that men receive as 'the patriarchal dividend' not only justify male domination" but also "lead them to defend the institution of patriarchy."[16] The consequence of denying their socially objective, male advantages is that a significant number of men lack any sense of accountability. They often present themselves as the victim of #MeToo, understood as an "unjust campaign," and of patriarchy more generally.[17] For instance, one of the alleged artist perpetrators in Iran described himself as follows: "One hour of my breathing equals six months of my critics and opponents' life."[18] Men like this artist are, therefore, surprised when gender rebellions challenge their privileges and question their allegedly "innate superiority." To preserve the privileges intrinsic to their social-gender position as men, they would thus employ various forms of gendered violence. According to the French materialist feminists, men act violently because they are motivated by maintaining the "material and symbolic benefits" that are derived from their social position of domination and developed through the lived experiences that primarily belong to men.[19] The gendered violence is not indeed an individual pathology but, rather, a logical consequence of "men's collective privilege."[20] They may consider even small losses of opportunities as large threats.[21] In the above example, the self-perception of the artist, which understands gender privileges as something intrinsic to their exceptional personality, can also reduce their willingness to change the present gendered orders. PettyJohn et al. have recently carried out an interesting research project on the impact of #MeToo on men's perception of masculinity. They analyzed over three thousand tweets by men and boys regarding the #MeToo campaign, identifying three primary groups of users: "the users committing actively engage in dismantling rape culture, users indignantly resistant to social change, and users promoting hostile resistance to social change."²² They demonstrate that the users' resistance to gender change manifests itself in different ways: from employing the rhetoric of "not all men" to the conviction that men are targeted "unfairly," from sexist and racist attitudes to the explicitly anti-feminist backlash. Likewise, in Iran's #MeToo campaign, men in general felt that the feminist critiques are not fair and thus did not hesitate to dismantle it. Various strategies are adopted by men to undermine and devaluate the survivors' narratives. They highlighted the false allegations that were merely exceptions to the campaign as a whole but misrepresented as the rule, thereby attacking the feminist platforms for publishing the narratives (Bidarzani, for example). What was ignored was the fact that "false allegations of violence and abuse are far less common than false denials of perpetration."²³

It is important for men to take care of their privileges carefully as they effectively provide them with different kinds of "gender impunity." As will be seen in further details, the alleged perpetrators with "special profiles" in Iran, often from the middle class, have more "male impunity" when committing violence: having a marital status, a superior work position, and an extended social network (in particular, with those who hold power and knowledge), media reputation, and being close to the "hard-core part" of the regime, including the security institutions. In distinction, the survivors have much less access to individual and institutional resources and support in order to defend themselves against male backlash. This is one of the reasons why Iran's #MeToo, lacking any social or legal lever to exercise pressure, had little objective or material impact on the individual and social lives of the alleged perpetrators who are accused of harassment and sexual or gender-based violence. Apart from a few cases that gained media attraction, in which the narratives led to paternalistic juridical intervention from the patriarchal state of the Islamic Republic, the accused men maintained their masculine privilege/power in their social and professional lives.²⁴ Indeed, #MeToo did not cost them much.

In some rare cases, #MeToo's narratives allegedly provided the accused men, ironically, with even greater legitimacy and higher social position in elite patriarchal circles, which is achieved via a kind of "masculine solidarity." One of the artists, for instance, asserted proudly that "the incident has even increased my followers on social media such as Instagram."²⁵ Another illuminating example is the big sale of the paintings by Aydin Aghdashloo during the #MeToo campaign, "an internationally acclaimed artist with ties to the ruling elite," as described in the *New York Times*.²⁶ According to the latter, this painter has been allegedly accused of manipulating and harassing at least thirteen women—the first narrative published on August 22, 2021.[27] Regardless of several accusations, other men supported him unconditionally and credited him with their gender solidarity simply because "men are dependent on each other to maintain that domination."[28] In this case, the backlash that men as a sex class mobilized was indeed the political warfare launched for defending their collective interests as being put into crisis by #MeToo. This implies more broadly that the feminist movements for stopping violence and achieving gender equality actually pose serious challenges to the gendered-collective interests of men and thus would appear to men as a major crisis to their masculinity.[29] Those who regard the #MeToo campaign as a threat to their hegemonic masculinity would not hesitate to marginalize or even downplay it. In this respect, such collective reactions are not specific to Iranian men only. It can also be assessed in the context of pervasive, masculinist responses to the advance of feminism around the world. The upshot is that one and the same logic is employed in all the transnational currents (social and political) that offer the patriarchal and homogeneous discourse on the "crisis of masculinity" and "excessive feminism."

The White-Collar Male Violence

While the #MeToo campaign in the "West" focused on the celebrity perpetrators, its counterpart in Iran concentrated mainly on the educated and urban middle-class men that possess various socioeconomic and cultural-symbolic capitals. The latter group has effective tools at their disposal to hide and deny their masculinity so that it cannot be easily identified. This social mechanism of rendering masculinity invisible is part of the process that can be articulated, sociologically, with the innovative concept of "white-collar male violence." Charles Wright Mills, the American sociologist of class structures, is one of the first to use this terminology in *White Collars: The American Middle Classes* for describing the middle-class actors who commit crimes by abusing their position and administrative influence in order to pocket economic benefits.[30] Similarly, the category of "white-collar crime" was introduced by Edwin Sutherland in criminological studies and defined as "a crime committed by a person of respectability and high social status in the course of his occupation."[31] The credibility, influence, and appearance of such a person make people not suspect him. Similar concepts can and should be employed in the field of feminist studies, which makes it possible to identify the "white-collar male middle-class violence." This sociological category is distinguished from the violence exercised by the two other social classes, that is, the workers ("blue collars") and the ruling classes, as much by its status and group-based privileges as by its political attitude, that is, as much by its cultural capital and its lifestyle as by its perception of itself. In what follows, I will attempt to "apply" this sociological category for the analysis of subtle forms of violence exercised by the middle-class men in Iran's #Metoo.

Part of the white-collar middle-class who were allegedly accused in Iran's #MeToo, ironically, acquired its effectiveness from positioning itself in favor of women's rights. These alleged perpetrators posed a gesture of feminism and adopted its discourse with an "acceptable" appearance and social status, thus granting themselves the impunity to commit complex, multifaceted, and lesser-known acts of violence against women. As an opportunist who learns to take advantage of his gendered position without being labeled as "troublemaker," the white-collar abuser is less likely to be exposed or punished, both socially and legally. With the well-groomed appearance, yet in the shadow of his socioeconomic power as well as his intellectual capital and social networks, the white-collar subject abuses the rights and interests of the others, imposing certain things on them without their consent, that is, harassing them.

The sexual harassment of Iranian white-collar men is expressed in various forms: manipulating the scene of sexual action, misusing their social and professional position, sexual misconduct and violating women's sexual freedom, using threats, intimidation, stigma, and lobbying to drop charges. However, white-collar men often oppose the bluntest forms and most grotesque abuses of masculine power such as violent "hypermasculinity"[32] and "aggressive frontier masculinity."[33] Yet, they do not have any problem, not at least in their practice, with less rigid types of masculinity. Thus, they experience some sort of "tension" between their "patriarchal interests" and "their (apparent) interest in undermining patriarchy."[34] The contradiction between the two is best exemplified by one of the cases in the #MeToo campaign. A famous musician at first completely denied the alleged accusations against him. A week later on April 17, 2021, due to social media pressures, he publicly apologized to the survivors.[35] However, just one hour after, a seventeen-minute audio was leaked anonymously. Recorded in the intimate gathering of friends, the harsh and explicitly masculine language of the audio file contradicted almost everything he stated with an "egalitarian" and "feminist" gesture in the previous video. The polite language and intellectual statements of the previous videos were suddenly replaced by the real patriarchal face of the allegedly accused musician. In the audio file, he called the survivors and feminist activists "mentally ill, sick, and distraught," "unsuccessful and uneducated" women who "lacked beauty," and accused the #MeToo campaign of being "noisy," that is, run by "jealous" women: "a year has passed, but I do not see a 'proper figure' in this campaign," he added.[36] Interestingly enough, he even defended Aghdashloo, calling the alleged accusations against him "insufficient."[37] Men like this musician enjoy the benefits of patriarchy without practicing an assertive version of male domination, thus adopting what is often described as "complicit masculinity"—a reference to the man "who admires or does not challenge hegemonic masculinity, even if he does not fit within the category."[38]

The legal-political procedures and regulations of the state institutions, mostly structured in favor of men, also pave the way for white-collar male middle-class violence. The legal code on gendered violence in Iran is fully based on Islamic doctrines and traditional family values.[39] For instance, many #MeToo survivors in Iran have published their narratives under pseudonyms without revealing their real identity because having sexual relation outside of marriage, under the Islamic law, is a crime and the survivors will be punished accordingly, if they could not prove that they have been sexually assaulted. In this context, the alleged white-collar perpetrators, taking advantage of their class-based access to juridical-legal information, already know that they can easily and safely escape the law when it comes to committing gendered violence. In September 2020, a famous academician who was allegedly accused as a part of the #MeToo campaign wrote in an open letter that "with the aim of casting a light on what has happened, I suggest the following mechanism: I would welcome any legal claim from anyone against me in the court."[40] Due to his field of research on women and children, this person is well aware of the structural and strong barriers that a woman encounters when she becomes a victim of sexual violence outside of marriage and attempts to exercise her right to have a recourse to law. The academic, intellectual, and artistic white-collar perpetrators achieve even more impunity when they are heavily tied to the ruling-class politicians, big economic players, and rentier elites. In this context, the formal and already limited law of the Islamic Republic is suspended, and the cases are no longer processed and thus dismissed forever. Profiting from such masculinist context, the white-collar presents the problem in purely legal terms, projecting their own masculinity onto the shortcomings of the existing male-centered judicial system as if they are not socially and individually responsible for their actions. This is how they justify and trivialize their intolerable behavior, thereby legitimizing their new forms of masculinity.

From Weakened Patriarchy to New Legitimized Forms of masculinity

The violence of white-collar men against women can be regarded as a response to the weakening of male domination and losing control over social reproduction and women's sexuality. This is best exhibited by the survivor middle-class women in #MeToo, wherein the male violence arises from the vulnerability of "hegemonic masculinity" (see earlier). This campaign shows that the dominant power of men is not self-sufficient or inherent to "men's nature" but historical-relational, depending on its acceptance and execution by the opposite sex. When women refuse to reproduce gendered hierarchies, that is, reject or challenge masculine dominant power, men start to forcibly regain what they believe they have lost.[41] In Iran's #MeToo, the weakened masculinity seeks revenge through more subtle forms of masculinity, thereby replacing the old forms of masculinity with new ones. By being mournful for their loss and grief, they adopt new strategies to resolve the crisis engendered by the partial erosion of male power.[42] The traditional paradigms of Iranian bourgeois masculinity such as religious commitment, rigid personal probity and marital loyalty, and harsh homophobia, which were more embedded in conservative culture, are now replaced with the secularized, hedonist, cultivated, calculative, egocentric, and more flexible modes of masculinity. They start to seek new accomplices, reproducing patriarchy in a fresh and more acceptable manner. While they may be forced to "condemn" certain forms of patriarchy and masculinity, nonetheless, they promote and normalize new forms of masculinity by stressing on women's responsibilities toward the question of gender violence. By doing so, the white-collar male creates the image of a "good and responsible man" wherein a certain level of violence and harassment against women is tolerated. Furthermore, the female survivor is blamed as much as the male perpetrator, as they are both equally responsible.

Following the wave of French #MeToo in 2017, one of the main polling centers in France investigates the question of whether the #MeToo movement had an impact on the extent and mode of masculine practice and mentality among French men. The result shows that "young" men have a more patriarchal view of their masculinity and are more committed to following its rules.[43] Contrary to popular belief, the research concludes, the new generation does not have essentially less masculinity than the previous one simply because of the level of their education and knowledge. What is changed above all in between these two generations is not masculinity per se but rather its modes of expression and determination. This is reminiscent of the famous Arabic proverb cited by the French historian Marc Bloch: "Men are more like their time than their father."[44] The patriarchal order reproduces itself at all costs, even at times of feminist progress in the present. Such reproduction is carried out not with defunct and traditional patriarchal methods but with "new legitimized masculinities," which makes their accusation more difficult than before.

Having failed to restore traditional patriarchal order and thus resorted to legitimated methods of masculinity, the allegedly accused intellectual perpetrators in Iran's #MeToo presented themselves as "advocates" of women, referring to their writings on gender, and employed arrogant philosophical definitions of gender issues in order to intimidate the public with their knowledge. In response to survivors, one of the alleged perpetrators, while denying the accusations, wrote on his Instagram page that

> I have been the messenger of vulnerable groups [i.e., women and children] whose patriarchal societies ignore their basic rights. Part of my goal has been for my work to be a reflection of the hidden voice of these groups, and I am proud of whatever extent this has been achieved.[45]

This new model of masculinity seeks to work out a nonthreatening accommodation with feminism by virtue of a greater tolerance for social conflict. This reminds us of how Balslev describes the masculine character of elite Iranian men in the early twentieth century, that is, those who were educated in "Western" or "Western-style" institutions and adopted Westernized manners, thus adding new aspects to their model of masculinity.[46] In this respect, women survivors in the twenty-first century are reduced by the perpetrators to "deceived objects" that lack the merit or ability to be associated with the educated men who know all about sexuality and sexual principles. It is, thereby, the men themselves who draw the border between the "right" and the "wrong" sexual interactions with their patriarchal and paternal standards, again presented as the "(only) relevant knowledge."[47] Consequently, the survivors in Iran were addressed as "the crazy persons who need to visit a therapist" and accused of "confusing sexual relationship with emotional one," "personalizing the problem," the "over- or poorly written," the labels that reminds one of gender stereotypes such as "women are talkative and emotional." Similarly, the feminist activists were also accused of being "banal," that is, not intellectual enough like men, and of "getting into people's beds"—the assertions by virtue of which men attempted to devalue the challenges posed by women and, thereby, maintain their hegemony.

In line with the same logic, and from the standpoint of perpetrators who regard the survivors as "too feminist" or "too radical," it is feminists' fault to mistakenly "identify" men's behavior as an expression of violence. In this way, perpetrators can commit violence and abuse their male power but disguise it under another name and thus be acquitted. The controversy over the act of "naming" in Iran's #MeToo sheds illuminating light on distinct ways in which the act of violence is defined and framed differently, depending on whether the subject is the dominant or the dominated. This mode of characterizing a social phenomenon, that is, "new definitions of violence and consent," is an important moment for the perpetrators who desire to legitimize/normalize new masculinities and renew the centrality of men. The phrase "a verbal joke and a pinch or something like that [which is not really considered an act of violence]" was uttered by a well-known artist to defend himself against the accusation of sexual harassment.[48] In another case that was reported by the *Guardian*, the accused, who grew up in Europe and spent the past decade in Iran conducting research on vulnerable women and children, wrote in his open letter:

> Looking back at the years passed, I find it to be a fair criticism of me that in some cases I had insufficient knowledge of the *cultural requirements*—due to being away for long—and relationships in the workplace so I did not properly observe the hierarchies of power and domination at work. I lacked social considerations and was too comfortable in my different views on relationships. In this way, it is possible to pave the way for misjudgments.[49]

The "sexual violence" is defined here by the alleged perpetrator who grew up in Europe as a kind of "cultural difference." According to the stories of the women survivors, he blamed, and indeed manipulated, numerous women for not being willing to have sexual relationship with him, indicating the latter as a sign of backward and traditional view of sexual freedom and the lack of "modern attitude" about new forms of sexual relations.[50] The new patriarchal mechanism that is at stake here is that the accused justifies his actions by attributing himself a kind of cultural and intellectual superiority and offering new definitions of sexual misconduct. By distorting the semantic of violence as "comfort behavior," the accused represented women as the main cause of abuse. In the same letter, he reduces sexual violence to the "inadvertent offences":

> During my lifetime I have made mistakes and offended some people. I have the courage to apologize to all of them ... But I am here speaking about inadvertent offences, which whether legal or verbal, are different from intentional harassment,

aggression, or relationships without consent. I would like to emphasize that I am not an intentional aggressor or abuser.[51]

As we can see here, even when the alleged perpetrator apologizes, he would prefer to do this for the "general" (nongendered) mistakes he made in his life, not addressing any "specific" survivor or violence he is accused of. The alleged accused is, therefore, as much guilty as everyone else who makes "general" mistakes in their lives, not as an alleged perpetrator. This is a case study example of new, legitimized masculinity that allows alleged perpetrators to deny the fact that the violence/harassment is specifically gendered and explicitly carried out against women.

Women's/Men's Rebellions against the Social Class of Men

The issue of violence in the social relationships between the sexes cannot be abolished until economic, social, and cultural equality is fully achieved.[52] The process of globalization and the rise of new global inequalities have massively transformed the local and regional gender orders in the Global South.[53] The unprecedented levels of poverty and precarity have caused men to lose to a large extent their social power and thus paved the way to form new gendered coalitions and solidarities among men themselves in order to compensate for their other socioeconomic failures. In a neoliberal and extremely polarized society like Iran, the collective protection of male superiority over the opposite sex has been playing a crucial role in the construction of their social identity and self-recognition as someone with "special ability." It is, thereby, not easy for them to stand up and say no to all the privileges they hold, especially in times of crisis when the tendency for gender domination is intensified. If men genuinely want to act against patriarchy in an effective manner, then they have no choice but to defend egalitarian interests in favor of women and subscribe to gender equality values. This entails betraying male solidarity and rebelling against their social class of men. In this regard, Bob Pease asserts the need for men to see beyond their socially constructed interests toward what he calls their "emancipatory interests," which is an ethical obligation to change gender relations.[54] Nonetheless, and in spite of strong male backlash, there is considerable evidence for accepting gender change by men as the male resistance is weakened.[55]

Since the interest or disinterest of men to change gendered hierarchies make an impact on the violence against women, some commentators have argued that men are part of the solution to the gender problem, the one that they themselves can also benefit from.⁵⁶ They propose to socially engage the passive and indifferent men and involve them with the egalitarian politics,⁵⁷ especially given that "the masculinity is implicated directly in men's widespread inaction or complicity in the face of men's violence against women."⁵⁸ In this regard, what is known as "positive masculinity study" emphasizes on the fact that men are capable of self-transformation, and thus there is no "shame" in participating in the politics of gender change.⁵⁹ As Michael Flood remarks, "The #MeToo campaign invites men to be prosocial bystanders who take action to prevent and reduce harm, including by strengthening the conditions that prevent initial perpetration or victimization."⁶⁰ In Flood's view, the #MeToo's call to action among men comprises three key tasks. First, it talks about listening to women, in order to recognize men's violence against women as common, serious, and wrong. Second, it demands from men to reflect on, and in fact invite them to change, their individual behavior in everyday situations with other men and women. Third, #MeToo encourages men contributing to wider social change, both by challenging other men as well as supporting larger efforts to transform the systemic gender inequalities as the foundation of sexual harassment and abuse.⁶¹ The transformation of men's subjectivity can, therefore, immensely facilitate the change in gendered relations and violence.

Due to absence of institutional support and the lack of experience in this new form of gender resistance, there is a sense of confusion among Iranian women on how to deal with male perpetrators and how to include them as part of the solution to the problem. This campaign, however, demonstrates well that the violence against women is not merely a "women issue" but rather an intersubjective and thus intersexual one, tied to social definitions of sex, gender, and masculinity/ femininity. The women during #MeToo in Iran have also invited men to "believe survivors" and encouraged them to understand the act of listening to women as a social responsibility, not as a "favor" to them. Nonetheless, the survey of this research suggests that only a minority of perpetrators started to have some sort of critical reflection on their gendered practices in the light of #MeToo, that is, the reassessment that led them to apologize publicly and accept their past mistakes or trying to make compensations.

While women have not been able to effectively involve men in the #MeToo campaign in Iran, they have nevertheless enabled some women to struggle against masculine domination. Women confronted with masculine hegemony by creating a kind of feminist solidarity parallel to that of male coalition, changing stereotypical definitions, and raising awareness in society. We should note, by way of conclusion, that narrating gendered violence in patriarchal society is by itself a courageous act of resistance, especially in an authoritarian regime like the Islamic Republic. Men's sexist attitudes and backlashes were not only challenged individually but also, and more creatively, through the open letters and stories written by a group of survivors and feminist activities collectively. In continuity with the #MeToo, independent collectives such as "The Council of Witches" had a direct action against the publication of photos and interviews of Aghdashloo, the allegedly accused artist mentioned earlier.[62] Other groups of women did not give up on gender justice to be realized through the already defunct juridical system of the regime and have insistently sued a few perpetrators who managed to escape from undertaking any responsibility toward the survivors. Although these collective efforts remained limited to only a few activist-feminist groups, they are growing in social, practical, and theoretical domains. We can conclude that the #MeToo campaign in Iran has been more effective in challenging individual harassment, backlash, and violence of white-collar middle-class men than the structural violence against women, which primarily concerns working-class women. Yet, this campaign has struggled to transform society by proposing the gender identity in which the hierarchical relations between the sexes are minimized and will ultimately disappear.

10

Hush! Girls Don't Scream (2013) by Puran Derakhshandeh and the #MeToo Movement in Iran

Maryam Zehtabi

It was only yesterday that I saw on the news the pictures of a man parading the severed head of his seventeen-year-old wife in the streets of Ahwaz. The "miscreant" wife, Muna Heydari, had fled the country in the hopes of getting away from her abusive husband. She was only twelve when she was married off to her cousin, only fourteen when she became a mother, and only seventeen when she fled the country and was brought back home by her father and decapitated by her husband.[1] The incident, showcasing the many injustices visited upon women in Iran, enraged the country, and the authorities not only arrested the culprit forthwith but also shut down the news agency that publicized the news as it was deemed to have offended public morality. Heartbreaking as this incident is, it is hardly singular in its atrocity or frequency or in the state's hasty attempt to sweep it under the rug.

In recent years, with the prevalence of social media platforms, the nation's attention has been drawn to the many girls of different ages and ethnicities who have been slaughtered invariably by their kin for allegedly besmirching the honor of their families. The tragedy of Muna is reminiscent of that of Rumina,[2] Shakiba,[3] Mubina,[4] and many other girls who fell through the cracks of a corrupt patriarchal sociopolitical system that banks on the commodification of women, their simultaneous fetishization and vilification, and eventual elimination.[5] This tragedy becomes even more poignant when we realize that in all these cases, it is the woman and not the male partner of this alleged relationship that has to pay the price for restoring honor to the family and reaffirming the virility and manhood of its male guardians.

The choice of decapitation as punishment for the woman in question is exceptionally apropos in a patriarchal culture such as Iran, which takes its legitimacy from its skewed interpretation of religion. Similar to the biblical story, the qur'anic Abraham was commanded by God in a vision to slay his son as part of a "a revealing test."[6] Although God saved Ishmael by replacing an animal for him, it is Abraham's unwavering faith and willingness in obeying God's orders that instituted sacrifice in Islam as a holy ritual performed year-round by Muslims all over the world and celebrated on a special occasion marked as the Eid al-Adha.[7] Women, such as Rumina and Muna, whose throats their father and husbands slit with such alacrity, are the modern-day sacrificial lambs on the altar of the alleged God-ordained male authority. While in the religious scriptures Ishmael is given a second lease of life when God intervenes on his behalf, Iranian women have received no such helping hand or divine intervention.

The response of the state to such crimes falls far short of ensuring justice for the victims and instead by handing down nominal sentences[8] to perpetrators of these crimes perpetuates the vicious cycle within which women are held accountable to their male kin for minor offenses and pay with their lives, while men can literally get away with murder and be celebrated within their macho circles as guardians of honor and morality.

As one of the very few countries that has not yet signed the Convention on Elimination of All Forms of Discrimination against Women (CEDAW), Iran can hardly claim to have women's best interests at heart. The fate of the notorious bill for the protection of women against violence is quite telling in this regard. The bill advocates for moderating, rather than abolishing, Iran's misogynistic laws. Caught, for over a decade, in an endless mire of bureaucratic red tape, the bill has been delayed and watered down innumerable times to appease its many hardline critics who deem it unnecessary and irrelevant in an Islamic culture where the guardianship of women is entrusted to their menfolk and the reason for the violence committed against them is their inability to accept this fact.[9]

With both the laws and traditions of the country condoning male authority, women's grievances, should they choose to air them, fall on deaf ears. This antipathy toward them explains the reluctance of women in reporting different forms of violence against them. This reluctance to report, however, is universal. Take the case of sexual crimes committed against women as an example. According to Mala Htun and Francesca R. Jensenius, this underreporting is

> attributable partially to attitudes that see violence as normal, common, and a private or family matter. Underreporting may also be strategic, as women

choose to avoid emotional, financial, and personal risks associated with police intervention and legal proceedings. Women who report incur costs, including disbelief and demeaning treatment by the authorities, retaliation, and ostracism by family and community.[10]

While all the reasons Hutn and Jensenius mention in the passage play a role in Iranian women's silence in the face of sexual harassment and abuse, there are other factors that push them even further to the extremes of this universal underreporting. According to Tara Sepehri Far, a researcher for Human Rights Watch based in New York, the problematic definition of rape in the Iranian criminal law is another major roadblock to women's reporting sexual assaults. By excluding marital rape and disbelieving women who were raped in a consensual extramarital relationship, the law refuses to extend victimhood status to a great many survivors of sexual assault. To add insult to injury, in telling the stories of sexual abuse perpetrated against them, Iranian women run the risk of incriminating themselves in the highly unjust judicial system in Iran where extramarital sex is criminalized and punishable by flogging.[11]

Those women who choose to go public with their stories do so in defiance of their history, culture, and politics, which espouse stoicism, self-censorship, and silence in the face of all calamities. Inquisitive, forbidding, draconian, and absurd, unbridled censorship hindering public expressions of thought and speech had been the defining characteristic of the Iranian cultural stage even before the Islamic Revolution of 1979 happened. This long reign of terror and censorship has given rise to a conservative, circumspect, and self-censoring culture that, in the words of Simin Daneshvar,[12] the first Iranian female novelist, "fears sincerity and honesty."[13] This paralyzing fear has led to the rigid and calculated separation of one's private self and public persona. Defined by restraint, an insurmountable separation between the public and the private, as well as silence and veiling, Iranian culture has produced a mystifying nation, men and women alike, whose aversion to self-revelation is construed as a virtue and for whom "the concept of honor is built around a woman's virginity, the token of her inaccessibility."[14]

But in a society where literal and psychological veils hinder even men's free expression, women can hardly fare better. This is particularly true in the case of Muslim/Iranian women whose voice has traditionally been "considered part of her '*Owrat* [pudenda] and subject to strict concealment"[15] and their silence "legitimized, spiritualized, fetishized, and idealized."[16] Lacking access to education until the twentieth century, being kept invisible and immobile in a predominantly patriarchal family, being veiled and maligned as the source of evil in a religious community were not particularly conducive to public expressions of thought, especially not to telling personal life narratives.

The act of forcibly veiling women in Iran, both in its literal and metaphorical sense, has been designed in such a way as to make sure that Iranian women would remain inaccessible, thus invisible and malleable, that they would not speak back to power, that they would not question the supremacy of men over them, that they would not sully their families' reputation by either their actions or words. It is against this backdrop that the outpouring of narratives by Iranian women survivors of sexual assault in the past few years gains extraordinary significance. Surmounting fear and long-standing cultural inhibitions in order to unveil one's voice, intimate thoughts, experiences, and emotions while anticipating the hefty price they will have to pay in the form of shaming, backlash, and legal repercussions for this cultural insubordination is nothing short of heroism.

The moment Iranian women chose for their daring outburst was in August 2020. Inspired by their global sisters, Iranian women came forward on social networking platforms to tell the heartbreaking stories of sexual harassment and abuse by men, some of whom were considered the pillars of their community.[17] With the #MeToo movement, as Jessica Bennett, the gender editor of *New York Times*, observes, "For perhaps the first time in history, powerful men [were] falling, like dominos, and women [were] being believed."[18] What the #MeToo movement did for Iranian women was to show them that they were not alone and breaking their silence on different forms of sexual violence is the first step toward healing and advocating for structural change. In solidarity with women across the world, they recognized that they "have the knowledge, skill, experience, imagination, vision, and creativity to identify, address, and bring radical transformation to our communities and institutions."[19]

Gone viral in 2017, the #MeToo movement was in fact founded more than a decade before by Tarana Burke, who was plagued by the fact that, when faced with a teenage survivor of sexual assault, she "could not muster the energy to tell her that I understood, that I connected, that I could feel her pain. I couldn't help her release her shame, or impress upon her that none of it was her fault," that she herself was also a survivor. Emphasizing leading with empathy and forming solidarity, Burke's vision was of helping "bring resources, support, and pathways to healing where none existed before" and empowering survivors "to disrupt the systems that allow sexual violence to proliferate in our world. This includes insisting upon accountability on the part of perpetrators, along with the implementation of strategies to sustain long term, systemic change."

When Alyssa Milano, the celebrity advocate of the movement, lent her support to it, she did so in order to bring to light "the magnitude of the problem."[20] According to the World Health Organization, one in three women have been subjected to sexual violence defined as

> any sexual act, attempt to obtain a sexual act, or other act directed against a person's sexuality using coercion, by any person regardless of their relationship to the victim, in any setting. It includes rape, defined as the physically forced or otherwise coerced penetration of the vulva or anus with a penis, other body part or object, attempted rape, unwanted sexual touching and other non-contact forms.

Refusing to release official data regarding the number of sexual assault reports filed by women and the number of convictions these allegations secure, the Islamic Republic has been directly responsible for keeping the nation in the dark regarding the enormity and prevalence of the problem.

The #MeToo movement in countries like the United States where it was founded has already led to changes in policies and laws. Financially restituting the survivors, reforming processes that hindered congressional staff from reporting harassment, setting up funds helping victims seek justice, instating protections for workers, and banning nondisclosure agreements that threaten victims with legal prosecution if they publicize their case are, according to Anna North, among the many measures undertaken by the government and the civil society to intervene on behalf of the survivors and to stop sexual harassment and abuse.[21] In Iran, however, despite the outrage caused by the outpouring of sexual assault stories on social media, little has been done to amend the situation other than arresting a few of the offenders and urging the victims to lodge complaints. What still needs to be accomplished in Iran is, according to Sepehri Far, adopting a gender-neutral definition of rape, which includes marital rape and any other form of coerced penetration and does not put the burden of saving another human being's life on the shoulders of the survivors.[22] The latter point refers to the death penalty stipulated in the Iranian penal code as the punishment of men found guilty of adultery. Many women are deterred from taking their cases to court as the trauma of causing another's death is hardly the resolution they need to the already traumatic experience of being a survivor of sexual assault. Furthermore, according to Marziyih Muhebi, a lawyer representing many sexual assault survivors pro bono, "Iran needs to introduce new legislation that would explicitly criminalize sexual assault and focus on providing mental and physical health support to victims."[23]

Although the movement in Iran did not garner the structural and systemic change required to pass new woman-friendly legislations and allocate resources necessary to mitigate the pervasiveness of violence against women, it was liberating in many ways. In the words of Muhebi, it was

> a wake-up call to a discourse that views victims as accomplices, culprits and provocateurs and at times, considers victims deserving of penalty. To a culture in which, at times, families eliminate the helpless and marginalised victims with the excuse of maintaining honour.[24]

Prior to the movement, rape was a taboo subject that hardly ever found its way into public debates. During the movement, however, women used public social networking platforms as "intimate publics" that united them based on their "shared feelings—that connect the personal to the political, and the national to the transnational, to confront the misogynist narratives that would seek to stifle those voices through practices of shaming, or the threat of being shamed."[25] The #MeToo movement gave women the platform they needed to break their silence, share their struggles, address the norms and laws enabling the offenders, and ask for their accountability. But more importantly, women bonded in solidarity to prevent what befell them from happening to others like them.

That Iran's own #MeToo moment happened three years after the movement went viral for the first time does not mean that it was completely part and parcel of an international alliance. Even prior to the movement, Iranian activists, writers, and filmmakers had been raising awareness regarding violence against women and the necessity of changing the social norms and laws to recognize such crimes as breaches of their human rights. In cinema, this activism led to making a number of movies revolving around the topic of rape. Probably the most internationally known example of Iranian movies tackling this topic is Asghar Farhadi's *The Salesman* (2016) which won the Academy Award for Best Foreign Language film in 2018. Manijeh Hekmat's *Old Road* (2018) followed on the heels of Farhadi and, very much like it, revolved around the story of a woman believed to be sexually assaulted and unwilling to tell her story. While *The Salesman* focuses on the reaction of people around the female protagonist to her plight, the *Old Road* displays the psychological trauma of being raped. Shahram Shah Hosseini's *The Girl's House* (2017) also leaves the audience in the dark regarding whether the protagonist has been raped and if so, who by. What all these movies have in common is their insistence on hinting at, rather than directly introducing, the issue of rape, which the whole movie is predicated upon. The exceptions to this case are *A Letter to My Mother* (2019) made by Amina Maher and *Hush! Girls Don't Scream* (2013) by Puran Derakhshandeh. A survivor of pedophilia, Amina portrays the psychological and emotional toll of being sexually assaulted as a child. Amina speaks of feeling "guilt, shame, helplessness" and also of suicidal thoughts that were not shared with family when still a child.²⁶ Like in Amina's story, the protagonist of *Hush! Girls Don't Scream* was sexually abused as a child and, rather than obfuscating her story by shrouding it in mysterious layers of obscurities, tells us the story directly. In what follows, I will closely study the latter movie to shed light on how, by problematizing the concepts of honor and shame, this movie laid the groundwork for the #MeToo awakening in Iran.

Belonging to the first generation of Iranian women filmmakers after the revolution of 1979, Derakhshandeh was born in March 1951 in Kermanshah, Iran. A director, screen writer, producer, and researcher, Derakhshandeh has never shied away from dealing with the concerns of the most marginalized and underprivileged groups of the Iranian society. Her cinematic career has spawned four decades and is replete with vocal statements against social injustice, poverty, corruption, exploitation, and the social maladies that they engender. A prolific documentary filmmaker as well, she has successfully brought to the limelight the lives and struggles of female heads of households, disease, economic depression, addiction, drug smuggling, mental and physical disabilities, divorce, and so on.

Based on a screenplay by Derakhshandeh and Mitra Bahrami, the award-winning *Hush! Girls Don't Scream* was made years before the heyday of the international #MeToo movement. The movie recounts the story of Shīrīn who commits murder hours before her wedding. The event remains a mystery to the detectives, her parents, her fiancé, and the multiple lawyers her parents hire to represent her as Shīrīn stops talking altogether after the perpetration of the crime. It is her last lawyer and a female one, Ms. Tavallāʾī, that eventually wins her confidence and breaks her silence.

Repeatedly molested as a kid by her mom's valet Murād, and photographed in the act, ever since she was eight years old, Shīrīn's pleas for help fall on deaf ears as her family, her teachers, and her physicians fail to recognize the symptoms of the abuse and dismiss her each time she tries to communicate her problems with them. One scene in particular stands out in this regard. Unable to admit to her mother that she is being sexually violated, she tries to recruit her help on behalf of an imaginary friend in need of saving. Her mother's response is quite telling as she shushes her and asks her to not only banish the thought but also stop talking to that friend. This dismissive attitude toward children and their concerns and the lack of sex education and open communication regarding sexual matters between parents and children explain why in subsequent investigations the police find Murād to be guilty of twenty-seven unreported counts of rape.

To prevent what befell her from happening to another girl, Shīrīn, now a woman in her mid-twenties, rushes to the aid of a young girl being dragged to a forsaken room by a man and, in her momentary insanity brought on by flashbacks of her own predicament as a child, kills him. The young girl's family never steps forward to help Shīrīn even after they find the molester's cellphone and all the nude photographs of their daughter on it, citing fear for their honor and reputation as the reason. Saving face and preserving reputation is also the main reason Shīrīn herself kept silent for years. Threatening that he would "ruin [her] reputation," Murād capitalized on the deep-rooted fear of jeopardizing one's good name instilled in children from a very young age. That a child of eight has to be concerned with the notion of reputation and honor is an irony not lost on the audience. Despite Ms. Tavallā'ī's desperate attempts to convince the all-male judges and the uncompassionate male prosecutor that there were mitigating circumstances that should be taken into account when handing down Shīrīn's sentence, she is found guilty of murder and sentenced to death by hanging.

The movie is the acme of Derakhshandeh's thriving career, further securing her reputation as a director who has dedicated her life to investigating social malaises and ways to alleviate them. This movie is as much about depicting the trauma of sexual assault as it is about challenging the misplaced emphasis on the notion of honor for whose preservation generations upon generations of survivors have been silenced into oblivion. The legal term used to refer to this crime in the movie is "tajāvuz be nāmūs," which roughly translates into "raping honor." That the word *nāmūs* has to even be mentioned is heartbreaking as it takes the woman as an individual out of the equation and makes the assault as a symbolic encroachment upon another man's property. Derakhshandeh, however, gives Shīrīn space and agency to reclaim her voice and tell us the story at her own pace without the mediation of a third-person narrator. During this unraveling, she has not only the unfailing support of her lawyer but also the devoted alliance of her prison mates who, if not victims of child abuse, are no strangers to being denied agency and voice and being trapped in the constrictive cage of cultural inhibitions.

Throughout the movie, we constantly hear the sound of the reporters' camera shutters clicking in the background and evoking the memories of the time Murād was taking photos of her. Purposefully merging these sounds and blending the past and the present through the use of intermittent flashbacks, Derakhshandeh reminds us that it is not only one criminal responsible for what befell Shīrīn but a whole society of bystanders who revel in objectifying her, documenting her miseries in photographs, and passively, pathologically, and voyeuristically looking at her.

Understandably, the theme of imprisonment in its both physical and psychological iterations is present throughout the movie and the motifs associated with it abound in it. Bars surround Shīrīn and their shadow haunts her. Doors that have the potential to offer new possibilities to her close in her face and stop the world from watching over her. Hands, both her abuser's and her mother's, cover her mouth to bury the story in her and with her. A refrain heard throughout the movie, hence its title, is "hush! girls don't scream." Contrast this with "men don't cry" said to Shīrīn's fiancé as he is mourning the loss of his marriage. While girls should refrain from raising their voice, men should hold back their emotions. Whereas girls are expected to be forbearing and suffer in silence, boys are to be tough and stoic. It seems as if sweeping things under the rug is a national coping mechanism the most recent example of which was shutting down the news agency that publicized Muna's death mentioned in the first paragraph.

The protagonist's imprisonment, isolation, and the consequent alienation from others are neatly summed up in her use of *chādur*, the cloth that covers a woman from head to toe. The only instances we see it used are within the court or in prison as a mandatory requirement. Shīrīn's female prison guards are clad in identical black chādurs making them, for the audience and probably for Shīrīn as well, completely indistinguishable from one another and thus, by erasing all their individualities, turning them into easily replaceable cogs in the unjust Iranian judicial machine.

The headscarf, reminding women at every turn of the societal conventions and expectations, is utilized symbolically multiple times in the course of the movie. Each time Shīrīn's lawyer is feeling suffocated, down, and in need of her own personal breathing space, she unties her scarf. The modesty codes governing Iranian cinema after the revolution of 1979 bar the actress from completely removing the scarf but by untying its knot, she shows the need to loosen its stifling grip around a woman's neck. Along with the noose that threatens to wrap around Shīrīn's neck and the hands of the abuser that threatened to break it if she did not keep silent, the headscarf is a potent symbol alluding to all the societal impositions and inscriptions on a woman's body.

The veil, however, is not the only garment vilified in the movie. The wedding dress also gets a mention. The bloody wedding gown becomes a fixture in the movie. We catch a glimpse of Shīrīn for the first time in her wedding dress, which is stained with the victim's blood. The next time we see a wedding dress is when she has decided to marry her cousin and leave Iran for good. It is in the bridal store that, upon seeing Murād, she slits her wrists in an attempt to take her own life while still wearing the white gown. Even as a kid, playing dress-up in her mother's bridal Maison did not end well for her. It is there that for the first time the character of Murād is introduced. Shīrīn's innocence, in her own eyes, is forever tainted. She has feelings of shame and guilt shared by many survivors who believe themselves to be complicit in their own abuse, and this presumed complicity hounds her. In her desperate attempt to find a man who can protect her and wrench her away from Murād's grip, Shīrīn almost marries three different men in the span of a few years only to realize at the end that her problem cannot be solved by escaping; instead, she must confront it and take charge of the situation. Furthermore, men in this movie are far from being saviors. They are inept, self-appointed agents of law and justice who fail her at every turn. Their initial inability to understand Shīrīn's motives for the murder shows the low esteem in which they hold women. The only explanation they could think of for why she committed the crime is that she was either in a relationship with the man and was being blackmailed for it or that she is insane. Otherwise, why would a girl with the prospect of a good marriage act up? They could not conceive of a woman being able to commit such a crime for a noble purpose, that she could take the law into her own hands and be the agent of true justice, hardly found in the misogynistic and anachronistic judiciary of the Islamic Republic.

In the absence of female judges in the courts of the Islamic Republic, it is once again left to men to make a decision regarding Shīrīn's life and death. The peculiar lack of compassion they show for her and the many times they endeavor to silence Ms. Tavallāʾī as she is defending her client make the audience wonder if Shīrīn would have met with a different fate had she been tried in a court with women in charge. Regardless of the gender of the judges, what remains equally problematic is the death penalty in general and its dependence on the will and decision of the bereaved family, in keeping with the penal code of the country. Shīrīn's life, similar to the lives of many others like her, hung in the balance as her lawyer and her fiancé looked for the brother of the man she killed so they could pay him off and stop her execution. That, of course, never happened, and the inequity and absurdity of this situation were enough to drive Shīrīn's interrogator to a spiritual crisis and to request a transfer to a judicial branch where he could question the sagacity of such laws. Shīrīn, however, as she herself explained, did not die at the gallows. She died when she suffered abuse and her cries for help were stifled by her family who should have been the closest to her and by her society that should have acted as her support network.

The end of the movie gives us no false hopes or redemptive promises. The very last scene takes us to a random street in front of a random girls' school. As the camera zooms in on the face of a very young girl, we hear children's laughter and babble in the background and realize that the director, in not so subtle a way, is introducing us to another potential Shīrīn. Derakhshandeh allowed us to see how one victim broke her silence to save other girls from suffering like her. Alone, however, she succumbed under the weight of unwieldy conventions and unsympathetic laws. Solidarity between the survivors and breaking taboos and stigmas regarding rape had to wait for seven more years until Iran's very own #MeToo movement.

Analyzing works such as *Hush! Girls Don't Scream* made by women and about women can be instrumental in recognizing the indigenous roots of Iranian women's gender equality consciousness. Although the global #MeToo movement created the momentum for Iranian women's bold move to publicize the stories of assaults on their persons, it was a long line of Iranian women poets, fiction writers, artists, filmmakers, and activists that brought to light the necessity of fighting for one's rights and freeing one's voice. It is vital to remind the readers once again that these stories were released on public platforms despite cultural, sociopolitical, religious, and legal obstacles, and for this tenacity and courage the bold women who jeopardized their life and reputation need to be celebrated.

Afterword

Patriarchalism, Male Abuse, and the Sources of the #MeToo Movement in the Muslim Middle East

Roger Friedland, Janet Afary, and Charlotte Hoppen

The #MeToo movement exploded on the American scene in 2017 with the desperate hope that women who had been sexually harassed, molested, or violated would finally be heard in the public sphere. Women hoped to change both male behavior and the law to protect them from men's sexual aggression. It has since become a transnational feminist movement. In 2018, just after the #MeToo movement burst onto the scene in the Middle East, we surveyed tens of thousands of primarily younger adults about their intimate lives, including their experiences with molestation and violence. Using Facebook (FB) banner ads in Algeria, Egypt, Iran,[1] Pakistan, Palestine, Tunisia, and Turkey, we were able to garner a large number of men who recounted whether they participated in these acts and women who reported such experiences. This chapter first reviews the #MeToo movement in the countries we surveyed and then analyzes both the extent of and the kinds of men most likely to engage in public molestation and domestic violence.

The Origins of the Movement in the United States

The #MeToo hashtag traces back to a civil rights activist who took her progressive movement public on social media—"me too" was created in 2006 by Tarana Burke, an African American activist concerned with sexual violence and other forms of oppression disproportionately impacting marginalized people, especially black women and girls.[2] Her goal was to empower women and girls who had experienced sexual violence by showing that there were thousands like them who had undergone a similar experience. Burke brought attention to the prevalence of misogyny and violence against women within civil rights organizations, showing that progressive organizations and social movements often ignored the conduct of their own abusive men, including clergy, who were important to the organization and often brought in substantial donations.

#MeToo broke out on the international scene eleven years later in October 2017. It began in the United States by exposing Hollywood moguls, media celebrities, politicians, and other high-ranking men. Among the celebrities accused were Hollywood producer Harvey Weinstein and actor Bill Cosby. Well-known politicians were also accused, including US president Donald Trump, who famously bragged about kissing and fondling any woman he wanted. Brett Kavanaugh, now a member of the US Supreme Court, was accused of attempted rape while in college. Alabama senate candidate Roy Moore was accused of having sex with a minor. Chairman and CEO of Fox News Roger Ailes and Fox news anchor Bill O'Reilly were both accused and forced to resign by female coworkers.

What was perhaps most surprising about the revelations of sexual abuse was the numerous liberal and progressive men accused of sexual violence. The *Washington Examiner* reported that "the #MeToo movement, which seeks to shine a light on systemic sexism and sexual harassment, has fallen disproportionately hard on Democratic lawmakers and other left-wing luminaries … Sexual harassment and abuse are clearly a bipartisan cancer."[3] Many of these men were known for their progressive stance on social issues, including promoting women in their field of work.[4]

Historical Justification for Violence against Women in the Middle East, North Africa, and South Asia

The experience of women in the Middle East was decidedly different than those of women in the West. Until the early twentieth century, respectable urban women did not appear in public unaccompanied. It was the men and the male servants, as well as female servants and slaves of both genders, who did the shopping, and as a result public sexual harassment of middle-class women was nonexistent and those of poorer classes and slaves were completely ignored. After World War II, unaccompanied urban women began to emerge in large numbers in public spaces, shopping in marketplaces, taking their children to school, going to beauty parlors, and socializing with other women. As women penetrated the public sphere, sexual harassment of and violence against urban middle-class women increased on the streets and in public areas. Many women in Muslim-majority cities are still concerned about traveling alone for fear of harassment and groping. In many of the countries of the region, including some in our survey, husbands maintain extraordinary powers within their households. They decide when and if their wives and daughters can go out to socialize, attend university or work, and they often use the prevalence of public harassment as justification for their controlling behavior. As elsewhere in the world, Muslim women in our survey indicate that they have been subjected to physical violence at home. Domestic violence is as common as elsewhere, with a global average of 30 percent of women having experienced domestic violence, notwithstanding national variations in its legality.[5] Thirty-eight percent of murders of women and girls around the world are by a family member or intimate partner.

In Algeria, Palestine, Pakistan, and Egypt, married men continue to hold certain rights over their wives and are permitted, by law, to perpetrate a certain level of domestic violence, so long as it does not lead to severe injury. The legal justification for this attitude continues to be the following Quranic sura (al-Nisa 4:34):

> Men have authority [*qawwama*] over women because Allah has made the one superior to the other, and because they [men] spend their wealth to maintain them [women]. Good women are obedient. They guard their unseen parts because Allah has guarded them. As for those [women] from whom you fear disobedience [*nushaz*], admonish them and send them to beds apart and beat them. Then if they obey you, take no further action against them. Allah is high, supreme.[6]

As Lisa Hajjar shows, the relationship among religion, the state, and women's rights can fall into one of four categories: (1) In countries with diverse religions, such as Palestine, Israel, and Lebanon, the state communalizes religion, so that each community is governed by sectarian laws, almost always with religious justification; (2) in countries such as Egypt, the government nationalizes religion, even though the state itself is secular; (3) in some countries, such as Iran and Saudi Arabia, the state theocratizes religion by declaring itself Islamic and governs on the basis of overtly theological grounds; and (4) in Tunisia, the state has liberalized religion by promoting gender equality as a foundation for family law. Thus, in three out of four categories of countries in our survey, family law is said to be derived from Islam.[7] But the sexism that finds textual sanction in Islam is by no means the only reason for the continuation of this violence. It is a choice to assert its contemporary applicability. There are other cases of subordination legitimated in the Qur'an, such as slavery, which are no longer invoked as justifications for the continuing exploitation of people. There is no logical reason that this same selective disregard would not apply here.

Since the late nineteenth century, pan-Islamists have used Islam as the central bulwark to mobilize their countrymen against the colonialism and imperialism of the West, which upheld its own treatment of women as central to their civilizing mission. Protecting the sexual honor of their wives, daughters, and sisters soon became the mantra of those Middle Eastern men who opposed the state's secular modernization. The colonizers often controlled everything else—the military, the economy, and the state, but not the family, a site where it was possible to fight the *kulturkampf* over men's untrammeled power over women's bodies.

Over the course of the twentieth century, the family has remained a privileged redoubt for those, particularly the Islamist parties, who seek to resist the state's efforts to modernize traditional gender structures and family law. Although colonialism and imperialism are no longer dominant issues, and public harassment of women and domestic violence have been declared illegal in most countries, public aggression toward women has increased. This might be interpreted as an expression of male anger and resistance to women's empowerment, their ability to go to school and university, to work and earn their own paychecks, to participate in political life, to divorce and receive alimony, to demand, exercise, and expand their legal rights to custody of their children—in short, to claim their right to be citizens of their nations.

#MeToo in the Middle East, North Africa, and South Asia Region

The #MeToo movement quickly went global, becoming a major social movement in a number of Middle East, North Africa, and South Asia (MENASA) countries, including the seven countries where we conducted our FB survey in 2018–19. The internet and social media have helped break the silence of tens of thousands of women who have been victims of public sexual harassment and private domestic violence, some of whom have used the anonymity of social media to tell their stories for the first time.

As in the West, in addition to the usual culprits—military and police officers, major entrepreneurs, clergymen, and conservative politicians—#MeToo in the Middle East has shed new light on leaders of charity and social welfare organizations, media figures, writers, academics, and artists who are generally on the progressive side of politics. Before turning to the results of our FB survey conducted at the time when #MeToo was spreading in the Middle East, we examine the most publicized cases of #MeToo in six of the seven countries we surveyed, excluding the Iranian case, which is discussed in great detail in this volume.

Pakistan

In Pakistan, on International Women's Day, in a march known as "Aurat," which has been held every year since 2019, women have brought sexual misconduct and the bullying of Pakistani women to greater public awareness. The website of Aurat showed that the cost of defending oneself against defamation prevented many women from filing cases and that filing one could even result in their being jailed or fined. The Pakistani #MeToo movement accused a number of offenders across the media, film industry, state, and political realms, including Pakistan's prime minister. In addition, it called attention to widespread sexual violence toward women by clerics, the judiciary, the Pakistani security establishments, such as the police and the military, as well as charity and social welfare institutions that are supposed to protect women and children. According to a study conducted by Human Rights Watch in 2009, between 10 and 20 percent of Pakistani women experienced domestic violence.[8] Pakistan and India have the highest rates of honor killings per capita of any country in the world.[9] In Pakistan, rape was institutionalized and even received the explicit approval of the state as a form of political intimidation. In addition, the rape and assault of Christian, Hindu, Sikh, and other minorities remained prevalent in Pakistan, just as child sexual abuse was widespread.[10] The stress on family honor and the shaming of women who came forward with their stories meant that the police often blamed the victims and did not take their reports seriously, while the criminal justice system protected powerful perpetrators.

One of the most notorious cases was that of actor Ali Zafar, who was accused of allegedly sexually harassing Meeshah Shafi, a singer and actor, as well as two dozen other women. In response, Zafar filed a civil defamation lawsuit against twenty-five women, including Shafi, and sought a billion rupees in damages. The court accepted his lawsuit, ignoring the allegations against him. Pakistani law enforcement accused the women who had come forward of staging a smear campaign and subsequently placed a gag order on Shafi. Meanwhile, Zafar went on numerous TV programs, sometimes accompanied by his wife, shedding tears and claiming that his accusers were funded by foreign money. In December of 2020, Zafar was awarded the Pride of Pakistan Award, one of the country's highest honors, by the country's president. In response, there was an explosion of anger by feminists with hashtags such as #BoycottAliZafar. Women and their male supporters held protests at screenings of the actor's films and at the Karachi premier of *Teefa in Trouble*.[11]

The #MeToo movement in Pakistan has experienced mixed results. There have been some reforms of existing sexual misconduct laws and greater public awareness. The Supreme Court of Pakistan directed federal and provincial legislatures to simplify and strengthen laws that deal with sexual misconduct, but activists continued to face backlash from former prime minister Imran Khan, who said feminism weakens motherhood, and from conservative legislatures, who called the women's actions shameful and obscene.[12]

Tunisia

Tunisia has some of the more progressive laws in the Middle East pertaining to women's rights. The law enables women to select their own spouse, get divorced, and access birth control and abortion.[13] However, until 2017, 97 percent of sexual harassment cases were never brought to court because the victim did not dare file an official complaint. In 2017, for the first time in the Arab world, the Tunisian parliament passed Law 58 outlawing all forms of violence against women and girls, including marital rape. It also made public sexual harassment punishable by to up a year in prison. As a result, at least on paper, it has become easier to prosecute cases of domestic violence and impose penalties for public sexual harassment.

In 2019 the Tunisian #MeToo movement was galvanized when a legislator was accused of public indecency and sexual harassment. A schoolgirl posted videos on social media of a newly elected member of Parliament, Zouhair Makhlouf, masturbating in his car outside her high school. Makhlouf belongs to the Democratic Progressive Party and is known for his strong support of environmental causes. This was one of the flashpoints that encouraged thousands of Tunisian women to share their personal experiences of sexual assault on #EnaZada Facebook, Tunisia's #MeToo movement. Makhlouf initially avoided prosecution by claiming parliamentary immunity. But in July 2021, when President Kais Saied introduced sweeping executive and legislative powers, he also lifted the political immunity of the members of Parliament. Makhlouf was summoned to court, and in November 2021, he was found guilty of indecent assault and sentenced to a year in prison. This was the first time an influential figure had faced prosecution for sexual abuse in Tunisia.[14]

Turkey

Turkey's #MeToo movement emerged in December 2020 when an anonymous Twitter user calling herself "Leyla Salinger" accused the celebrated novelist Hasan Ali Toptas of sexually harassing her when she was in college. The tweet led many other Turkish women to share similar accusations against Toptas. Subsequent tweets accused several other authors of sexual violence, as well as publisher Ibrahim Colak, who committed suicide in December 2020, leaving behind a suicide note: "After this hour, I cannot look at the face of my wife, children and friends."[15]

Under the hashtag #Uykularimiz Kacsin (#MayYouLoseSleep), survivors of sexual abuse began to share their stories, which they had not formerly done because of fear and shame. When backlash began to grow against Leyla Salinger, the famous journalist and feminist Melis Alphan also shared her story of how as a child she had been violated by a friend of her grandfather's and how the scars of that incident remained with her.[16]

Women struggling for equality in Turkey came under assault with the rise in 2002 of the Islamist Adalet ve Kalkınma Partisi, known in English as the AKP, the Justice and Development Party. In 2014, President Erdogan urged women to have three and then five children. In 2015, Turkey's liberal abortion law was undone, making it nearly impossible to have an abortion in state or private hospitals. Turkish women have suffered dramatically under the current authoritarian nationalist and Islamic fundamentalist government. Femicide has increased since the rise of the AKP. From 2008 to 2017, some 2,500 women were killed. A majority of them (62 percent) were killed by husbands, former husbands, or boyfriends, while 28 percent were killed by relatives.[17]

The high rates of sexual harassment are likely manifestations of this confrontation between female empowerment and Islamist rule. There are laws in Turkey that allow women to press charges of sexual harassment. Perpetrators can be jailed for three months to two years if found guilty, yet the courts do not enforce the law, and in a majority of cases the accused is often found not guilty or the verdict is "postponed."[18] The Turkish government further escalated attacks on women's rights in 2021 by provocatively withdrawing from the 2012 Istanbul Convention Against Domestic Violence, claiming it was a threat to national sovereignty. It did so despite widespread protests, including by the president's own daughter Sumeyye Erdogan Bayraktar, who served on the board of the Woman and Democracy Association.[19]

Egypt

Egypt passed laws against sexual violence and harassment in 2014. The regime of Abdel el-Sisi, a devout Muslim, authorized a National Strategy for Combating Violence Against Women in 2015.[20] But victims generally do not come forward. If a woman brings an accusation of molestation against an unrelated man, authorities often subject her to "virginity tests" and ask about her sexual history. As Alaa Alaswany, an Egyptian novelist, shows in his *Republic of False Truths* (2021), these strategies are also used to politically intimidate women.[21] During the Arab Spring (2011), the police subjected protesting female students to virginity tests as a tactic to traumatize and humiliate them. Rates of domestic violence are also high and seem to be going up. In 1995, one out of every three ever-married women reported being beaten at least once in her marriage. In 2015, 46 percent of ever-married women had experienced violence by their husbands.[22]

Egypt's #MeToo movement began in the midst of the COVID-19 pandemic after Sabah Khodir saw a social media post in which a female student at the American University of Cairo accused classmate Bassam Zaki of being a sexual predator and of blackmailing women. Khodir subsequently took a picture of Zaki and gathered details of alleged sexual abuse about him from countless other women through text messages and voice recordings, which she posted online in June 2020. The post went viral, and the authorities were alarmed. In December 2020, Zaki was sentenced to eleven years in prison for the attempted rape of three women and for drug possession. This led to networks of women joining forces to single out other men who had committed sexual assault. The Egyptian National Council of Women urged women to report their stories and received four hundred complaints within days. An Instagram account called Assault Police was created, providing Arab women everywhere with the opportunity to report assaults and seek resources. The Egyptian Parliament approved a law guaranteeing the anonymity of the participants. By November 2020, Assault Police had more than two hundred thousand followers. Khodir began connecting victims to psychiatrists, while Noor El-Gohary, a female attorney, took cases to the National Council of Women and the prosecutors' offices. Since then, there has been a push to have more women in the judiciary, since women had been banned from applying for the judiciary for a number of years.[23]

Perhaps the most vocal Egyptian spokesperson of #MeToo is Mona Eltahawy, a *New York Times* journalist who divides her time between New York and Cairo. She was beaten and abused by the Egyptian police while reporting from Tahrir

Square in 2011. She went on to write a highly provocative article in April 2012 for *Foreign Policy* titled "Why Do They Hate Us: The Real War on Women Is in the Middle East," which explored women's lack of freedom and equality in the Arab-Muslim world.[24] Eltahawy also wrote about experiencing molestation during Hajj pilgrimage in Mecca when she was fifteen, and she invited fellow Muslim women to share similar stories of assault using #MosqueMeToo. The hashtag went viral within days, receiving both support and backlash from the global Muslim community. In 2017, she directly confronted Tariq Ramadan, a progressive Swiss-Muslim intellectual and faculty member at Oxford's Saint Anthony's College, who was charged with the rape of two women. Ramadan, an important public intellectual, is the grandson of Hasan al-Banna, founder of the Muslim Brotherhood of Egypt. In 2004, he was featured by *Time Magazine* as one of the hundred most influential people of the world. After the investigation into the charges, he went on a leave of absence from his job and has since been convicted of the rape of five women.[25] In writing about the challenges that Muslim feminists face, such as when she was dissuaded from speaking out against Ramadan because he is a prominent Muslim intellectual who has been under attack by Western Islamophobes, Eltahawy wrote,

> We Muslim women are caught between a rock and a hard place—a trap presenting near-impossible obstacles for exposing sexual violence. The rock is an Islamophobic right wing in other cultures that is all too eager to demonize Muslim men ... The hard place is a community within our own faith that is all too eager to defend Muslim men against all accusations.[26]

Algeria

In Algeria, #WeWillNoLongerProtectSexualAbusersAfterToday was launched in response to the widespread harassment of women in public spaces with the complicity of the police. Blogger Ryma posted a tearful Instagram video stating that she was on the streets at 6:00 p.m. when a passerby harassed her by telling her she should be in the kitchen. When she filed a complaint, she was told by the police that she should not have been out at that time of the day anyway. The video sparked an explosion among Algerian women, who said such instances were all too common and that it did not matter if the women observed the hijab. One wrote,

> When you can't ride a bus or train without the occasional groping
> When you can't walk a few meters in town without someone harassing you

When you don't feel safe in your skin anymore

Enough is enough.²⁷

In November 2020, a group of Algerian actresses joined these protests. They listed cat calls, hissing, and other misogynistic expressions that women experience daily while walking on the streets, along with verbal expressions such as "Where's that dinner?," "Put down your brother's bike and go home!," and "When you're married, you'll stop working at the university," or hateful ones such as "If he hit her, she must have been asking for it."²⁸

Palestine

In Palestine, the public struggle against harassment began with Yasmeen Mjalli, a 21-year-old Palestinian woman. She had started her #NotYourHabibti (Not Your Sweetheart) a few months before #MeToo took off by painting her slogan on T-shirts and denim jackets sewn by women from across the West Bank and Gaza. As interest grew, she sat behind a black typewriter in front of the City Hall of Ramallah, the de facto capital of the West Bank, and asked women passing by to anonymously tell her their stories of harassment, which she then typed up and posted on social media. The black typewriter is well known for its original use by the Israeli authorities, who typed up permissions for Palestinians wanting to enter or exit the territories. Mjalli used it as a tool for bringing greater attention to the subject of violence against women, not so subtly comparing Palestinian men who harass women with the Israeli soldiers who occupy the Palestinian territories.

Her stories have had a great impact, even among children. An eight-year-old boy, for instance, was excited because someone was fighting to give "his mom and his sisters their rights."²⁹ While the violence of the Israeli state against Palestinian women activists is well documented in regional and international media, discussions of domestic violence and honor killings and public sexual harassment remain taboo issues within the Palestinian community. Not everyone has reacted positively to #NotYourHabibti. Some dismissed Mjalli as a "foreigner," despite her local roots; others denied that sexual harassment was a real issue or, worse, blamed the women for bringing it upon themselves. Mjalli complained that "often, the occupation is used as an excuse to hide social issues in Palestine."³⁰

The following year in September 2019, another feminist movement known as Taliaat, "Coming Out," brought a hundred women together in Ramallah to protest against domestic violence. Similar demonstrations were organized in Jerusalem, Haifa, Jaffa, Nazareth, and the Gaza Strip, as well as in Beirut and Berlin, calling for a "unified cry" to support Palestinian women. The demonstrations protested the growing rates of femicide in the West Bank and Gaza, as well as among Palestinians inside Israel. The movement was attacked by Palestinian conservatives who accused it of "distorting the image of the Palestinian man to serve outside agendas" and betraying the Palestinian cause. However, Palestinian women continue to insist that their movement is an essential part of the national liberation movement and that "the Freedom of Palestinian women is at the heart of the Palestinian national liberation project."[31]

Who Abuses Women? Who Is Abused?

In our research, we have been interested in the role of patriarchalism, sexism, Islamic piety, and Islamist politics as potential determinants of individual abuse of women. A number of female commentators have pointed to what they understand as fear and hostility toward women within Islamic sharia, and particularly within the Islamist community.[32] Is Islam per se an actual source of men's abuse of women? We will argue that it is patriarchalism—the belief that men have the right and obligation to control women—and sexism—sexual objectification of and discrimination against women—that drive men's abuse of women in the region.

In 2018–19, we used FB banner advertisements[33] to recruit respondents in seven Muslim-majority countries with which they self-identified by having signed up for the FB homepage designed specifically for Algeria, Egypt, Iran, Pakistan, Palestine, Tunisia, and Turkey (Figure A.1). In the case of Iran, which did not allow us to advertise, we used both the blogosphere, which tends to be more liberal, and FB pages created by students from the campuses of the private Azad universities, which draw more traditional middle-class students. Our respondents in these analyses grew up in Muslim homes, were overwhelmingly raised as Muslims, and were all older than eighteen.

Our survey was submitted to two IRB panels, one at the University of California, Santa Barbara, and the other at NYU-Abu Dhabi. Sexual surveys in Muslim-majority nations have typically been done based on convenience samples in institutions of higher education using paper surveys administered in class after obtaining informed-consent forms. These surveys typically find very low levels of intimate female behavior. The fact that one has taken such a survey is visible

Figure A.1 Banner ad used in our FB survey aimed at Iranians: "How do we Love?" Photo credit: Jade Borgeson.

to others, there is a personally identifiable record of one's participation, and there is the possibility that someone can see one's response to sensitive items when filling out the survey or handing in the questionnaire. All of these visibilities are eliminated through an online anonymous survey such as the one we used, where not even an IP address was collected, so that no survey could be linked to a specific computer. Given the sensitivity of the questions asked, and the fact that female respondents are more likely to use computers at home, we provided an exit button on every page in the event that somebody came into the room unexpectedly. We also provided an email address for respondents to communicate their concerns about the survey. The responses we received were overwhelmingly positive, enormously curious about the results, often grateful that we were gathering the data and that our results would eventually become public knowledge.

A total of 4,694 women and 6,133 men completed the survey. We were not sampling young people; we were sampling young national FB users. This meant that respondents were sampled from those who had registered themselves under a particular nation's FB service with which they identified; it did not necessarily mean that they lived there, although 95 percent of our sample did live in the FB country in which they had registered.[34] FB posted our banner advertisements on samples of FB users from these country pages, which took respondents to a landing page where they could take the survey. It was entirely anonymous, and protections were built in that allowed respondents to immediately exit the page.. The survey was fielded in Arabic, Persian, Turkish, and Urdu, with translation and back-translation by native speakers (Table A.1).

Table A.1 Descriptive Statistics of Respondents by Gender

	Women (N = 4,694)		Men (N = 6,133)		Total (N = 10,827)	
	N	%	N	%	N	%
Education						
Primary school or lower	191	4	934	15	1,125	11
Some secondary school	467	10	1,203	20	1,670	16
Finished secondary school	772	17	1,490	25	2,262	21
Some nonreligious university	1,170	25	850	14	2,020	19
Some religious university	21	1	16	0.3	37	0.3
Finished nonreligious university	1,276	27	873	14	2,149	20
Finished religious university	28	1	45	1	73	1
Some graduate education	234	5	205	3	439	4
Finished graduate school	505	11	468	8	973	9
Marital status						
Single	2,731	59	2,740	46	5,471	51
Engaged	351	8	353	6	704	7
Married	1,090	24	2,401	40	3,491	33
Separated	114	3	237	4	351	3
Divorced	233	5	172	3	405	4
Widowed	115	3	101	2	216	2
Age (y)						
19–22	1,487	32	1,163	20	2,650	26
23–30	1,571	34	1,793	31	3,364	32
31–40	878	19	1,450	25	2,328	22
41–50	479	10	881	15	1,360	13
51–58	188	4	505	9	693	7

Note: The N values listed in this table indicate the total number of women, men, or total respondents in our Facebook sample who fall into a category.

Source: Data gathered from the authors' surveys.

To get a basic sense of the sample, we present descriptive statistics of select demographics in Table A.1. Our sample comprises all educational levels. The women in the sample are, on average, much more educated than the men. Four percent of the women had only primary education compared to 15 percent of the men. Thirty-one percent of the women only had secondary education or less whereas 60 percent of the men were in this position, twice the female proportion. The gender gap was also evident in higher education. Twenty-seven percent of female respondents had finished nonreligious university compared to 14 percent of the men.

In terms of marital status, more than half of the female respondents were single, whereas less than half of the men were single. The men in the sample were much more likely than the women to be married—40 percent men versus 24 percent women. The women in our sample were much younger than the men. Thirty-two percent of women were in the age range 19–22 compared to 20 percent of the men. We found the same thing at the other end of the age distribution, where 14 percent of the women were over age 40 compared to 24 percent of the men. These demographic variables had no significant effects on men's reported rates of abuse.

Men's Abuse of Women: The Data

In the Middle East, data on sexual behavior has long been sparse, typically based on convenience samples of students. Data on sexual abuse by men is even more difficult to find. Neither public nor private incidents are regularly reported to authorities, and if they are reported, they are often neither recorded nor acted upon. We wanted to know what kind of men engage in the abuse of women in these societies. Our data centered on two forms of abuse, both involving a woman's body: sexual molestation, that is, touching a woman's body in a public space, and domestic abuse, striking one's wife or partner in private. Male respondents, regardless of marital status, were asked the following questions:

1. Have you ever touched a woman's body in a public place (work, street, public transportation, school, university, or a religious institution)?
2. Have you ever hit your partner in the course of an argument?

A total of 698 men responded that they had touched a woman's body in a public place, while 3,698 men had not. This means around 16 percent of the men in our sample who answered these questions reported having sexually molested a woman in public. A total of 995 men responded that they had hit their wife or partner in the course of an argument, while 1,916 men had not. Thus, around 34 percent of the men in our sample reported having hit their wife or partner. There were 169 men in the sample who reported having both molested a woman in public and hit their wife or partner, which comprises about 3 percent of the sample of men.[35]

Abuse varies by country (see Table A.2). The rate of male self-reported molestation of women in public is highest in Turkey (23.6 percent), Tunisia (21.8 percent), and Algeria (20.4 percent) and lowest in Pakistan (7.9 percent), Iran (11 percent), and Palestine (13.7 percent).[36] The rate of self-reported domestic violence is highest in Algeria (40.5 percent), Egypt (37.4 percent), and Turkey (36 percent) and lowest in Palestine (27.1 percent). The intercountry variation of public molestation is greater than that of domestic abuse, where country rates are more tightly clustered together. The rates of these two forms of abuse have remained stable between our unreported 2012 sample wave and our 2018 wave.

In every country, the percentage of men sampled who engaged in public molestation is lower than the percentage who hit their wives or partners in the private domestic sphere. Men are much more likely—even two, three, or four times more likely—to have hit their wives than to have molested a woman in the street or on public transit. The reason why rates of violence in private toward

Table A.2 Cross-Tabulation of Male Abuse and Respondent Country

	Public molestation***		Domestic violence***	
	N	%	N	%
Algeria ($N = 1,567$)	224	20	229	41
Egypt ($N = 879$)	129	20	205	37
Iran ($N = 444$)	42	11	80	31
Pakistan ($N = 1,937$)	94	8	288	31
Palestine ($N = 418$)	43	14	70	27
Tunisia ($N = 584$)	94	22	73	33
Turkey ($N = 304$)	52	24	50	36

*$p < 0.05$, **$p < 0.01$, ***$p < 0.001$

Note: Chi² tests were used to calculate p-values. N values listed next to the country indicate the total number of male respondents located in each country. The total Ns and percentages indicate the total number of men in our sample who reported perpetrating the listed type of violence. For example, in Algeria, 20.4 percent of men have publicly molested a woman.

Source: Data gathered from the authors' surveys.

wives and partners are so much greater than rates of molestation of female strangers in public, we suggest, is due to two factors. First, the public nature of molestation increases the likelihood that the act will be visible to others. There is a greater risk of detection. Second, when a man molests a woman in public, he is violating the honor of a woman who is under the protection of another man. Not only is there potentially another man—whether father, husband, or brother—who will respond to his infraction on his honor, but if the perpetrator subscribes to patriarchal norms, he will be constrained not to engage in such behavior. This is not because he respects the woman's rights, but because he respects other men's rights over women.

The first thing that we did was to see whether a man's occupation had any effect on his propensity to engage in either form of abuse. There were only three occupational categories—creatives (artists, musicians, actors, and writers), executives and CEOs of private firms, and vendors—that were significantly more likely to engage in public molestation of women. Creatives and vendors were far and away the most likely to engage in sexual molestation in public places.[37] In terms of domestic violence toward women, there were no significant differences between occupations. This confirms the centrality of creatives as perpetrators of sexual aggression singled out by the #MeToo movement in Iran and elsewhere, but only toward strangers in public, not violence toward women in private unions. Occupation does not explain violence toward one's wife. We do not have a good explanation why these three occupations would increase the likelihood of public molestation. It may be that CEOs regard the women who work for them as their property, since the women and their families depend on the CEO for survival, and for this reason these powerful men ignore the patriarchal custom of respecting the property rights of the men whose female relatives work for them. Vendors are in constant contact with women, particularly highly vulnerable domestic workers, a fact that might facilitate their molestation. But the more secular and individualistic creatives/writers/ are in an entirely different category. They are least bound by patriarchal obligations as they are more likely to regard women as individuals and not as the property of the men in their family. Yet paradoxically this very attitude may increase their public molestation of women. Whatever the case, we did not include occupation in our regression models.

Table A.3 examines violence experienced and perpetrated by gender. Given strong modesty norms in the region and sexism in the Middle East more generally, women are viewed as naturally seductive and men as powerless to resist their temptations. Women's sexuality is considered a source of social disorder or

Table A.3 Cross-Tabulation of Abuse Experienced and Perpetrated by Respondent Gender

	Women who were …		Men who have …	
	N	%	N	%
Sexually molested in public	878	24	698	16
Hit by partner***	489	33	351	12
Hit partner***	286	19	995	34

*p < 0.05, **p < 0.01, ***p < 0.001

Note: Chi² tests were completed to calculate p-values. Respondents were asked if they had experienced each of these, so it is possible for people to have experienced multiple forms of violence and to have perpetrated multiple forms of abuse. N values and percentages within the cross-tabulation indicate the N or percentage of the listed gender who have either experienced or perpetrated the listed type of violence. For example, 24.1 percent of women in our sample reported having been sexually molested in public. Additionally, 35.2 percent of women in our sample reported experiencing one or multiple forms of these violence or having perpetrated violence.

Source: Data gathered from the authors' surveys.

fitna. When a woman suffers such aggression, there is often a taint that she must somehow be responsible for the unwanted sexual aggression she received from a man. In an Egyptian survey, taken in 2008, most women believed that women should not report their experiences of sexual harassment to "avoid ruining their reputations" and thus their ability to stay or get married.[38]

It is therefore notable that large numbers of women in our survey nevertheless answered that they had been "sexually molested in a public place (work, street, public transportation, school, university or religious institution." Because our survey was completely anonymous—both in its registration and remote implementation—it seems a much larger number of women admitted to having been publicly molested, as well as hit by their male partners than one might have expected. It may also reflect the impact of the #MeToo movement, which has urged women to come forward to report their abuse. It is important to note that these rates of abuse are based on self-reported behavior. Given the differential stigma in the MENASA region that attaches to female victims as opposed to male perpetrators, we would expect women's self-reports to be much lower than those of men. Undoubtedly, some men who did engage in abuse of women checked that they had not engaged in any of these forms of violence, while they indeed had done so. This appears to be most pertinent to public molestation of women. That the percentage of men who reported molesting women in public is significantly lower than the percentage of women who reported being molested in public suggests an asymmetrical reporting bias, where men underreport their violations.

To get a sense of the validity of our data, we compared the male rates of abuse with female rates of being abused (see Table A.3). While male respondents' self-reported physical violence toward their wives and partners is comparable to what women report (34 percent vs. 33 percent), men's self-reported public molestation of women is much lower than what women report (16 percent vs. 24 percent). There is, of course, a likelihood of underreporting for both women and men for both kinds of event, given the perception of shame involved. That shame is likely to be greatest for women who are molested and men who molest in public, given that this practice is clearly forbidden, while husbands' violence toward women is an expected occasional occurrence in marriage, despite laws against it in many of the countries surveyed. Our results on the rates of domestic violence conform almost exactly with the findings about ever-married Egyptian women two decades ago.[39]

In the case of domestic abuse, the consonance of self-reports of men hitting and women being hit at home are quite close, while men are much less likely to report being hit than women are to report having hit their husbands. The percentage of women who report having hit their husbands (19 percent) is surprising. That almost one in five women has done this suggests that women are far from passive in intra-marital conflicts. For their husbands, this extreme manifestation of disobedience is likely shameful, suggesting that the husband is not the master of his household, which is likely part of the reason only 12 percent of the men report having been hit by their spouses, fiancées, and girlfriends. The stigma for men to admit that their wives struck them is likely greater than that for wives to report that their husbands have struck them.

Two Axes of Division: Islamism and Socialism

There are two major axes of political division in the contemporary Muslim world: Islamism and socialism. We were concerned that our survey would attract modern laicists, the kind of liberal secularists who often offer themselves to and/or are chosen by Western media outlets. We asked our respondents their position on Islamist politics, here measured in terms of their attitude about the extent to which Islamic law should be the, or a, basis of state law. All respondents were asked the following:

1. How would you define your political position?

    a. I support the principle of complete separation of religion and state.

Table A.4 Descriptive Statistics of Support for Islamic Law by Respondent Gender

	Women (N = 2,803)		Men (N = 3,444)		Total (N = 6,247)	
	N	%	N	%	N	%
No Islamic law	785	28	873	25	1,658	27
Some Islamic law	1,069	38	1,143	33	2,212	35
Only Islamic law	949	34	1,428	42	2,377	38

Note: Chi^2 tests were completed to calculate p-values, but no significant values were present. The N values at the top of each gender column count the total number of women, men, or respondents in our sample who answered the Islamic law question. N values and percentages within the cross-tabulation list the number of women or men who support the corresponding level of Islamization of the law. For example, 785 (28 percent) women in our sample oppose any Islamic law in their country. In the sample as a whole, 1,658 (26.5 percent) respondents support a complete secularization of the law. Numbers have been rounded off to the next whole number.

Source: Data gathered from the authors' surveys.

    b.   I believe Islamic law should be one source of the nation's law.
    c.   I believe Islam should be the sole source of the law.

Table A.4 shows that liberal secularists comprise a minority of our respondents. For men, only a quarter of the respondents want a complete separation of mosque and state, with no Islamic law adopted by the nation-state. Another third prefer to have some Islamic law enforced, typically those laws that concern the life cycle and family: marriage and divorce, inheritance and spousal support, child custody, birth, and death. The largest percentage among men, 41.5%, were among Islamists, those who supported the state's adoption of only Islamic law. Women were less likely than men to favor only Islamic law (34 percent) and more likely to favor only some Islamic law (38.1 percent for women; 33.2 percent for men). This difference suggests that there are elements of Islamic law that women do not want enforced by the state. Let us see whether women's selective endorsement of Islamic law is related to its patriarchal aspects.

Islamism, Patriarchalism, and Sexist Eroticism

We analyze acts of male sexual aggression and physical violence toward women. We are particularly interested in untangling the roles of religion, patriarchy, and sexism in conditioning or priming these abusive behaviors. There is no question that many religions, including Islam, Judaism, Christianity, and Hinduism, are associated with highly patriarchal views. The modern religious right, often called "fundamentalist," is associated with patriarchal laws that reinforce those relations, especially subjugation of a wife to her husband.

Is there a relationship between Islamism and support for/engagement in patriarchal and sexist practices? Support for patriarchal familial structures is the bread and butter of Islamist parties.[40] Table A.5 indicates that, for men, there are strong and statistically significant relations between Islamism, understood here as making Islamic law the basis of legislation, and patriarchal beliefs. We have made Islamism into an ordinal variable, such that those who want to apply Islamic law to certain sectors of life are considered somewhat Islamist, those who want to apply only Islamic law are considered Islamist, and those who do not want to apply any Islamic law are considered secularists

Every patriarchal position in our sample garners more male support among Islamists than among those who hold less Islamist positions. We asked respondents the following five items to test this hypothesis (see Table A.5):

1. Should honor killing not be considered the same as murder? That is, be given a more lenient punishment?
2. Should polygamy remain/be legalized?
3. Should men be able to divorce their wives at will?
4. Should husbands be able to determine whether their wives work?
5. Should Muslim women wear the hijab?

Table A.5 Cross-Tabulation of Support for Islamic Law by Patriarchal Beliefs for Men

	No Islamic Law		Some Islamic Law		Only Islamic Law	
	N	%	N	%	N	%
Honor killing is not murder***	417	49	699	63	916	66
Polygamy should be legal***	379	44	785	70	1,050	75
Men should divorce at will***	298	35	453	40	648	46
Men decide if wife works***	345	40	685	61	977	70
Women should wear hijab***	342	40	874	77	1,301	92
Uses the internet for sex	100	12	108	10	127	9
Watches pornography***	238	27	166	15	196	14

*p < 0.05, **p < 0.01, ***p < 0.001

Note: Chi^2 tests were used to calculate p-values. N values and percentages in the cross-tabulation indicate men who support different levels of Islamic law and agree with the listed statements or engage in the listed behaviors. For example, of men who oppose any Islamic law, 11.5 percent use the internet to arrange for sex.

Source: Data gathered from the authors' surveys.

To analyze sexism, we used two indicators, both of which point to the objectification of women as sexual bodies, as opposed to a discriminatory and controlling orientation toward women. We asked respondents the following:

1. Do you use the internet to arrange for sex?
2. Do you watch pornography on the internet?

It is important to note that honor killings are not religiously sanctioned practices but have their roots in tribal Middle Eastern cultures and can be found among all religious denominations of the region. The evidentiary basis required by Islamic law for a lawful killing of a married woman who has voluntarily had sex with a man who is not her husband is so stringent that such executions rarely took place. Historically, fathers and brothers were guardians of a daughter's or sister's chastity, and a family's honor depended on the chastity of the women in that family. Islamist men are much more likely than secularist men (66 percent vs. 49 percent) to think honor killing should not be regarded as murder and that, instead, there should be greater leniency when such killings take place. This does not mean that secularist men oppose sanctions against men who engage in femicide to protect the honor of their families. Forty-nine percent of men who support a secularist position, the belief that Islam should have no bearing on legality, also believe that honor killings should not be considered equivalent to murder. This is a crucial finding that threads through this afterword. Support for patriarchy is relatively independent of Islam and Islamism. A large proportion of men who support the complete separation of religion and state still hold to highly patriarchal views, including laws that exculpate men who murder their kinswomen to salvage their family's honor. And reciprocally, a substantial percentage of Islamist men believe that honor killings are murder and should be treated as such. That Islamist men are significantly less likely to take this position suggests that the Islamist viewpoint is more patriarchal and thus attracts or socializes men who wish this right to be legalized. It does not, however, make Islamism the sole source of patriarchalism.

On the subject of polygamy, explicitly endorsed in the Qur'an, we see a similar phenomenon. Male Islamists are much more likely than secularists to believe that polygamy should be legalized. Almost 75 percent of the Islamists support the legalization of polygamy, including men in countries such as Turkey and Tunisia, where the practice has long been banned. The independent influence of patriarchalism is again evident. Forty-four percent of the secularists in our sample also support the legalization of polygamy. That support for the legalization of polygamy is much greater among Islamists again suggests greater patriarchalism among Islamists. It does not however support the identity of patriarchalism and Islamism. A not insubstantial proportion (25 percent) of Islamist men also oppose the legalization of polygamy.

Polygamous practice itself, as opposed to support for its legality, is not particularly Islamist. Islamist men, men who want the law of the nation-state to be based on Islamic jurisprudence alone, are as likely to be in a polygamous marriage as secularists (see Table A.6). It is support for the legalization of polygamy, not actual engagement in it, that is differentially associated with Islamism. Most men who support the legalization of polygamy do not actually practice it. It is not surprising then that among those who want to exclude Islam as a basis of state law, many still want to keep polygamy legal.

Gender makes a difference in the support for legalization of polygamy. Polygamy is explicitly endorsed in the Qur'an. Yet, men and women do not respond similarly to the contemporary legitimacy of this religious dictate. Sixty-three percent of male Muslim respondents think polygamy should be legal, as opposed to 36 percent of Muslim women (see Table A.7). Polygamy was generally a marker of wealth and a class marker among both the rural and the urban well-to-do. It meant a man had acquired sufficient wealth to take a second wife and hold a major celebration for the event and support any children from such a union. In a world in which men had access to concubines and slaves, historically only a small percentage of them took another wife, such as members of royal families, tribal leaders, and well-to-do merchants and clerics.[41]

Table A.6 Cross-Tabulation of Support of Islamic Law and Polygamous Marriage for Men Who Are in Such Relationships

	No Islamic Law (N = 434)		Some Islamic Law (N = 493)		Only Islamic Law (N = 578)	
	N	%	N	%	N	%
One wife (N = 1,447)	416	96	477	97	554	96
More than one wife (N = 58)	18	4	16	3	24	4

Note: Chi² tests were used to calculate p-values, but there were no significant values present. N values listed under each support for Islamic law column indicate the number of men who support different levels of Islamic law. N values listed next to each polygamous marriage status row indicate the number of men in our sample who have either one wife or more than one wife. The N values and percentages in the cross-tabulation indicate the number of men who support the form of Islamic law and have either one wife or more than one wife. For example, 95.9 percent of men in our sample who do not support any Islamic law have one wife.

Source: Data gathered from the authors' surveys.

Table A.7 Cross-Tabulation of Support of Patriarchalism by Respondent Gender

	Women		Men	
	N	%	N	%
Honor killing is not murder***	1,572	45	2,697	64
Polygamy should be legal***	1,302	36	2,764	63
Men should be able to divorce at will***	845	23	1,770	39
Men decide if wife works***	949	25	2,585	58
Women should wear hijab***	2,588	70	3,271	74
Uses the internet for sex***	35	1	565	9
Watches pornography***	207	4	912	15

*p < 0.05, **p < 0.01, ***p < 0.001

Note: Chi² tests were used to calculate p-values. N values and percentages in the cross-tabulation indicate respondents who agree with the listed statements or engage in the listed behaviors. For example, 4.4 percent of women watch pornography.

Source: Data gathered from the authors' surveys.

In the modern world, polygamy is more a weapon, a powerful threat husbands can use, as opposed to something they actually do. In the event of a conflict with his wife, a husband can threaten her that he will take another wife, even if he will not do it given its high cost and familial complications.[42] In the twenty-first century, polygamy is less something a man does than something he wants to know is possible for him. It can be compared to the way many median-income American men oppose imposing high taxes on the very wealthy because they want to keep that option open for themselves, even as a utopian dream.

The legal right of men to divorce at will is called *talaq*, considered a "reprehensible" act in the Qur'an but still a legal form of divorce within Islamic law. *Talaq*, meaning release, is divorce and is effected by the husband's simple repeated uttering of the formulation of divorce. A man can invoke *talaq* only twice, because upon the third repudiation, the marriage is no longer resumable, unless his former wife marries someone else and then gets a divorce from that man, at which point she can remarry her first husband if she chooses to do so. The tradition goes back to pre-Islamic Arabia, where women could have multiple male partners, just as men could have multiple female partners, so long as they were in different regions.[43] A woman could declare her desire to leave a relationship just as a man could. The children of unions were brought up by the maternal family as the prophet Muhammad himself was until his mother died. The introduction of Islam brought two new changes to the region. Women could no longer have multiple partners (now called *zina*, translated as "adultery"), while men could continue to do so and leave them just as freely as before. In addition, men could have these multiple partners in one location, even in one house.[44] Several countries in our survey have ended the practice of *talaq* and require that divorce proceedings take place in courts (Iran, Tunisia, Turkey), while others (Egypt, Palestine) have not.

Once again (see Table A.8), we see that support for men's right to *talaq*, divorce at will, is associated with Islamism. Islamist men are more likely to support such divorce (46 percent of Islamist men as opposed to 35 percent of secularists). We see that there is support for *talaq* even among secularists. An astonishing proportion of men who believe in separation of religion and state still would like men to have the right to *talaq*. We also see a gender difference in support of *talaq*. Women are more likely to oppose *talaq* than are men as a whole (77 percent vs. 61 percent) (see Table A.7). As with polygamy, Islamism contributes to patriarchalism; it does not explain it. What makes *talaq* different from polygamy is that a much larger percentage of Islamist men, indeed a majority of men who affirm that state law should follow the Qur'an, oppose the legalization of *talaq*.

Table A.8 Cross-Tabulation of Support for Islamic Law by Patriarchal Beliefs for Men

	No Islamic Law		Some Islamic Law		Only Islamic Law	
	N	%	N	%	N	%
Honor killing is not murder***	417	48.8	699	62.8	916	66.1
Polygamy should be legal***	379	44.0	785	69.5	1,050	74.5
Men should divorce at will***	298	34.5	453	40.1	648	46.1
Men decide if wife works***	345	40.1	685	60.7	977	69.5
Uses the internet for sex	100	11.5	108	9.5	127	9.0
Watches pornography***	238	27.4	166	14.6	196	13.8

*p < 0.05, **p < 0.01, ***p < 0.001

Note: Chi^2 tests were used to calculate p-values. N values and percentages in the cross-tabulation indicate men who support different levels of Islamic law and agree with the listed statements or engage in the listed behaviors. For example, of men who oppose any Islamic law, 11.5 percent use the internet to arrange for sex.

Source: Data gathered from the authors' surveys.

Opposition to *talaq* has a long history and is quite widespread, even among pious Muslims because of the way in which husbands have historically used it to abandon women and children. Men have resorted to *talaq* because they no longer wanted the financial responsibility or did not want to have to accommodate or even listen to their spouse's demands. In a number of countries, *talaq* still remains a far more real possibility in a marriage than polygamy or honor killing. For Islamist men, *talaq* may involve not only his own marriage but that of his mother, sisters, daughters, or nieces, making him (the father, son, brother, or uncle) responsible for maintenance of the divorced woman and perhaps her children. It is evident that what gets thematized by Islamist men does not follow the dictates of Islamic law; a considerable number of Islamist respondents are willing to oppose elements of Islamic family law in the Qur'an that they understand as contrary to the interests and preferences of their female family members.

In contrast, a majority of such men support the position that honor killing is not murder, something not prescribed by Islamic law. Honor killing, like polygamy, is more aspirational than real, an imagined actionable potentiality, not something that is actually done with any frequency. Their possibility acts as a source of patriarchal power, indicating the kinds of weapons a father could use to control the intimate life and marital choices of his daughter or the threat that lies there to eliminate the exclusive claims of his wife to his affection and sexual life.

We also examined a husband's right to determine whether his wife should be able to work outside the household. Women in these countries are often highly educated, but their formal rates of participation in the labor force are much smaller than in the rest of the world (Tunisia, 26 percent; Egypt, 15 percent; Palestine, 16 percent, for example).[45] There remains a great deal of opposition to women's work outside the house, not just by husbands but by in-laws and relatives on both sides. Islamist men are much more likely to believe that men should have this authority over their wives than do secularist men (70 percent of the Islamists compared to 40 percent of the secularists; see Table A.8). We find that Islamist men are more likely to believe that husbands should have this right, yet a large proportion of secularist men think so too.

The final patriarchal practice we examined was the obligation of Muslim women to wear the hijab, typically a scarf covering a woman's hair. The hijab is not only a public signal of modesty, and hence of rejection of touching, talking, or being alone with men outside the family, it is also part of the praxis of piety, cultivating a modest self who feels close to God.[46] The hijab has other potential uses for women, from signaling piety to potential Muslim marriage partners, to signaling to men that a woman who observes it should not be harassed, thus allowing Muslim women, particularly daughters from traditional families, to maneuver more easily in mixed-sex public spaces, whether the university, the workplace, cafes, and concerts.[47] Underlying all these uses is the assumption that women's uncovered hair is sexually arousing for men who cannot control themselves and that women's bodies must consequently be controlled to prevent social disorder and the violation of husbands' honor.[48] The requirement that women wear the hijab, strongly promoted by Islamist movements, has become a central symbol of Islamism throughout the Muslim world, a mark of distinct, authentic identity and difference from the West's sensuous commodity culture.

And indeed, it is upon this patriarchal practice that Islamism makes the largest difference in men's and women's support. Islamist men are almost unanimous in their belief that Muslim women wear the hijab (92 percent) as opposed to the division among secularist men, with 40 percent support. Unlike patriarchal restrictions on women working, husband's right to divorce at will, polygamy, and honor killing, women in general are overwhelmingly supportive of the women's obligation to wear the hijab in public, some 70 percent. Where once a voluntary choice by women in traditional families, and then forbidden by authoritarian modernizing regimes like that of the Pahlavi Shah in Iran (1941–79), this suggests that this practice of female public modesty promoted by Islamist parties has become normative, taken for granted among many Muslim women.

That for many young women, however, it is something one must do, not necessarily something one wants to do, is revealed by the explosive country-wide protests led by women in Iran in 2022. That opposition appears to be driven not by opposition to the practice per se but to the state's enforcement of it as well as many other restrictions imposed on women in family law and in the public sphere. It should be, in their view, a woman's choice, neither enforced nor forbidden by the state.

Sexism, Pornography, and Using the Internet for Sex

Turning to sexism, we looked at two indicators: whether men used the internet to watch pornography and whether they used it to arrange for sex. In contrast to the patriarchalism indicators, which measure beliefs, the sexism variables capture actual behavior. These are not indicators of patriarchalism, which involves male power within familial structures. These are extrafamilial practices, both of which entail the objectification of women's bodies as sexual commodities as opposed to the embodiment of a person. In Muslim societies, pornography is generally considered a form of vicarious adultery, as *zina*, or fornication "of the eye," looking at what is forbidden. In the case of pornography, religious cosmology does make a significant and substantial difference. Islamists are dramatically less likely than secularists to report that they watch pornography (14 percent vs. 27 percent; see Table A.8). This does not mean that they never do it. One in seven Islamist men admits to watching pornography. Islamism does not support such erotic sexism; if anything, it suppresses it. Secularist men are twice as likely to report that they watch pornography as Islamist men.

In regard to men's use of the internet to arrange sex, presumably with strangers who offer sexual services in exchange for payment, or the use of social media to arrange casual sexual encounters, a relatively small percentage (9 percent) of Islamist men engage in this practice (see Table A.8). Although Islamist men are marginally less likely (11 percent) than secularists to do so, the difference between Islamist and secular men is not statistically significant. In terms of the normative dictates of Islamic practice, these results are not surprising. In fact, Islamist men are much more likely to foreswear pornography and just as likely as secular men to use the internet to obtain one or another form of sexual access. Islamist men are much more likely to support patriarchal practices and less likely to engage in erotic objectification of women's bodies. Islamism dramatically reinforces patriarchalism but does offer some protection against the commodification of women's erotic bodies.

What about women? We first looked at the aggregate difference between women and men, regardless of their political stance on the Islamization of state law. There is a gender difference in support for patriarchal practices (see Table A.7). Muslim women overwhelmingly oppose honor killing, polygamy, men's ability to divorce at will, and a husband's right to decide if his wife works. Although the difference is statistically significant, the magnitude of the gender difference for the hijab is not that great. Aside from this item, there is an explosive gender divide around patriarchal practices.

Irrespective of women's stance on the role of Islamic law, thus aggregating both Islamists and secularists—the data show that women are much less supportive of patriarchal practices: honor killing (45 percent vs. 64 percent), polygamy (36 percent vs. 63 percent), divorce at will (23 percent vs. 39 percent), a husband's right to decide if his wife works (25 percent vs. 58 percent), and wearing the hijab (70 percent vs. 74 percent). The general differences between men and women are all quite large, with the exception of the hijab, where there is only a 4 percent difference between male and female support. With regard to using the internet to arrange for sex, the proportionate gender differences are even greater: less than 1 percent of women use the internet to find sex compared to 9 percent of the men, and 4 percent watch pornography compared to 15 percent of the men.

Gender differences of such magnitudes need to be decomposed. Just as we saw support for patriarchal practices among non-Islamist men, indicating the relative autonomy of patriarchalism from Islamism, the question is whether we will see a parallel phenomenon among Islamist women, where Islamist women are more likely to support some women's rights positions, indicating the relative autonomy of gender politics from Islamism. To assess this possibility, we did the same cross-tabulation of women's support for Islamism and attitudes about patriarchal practices and engagement in sexist eroticism that we conducted for men (see Table A.9).

Does Islamism have the same effect on women's support for patriarchal practices as it did for men? Support for Islamism, here the state's application of Islamic law, has exactly the same pattern of significant effects on support for patriarchal practices among women that it did among men (see Table A.9). Women who support Islamism are more likely than their secularist counterparts

Table A.9 Cross-Tabulation of Support for Islamic Law by Patriarchal Beliefs for Women

	No Islamic Law		Some Islamic Law		Only Islamic Law	
	N	%	N	%	N	%
Honor killing is not murder***	223	29	474	45	457	50
Polygamy should be legal***	129	18	412	39	482	52
Men should divorce at will***	139	18	262	25	260	29
Men decide if wife works***	72	9	259	24	291	31
Women should wear hijab***	230	30	839	79	875	93
Uses the internet for sex	9	1	9	1	7	1
Watches pornography***	69	9	44	4	23	2

*$p < 0.05$, **$p < 0.01$, ***$p < 0.001$

Note: Chi^2 tests were used to calculate p-values. N values and percentages in the cross-tabulation indicate women who support different levels of Islamic law and agree with the listed statements or engage in the listed behaviors. For example, of women who oppose any Islamic law, 1.2 percent use the internet to arrange for sex.

Source: Data gathered from the authors' surveys.

to contend that honor killing is not murder, that divorce at will by men is acceptable, that husbands should have the ultimate authority to decide if their wives work, that women should don the hijab, and to support the legalization of polygamy. Islamist women are much less likely to watch pornography than their secularist counterparts. And there is no significant difference in the use of the internet to arrange for sex, a very marginal practice for both. Islamism matters for women's support for patriarchal practices, just as it does for men.

But there is a distinction in these differences: the difference that Islamism makes is not the same for women and men. Islamist women differ from Islamist men in their degree of support for patriarchal practices both in terms of the raw magnitude of their support and in terms of the impact of Islamism on such support (see Table A.10). We looked at the gap between the percentage of Islamist men and women who support and/or engage in patriarchal practices and sexist eroticism. And we also looked at the difference that men and women's Islamism made to their support/engagement by calculating the disparity in the Islamist effect on such support between Islamist and secularist men and women (see Table A.10). The first is a measure of gender difference between Islamist men and women; the second, a measure of the disparity Islamism makes by gender.

With one exception, for every patriarchal practice, Islamist women are less likely to support it than are their male Islamist counterparts. For example, 66 percent of Islamist men support honor killing compared to 50 percent of

Table **A.10** Gender Differences Among Islamists in terms of Patriarchal Practices

	Women (%)	Men (%)	Islamist-Secularist Difference Men (%)	Islamist-Secularist Difference Women (%)
Honor killing is not murder	50	66	21	17
Polygamy should be legal	52	75	34	31
Men should be able to divorce at will	29	46	11	11
Men decide if wife works	31	70	22	29
Women should wear hijab	93	92	62	50

Note: The first two columns indicate the percentage of Islamist women and men who support patriarchal practices. The second two columns indicate the metric difference in the percentage of women and men supporting each patriarchal practice for Islamists and secularists.

Source: Data gathered from the authors' surveys.

Islamist women. Within the Islamist community, the gender difference in support for a husband's right to determine whether his wife works is particularly large, 70 percent of Islamist men compared to 31 percent of Islamist women, a 39 percent gap.

The one exception is support for the hijab: Islamist women are overwhelmingly supportive, even slightly more than the men: 93 percent of women versus 92 percent of men. This is also the patriarchal practice where Islamism makes the greatest difference, a 62 percent difference between Islamists and secularists for men and a 50 percent difference for women. Support for the hijab appears to be the anchor of Islamist political identity, shared widely within the Islamist community by men and women alike. On this policy alone, there is a clear gender consensus within the Islamist community. But for every other patriarchal policy, there is a significant gender gap in support even within the Islamist community.

Islamist women who support such practices may have different motives. One might argue that they, like their male counterparts, understand Islamic law as divinely mandated. One cannot pick and choose which laws one wants everybody to follow and which law one does not. This does not, however, explain why women would be less likely to support honor killing, which is not within the ambit of Islamic law. Another possibility is that patriarchalism itself comes as a package and that women understand the costs they must bear as offset by the advantages they are awarded, whether it is the ability to find an appropriate husband, remain at home and receive financial support as they raise the couple's children, or in general the right to expect to be protected and provided for by their husbands and male folks. If this is the case, then our data suggest that for a large percentage of Islamist women, this package has become unacceptable. Only 29 percent of Islamist women, for example, believe that their husbands should have the legal right to divorce them at will; only 31 percent believe that husbands should have the right to decide whether or not they work. The data suggest that these forms of disempowerment of women are not acceptable to a large percentage not just of women but Islamist women as well.[49] It accords with our finding that a larger percentage of women, as opposed to men, want only *some* Islamic laws, not all of them, to be the law of the land. All of the practices where there is a large gender difference within the Islamist community are those that explicitly grant men control over women and differentially benefit them. Islamist women do not approve.

Six themes emerge from this data. First, there is a significant relationship between Islamism and support for patriarchalism. Islamist men and women were much more likely than secularist men to endorse patriarchal practices.

Second, there are both large percentages of non-Islamist men who similarly support patriarchalism and large percentages of Islamist men who oppose these patriarchal elements. Third, men are much more likely than women to support patriarchal practices. This is true for honor killing, polygamy, divorce at will, and the husband's right to decide if his wife is allowed to work outside the home. Fourth, women are more likely to oppose patriarchal practices, and are less likely to support the wholesale application of Islamic law in general. Fifth, *talaq*—divorce at a man's will—is the element of practice that elicits most opposition by all men, including Islamist men. And finally, secularist men are much more likely to engage in the erotic sexist practice of pornography than are Islamist men.

Support for patriarchal practices is shared by Islamist and secularist Muslims. Although Islamists are more supportive of patriarchalism than secularists, Islamism cannot be conflated with patriarchalism.[50] The relations of Islamism to patriarchalism and to sexism are not the same. Islamism indicates support for protective—read "controlling"—forms of patriarchalism but not for erotic sexism. We also found that sexism is not an important determinant of sexual abuse of women. Pornography objectifies unknown women's bodies with whom one has an imaginary sexual relationship. In the Muslim legal tradition, it easily assimilates to fornication of the eye or simulated adultery. Having a relationship with a woman who is understood to be under the protection of another male is haram, forbidden, in Islamic law. Here, Islamism makes a big difference, cutting the rate of watching pornography in half.

Most men in our survey do not abuse women, either in public or private. As stated earlier, around 16 percent of men reported having sexually molested a woman in public, while 34 percent of men reported having hit their wife or partner. We examined what beliefs and actions affect the propensity of men to perpetrate violence against women. Islamism has long been associated with fighting Western feminism, which is perceived to be a neocolonial violation of a distinctive Muslim culture, where men and women are understood to have God-given gender roles in which women are expected to subordinate their personal interests to those of the family and their preferences to those of their husbands.[51] Islamists have consistently pushed for laws that subordinate women to men through personal status and family law. Given these reasons, we tried to see if individual Islamist men in our survey were more likely than other men to abuse women in public, because the women's presence as independent, unaccompanied beings in public space offend them. We concluded that Islamist men in our survey were not more likely than other men to molest women in public. This would suggest that sexual molestation, beyond the play of individual desire, might be a personal political tool of men from various religious persuasions to fight feminism and to express the sense of resentment some men feel as they witness the erosion of male privileges.

Socialism, Sexism, and Patriarchy

Socialism is the other major axis of political division in the modern Muslim world. Does political-economic ideology have an impact on the way Muslim men treat women? Socialism generally involves a commitment to economic equality between classes, races, regions, and genders. In the Muslim world, socialist regimes and political parties, such as Nasser's Egypt, the Syrian or Iraqi Arab Socialist Ba'athist regime, or the Iranian communist Tudeh Party, notably increased opportunities for women to achieve higher levels of education and professional, managerial, and technical positions.[52]

One might expect that men who hold socialist views would be less likely to abuse women, since they should believe that women have the same inherent rights as they do. Yet there is considerable evidence, despite their avowed commitment to the equality of women and men, that left parties and movements around the world have operated in a sexist manner, because not only is the leadership dominated by men but because women are also predominantly confined to subordinate, gender-typed roles. Furthermore, there is evidence that female comrades are often subject to precisely the harassment and molestation we are attempting to predict.[53] Few have pointed to these experiences as a spur to the emergence of the feminist movement in the United States and elsewhere in the 1970s and today among African American feminists in the United States.[54]

We asked respondents about their ideal form of political economy. Our survey question reads as follows:

1. What is your ideal form of political economy for your country?

    a. A free market economy with very low taxes where health care, education, and housing are not guaranteed.
    b. A social democracy with higher taxes and a high level of government-provided health care, education, and housing.
    c. A socialist state control of the economy where health care, education, and housing are free.

Table A.11 Cross-Tabulation of Male Political Economy Beliefs and Patriarchal Beliefs

	Free Market		Social Democracy		Socialist State	
	N	%	N	%	N	%
Honor killing is not murder	451	56	537	57	537	61
Polygamy should be legal***	563	69	563	59	573	65
Men should have the right to divorce at will*	375	46	372	39	376	42
Men decide if wife works***	476	59	479	50	561	63
Uses the internet for sex	96	12	85	9	95	11
Watches pornography***	151	18	216	23	141	16

*p < 0.05, **p < 0.01, ***p < 0.001

Note: Chi² tests were used to calculate p-values. Each N value and percentage in the cross-tabulation lists the number of men in the sample who hold the corresponding political economy belief and engage in the listed behavior or hold the patriarchal belief. For example, of men who believe in a free market economy, 11.7 percent use the internet to arrange for sex.

Source: Data gathered from the authors' surveys.

We wanted to know if socialists are less likely to support patriarchalism and engage in erotic sexism. Table A.11 cross-tabulates support for socialism, social democracy, and a free market with patriarchal and sexist beliefs. Those who support a free market, grounded in the play of individual desires and the supply of commodities that are the objects of those desires, are more likely to watch pornography compared to socialists but less likely to do so than social democrats. Although the magnitude of the difference is not great, particularly when compared to the effects of Islamist belief, the free-marketeers are also most likely to support the legality of polygamy, but again the substantive difference is small, a 4 percent difference between the free-marketeers and socialists.

The same goes for their large support for divorce at will. Supporters of the free market are less likely to believe a husband has the right to decide whether his wife enters the labor market than socialists but more likely than social democrats to believe so. This difference is consistent with the liberal ideology; however, once again the difference is relatively small, 4.3 percent compared to socialists. These small differences were wiped out in the regression analyses, such that support for socialism had no effect on men's propensity to control or abuse women. We subsequently dropped this variable from the analysis, not only because it has no effect on our dependent variable but also because its inclusion both reduced our N and also the significance of the patriarchal and sexist independent variables.

Table A.12 Cross-Tabulation of Political Position and Islamic Beliefs of Men

	No Islamic Law		Some Islamic Law		Only Islamic Law	
	(N = 710)		(N = 852)		(N = 905)	
	N	%	N	%	N	%
Free market (N = 748)***	245	35	254	30	249	28
Social democracy (N = 892)***	285	40	337	40	270	30
Socialist state (N = 827)***	180	25	261	31	386	43

*p < 0.05, **p < 0.01, ***p < 0.001

Note: Chi^2 tests were used to calculate p-values. The N values under each column indicate the number of men who reported believing in the listed type of Islamism and also answered the political economy question. The N value next to each row header indicates the number of men who believe in the corresponding type of political economy and also responded to the Islamic law question. Each N and percentage in the cross-tabulation list the number of men who support or reject Islamism and have particular beliefs about the political economy. For example, of men who hold secular beliefs, 34.5 percent believe in the free market.

Source: Data gathered from the authors' surveys.

To get a sense of the political cosmologies of our male respondents—the ways in which our respondents position themselves on these two axes of worldview—we cross-tabulated male responses with the Islamist and socialist scales (see Table A.12). We already discovered that patriarchalism is shared across the Islamist-secular divide. Do Islamists and secularists differentially support different political-economic ideologies? Secularists were most likely to support social democracy, as were those who favor that Islamic law be confined to family and life-cycle matters. Islamists, on the contrary, were most strongly supportive of socialism. On its face, this is a surprising result. Islam has a long history of support for private property,[55] a tenet shared by the merchant class from whose communities Islamist movements have drawn many of their most ardent supporters.[56] Moreover, Islamists have a long history of hatred for communist ideology, which their thinkers denounce as materialistic and animalistic. In *Milestones*, Sayyid Qutb, the Egyptian -Islamist scholar who wrote the most important theological mandate for jihad against Nasser's Arab Socialism, condemned the communist grounding of political order in nature, such that "the basic needs of human being are considered identical with those of animals, that is, food and drink, clothing, shelter, and sex."[57] Nonetheless, since the late 1920s, and influenced by Soviet Russia, communist themes of social justice and anti-imperialism have made their way into the Islamist discourse, as evidenced even half a century later by the centrality of the sociologist Ali Shariati in the 1979 Iranian Revolution.[58]

In our sample, there is no majority support for a free market, whether among secularists or Islamists. One might have expected more support for a free-market society among Islamists given the long tradition of respect for private property and the strong support of Islamism among the merchant class. In fact, only 28 percent of Islamists support the neoliberal position (see Table A.12). Among secularists and those who confine the legal applicability of Islam to personal status issues, the most popular position is social democracy, a market economy moderated by a welfare state. Among Islamists, the most popular political position is socialism, with close to 43 percent supporting this option. Given the long durée of hostility to communism, with its derogation of the public status of religion, if not the permissibility of religious practice and education per se, this is surprising, though it does confirm the view that Islamism took many of its economic doctrines from earlier communist or socialist movements of the region, including Russian Communism, the Tudeh Communist Party of Iran, the Arab Socialism of Nasser, and the Ba'athists of Iraq and Syria.[59] Indeed, 73 percent of Islamists in our sample do not support the neoliberal position. This suggests that the Islamists in the countries we sample are not necessarily against certain progressive political-economic policies with regard to the economy, including those measures that benefit poor women (e.g., women's elementary and high school education, child and maternity care, greater access to clean water, electricity, public transportation, food, etc.). Islamists, starting with the Muslim Brotherhood of Egypt, which began in the late 1920s, have supported such measures in Egypt[60] and also did so after the 1979 Iranian Revolution.[61]

Accounting for Variation in Muslim Male Abuse

Secularism and socialism, do these epic cosmologies that have animated Muslim modernity, protect women? The issue is whether acts of male abuse in public and private actually have anything to do with men's support for Islamism or socialism per se, and/or does abuse have patriarchalism and sexism as their deeply penetrated sources. Islamist men are more likely to have patriarchal views, but so do large proportions of non-Islamist men. We seek to isolate the net effect of patriarchalism from that of support for an Islamist state. To do so, we use nested logistic regression analyses in which we estimated equations predicting the likelihood of individual men in our survey perpetrating sexual molestation in public and domestic violence in private based on patriarchal and sexist beliefs and actions, controlling for support for Islamism and socialism. In the nested models, we initially included measures of the two political cosmologies: Islamism, the notion that all the laws of the state should be consistent with the dictates of the Qur'an, and socialism, the notion that the state should regulate the economy in the interests of collective needs rather than private interests, as in the capitalist market. Support for political Islam is very different from one's piety and commitment to Islam. We also controlled for Islamic piety, measured by how frequently male respondents pray. The practice of prayer affords and signals the desire for a personal relationship with God. It is not a political stance on the position of Islam within the state, but in the soul of the adherent. Including it allows us to parse the effects of Islamic piety as opposed to Islamism.

Because our dependent variables, the variables whose variation we seek to account for, are dichotomous binaries—yes, I have molested a woman in public (coded 1); no, I have not (coded 0)—we use logistic regression models. Unlike a standard regression, which has a linear functional form, this form approximates an S-curve, which is more consonant with a dichotomous dependent variable. When considering logistic regression, the reader should think of the odds in gambling, not the percentage of men who engage in a particular practice. Logistic regression generates odds ratios, which indicate the odds of engaging in molestation of, or physical violence against women based on any of the independent variables, such as belief in polygamy or watching pornography. The odds ratio is estimated at the sample average of each independent variable. The coefficients measure the shift in the odds due to a one-unit change in the independent variable. For dichotomous independent variables, there is only one unit change, no to yes, 0 to 1. An odds ratio coefficient of less than 1 indicates a negative relationship, in which the odds decline with changes in the independent variable; a ratio of more than 1 indicates a positive relationship, in which the odds increase with changes in the independent variable. Logistic regression results are displayed in Table A.13. For example, those men who use the internet to arrange for sex are 170 percent more likely to engage in public molestation than men who do not (2.70 − 1.00 = 1.70). Men who pray more frequently are 27 percent less likely to engage in public molestation of women (.73 − 1.00 = −.27).

The analyses of public molestation and private physical violence in Table A.13 are based on the sample of men currently or formerly in a relationship. We included only those men who are married, whether formally or informally, are in a relationship, or have been divorced, separated, or widowed.

Table A.13 Nested Logistic Regression Predicting Sexual Abuse Behaviors by Patriarchal Beliefs of Male Respondents Currently or Formerly in Relationships, Odds Ratios

	Public 1	Public 2	Private 1	Private 2
Honor killing is not murder	1.13	1.15	1.60***	1.61***
	(0.18)	(0.19)	(0.20)	(0.20)
Polygamy beliefs				
Polygamy should be legal	0.90	0.98	1.26	1.32*
	(0.16)	(0.18)	(0.18)	(0.19)
In a polygamous marriage	1.73	1.57	2.19*	2.07*
	(0.62)	(0.57)	(0.67)	(0.64)
Men should divorce at will	0.92	0.93	1.28*	1.29*
	(0.15)	(0.15)	(0.16)	(0.16)
Husband decides if wife works	1.45*	1.50*	1.37*	1.39*
	(0.25)	(0.26)	(0.18)	(0.18)
Women should wear the hijab	0.70	0.86	1.15	1.29
	(0.13)	(0.18)	(0.18)	(0.22)
Internet uses				
To arrange for sex	2.86***	2.70***	1.31	1.23
	(0.66)	(0.62)	(0.28)	(0.27)
Watches pornography	1.85**	1.77**	1.52*	1.47*
	(0.35)	(0.34)	(0.25)	(0.24)
Islamism and piety				
Only Islamic law		0.82		0.98
		(0.19)		(0.17)
Some Islamic law		0.92		0.94
		(0.20)		(0.16)
# Times pray per day		0.73***		0.80**
		(0.06)		(0.05)
Constant	-1.790***	-1.526***	-1.455***	-1.248***
	(0.19)	(0.20)	(0.16)	(0.17)
Observations	1,279	1,279	1,279	1,279
Log Likelihood	-558.1	-550.5	-820.1	-814.5

*p < 0.05, **p < 0.01, ***p < 0.001

Note: Chi² tests were used to calculate p-values. Public models (Public 1 and Public 2) analyze public molestation behaviors. Public 1 analyzes public molestation without Islamism and piety included in the regression, while Public 2 includes these variables in the analyses. Private models (Private 1 and Private 2) analyze domestic violence behaviors. Private 1 analyzes domestic violence without Islamism and piety included in the regression, while Private 2 includes these variables in the analyses. We nest these regressions to determine the influence of Islamism and piety on public molestation and domestic violence outcomes. Standard errors are in parentheses.

Source: Data gathered from the authors' surveys.

Support for Islamism, in itself, has no effect on whether an individual man molests women in public places or hits them in private. Islamic piety, as indicated by the frequency of prayer, actually reduces the likelihood of an individual man's violence toward women, both in public and private. It is patriarchalism that sustains male aggression toward women, but only at home. Patriarchal beliefs have only one significant effect on variations in sexual molestation of women in public places. Belief that a husband has the right to keep his wife from working increases the odds of molestation by 50 percent when controlling for Islamism. Patriarchalism has no other significant effects on public molestation.

But patriarchal beliefs do, with one exception, have consistently significant and substantial effects on physical violence toward one's own wife or partner. Belief in the legalization of polygamy increases the odds of hitting one's wife by 32 percent when controlling for Islamism. Being in a polygamous marriage dramatically increases the odds of abusing one's wife by 107 percent. Believing that honor killing is not murder increases the odds of spousal violence by 61 percent. Believing that a man should legally be able to divorce his wife by unilateral repudiation increases the odds of violence by 29 percent. Marriage to a patriarchal husband puts a woman at risk.

That patriarchalism has no significant effect on molestation of women in public, while having significant and substantial effects on violence toward one's wife in private, calls for an explanation. One possibility is that patriarchalism works through the sense that wives and daughters are viewed as the private property of husbands and fathers, to be controlled, guarded, and protected. Those with such views see their wives and partners as necessarily subordinate to them. If these women lead their own lives without obtaining the approval of their husbands and, worse, do not obey them when they are forbidden from, for example, wanting to work outside the house, men may feel that they are entitled, indeed expected, to discipline them.

In contrast, in the case of public molestation, the women targeted in public are strangers, over which these men have no rights. Moreover, these women are assumed to be the responsibility of, and to have to answer to, some other man, whether father, brother, or husband. To molest them would be to encroach on the property rights of other men—indeed, to undermine these men's exclusive right to control them. This might be the reason patriarchalism does not convert to personal abuse of anonymous women in public, while having a strong relation to violence at home. When we control for these patriarchal beliefs, we see that it is patriarchalism, not political Islam per se, that drives men's abuse of women.

This indicates that men who are not Islamists are just as likely to engage in violence against women as Islamist men.

Islamist State Ideology

In terms of Islamism, our analysis has centered on the Islamist attitudes of individual men, not on the effect of an Islamist state on abusive male behaviors. The practices of Islamist states make a huge difference to women's safety and even her survival. For example, in the case of Iran, human rights attorney Mehrangiz Kar documented the dramatic increase in domestic violence after the 1979 Islamic Revolution by studying court cases of men charged with extreme violence and murder against their wives. Rates of child marriage shot up; men regained the right to *talaq* and to polygamy; tolerance of honor killings was restored; and guardianship of children reverted to fathers. In addition, according to the sharia, the monetary value of the life of a woman (*dīyah*) was declared to be worth half of a man's. This meant that when a husband killed his wife, her family had to pay the man's family a substantial sum before he could be punished. Since most families could not come up with that kind of money, the murderer was eventually set free. As Kar recalled, a young girl would be forced into marriage by her parents. After marriage, it was not uncommon for a husband who had lost interest in his wife to torment her, usually by severe beatings and burning parts of her body with cigarettes and kabab skewers, in order to force her to renounce her financial compensation upon divorce, known as *mahr*. She could not leave him, because her parents and the authorities would ignore her pleas and she did not want to lose custody of her children. She had no money, because she was not allowed to work without her husband's permission. At a certain point, the beatings would become intolerable. If she still did not agree to give up her *mahr*, her husband might accuse her of infidelity and murder her. When the authorities charged him with the murder, he claimed it was a justified honor killing. When his claim was proved to be false, the family of the woman would be told to come up with the *dīyah* compensation to make up for the difference in the value of the life of a woman and a man. The family either could not or did not want to pay such a hefty price for an already dead daughter, and so the case would be dropped, and the murderer would get off with a minimal sentence. The accounts given by the male perpetrators, and compiled by Kar, are filled with patriarchal intent—accusations of infidelity, their desire to control the women's movements, the men's efforts to expropriate their wife's inherited jewelry or property, complaints that they talked to neighbors or burnt the food.[62] There is no recourse to irreligiosity—for example, that a woman did not pray or fast. Indeed, most of the men did not seem particularly religious themselves.

The practices of Islamist states do dramatically affect patterns of male abuse, effects that we can see in our data. Take the case of sexual molestation of women in public. In Islamist states such as Iran and Pakistan, sex segregation is enforced in many public spaces, thereby reducing the opportunity for molestation. In Iran, for example, in the early years of the revolution, any unauthorized form of contact between a man and woman, be it sexual harassment or a simple consensual date, could result in draconian punishments by the state. In the first case, only the man was punished, while in the second, both were punished. Moreover, sexually aggressive behavior by men in public is often seriously sanctioned by the police. Sometimes, as in Iran, special agents are specifically charged with monitoring such things.

Looking at the country-specific rates of public molestation of women in our sample, we see they are lowest in Iran, Palestine, and Pakistan, three states in which family law is heavily derived from the sharia. In the case of men's abuse of women in private, here, too, the patriarchal practices of Islamist regimes seem to make a difference. Recall that it was here that patriarchal attributes mattered most to male behavior. Examining the Iranian case, the Islamic Republic dramatically transformed the ability of married women to obtain divorce in the event that their husbands abused them. Before the 1979 Revolution, women whose husbands beat them could sue for divorce and then barter their alimony in return for custody of their children. After the revolution, the conditions under which women could sue for divorce were radically constricted. Being hit by your husband was not a sufficient reason for divorce. This eliminated a major constraint on husbands striking their wives. Looking at country-specific rates of private abuse of women, Palestine, Iran, and Pakistan, the three states which have historically drawn heavily on sharia to limit women's rights—including allowing polygamy, divorce at will, wife beating, and honor killings—have significantly lower rates of domestic violence.[63] We can conjecture that women in these countries are more likely to silently endure their subordination, partly to give their husbands less opportunity to inflict violence upon them.[64]

Sexism also matters, and for both forms of abuse. Men who regularly watch pornography are significantly more likely both to sexually molest women in public and to beat them up in private. Research suggests that men who regularly watch pornography are more likely to regard women as "objects and orifices—something to be penetrated, slammed against, ejaculated on."[65] This finding suggests that those who derive pleasure from such sexual objectification of women are more likely to be violent toward women as well. Men who use the internet to arrange for sex are also more likely to sexually molest women in public, but they are not more likely to hit them in private.[66]

Finally, we analyzed the net effect of political economic ideology. Like Islamism, support for socialism has absolutely no significant net effects on either form of abuse. What this means is that men who consider themselves socialists are just as likely as other men to engage in both public harassment and domestic violence.

Conclusion and Discussion

Muslim men's violence toward women does not have a religious color. In fact, men who pray regularly are less likely to sexually harass women in public or physically abuse them in private. Nor does male violence have, in itself, a clear political color. Islamists and secularists, socialists and neoliberals all engage in violence. Socialist men are just as likely to engage in public and private abuse of women as other men.

Patriarchalism, the belief that men have the right and obligation to control women, and sexism, the sexual objectification of women, are primary vectors of risk for women. But they are very different in their effects. Patriarchalism is strongly associated with domestic violence toward women, while sexism is strongly associated with both public molestation of women and violence toward them at home. Islamism contributes to the abuse of women by promoting patriarchalism.

We found that men who want to live under a socialist state were not that different from those who preferred a free-market economy in terms of their support for patriarchal practices. The one area where there was a significant difference was in terms of men's right to control whether their wives worked outside the house: Socialist men, a significant number of whom were Islamists as well, were much more likely to support a man's right to control their wives than those who idealized the free market. This makes sense in that in free markets, both men and women are regarded as independent actors equally able to act upon their preferences. A socialist state, in contrast, can legitimately override market processes in order to achieve social goods, here a God-given essential difference between women and men. Our survey indicates that neither secularism nor socialism, as currently understood, are antidotes to men's abuse of women. Both sexism and patriarchalism are ancient and based on our results are to some extent independent of both Islamism and socialism. The sharing of sexism and patriarchalism between the Islamists and secularists is much more extensive than we had assumed. This points to the possibility that legal reforms against abuse of women can potentially cross the ideological lines that have ripped Muslim nation-states into shreds. But it also reveals a well of support for patriarchal policies that both secular and nonsecular male voters will approve.

While there is little gender difference in support for Islamism as an abstract principle, there is a huge gender difference in terms of support for specific patriarchal practices that are supported by Islamist parties and movements, including legalization of polygamy, divorce by men at will, a husband's right to decide whether his wife works, and support for honor killing. This implies that gender is a very important wedge for the liberalization of Islamic law. But it may also suggest that most women are not aware of the full ramification of what institutionalized Islamism entails for them, as against the Islam they have known and practiced since childhood. This suggests that advocates of women's rights could productively start a campaign that would alert women to the fact that Islamists embrace a far harsher position on all of these sensitive issues and that men in general, and Islamist men in particular, are to a significant degree attracted to this ideology because it gives free reign to their patriarchalism.

As we saw in the first part of this afterword, the #MeToo movement has shown that toxic masculinity has no political party. In the United States, a significant number of men who were accused of sexual violence toward women and children were progressives with impressive pedigrees on social justice. These included clerics known for their support of the poor, directors and producers known for their progressive films, and powerful media personalities known for their promotion of female subordinates.

Our brief exploration of the #MeToo movement during the past four years in six Muslim majority countries, as well as in Iran as discussed in this volume, shows a similar pattern. Men with liberal and socialist leanings are just as likely as others to engage in public molestation and violence toward their own partners, while pious male Muslims are less likely to engage in such abuses. Sexist eroticism, particularly consumption of pornography, increases the likelihood of perpetrating both public molestation and domestic violence, while patriarchal beliefs significantly increase the likelihood of perpetrating domestic violence. The primary mechanism we have been able to identify in our survey of individuals by which Islamism shapes individual violence toward women is through its promotion of patriarchalism, both as a worldview and in terms of laws that bolster male power over women in the public and private spheres. Islamism, when translated into state law, institutionalizes patriarchalism, encouraging a toxic masculinity that gives free reign to these actions with dramatic social implications for women. There is an irony here because, in reality, Islamist states like Iran, by enforcing policies that subordinate women, end up actually substituting for the authority of fathers and husbands. The state becomes a coercive, collective father.[67]

While future research must further explore the pathways to male violence toward women, this study provides an initial framework for understanding the sources of violence against women. The simple talk offered by secular and socialist men that if they were to assume power, mistreatment of women would suddenly end is a self-satisfied talking point, one not based on reality. It does nothing to either diagnose sexist and patriarchal practices or to identify how to get rid of them. Instead, we must look more carefully at the relatively independent logic of patriarchalism and sexism themselves, rather than load them down with other ideological baggage.

Our study, including our finding that many Islamists do not support neo-liberalism, and indeed are quite supportive of a socialist (43%) or a social democratic model (30%) of political economy, points to an analytic challenge for future research. The rise of authoritarian populisms in the West has been characterized by the competing explanations as a revolt against non-traditional cultural changes of gender and racial equality, or a response to the economic insecurity and downward mobility caused by globalization of supply chains and Schumpeterian technological changes.[68] Yet the religious right in the US is against the expansion of the welfare state, let alone social democratic alternatives. In contrast, in the MENASA region Islamists endorse more "traditional" gender values, particularly patriarchal ones, and various degrees of authoritarianism, but they also reject the liberal market as an exclusive mechanism to order production and distribution.[69]

In the 1970s, Islamist political movements assumed power in part by giving the impression that they would be the guardians of morality both by controlling what was considered women's provocative clothing and behavior and by clamping down on sexual harassment in the streets. This is why more than forty years after the Islamic Revolution, the conduct of the "guardians of morality" on the streets of Iran has ignited such an explosive reaction. Young women have been arrested on various charges, including improper hijab, then severely beaten and even killed (as in the case of the 22-year-old Kurdish Iranian woman Mahsa Jina Amini) or raped in police custody (as in the case of the anonymous 15-year-old girl in Zahedan). These actions by the police and the "guardians of morality" are obscene violations of the mandate and the raison d'etre of the Islamic regime, which came to power in the name of protecting morality. The outpouring of protests by Iranian women, and the support they have received from many young men, originate in the new generation's opposition to many patriarchal practices. They are demanding a separation of religion and state, not because they are opposed to Islam but because Islam has been used to oppress women and regulate gender relations, and create a highly corrupt and militarized state that no longer can provide a basic standard of living for a majority of its citizens.

Notes

Prologue

1 Tarana Burke and Elizabeth Adetiba, "Tarana Burke Says #MeToo Should Center Marginalized Communities," in *Where Freedom Starts: Sex Power Violence #MeToo* (Brooklyn, NY: Verso, 2018), 28–38.
2 Nadja Sayej, "Alyssa Milano on the #MeToo Movement: 'We're Not Going to Stand for It Any More,'" *Guardian*, Guardian News and Media, December 1, 2017, https://www.theguardian.com/culture/2017/dec/01/alyssa-milano-mee-too-sexual-harassment-abuse
3 Victim blaming can be defined as someone saying, implying, or treating a person who has experienced harmful or abusive behavior (such as a survivor of sexual violence) as if it were a result of something they did or said, instead of placing the responsibility where it belongs: with the person who harmed them.
4 Ashifa Kassam, "Margaret Atwood Faces Feminist Backlash on Social Media over #Metoo," *Guardian*, Guardian News and Media, January 15, 2018, https://www.theguardian.com/books/2018/jan/15/margaret-atwood-feminist-backlash-metoo
5 Chaminda Jayanetti, "New Equalities Commissioner Attacked 'Modern Feminism' and #Metoo," *Guardian*, Guardian News and Media, November 22, 2020, https://www.theguardian.com/society/2020/nov/22/new-equalities-commissioner-attacked-modern-feminism-and-metoo
6 Mohamad Mehdi Shoayb, "Jurisprudential Analysis of Article 102 of the Criminal Procedure Code with Emphasis on the Concepts and Examples of Private Plaintiff." *Rasail Journal* 8 (2017): 69.
7 Fazel Hadadi, "Unconscious Sexual Assault; Criticism of Article 224 of the Islamic Penal Code 2013," *Rasail Journal* 2 (2016): 78.
8 The Bill on Dignity and Protection of Women against Violence. The latest stage: sending from the government to the Parliament for legal formalities on October 24, 2013. https://www.ekhtebar.ir/لایحه-حفظ-کرامت-و-حمایت-از-زنان-در-برابر/
9 "Slavoj Žižek on #MeToo Movement," Russia Today, YouTube, January 17, 2019.
10 Jim Middlemiss, "Navigating Sexual Harassment in a #Metoo World," Canadian Lawyer, September 21, 2018, https://www.canadianlawyermag.com/news/opinion/navigating-sexual-harassment-in-a-metoo-world/275467

11 Anastasia S. Burelomova, Marina A. Gulina, and Olga A. Tikhomandritskya, "Intimate Partner Violence: An Overview of the Existing Theories, Conceptual Frameworks, and Definitions," *Psychology in Russia: State of the Art* 11, no. 3 (2018): 128–44.
12 Stoning is punishable under Iranian law in cases where a married person has sex with someone other than his or her spouse, and this relationship is based on testimony. Four witnesses found to be fair by the court or four confessions of the person who committed the act are needed for proving it.
13 "Ayatollah Bayat Zanjani: The Stoning Ruling Is Not in the Quran," Radio Farda, July 12, 2010, https://www.radiofarda.com/a/F11_Iran_adultery_stoning_Ayatollah_Bayat_statement/2096964.html
14 "Bayat Zanjani: The Stoning Ruling."
15 Rahim Ghomeishi, "Captivity in Captivity," @ghomeishi3—All Telegram Channel Posts, telemetr.io, https://telemetr.io/en/channels/1115454551-ghomeishi3/posts (accessed March 12, 2022).
16 "The Statement of Iranian Women in Cinema in Protest to Violence against Women in Cinema," Akhbar Rooz, April 1, 2022. https://www.akhbar-rooz.com/148050/1401/01/12/

Introduction: Bodies, Spaces, and Places

1 Chris Snyder and Linette Lopez, "Tarana Burke on Why She Created the #MeToo Movement—and Where It's Headed," *Business Insider*, December 13, 2017, https://www.businessinsider.com/how-the-metoo-movement-started-where-its-headed-tarana-burke-time-person-of-year-women-2017-12
2 See Janet Afary, *Sexual Politics in Modern Iran* (Cambridge: Cambridge University Press, 2009); Mahnaz Afkhami, "A Future in the Past: The 'Prerevolutionary' Women's Movement," in *Sisterhood Is Global*, ed. Robin Morgan (New York: Anchor Books, 1984); K. S. Batmanghelichi, *Revolutionary Bodies: Technologies of Gender, Sex, and Self in Contemporary Iran* (London: Bloomsbury Press, 2020); Homa Hoodfar, *The Women's Movement in Iran: Women at the Crossroad of Secularization and Islamization* (Montpellier: Women Living Under Muslim Laws, 1999); Afsaneh Najmabadi, *Women with Moustaches and Men without Beards: Gender and Sexual Anxieties of Iranian Modernity* (Berkeley: University of California Press, 2005); Zahra Tizro, *Domestic Violence in Iran: Women, Marriage and Islam* (London: Routledge, 2012).
3 Carine M. Mardorossian, "Toward a New Feminist Theory of Rape," *Signs* 27, no. 3 (2002): 768.

4 Claudia Yaghoobi, "Over 40 Years of Resisting the Compulsory Veiling: Relating Literary Narratives to Text-Based Protests to Cyberactivism," *Journal of Middle East Women's Studies* 17, no. 2 (2021): 220.
5 Moha Ennaji and Fatima Sadiqi, "Introduction: Contextualizing Gender and Violence in the Middle East," in *Gender and Violence in the Middle East*, ed. Moha Ennaji and Fatima Sadiqi (London: Routledge, 2011), 1–2.
6 N. Al-Ali, "Reconstructing Gender: Iraqi Women between Dictatorship, War, Sanctions and Occupation," *Third World Quarterly* 26, no. 4/5 (2005): 740.
7 Zahra Tizro, *Domestic Violence in Iran: Women, Marriage and Islam* (London: Routledge, 2012), 1.
8 F. El-Zanaty, E. Hussein, G. Shawky, A. Way, and S. Kishor, *Egypt: Demographic and Health Survey 1995* (Calverton, MD: National Population Council and Macro International, 1996), 206.
9 S. Tomaselli and R. Porter, *Rape: An Historical and Cultural Enquiry* (Oxford: Blackwell, 1986).
10 Claudia Yaghoobi, *Temporary Marriage in Iran: Gender and Body Politics in Modern Iranian Film and Literature* (Cambridge: Cambridge University Press, 2020), 17.
11 Tizro, *Domestic Violence in Iran*, 9.
12 Pierre Bourdieu, *Distinction: A Social Critique of the Judgement of Taste* (London: Routledge, 1984), 466.
13 Bourdieu, *Distinction*, 474.
14 Janet Wolff, "Reinstating Corporeality: Feminism and Body Politics," in *Feminine Sentences: Essays on Women and Culture*, ed. Janet Wolff (Berkeley: University of California Press, 1990), 120–40; Michel Foucault, *Discipline and Punish: The Birth of the Prison* (New York: Vintage Books, 1977); Alphonso Lingis, "The Subjectification of the Body," in *The Body: Classic and Contemporary Readings*, ed. Donn Welton (Oxford: Blackwell, 1999), 296; Sandra L. Bartky, "Foucault, Femininity, and the Modernization of Patriarchal Power," in *Writing on the Body: Female Embodiment and Feminist Theory*, ed. K. Conboy, N. Medina, and S. Stanbury (New York: Columbia University Press, 1997), 132.
15 Linda McDowell, *Gender, Identity and Place: Understanding Feminist Geographies* (Minneapolis: University of Minnesota Press, 1999), 56.
16 Banu Gökarıksel, "Beyond the Officially Sacred: Religion, Secularism, and the Body in the Production of Subjectivity," *Social and Cultural Geography* 10, no. 6 (2009): 666.
17 Masserat Amir-Ebrahimi, "Transgression in Narration: The Lives of Iranian Women in Cyberspace," *Journal of Middle East Women's Studies* 4, no. 3, Special Issue: Innovative Women: Unsung Pioneers of Social Change (2008): 90–1.
18 Amir-Ebrahimi, "Transgression in Narration," 98–101.

1 Like a Wrapped Chocolate: The Islamic Republic's Politics of Hijab and the Normalization of Sexual Harassment

1 Neda Sanij, "Iranian Women Who Shouted: That Man Assaulted Us," BBC News Farsi, BBC, August 22, 2020, https://www.bbc.com/persian/iran-features-53873273 (accessed January 17, 2022).
2 "Increase in Reports of Violence against Women," Pupils Association News Agency, November 24, 2019, https://www.pana.ir/news/970848
3 "66% of Iranian Women Are Exposed to Violence," *ISNA*, November 16, 2018, accessed November 12, 2022, https://www.isna.ir/news/97082512283
4 SepanoData.Ir, "The Domestic Violence Situation in Iran Based on Two National Research Projects," *Center for the Study of Women and Family*, December 9, 2015, https://jwdp.ut.ac.ir/news?newsCode=1218 (accessed January 15, 2022).
5 Mohammad Esmaeil Riahi and Tahereh Lotfi Khachaki, "Social Analysis of the Influencing Factors on the Experiencing Street Harassment by Female Students of University of Mazandaran," *Strategic Research on Social Problems in Iran University of Isfahan* 5, no. 2 (2016): 69–88.
6 Celia Kitzinger, "Heteronormativity in Action: Reproducing the Heterosexual Nuclear Family in After-Hours Medical Calls," *Social Problems* 52, no. 4 (2005): 478.
7 Afsaneh Najmabadi, *Women with Moustaches and Men without Beards: Gender and Sexual Anxieties of Iranian Modernity* (Berkeley: University of California Press, 2005), 3–4.
8 Najmabadi, *Women with Moustaches*, 26.
9 Gil Z. Hochberg, *Visual Occupations* (Durham, NC: Duke University Press, 2015), 7.
10 Najmabadi, *Women with Moustaches*, 39.
11 Mohamad Tavakoli-Targhi, *Refashioning Iran* (Basingtoke: Palgrave, 2001), 36.
12 Houchang E. Chehabi, "Staging the Emperor's New Clothes: Dress Codes and Nation-Building under Reza Shah," *Iranian Studies* 26, nos. 3–4 (1993): 213–14.
13 Chehabi, "Staging the Emperor's New Clothes," 215.
14 Janet Afary, *Sexual Politics in Modern Iran* (Cambridge: Cambridge University Press, 2009), 156.
15 Chehabi. "Staging the Emperor's New Clothes," 223.
16 Laura Mulvey, *Visual and Other Pleasures* (New York: Palgrave, 1989), 140.
17 Ali Behdad, *Camera Orientalist: Reflections on Photography of the Middle East* (Chicago: University of Chicago Press, 2016), 111.
18 Behdad, *Camera Orientalist*, 111–13.
19 Wendy DeSouza, *Unveiling Men: Modern Masculinities in Twentieth-Century Iran* (New York: Syracuse University Press, 2019), 27.

20 Afsaneh Najmabadi, "The Erotic Vaṭan [Homeland] as Beloved and Mother: To Love, to Possess, and to Protect," *Comparative Studies in Society and History* 39, no. 3 (1997): 444.
21 Minoo Moallem, *Between Warrior Brother and Veiled Sister: Islamic Fundamentalism and the Politics of Patriarchy in Iran* (California: University of California Press, 2005), 81.
22 Moallem, *Between*, 64–5.
23 Robert W. Connell and James W. Messerschmidt, "Hegemonic Masculinity: Rethinking the Concept," *Gender & Society* 19, no. 6 (2005): 838. Connell explains that "hegemonic masculinities can be constructed that do not correspond closely to the lives of any actual men. Yet these models do, in various ways, express widespread ideals, fantasies, and desires. They provide models of relations with women and solutions to problems of gender relations. Furthermore, they articulate loosely with the practical constitution of masculinities as ways of living in everyday local circumstances. To the extent they do this, they contribute to hegemony in the society-wide gender order as a whole."
24 DeSouza, *Unveiling Men*, 4.
25 Shahin Gerami, "Mullahs, Martyrs, and Men: Conceptualizing Masculinity in the Islamic Republic of Iran," *Men and Masculinities* 5, no. 3 (2003): 262–4. Gerami identifies these masculine prototypes: the merchants (*bazzaris*); the professionals—engineers, doctors, and professors (*doctor-o-mohandes*); military officers (*sarhang-va- afsar*); civil service employees (*karmands*); workers (*kargar* and *amaleh*); and peasants (*dehati*). Less significant peripheral prototypes were urban cowboys (*jahel*) and misfits (*lat-ha*).
26 Kaveh Bassiri, "Masculinity in Iranian Cinema," *Global Encyclopedia of Lesbian, Gay, Bisexual, Transgender, and Queer (LGBTQ) History* (2019): 1018.
27 Gerami, "Mullahs," 260.
28 Gerami, "Mullahs," 262.
29 Examples of collective political groups: one million signatures campaign, Inqilab daughters. To name a few: Nasrin Sotoudeh, Narges Mohammadi, Bahareh Hedayat, Shirin Ebadi, Mujaheddin opposition leader, Maryam Rajavi.
30 To promote hijab and correct veiling, the Morality Police was founded on December 4, 2005, during Mahmoud Ahmadinejad's administration.
31 Riaz Hassan, *Attitudes toward Veiling and Patriarchy in Four Muslim Societies: An Exploratory Study*, GE von Grunebaum Center for Near Eastern Studies (California: University of California Press, 2000), 19.
32 Ziba Mir-Hosseini, "The Conservative Reformist Conflict over Women's Rights in Iran," *International Journal of Politics, Culture, and Society* (2002). Mir-Hosseini

writes, "In their Friday sermons, lectures and writings, political clerics often spoke of the success and the authority of the Islamic Republic with reference to the policy of compulsory hijab" (42).

33 Ziba Mir-Hosseini, "The Politics and Hermeneutics of Hijab in Iran: From Confinement to Choose," *Muslim World Journal of Human Rights* 4, no. 1 (2007): 4.

34 Faegheh Shirazi-Mahajan, "The Politics of Clothing in the Middle East: The Case of Hijab in Post-revolution Iran," *Critique: Journal of Critical Studies of Iran & the Middle East* 2, no. 2 (1993): 60.

35 Mir-Hosseini, *Islam and Gender*, 65–71.

36 Men lowering their gaze was a part of the hijab discourse when I was growing up in the Islamic Republic, and during my adolescent years. State officials and religious men would avoid looking at *nā-mahram* women while conversing. The practice is also present in the cultural productions of the 1990s and early 2000s. This attitude was virtually nonexistent during 2008 and 2009.

37 Saeid Golkar, *Captive Society: The Basij Militia and Social Control in Iran* (New York: Columbia University Press, 2015).

38 Rebecca Tan, "For the First Time since 1980, Iranian Women Allowed to Watch World Cup in Same Stadium as Men," *Washington Post*, June 20, 2018, https://www.washingtonpost.com/news/worldviews/wp/2018/06/20/for-the-first-time-since-1980-iranian-women-allowed-to-watch-world-cup-in-same-stadium-as-men/?utm_term=.7518db959335. They have even disguised themselves as men to avoid these discriminatory restrictions. Over the past few years, Iranian women and rights organizations have also tried to reverse the policy through direct appeals to FIFA and the international volleyball federation (FIVB). Women have campaigned and lobbied parliament until finally in June 2018 with FIFA's pressure and threat women were allowed to enter the landmark stadium of Azadi to watch a live screening of the last two games of Iran's national football team at the 2018 World Cup.

39 See Naser Makarem Shirazi's information station for further info: https://makarem.ir/main.aspx?typeinfo=21&lid=0&mid=250249

40 Claudia Yaghoobi, *Temporary Marriage in Iran: Gender and Body Politics in Modern Iranian Film and Literature* (Cambridge: Cambridge University Press, 2020), 254.

41 Yaghoobi, *Temporary Marriage in Iran*, 237–8.

42 Claudia Yaghoobi, "Socially Peripheral, Symbolically Central: Sima in Behrouz Afkhami's Shokaran," *Asian Cinema* 27, no. 2 (2016): 156.

43 Yaghoobi, *Temporary Marriage in Iran*, 10.

44 Yaghoobi, *Temporary Marriage in Iran*, 224.

45 Yaghoobi, *Temporary Marriage in Iran*, 257.

46 Ali Mirsepassi, *Intellectual Discourse and the Politics of Modernization: Negotiating Modernity in Iran* (Cambridge: Cambridge University Press, 2000), 10–11.

47 Moallem, *Between Warrior Brother and Veiled Sister*, 70.
48 Janet Afary, "The Sexual Economy of the Islamic Republic," *Iranian Studies* 42, no. 1 (2009): 15–16.

2 The Iranian #MeToo and the Double Bind of Iranian Feminism: Between Religion, the Global Gender Struggle, and Liberal Feminism

1 For English-language discussion of this bill, see Farnaz Fasihi, "Iran Moves to Outlaw Sexual Violence and Harassment of Women," *New York Times*, January 5, 2021, https://www.nytimes.com/2021/01/05/world/middleeast/iran-sexual-violence-metoo-women.html. For Persian-language discussion of the legal changes, see Sarvenaz Rastegar, "10 Years of Waiting for Nothing: Take a Look at the Protection, Dignity, and Security of Women Against Violence Bill," *Iran Human Rights*, February 7, 2021, https://iranhr.net/fa/articles/4613/; "The Iranian Government Passed a Bill Banning Violence against Women after a Decade of Controversy," *euronews*, January 4, 2021, https://per.euronews.com/2021/01/04/the-iranian-government-passed-a-bill-banning-violence-against-women-after-a-decade-of-cont; Mitra Shojaee, "Women's Protection against Violence Bill: The Lion without Mane, Tail and Belly," *Deutsche Welle*, November 25, 2021, https://www.dw.com/fa-ir/لایحه-حمایت-از-زنان-در-برابر-خشونت-شیر-بی-یال-و-دم-و-اشکم/a-59931740

2 While protocols for research handling of social media data are constantly evolving, our institution, McMaster University, at the time of writing, does not require further ethical screening on publicly available data. Tweets from public accounts are considered public data. However, we have anonymized the tweets (delinked them from any potential reference to real people) and paraphrased testimonies as a further step in protecting the identity of the women whose public testimonies have been cited. We have in writing the permission of Shima Ghooshe to translate and cite her words directly in the chapter. The other sources that we use are also legacy media: public documents, interviews in legacy media, statements from organizations' websites, and so on, which, according to our ethical protocols, are free from any further screening.

3 A recent controversy, centered around Masih Alinejad's opposition to a bill that criminalizes Islamophobia in the United States, is a case in point. Accused by Congresswoman Ilhan Omar and her husband, Tim Mynett, of spreading Islamophobia, Alinejad has been quick to note that her criticism of the Iranian religious regime is based on lived and embodied experiences of forced veiling, jail, and torture in the name of religious piety; that she respects Islam and pious Muslim women who choose Islam first (her mother, Alinejad points out, is one of them)

but insists on a clear differentiation between hate crimes against Muslims and the opportunity for open and rigorous critique of oppressive regimes that derive their legitimacy from Islam. See the enormous debate that happened on Twitter: Masih Alinejad (@AlinejadMasih), "1—In response to my @washingtonpost op-ed on how @IlhanMN's proposed legislation against Islamophobia could silence legitimate concerns about Islamist extremism, her husband defamed me" (Twitter, January 29, 2020, https://twitter.com/AlinejadMasih/status/1487446697915650057). See our analysis of this debate via a critique of the native informant angle in the last section of this chapter.

4 All appropriations of Muslim testimonies of female suffering under the banner of "saving Muslim women from Muslim men" have been discussed in fascinating detail by postcolonial scholarship. Some notable publications include: Saba Mahmood, "Secularism, Hermeneutics and Empire: The Politics of Islamic Reformation," *Public Culture* 18, no. 6 (2006): 323–47; Jasmin Zine, "Between Orientalism and Fundamentalism: The Politics of Muslim Women's Feminist Engagement," *Muslim World Journal of Human Rights* 3, no. 5 (2006): 1–24; and Leila Abu-Lughod, *Do Muslim Women Need Saving* (Boston, MA: Harvard University Press, 2015).

5 Atena Kamel, "Can the Victim Speak?" *Zanan Emrooz*, no. 41 (2021): 8–14.

6 Sahar Maranloo, "Legal Reflections of the Women's Campaigns against Sexual Harassment," *Zanan Emrooz*, no. 41 (2021): 36–41.

7 With regard to Emamverdi's case, see the analysis by Roghayeh Rezaei, "#MeToo Branded a Zionist Movement in High-Profile Tehran Rape Trial," *Iran Wire*, January 4, 2022, https://iranwire.com/en/features/11035. For a more comprehensive exchange of arguments between Iranian feminists, secular and religious, see: Haideh Moghissi, "Islamic Feminism Revisited," *Comparative Studies of South Asia, Africa and the Middle East* 31, no. 1 (2011): 76–84. See also: Laila Mouri and Kristin Soraya Batmanghelichi, "Can the Secular Iranian Women's Activists Speak? Caught between the Political Power and the Islamic Feminist," in *Gender and Sexuality in Muslim Countries*, ed. Gul Ozyegin (Farnham: Ashgate, 2015), 331–54.

8 Rezaei, "#MeToo Branded a Zionist Movement."

9 Shahin Gholami, "Analysis of the Neglected Dimensions of #MeToo in Iran," *Harasswatch*, https://harasswatch.com/news/1706/صدایی-علیه-سکوت%E8%80%2C (accessed November 11, 2021).

10 Aydin Aghdashloo and Kamil Ahmadi are among the prominent names that got caught up in public controversies during the Iranian #MeToo. See Farnaz Fassihi, "A #MeToo Awakening Stirs in Iran," *New York Times*, October 22, 2020, https://www.nytimes.com/2020/10/22/world/middleeast/iran-metoo-aydin-aghdashloo.html

11 Islamic penal law in Iran, in the words of Ghooshe, defines adultery as "the insertion of a man's penis into a woman's body from front or back to the extent beyond the circumcision site, that is, if the head of the penis enters by force and

does not reach the circumcision site, there is no adultery at all, and it is not a crime." Exact word in Farsi: زنا

12 Twitter, توی فکر بودم که مسعود کاظمی اومد کنار من روی مبل دونفره نشست و بازوم رو گرفت, December 18, 2020, https://twitter.com/Shadishaaaaad/status/1339814458395402 241.

13 Interview published in Farsi on the site of the Iranian Women Association: Shahrzad Hemmati, "Missing Criteria in the Iranian #MeToo Movement," *Iranian Women Association*, November 27, 2020, https://ir-women.com/17293

14 Interview published in Farsi on the site of the Iranian Women Association: Shahrzad Hemmati, "Verification Methods of Harassment Narratives in Conversation with Samaneh Savadi, a Women Activist," *Iranian Women Association*, November 27, 2020, https://ir-women.com/17254

15 For a comprehensive overview of the main terms, concepts, and legal dimensions of the #MeToo movement, see Deborah Tuerkheimer, "Beyond #MeToo," *New York University Law Review* 94, no. 1146 (2019): 1147–208. See also Sarah Jaffe, "The Collective Power of #MeToo," *Dissent* 65, no. 2 (2018): 80–7. Specifically, the concepts that emerged globally in the movement are discussed in an editorial article by Dubravka Zarkov and Kathy Davis, "Ambiguities and Dilemmas Around #MeToo: #ForHowLong and #WhereTo?," *European Journal of Women's Studies* 25, no. 1 (2018): 3–9. The force and gist of the Iranian debate comes a bit later in time, and it reflects to a certain extent, particularly in its diasporic articulations in the legal, ethical, and systemic dimensions, much of the dynamics in the Western setting.

16 For comprehensive historical review of the various waves and dilemmas, see Deborah Cameron, *Feminism: A Brief Introduction to the Ideas, Debates and Politics of the Movement* (Chicago: University of Chicago Press, 2019).

17 Roya Hakakian, "A UN Farce Has Tragic Implications for Feminist Activists in Islam," *Washington Post*, April 27, 2021, https://www.washingtonpost.com/opinions/2021/04/27/un-farce-has-tragic-implications-feminist-activists-iran/. See also Masih Alinejad and Roya Hakakian, "Iranian Women Are Staging Offensive against Sexual Abuse: It's Long Overdue," *Washington Post*, August 26, 2020, https://www.washingtonpost.com/opinions/2020/08/26/iranian-women-are-staging-an-offensive-against-sexual-abuse-its-long-overdue/

18 Roya Hakakian, "The Flame of Feminism Is Alive in Iran: While Western Activists Defend the Right of Muslim Women to Wear the Veil, Iranian Women Are Fighting for a Bigger Cause: Choice," *Foreign Policy*, March 7, 2019, https://foreignpolicy.com/2019/03/07/the-flame-of-feminism-is-alive-in-iran-international-womens-day/

19 Roya Hakakian, "Unveiling Iran," *New York Review of Books*, March 8, 2021, https://www.nybooks.com/daily/2021/03/08/unveiling-iran/

20 Yale Law School has hosted both Hakakian and Alinejad as speakers in February 2019; see "Masih Alinejad and Roya Hakakian on Feminism and Freedom in Iran," *Yale Law School*, February 8, 2019, https://law.yale.edu/yls-today/news/masih-alinejad-and-roya-hakakian-feminism-and-freedom-iran

21 A comprehensive report from the Atlantic Council, written by Mehrangiz Kar and Azadeh Pourzand in April 2021, clearly captures the rights-based language of Iranian feminism written in the diaspora. See by Mehrangiz Kar and Azadeh Pourzand, "Iranian Women in the Year 1400: The Struggle for Equal Rights Continues," *Atlantic Council*, April 2021, https://www.atlanticcouncil.org/wp-content/uploads/2021/04/Iranian_Women_in_the_Year_1400-The_Struggle_for_Equal_Rights_Continues.pdf

22 Ziba Mir Hosseini, "Beyond Islam versus Feminism," *IDS Bulletin* 42, no. 1 (2011): 67–77.

23 Roya Hakakian and Masih Alinejad, "There Are Two Types of Hijabs: The Difference Is Huge," *Washington Post*, August 4, 2019, https://www.washingtonpost.com/opinions/global-opinions/there-are-two-types-of-hijabs-the-difference-is-huge/2019/04/07/50a44574-57f0-11e9-814f-e2f46684196e_story.html

24 Link to Mynett's derogatory tweet, which unleashed an avalanche of responses: Tim Mynett (@TimMynett), "So this lady doesn't want to combat Islamophobia because she doesn't like Muslims. Understood!," Twitter, January 26, 2022, https://twitter.com/TimMynett/status/1486354013612302338

25 Masih Alinejad, "Why I Am Opposed to Ilhan Omar's Bill against Islamophobia," *Washington Post*, January 25, 2022, https://www.washingtonpost.com/opinions/2022/01/25/why-im-opposed-ilhan-omars-bill-against-islamophobia/

26 Elnaz Sarbar, "Caught in Identity Politics, I Will Not Be Silenced," MyStealthyFreedom.Org, January 23, 2022, https://www.mystealthyfreedom.org/caught-in-identity-politics-i-will-not-be-silenced/. A particularly critical article of Ilhan Omar's politics appears on the blog of Nervana Mahmoud, a British Egyptian commentator and activist on Middle Eastern topics. See "Ilhan Omar's Ill-Advised Dismissal of Masih Alinejad," Nervana (blog), January 30, 2022, https://nervana1.org/2022/01/30/ilhan-omars-ill-advised-dismissal-of-masih-alinejad%EF%BF%BC/

27 Masih Alinejad has been imprisoned, abused, and exiled by the Iranian state. Currently, her brother is threatened with eight years in prison for refusing to publicly denounce her. See Yaghoub Fazeli, "Iranian Journalist Masih Alinejad's Brother Sentenced to 8 Years in Prison," *Al Arabiya English*, July 16, 2020, https://english.alarabiya.net/News/middle-east/2020/07/16/Iranian-journalist-Masih-Alinejad-s-brother-sentenced-to-8-years-in-prison-Lawyer. See also Robyn

Wright, "Iran's Kidnapping Plot Exposes Its Paranoia," *New Yorker*, July 19, 2021, https://www.newyorker.com/news/daily-comment/irans-kidnapping-plot-exposes-its-paranoia. Roya Hakakian writes a memoir where she explains how the religious state controls female sexuality, honor, and life trajectories. See Roya Hakakian, *Journey from the Land of No: A Girlhood Caught in Revolutionary Iran* (New York: Random House USA, 2005).

28 https://women.gov.ir/fa/news/14159/متن-لایحه-حفظ-کرامت-و-حمایت-از-زنان-در-برابر-خشونت-منتشر-شد. Presentation of the bill and how it delivers progress and compromise is available in Maziar Motamedi, "Protecting Dignity: Iran's Push to Fight Violence against Women," *Al Jazeera English*, February 28, 2021, https://www.aljazeera.com/features/2021/2/28/protecting-dignity-irans-push-to-fight-violence-against-women

29 Zahra Ayatollahi, "Security of Women against Violence Bill or the Implementation of Fifth Goal of the 2030 Document," *Keyhan Newspaper*, January 20, 2018, https://kayhan.ir/fa/news/121939/لایحه-امنیت-زنان-در-برابر-خشونت-یا-اجرای-هدف-5-سند-2030یادداشت-میهمان

30 Ziba Mir Hosseini is the author of numerous influential texts and exegetical interpretations of Islamic scriptures. A groundbreaking text for her Islamic feminist methodology is an article initially published in English in 2006. See Ziba Mir Hosseini, "Muslim Women's Quest for Equality: Between Islamic Law and Feminism," *Critical Inquiry* 32, no. 4 (2006): 629–45.

31 Ziba Mir Hosseini, "What Is Islamic Feminism," CILE Seminar on Ethics and Gender at the University of Oxford, June 17, 2015, https://www.youtube.com/watch?v=Fzf2D43wcTc

32 Ziba Mir Hosseini, "Feminist Voices in Islam: Promise and Potential," *Open Democracy*, November 19, 2012, https://www.opendemocracy.net/en/5050/feminist-voices-in-islam-promise-and-potential/

33 A somewhat comprehensive review of the debates could be found in: Zora Hesova, "Secular, Islamic or Muslim Feminism?" *Gender and Research* 20, no. 2 (2019): 26–46. For a detailed layout of Islamic feminism, see Haideh Moghissi, "Islamic Feminism Revisited," *Comparative Studies of South Asia, Africa and the Middle East* 31, no. 1 (2011): 76–84.

34 Leila Mouri and Kristin Soraya Batmanghelichi, "Can the Secular Iranian Women's Activists Speak? Caught between the Political Power and the Islamic Feminist," in *Gender and Sexuality in Muslim Countries*, ed. Gul Ozyegin (Farnham: Ashgate Publishing, 2015), 331–54.

35 Dilyana Mincheva, "#DearSister and #MosqueMeToo: Adversarial Islamic Feminism within the Western-Islamic Public Sphere," *Feminist Media Studies*, doi: 10.1080/14680777.2021.1984273 (online).

3 Rhetorical Listening to the Iranian #MeToo Movement in Diaspora

1. In an article titled "Cyberfeminism, Iranian Style: Online Feminism in Post-2009 Iran," K. Soraya Batmanghelich and Laila Mouri elaborate on how, as a result of the pressure and censorship of the Islamic state, different groups of Iranian feminist activists decided to leave the country (some remained inside Iran) and continue their activism in the online sphere. These were among some of the prominent groups who also paid attention and raised voices of Iranian #MeToo movement in the diaspora. However, because in this chapter I focus on rhetorical listening to #MeToo by Iranian academic feminists, it does not analyze their activisms in this regard. See K. Soraya Batmanghelichi and Leila Mouri, "Cyberfeminism, Iranian Style," *Feminist Media Histories* (2017): 50–80.
2. Valentine Moghadam, "Transnational Feminist Activism and Movement Building," in *Oxford Handbook of Transnational Feminist Movements*, 1st ed., ed. Rawwida Baksh and Wendy Harcourt (Cary, NY: Oxford University Press, 2015), 53–81.
3. As I will mention in the text, Zahra Tizro's *Domestic Violence in Iran: Women, Marriage and Islam*, Iranian Studies 11 (Abingdon, Oxon: Routledge, 2012); and Claudia Yaghoobi's *Temporary Marriage in Iran: Gender and Body Politics in Modern Iranian Film and Literature*, The Global Middle East 12 (Cambridge: Cambridge University Press, 2022) are among the few works that address gender-based violence and domestic abuse directly.
4. Rebecca Jane Hall, "Feminist Strategies to End Violence against Women," in *Oxford Handbook of Transnational Feminist Movements*, 1st ed. (Cary, NY: Oxford University Press, 2015), 396–7.
5. Margaret Atwood, *The Handmaid's Tale* (Boston: Houghton Mifflin, 1986).
6. Ruby Hamad, *White Tears/Brown Scars: How White Feminism Betrays Women of Color* (New York: Catapult, 2020), 170.
7. Kumari Jayawardena, *Feminism and Nationalism in the Third World* (London: Zed, 1985).
8. Firoozeh Kashani-Sabet, "Patriotic Womanhood: The Culture of Feminism in Modern Iran, 1900–1941," *British Journal of Middle Eastern Studies* 32, no. 1 (2005): 29–46.
9. Camron Michael Amin, "Globalizing Iranian Feminism, 1910–1950," *Journal of Middle East Women's Studies* 4, no. 1 (2008): 1, https://doi.org/10.2979/mew.2008.4.1.6
10. Moghadam, "Transnational Feminist Activism," 54.
11. Moghadam, "Transnational Feminist Activism," 60.

12 Mary Shanti Dairiam, "CEDAW, Gender, and Culture," in *The Oxford Handbook of Transnational Feminist Movements*, 1st ed. (Oxford: Oxford University Press, 2015), 367–93.
13 Zakia Salime, *Between Feminism and Islam: Human Rights and Sharia Law in Morocco*, 1st ed. (Minneapolis: University of Minnesota Press, 2011).
14 Moghadam, "Transnational Feminist Activism," 63.
15 Inderpal Grewal, *Transnational America Feminisms, Diasporas, Neoliberalisms* (Durham, NC: Duke University Press, 2005), 137; https://doi.org/10.1515/9780822386544
16 Hall, "Feminist Strategies," 405.
17 Dana Olwan, "Gendered Violence, Cultural Otherness, and Honour Crimes in Canadian National Logics," *Canadian Journal of Sociology* 38, no. 4 (2013): 533–56; https://doi.org/10.29173/cjs21196
18 Dana M. Olwan, "Pinkwashing the 'Honor Crime': Murdered Muslim Women and the Politics of Posthumous Solidarities," *Signs: Journal of Women in Culture and Society* 44, no. 4 (June 1, 2019): 905–30, https://doi.org/10.1086/702311
19 Sima Shakhsari, "From Homoerotics of Exile to Homopolitics of Diaspora: Cyberspace, the War on Terror, and the Hypervisible Iranian Queer," *Journal of Middle East Women's Studies* 8, no. 3 (2012): 14–40, https://doi.org/10.2979/jmiddeastwomstud.8.3.14
20 Maryamossadat Torabi 2020, 255–6. Maryamossadat Torabi, "Sexual Harassment and Iranian Law's Coverage," in *The Global #MeToo Movement: How Social Media Propelled a Historic Movement and the Law Responded*, ed. Ann M. Noel and David B. Oppenheimer (Fastcase: Full Court, 2020), 255–60.
21 Quoted by Farnaz Fassihi, "A #MeToo Awakening Stirs in Iran," *New York Times*, October 22, 2020, sec. World, https://www.nytimes.com/2020/10/22/world/middleeast/iran-metoo-aydin-aghdashloo.html
22 It does not mean that the law refuses to protect sexually assaulted women. However, Torabi (2020) elaborates that because the law only considers assault that happened in public as provable and punishable, it leaves out almost all of the incidents of sexual harassment and women's #MeToo stories.
23 Mariz Tadros, "From Secular Reductionism to Religious Essentialism: Implications for the Gender Agenda," in *Oxford Handbook of Transnational Feminist Movements*, 1st ed. (Cary, NY: Oxford University Press, 2015), 659.
24 Tadros, "From Secular Reductionism," 653.
25 Valentine Moghadam, "Gender and Revolutionary Transformation: Iran 1979 and East Central Europe 1989," *Gender and Society* 9, no. 3 (1995): 328–58.
26 Haleh Afshar, "Khomeini's Teachings and Their Implications for Women," *Feminist Review*, no. 12 (1982): 61, https://doi.org/10.2307/1394882

27 Haleh Afshar, *Islam and Feminisms: An Iranian Case-Study* (New York: St. Martin's, 1998).
28 Haideh Moghissi, "Islamic Cultural Nationalism and Gender Politics in Iran," *Third World Quarterly* 29, no. 3 (2008): 551–4; http://www.jstor.org/stable/20455056
29 Zahra Tizro, *Domestic Violence in Iran: Women, Marriage and Islam* (London: Routledge, 2012), 89–121.
30 Nahid Yeganeh, "Women, Nationalism and Islam in Contemporary Political Discourse in Iran," *Feminist Review*, no. 44 (1993): 3–18, https://doi.org/10.2307/1395192; Parvin Paidar, *Women and the Political Process in Twentieth-Century Iran* (Cambridge: Cambridge University Press, 1995).
31 Janet Afary, *Sexual Politics in Modern Iran* (Cambridge: Cambridge University Press, 2009).
32 Janet Afary, "The Sexual Economy of the Islamic Republic," *Iranian Studies* 42, no. 1 (2009): 5.
33 Yaghoobi, *Temporary Marriage in Iran*.
34 Afsaneh Najmabadi, "Feminism in an Islamic Republic: Years of Hardship, Years of Growth," in *Islam, Gender, and Social Change*, ed. Yvonne Yazbeck Haddad and John L. Esposito (New York: Oxford University Press, 1998), 59–84.
35 Najmabadi, "Feminism in an Islamic Republic," 65.
36 Ziba Mir-Hosseini, *Islam and Gender: The Religious Debate in Contemporary Iran* (London: I.B. Tauris, 2000).
37 Ziba Mir-Hosseini, "The Conservative: Reformist Conflict over Women's Rights in Iran," *International Journal of Politics, Culture, and Society* 16, no. 1 (2002): 37–53.
38 Valentine Moghadam, "Islamic Feminism and Its Discontents: Toward a Resolution of the Debate," *Signs* 27, no. 4 (2002): 1135–71, https://doi.org/10.1086/339639
39 Moghadam, "Transnational Feminist Activism," 63.
40 Afsaneh Najmabadi, "Mapping Transformations of Sex, Gender, and Sexuality in Modern Iran," *Social Analysis: The International Journal of Social and Cultural Practice* 49, no. 2 (2005): 54–77.
41 Afsaneh Najmabadi, *Women with Mustaches and Men without Beards: Gender and Sexual Anxieties of Iranian Modernity* (University of California Press, 2005).
42 Afsaneh Najmabadi, "Transing and Transpassing across Sex-Gender Walls in Iran," *Women's Studies Quarterly* 36, no. 3/4 (2008): 23–42; "Verdicts of Science, Rulings of Faith: Transgender/Sexuality in Contemporary Iran," *Social Research* 78, no. 2 (2011): 533–56; "Genus of Sex or the Sexing of 'Jins,'" *International Journal of Middle East Studies* 45, no. 2 (2013): 211–31; *Professing Selves: Transsexuality and Same-Sex Desire in Contemporary Iran* (Durham, NC: Duke University Press Books, 2013).

43 Minoo Moallem, "The Texualization of Violence in a Global World: Gendered Citizenship and Discourses of Protection," *Review of Japanese Culture and Society* 11/12 (1999): 9–17.
44 Minoo Moallem, "Universalization of Particulars: The Civic Body and Gendered Citizenship in Iran," *Citizenship Studies* 3, no. 3 (November 1, 1999): 319–35, https://doi.org/10.1080/13621029908420718; "'Foreignness' and Be/Longing: Transnationalism and Immigrant Entrepreneurial Spaces," *Comparative Studies of South Asia, Africa and the Middle East* 20, no. 1 (2000): 200–10; "Iranian Immigrants, Exiles and Refugees: From National to Transnational Contexts," *Comparative Studies of South Asia, Africa and the Middle East* 20, no. 1 (2000): 161–4; "Whose Fundamentalism?," *Meridians* 2, no. 2 (2002): 298–301.
45 Minoo Moallem, *Between Warrior Brother and Veiled Sister: Islamic Fundamentalism and the Politics of Patriarchy in Iran* (Berkeley: University of California Press, 2005).
46 Paola Bacchetta, Tina Campt, Inderpal Grewal, Caren Kaplan, Minoo Moallem, and Jennifer Terry, "Transnational Feminist: Practices against War," *Meridians: Feminism, Race, Transnationalism* 19, no. 3 (2020): 131–8.
47 Sima Shakhsari, "Weblogistan Goes to War: Representational Practices, Gendered Soldiers and Neoliberal Entrepreneurship in Diaspora," *Feminist Review*, no. 99 (2011): 6–24.
48 Sima Shakhsari, "From Homoerotics of Exile to Homopolitics of Diaspora: Cyberspace, the War on Terror, and the Hypervisible Iranian Queer," *Journal of Middle East Women's Studies* 8, no. 3 (2012): 14, https://doi.org/10.2979/jmiddeast womstud.8.3.14
49 Sima Shakhsari, "Transnational Governmentality and the Politics of Life and Death," *International Journal of Middle East Studies* 45, no. 2 (2013): 340–2; "The Queer Time of Death: Temporality, Geopolitics, and Refugee Rights," *Sexualities* 17, no. 8 (December 1, 2014): 998–1015, https://doi.org/10.1177/1363460714552 261; *Politics of Rightful Killing: Civil Society, Gender, and Sexuality in Weblogistan* (Durham, NC: Duke University Press, 2020).
50 Roksana Bahramitash, "Islamic Fundamentalism and Women's Employment in Indonesia," *International Journal of Politics, Culture, and Society* 16, no. 2 (2002): 255–72; "Islamic Fundamentalism and Women's Economic Role: The Case of Iran," *International Journal of Politics, Culture, and Society* 16, no. 4 (2003): 551–68; "Myths and Realities of the Impact of Political Islam on Women: Female Employment in Indonesia and Iran," *Development in Practice* 14, no. 4 (2004): 508–20; "Iranian Women during the Reform Era (1994–2004): A Focus on Employment," *Journal of Middle East Women's Studies* 3, no. 2 (2007): 86–109, https://doi.org/10.2979/mew.2007.3.2.86
51 Valentine Moghadam, "Patriarchy in Transition: Women and the Changing Family in the Middle East," *Journal of Comparative Family Studies* 35, no. 2 (2004): 137–62.

52 Valentine Moghadam, "Women's Economic Participation in the Middle East: What Difference Has the Neoliberal Policy Turn Made?," *Journal of Middle East Women's Studies* 1, no. 1 (2005): 110–46.

53 Valentine Moghadam, "Hidden from History? Women Workers in Modern Iran," *Iranian Studies* 33, no. 3/4 (2000): 377–401.

54 Tarana Burke, *Unbound: My Story of Liberation and the Birth of the Me Too Movement* (New York: Flatiron Books, 2022).

55 Krista Ratcliffe, *Rhetorical Listening: Identification, Gender, Whiteness* (Carbondale: Southern Illinois University Press, 2005), 17.

56 Ratcliffe, *Rhetorical Listening*, 26.

57 Neda Maghbouleh, *The Limits of Whiteness: Iranian Americans and the Everyday Politics of Race*, 1st ed. (Stanford, CA: Stanford University Press, 2017).

58 Rebecca Dingo, "Linking Transnational Logics: A Feminist Rhetorical Analysis of Public Policy Networks," *College English* 70, no. 5 (2008): 490–505, https://doi.org/10.2307/25472285; *Networking Arguments: Rhetoric, Transnational Feminism, and Public Policy Writing*, 1st ed. (Pittsburgh, PA: University of Pittsburgh Press, 2012); "Networking the Macro and Micro: Toward Transnational Literacy Practices," *JAC* 33, no. 3/4 (2013): 529–52.

4 Structural and Material Considerations and the Nexus of Power and Sexuality in the Iranian #MeToo Movement

1 The topic of this chapter might raise ethical and legal questions. However, it does not involve human participants, which would necessitate an ethical review. My focus will be theoretical and my arguments are based exclusively on publicly available information (print and online publications in the public domain) with no interaction between the author and any human subject. The persons are not the unit of analysis in this study, and no individuals accused of alleged sexual crimes are mentioned or hinted at.

2 Jean-Claude Milner, "Reflections on the MeToo Movement and Its Philosophy," *Problemi International* 3, no. 3 (2019): 65–89.

3 For a discussion of these differences, see Milena Popova, *Sexual Consent* (Cambridge, MA: MIT Press, 2019), 21.

4 Sue Lees, "Judicial Rape," *Women's Studies International Forum* 16, no. 1 (1993): 11–36.

5 Zahra Tizro, *Domestic Violence in Iran: Women, Marriage and Islam* (London: Routledge, 2012), 133.

6 Maryam Fūminī, "*Mushkilāt-i Shekāyat az Tajāvuz-i Jinsī dar Dastgāh-i Qaḍāei Irān*," 1399/2020.

7 For some statistics on domestic violence in Iran, see Tizro, *Domestic Violence in Iran*, 16–19.
8 "The Criminal Justice System: Statistics," *Rape, Abuse and Incest National Network*, n.d.
9 Nafīsih Bāqirī, "Sīyāsat-i Kaifarī-i Irān dar Rābiṭih bā Āzār-i Jinsī," *Faṣlnāmih-i 'Ilmī-Huqūqī-i Qānūnyār* 2, no. 6 (1397/2019): 428.
10 Fūminī, "*Mushkilāt-i Shekāyat*." For a discussion of the definition of rape in Western legal context, see Ann J. Cahill, *Rethinking Rape* (Ithaca, NY: Cornell University Press, 2001), 10–12.
11 Fūminī, "*Mushkilāt-i Shekāyat*."
12 See Arzoo Osanloo, *Forgiveness Work* (Princeton, NJ: Princeton University Press, 2020), 46.
13 L. Tarighi, ed., "Annual Report on the Death Penalty in Iran 2020," *Iran Human Rights Report*, 2020.
14 Popova, *Sexual Consent*, 6.
15 Popova, *Sexual Consent*, 4.
16 Popova, *Sexual Consent*, 10.
17 Popova, *Sexual Consent*, 9.
18 C. K. Egbert, "Why Consent Is Not Enough," *Feminist Current*, June 25, 2014.
19 Serene J., Khader, *Adaptive Performances* (Oxford: Oxford University Press, 2011), 4, 20; original emphasis.
20 Popova, *Sexual Consent*, 15.
21 Popova, *Sexual Consent*, 18–19.
22 Popova, *Sexual Consent*, 21; original emphasis.
23 Rosemarie Tong, *Feminist Thought: A More Comprehensive Introduction* (Boulder, CO: Westview, 2009), 2.
24 bell hooks, *The Will to Change: Men, Masculinity, and Love* (New York: Atria, 2004), 95.
25 Tong, *Feminist Thought*, 96–127.
26 Popova, *Sexual Consent*, 15.
27 Popova, *Sexual Consent*, 142.
28 Milner, "Reflections," 64.
29 Popova, *Sexual Consent*, 170.
30 Zillah Eisenstein, "Developing a Theory of Capitalist Patriarchy: and Socialist Feminism," in *Capitalist Patriarchy and the Case for Socialist Feminism*, ed. Zillah Eisenstein (New York: Monthly Review Press, 1979), 5.
31 Mark Fisher, *Capitalist Realism: Is There No Alternative* (Hants: Zero, 2009).
32 Karl Marx, *Capital: A Critique of Political Economy, Vol. 1*, trans. Ben Fowkes (New York: Vintage, 1976), 280.

33 Ernesto Screpanti, *Labour Value: Rethinking Marx's Theory of Exploitation* (Cambridge: Open Book, 2019), 13, 26.
34 Kathi Weeks, *The Problem with Work: Feminism, Marxism, Antiwork Politics, and Postwork Imaginaries* (Durham, NC: Duke University Press, 2011), 19.
35 Catherine A. MacKinnon, *Toward a Feminist Theory of the State* (Cambridge, MA: Harvard University Press, 1989), 3.
36 Milner, "Reflections," 74–5.
37 Leigh Goodmark, *Decriminalizing Domestic Violence: A Balanced Policy Approach to Intimate Partner Violence* (Oakland: University of California Press, 2018), 135. One of the main causes of sexual violence against women within the context of marriage in Iran remains economic dependence of women on their husbands; see Tizro, *Domestic Violence in Iran*, 131.
38 Sara Markowitz, "The Price of Alcohol, Wife Abuse, and Husband Abuse," *Southern Economic Journal* 67, no. 2 (2000): 299.
39 Mimi E. Kin, "From Carceral Feminism to Transformative Justice: Women-of-Color Feminism and Alternatives to Incarceration," *Journal of Ethnic and Cultural Diversity in Social Work* 27, no. 3 (2018): 219–33.
40 Carol P. Christ, "A New Definition of Patriarchy: Control of Women's Sexuality, Private Property, and War," *Feminist Theology* 24, no. 3 (2016): 222.
41 George G. Brenkert, "Freedom and Private Property in Marx," *Philosophy and Public Affairs* 8 (1979): 123.
42 Silvia Federici, "Marx and Feminism," *tripleC* 16, no. 2 (2018): 469.
43 Simone De Beauvoir, *The Second Sex*, trans. and ed. H. M. Parshley (London: Jonathan Cape, 1956), 80.
44 Popova, *Sexual Consent*, 13.
45 Popova, *Sexual Consent*, 13.
46 Kecia Ali, *Sexual Ethics and Islam: Feminist Reflections on Quran, Hadith, and Jurisprudence* (London: One World, 2016), 57. For discussions about the link between Islamic jurisprudence, present-day legal practices, and their impact on lived experiences of Muslim women, see various essays in Ziba Mir-Hosseini, Mulki Al-Sharmani, and Jana Rumminger, *Men in Charge? Rethinking Authority in Muslim Legal Tradition* (London: One World, 2015).
47 Tizro, *Domestic Violence in Iran*, 21.
48 Tizro, *Domestic Violence in Iran*, 40.
49 Tizro, *Domestic Violence in Iran*, 38.
50 For a discussion of these rights, see Tizro, *Domestic Violence in Iran*, 38.
51 Tizro, *Domestic Violence in Iran*, 117.
52 See Natasha Bakht, "The Incorporation of Shari'a in North America: Enforcing the Mahr to Combat Women's Poverty Post-relationship Dissolution," in *The Oxford*

Handbook of Islamic Law, ed. Anver M. Emon and Rumee Ahmed (Oxford: Oxford University Press, 2015), 1–30.
53 Ali, *Sexual Ethics and Islam*, 4.
54 Hina Azam, *Sexual Violation in Islamic Law: Substance, Evidence, and Procedure* (Cambridge: Cambridge University Press, 2015), 10.
55 Azam, *Sexual Violation in Islamic Law*, 86.
56 Tizro, *Domestic Violence in Iran*, 51.
57 Tizro, *Domestic Violence in Iran*, 52.
58 See Mahdi Tourage, "Affective Entanglements with the Sexual Imagery of Paradise in the Qur'an," *Body and Religion* 3, no. 1 (2019): 52–70.
59 Slave concubinage is sanctioned by the Qur'an. See the Qur'an 33:50 and 23:5-6. All translations of the Qur'an are mine.
60 Kecia Ali, *Marriage and Slavery in Early Islam* (Cambridge, MA: Harvard University Press, 2010), 164.
61 Tizro, *Domestic Violence in Iran*, 33; Azam, *Sexual Violation in Islamic Law*, 10.
62 Azam, *Sexual Violation in Islamic Law*, 24–5.
63 Ali, *Marriage and Slavery in Early Islam*, 120.
64 Nāzlī Kāmvarī, "*Kunish-i Guftār-i Ta'sīrguẕār bar Kampainhāy-i Ānlīn va Āflīn 'Alayh-i Qatl-i Nāmūsī, Tajāvuz-i Jinsī va Ḥijāb-i Ijbārī*." In Nāzlī Kāmvarī, ed. *Dar Mīyānih – Dar Ḥāshīyih: Dar Bāreh-i Lāyihay-i Faqr-i Ṭabaqih-i Mīyānī dar Iran* (Zamānih Media, 1400/2022), 235–80.
65 Tizro, *Domestic Violence in Iran*, 100.
66 Popova, *Sexual Consent*, 28.
67 Puran Sen, "'Crimes of Honour', Value and Meaning," in *Honour: Crimes, Paradigms, and Violence against Women*, ed. Lynn Welchman and Sara Hossain (London: Zed, 2005), 59.
68 Kāmvarī, "*Kunish-i Guftār-i*," 247.
69 Eisenstein, "Developing a Theory of Capitalist Patriarchy."
70 Cahill, *Rethinking Rape*, 4.
71 Marx, *Capital*, 326.
72 Claudia Yaghoobi, *Temporary Marriage in Iran: Gender and Body Politics in Modern Iranian Film and Literature* (Cambridge: Cambridge University Press, 2020), 196.
73 hooks, *The Will to Change*, 52.
74 Popova, *Sexual Consent*, 4, 23, 24.
75 Abu Ameenah Bilal Philips and Jameelah Jones, *Polygamy in Islam* (Riyadh, Saudi Arabia: International Islamic Publishing House, 2005), 48–9.
76 Fatima Seedat, "Sexual Economies of War and Sexual Technologies of the Body: Militarised Muslim Masculinity and the Islamist Production of Concubines for the Caliphate," *Agenda: Special Volume on Women, Religion and Security* 30, no. 3 (2017): 3.

77 Cahill, *Rethinking Rape*, 2.
78 Lisa Kemmerer, "Introduction," in *Sister Species: Women, Animals, and Social Justice*, ed. Lisa Kemmerer (Urbana: University of Illinois Press, 2011), 16.
79 Carol J. Adams, *The Sexual Politics of Meat: A Feminist-Vegetarian Critical Theory* (New York: Continuum, 2010).
80 Kecia Ali, "Muslims and Meat-Eating: Vegetarianism, Gender, and Identity," *Journal of Religious Ethics* 43, no. 2 (2015): 269.
81 Kemmerer, "Introduction," 25.
82 Carol J. Adams, "Woman-Battering and Harm to Animals," in *Animals and Women: Feminist Theoretical Explorations*, ed. Carol Adams and Josephine Donovan (Durham, NC: Duke University Press, 1995), 72.
83 "Gurbih," *Farhang-i Farsi-i Mo'in*, n.d.
84 Cahill, *Rethinking Rape*, 2, 28.
85 Popova, *Sexual Consent*, 17.
86 Kāmvarī, "*Kunish-i Guftār-i*," 259.
87 Tamura A. Lomax, "Occupy Rape Culture," *Feminist Wire*, November 5, 2011.
88 Patrick Kingsley, "80 Sexual Assaults in One Day—the Other Story of Tahrir Square," *Guardian*, July 5, 2013.
89 Stuart Kirby, Brian Francis, and Rosaline O'Flaherty, "Can the FIFA World Cup Football (Soccer) Tournament Be Associated with an Increase in Domestic Abuse?" *Journal of Research in Crime and Delinquency* 51, no. 3 (2014): 259–76.
90 Fae Chubin, "You May Smother My Voice, but You Will Hear My Silence: An Autoethnography on Street Sexual Harassment, the Discourse of Shame and Women's Resistance in Iran," *Sexualities* 17, no. 1/2 (2014): 176–93. Fae Chubin is the pseudonym of the author altered in the original publication in order to protect their identity.
91 Eve Kosofsky Sedgwick, *Epistemology of the Closet* (Berkeley: University of California Press, 1990), 21.
92 "LGBTQ+ 'Panic' Defense," n.d.
93 Susanna Paasonen, Feona Attwood, Alan McKee, John Mercer, and Clarissa Smith. *Objectification: On the Difference between Sex and Sexism* (London: Routledge, 2021), 29.
94 Martha C. Nussbaum, "Objectification," *Philosophy and Public Affairs* 24, no. 4 (1995): 257.
95 Claudia Yaghoobi, "Yusuf's 'Queer' Beauty in Persian Cultural Productions," *Comparatist* 40 (2016): 245–66.
96 Barbara Freyer Stowasser, *Women in the Qur'an, Traditions, and Interpretation* (Oxford: Oxford University Press, 1994), 50–6.
97 Stowasser, *Women in the Qur'an*, 52.
98 MacKinnon, *Toward a Feminist Theory of the State*, 124.

99 Popova, *Sexual Consent*, 10.
100 Yaghoobi, *Temporary Marriage in Iran*, 54.
101 Weeks, *The Problem with Work*, 4.
102 Yaghoobi, *Temporary Marriage in Iran*, 48–50.
103 Milner, "Reflections," 76.
104 "Apostolic Letter *Ordinatio Sacerdotalis* of John Paul II to the Bishops of the Catholic Church on Reserving Priestly Ordination to Men Alone," 1994.
105 R. W. Connell, *Masculinities* (Cambridge: Polity, 2005), 79.
106 Ruth Pearce, Sonja Erikainen, and Ben Vincent, "TERF Wars: An Introduction," *Sociological Review Monographs* 68, no. 4 (2020): 8–15.
107 Abbas Kiarostami, *Dah* (Ten), 2002.
108 Kiarostami, *Dah* (Ten), my translation. Similar argument is put forth by Nawal El Saadawi, in her *The Hidden Face of Eve: Women in the Arab World*, trans. Sherif Hetata (London: Zed, 2007), 102–26.
109 Martha C. Nussbaum, "'Whether from Reason or Prejudice': Taking Money for Bodily Services," *Journal of Legal Studies* 27, no. 2 (1998): 693.
110 Alara Efsun Yazicioglu, *Pink Tax and the Law: Discriminating against Women Consumers* (London: Routledge, 2018).
111 Yazicioglu, *Pink Tax and the Law*, 7, 25.
112 Popova, *Sexual Consent*, 152, 164, 179.
113 hooks, *The Will to Change*, 105, 72, 145, 166, 109.
114 hooks, *The Will to Change*, 143.
115 hooks, *The Will to Change*, 28.

5 Twitter Data Analysis on #MeTooIran

1 Khamenei.ir. "The Disaster of Countless Sexual Assaults on Western Women—Including Incidents Leading to #Metoo Campaign—and Islam's Proposal to Resolve It Http://English.Khamenei.Ir/News/5986/10-Facts-by-Ayatollah-Khamenei-Can-Hijab-Save-Western-Women Https://T.Co/TV1TzFcra4." Tweet. @*khamenei_ir* (blog), October 3, 2018. https://twitter.com/khamenei_ir/status/1047540289265647616.

2 Judith Rudakoff, ed., *Performing #MeToo: How Not to Look Away* (United Kingdom: Intellect, 2021); "Semantic Network Analysis of the International Communication Association | Human Communication Research | Oxford Academic," https://academic.oup.com/hcr/article-abstract/25/4/589/4554809?redirectedFrom=fulltext (accessed February 21, 2022).

3 Yasamin Rezai, "#MeToo in Iran: Lessons & Questions across Platforms," Instasociety, https://instasociety.org/issues/issue-ii/metoo-iran/ (accessed November 11, 2022).
4 Faranak Amidi, "100 Women: Muslim Women Rally Round #Mosquemetoo," BBC News, BBC, February 9, 2018, https://www.bbc.com/news/world-43006952
5 Rudakoff, *Performing #MeToo*.
6 Rudakoff, *Performing #MeToo*.
7 Farnaz Fassihi, "A #MeToo Awakening Stirs in Iran," *New York Times*, October 22, 2020, sec. World, https://www.nytimes.com/2020/10/22/world/middleeast/iran-metoo-aydin-aghdashloo.html
8 Anabel Quan-Haase, Kaitlynn Mendes, Dennis Ho, Olivia Lake, Charlotte Nau, and Darryl Pieber, "Mapping #MeToo: A Synthesis Review of Digital Feminist Research across Social Media Platforms," *New Media & Society* 23, no. 6 (June 1, 2021): 1700–20, https://doi.org/10.1177/1461444820984457
9 Ying Xiong, Moonhee Cho, and Brandon Boatwright, "Hashtag Activism and Message Frames among Social Movement Organizations: Semantic Network Analysis and Thematic Analysis of Twitter during the #MeToo Movement," *Public Relations Review* 45, no. 1 (2019): 10–23, https://doi.org/10.1016/j.pubrev.2018.10.014
10 Heather Lang, "#MeToo: A Case Study in Re-embodying Information," *Computers and Composition*, Digital Technologies, Bodies, and Embodiments, 53 (September 1, 2019): 9–20, https://doi.org/10.1016/j.compcom.2019.05.001
11 Quan-Haase et al., "Mapping #MeToo."
12 Xiong et al., "Hashtag Activism."
13 Marya L. Doerfel and George A. Barnett, "A Semantic Network Analysis of the International Communication Association," *Human Communication Research* 25, no. 4 (June 1, 1999): 589–603, https://doi.org/10.1111/j.1468-2958.1999.tb00463.x
14 Aimei Yang and Shari R. Veil, "Nationalism versus Animal Rights: A Semantic Network Analysis of Value Advocacy in Corporate Crisis," *International Journal of Business Communication* 54, no. 4 (October 1, 2017): 408–30, https://doi.org/10.1177/2329488415572781; Staci M. Zavattaro, P. Edward French, and Somya D. Mohanty, "A Sentiment Analysis of U.S. Local Government Tweets: The Connection between Tone and Citizen Involvement," *Government Information Quarterly* 32, no. 3 (July 1, 2015): 333–41, https://doi.org/10.1016/j.giq.2015.03.003
15 James A. Danowski, "Network Analysis of Message Content," *Progress in Communication Sciences* 12 (1993): 198–221; Doerfel, Marya L. "What Constitutes Semantic Network Analysis? A Comparison of Research and Methodologies," *Connections* 21, no. 2 (1998): 16–26, http://citeseerx.ist.psu.edu/viewdoc/download?doi=10.1.1.211.9021&rep=rep1&type=pdf#page=18
16 Xiong et al., "Hashtag Activism."
17 Xiong et al., "Hashtag Activism."

18 Xiong et al., "Hashtag Activism."
19 Xiong et al., "Hashtag Activism."
20 Xiong et al., "Hashtag Activism."
21 Sepideh Modrek and Bozhidar Chakalov, "The# MeToo Movement in the United States: Text Analysis of Early Twitter Conversations," *Journal of Medical Internet Research* 21, no. 9 (2019): e13837, https://www.jmir.org/2019/9/e13837/
22 Hossein Kermani and Marzieh Adham, "Mapping Persian Twitter: Networks and Mechanism of Political Communication in Iranian 2017 Presidential Election," *Big Data & Society* 8, no. 1 (2021): 20539517211025568.
23 The code can be accessed at https://github.com/mspayam/MeTooIran.
24 Mordek and Chakalov, "The# MeToo Movement."
25 Maciej Eder, Jan Rybicki, and Mike Kestemont, "Stylometry with R: A Package for Computational Text Analysis," *The R Journal* 8, no. 1 (2016): 107–21.

6 #Unveiling_the_Iranian_MeToo: Symptomatic Reading of Iranian MeToo through the Lens of Political Economy

1 Abby Ohlheiser, "The Woman behind 'Me Too' Knew the Power of the Phrase When She Created IT—10 Years Ago," *Washington Post* (WP Company, October 26, 2021), https://www.washingtonpost.com/news/the-intersect/wp/2017/10/19/the-woman-behind-me-too-knew-the-power-of-the-phrase-when-she-created-it-10-years-ago/
2 I insist that #MeToo is not a movement and should not be addressed by this term. It is a pure instance of feminist hashtag activism, and like any other activist forms of collective action must be conceived as merely a part of the feminist movement. I do prefer not to use the term "movement" in this text.
3 Chris Snyder and Linette Lopez, "Tarana Burke on Why She Created the #MeToo Movement—and Where It's Headed," *Business Insider Australia*, December 13, 2017, https://www.businessinsider.com.au/how-the-metoo-movement-started-where-its-headed-tarana-burke-time-person-of-year-women-2017-12.
4 Heather Berg, "Left of #Metoo," *Feminist Studies* 46, no. 2 (2020): 259–84, https://doi.org/10.15767/feministstudies.46.2.0259
5 "Marxism, Feminism and #Metoo," 1917: Journal of the International Bolshevik Tendency (No. 41—Marxism, Feminism and #MeToo, 2019), http://www.bolshevik.org/1917/no41/ibt_1917_41_08_me_too.html

6 Tarana Burke and Elizabeth Adetiba, "Tarana Burke Says #MeToo Should Center Marginalized Communities," in *Where Freedom Starts: Sex Power Violence #MeToo* (Brooklyn, NY: Verso, 2018), 28–38.
7 Qtd in Mary McKenna and Myles Baker, "Silvia Federici Challenges #MeToo Movement to Look at the Systemic, Economic Causes of Sexual Violence," *Works in Progress*, March 31, 2018, https://olywip.org/silvia-federici-challenges-metoo-movement-look-systemic-economic-causes-sexual-violence/
8 "Slavoj Zizek on #MeToo Movement," *Russia Today* (YouTube, January 17, 2019), https://www.youtube.com/watch?v=ai_UAPaoEW4
9 Rosalind Gill and Shani Orgad, "The Shifting Terrain of Sex and Power: From the 'Sexualization of Culture' to #Metoo," *Sexualities* 21, no. 8 (April 2018): 1313–24, https://doi.org/10.1177/1363460718794647
10 See Prohibition of Domestic Violence campaign, https://pdvc.bidarzani.com/. This activist practice has lost its momentum in recent years.
11 Paria Rahimi, "The Study of Cyber Activity Patterns of Women's Rights Activists and Their Relation to Activism in the Real Space" (MA dissertation, University of Tehran, Tehran, 2018).
12 "MeToo Movement in Iran," Wikipedia, February 22, 2023, https://fa.wikipedia.org/wiki/جنبش_من_هم_در_ایران.
13 Paul Ricoeur, "The Model of the Text: Meaningful Action Considered as a Text," *New Literary History* 5, no. 1 (1973): 91–117, https://doi.org/10.2307/468410
14 Robert Paul Resch, *Althusser and the Renewal of Marxist Social Theory* (Berkeley: University of California Press, 1992).
15 Louis Althusser and Étienne Balibar, *Reading Capital: The Complete Edition* (London: Verso, 2016), 2.
16 Martin Heidegger, *Being and Time: A Translation of Sein Und Zeit*, trans. Joan Stambaugh (Albany: State University of New York Press, 2010).
17 Robert J. C. Young, "Rereading the Symptomatic Reading," in *The Concept in Crisis: Reading Capital Today*, ed. Nick Nesbitt (Durham, NC: Duke University Press, 2017), 35–48.
18 Gregory Elliott, "Symptomatic Reading," in *A Dictionary of Cultural and Critical Theory*, ed. Michael Payne and Jessica Rae Barbera (Malden, MA: Wiley-Blackwell, 2013), 679.
19 The parasite is a term that Derrida himself has used to clarify "Deconstruction" in his letter to the Japanese philosopher Toshihiko Izutsu. See Jacques Derrida, "Letter to a Japanese Friend," in *Derrida and Différance*, ed. David O. Wood and Robert Bernasconi (Evanston, IL: Northwestern University Press, 1988), 1–6.
20 Nesbitt and Young, "Rereading the Symptomatic Reading."
21 Aida Qajar, "An Iranian Star Who Doesn't Understand No Means No," IranWire, April 21, 2021, https://iranwire.com/en/features/69391/

22 "The Shocking Words of Mohsen Namjoo among His Friends and Fans," *Feminism Everyday*, April 17, 2021, https://facebook.com/100048665487265/videos/283104060106230/?refsrc=deprecated&_rdr
23 Pierre Bourdieu, *Outline of a Theory of Practice* (Cambridge: Cambridge University Press, 2013), 178.
24 Erik Neveu, "Bourdieu's Capital(s): Sociologizing an Economic Concept," in *The Oxford Handbook of Pierre Bourdieu*, ed. Thomas Medvetz and Jeffrey J. Sallaz (Oxford: Oxford University Press, 2018), 417–51.
25 Bourdieu, *Outline of a Theory*.
26 Mairi Maclean, Charles Harvey, and Gerhard Kling, "Pathways to Power: Class, Hyper-Agency and the French Corporate Elite," *Organization Studies* 35, no. 6 (2014): 825–55, https://doi.org/10.1177/0170840613509919
27 Bourdieu, *Outline of a Theory*.
28 Pierre Bourdieu, "The Forms of Capital," in *Handbook of Theory and Research for the Sociology of Education*, ed. John Richardson (Westport, CT: Greenwood, 1986), 242; emphasis added.
29 Bourdieu, "The Forms of Capital."
30 Bourdieu, "The Forms of Capital."
31 Bourdieu, *Outline of a Theory*.
32 Bridget Fowler, "Pierre Bourdieu: Unorthodox Marxist?," in *The Legacy of Pierre Bourdieu: Critical Essays*, ed. Simon Susen and Bryan S. Turner (London: Anthem, 2011), 33–58.
33 Bourdieu, *Outline of a Theory*.
34 Farnaz Fassihi, "A #MeToo Awakening Stirs in Iran," *New York Times*, October 22, 2020, https://www.nytimes.com/2020/10/22/world/middleeast/iran-metoo-aydin-aghdashloo.html
35 "Aydin Aghdashloo," Wikipedia, Wikimedia Foundation, November 15, 2022, https://en.wikipedia.org/wiki/Aydin_Aghdashloo
36 "Iranian Artworks Go under Hammer at Tehran Auction," Kayhan International, August 15, 2021, https://kayhan.ir/files/en/publication/pages/1400/5/23/2078_16 577.pdf
37 Qtd in Bridget Fowler, "Pierre Bourdieu: Unorthodox Marxist?," in *The Legacy of Pierre Bourdieu: Critical Essays*, ed. Simon Susen and Bryan S. Turner (London: Anthem, 2011), 34.
38 Qtd in Dale Southerton, "Symbolic Capital," in *Encyclopedia of Consumer Culture*, ed. Dale Southerton (Thousand Oaks, CA: SAGE, 2011), 1418–20, https://dx.doi.org/10.4135/9781412994248.n532
39 Bourdieu, *Outline of a Theory*, 183.
40 Dale, "Symbolic Capital."

41 Cheleen Mahar, Richard Harker, and Chris Wilkes, "The Basic Theoretical Position," in *An Introduction to the Work of Pierre Bourdieu: The Practice of Theory*, ed. Richard Harker, Cheleen Mahar, and Chris Wilkes (Houndmills, Basingstoke: Palgrave Macmillan, 2003), 14.

42 Editorial, "12 Billion Sales Logic," Artmag, January 31, 2021, https://artmag.ir/en/painting/281-12-billion-sales-logic.

43 "Who Is the Buyer of the 12 Billion Toman Painting?," Tabnak Javan, tabnakjavan, January 17, 2021, https://tabnakjavan.com/fa/news/33521/ خریدار-تابلوی-۱۲-میلیارد-تومانی-کیست

44 "The trial of Keivan Emamverdi who is accused of dozens of rape cases is postponed," Radio Farda, September 26, 2021, https://www.radiofarda.com/a/31478617.html

45 Qtd in "Why Is the Judiciary Stalling on the Trial of Alleged Rapist Keyvan Emamverdi?," *Iran Wire*, June 3, 2020, https://iranwire.com/en/society/104816-why-is-the-judiciary-stalling-the-trial-of-alleged-serial-rapist-keyvan-emamverdi/

46 "As a Serial Rapist Is Sentenced to Death, Victims Slam Lack of Justice," *IranWire*, July 11, 2022, https://iranwire.com/en/women/105617-as-serial-rapist-is-sentenced-to-death-victims-slam-lack-of-justice/

47 Harker et al., "The Basic Theoretical Position," 1–25.

48 Fowler, "Pierre Bourdieu."

49 Bourdieu, *Outline of a Theory*.

50 Qtd in Dale. "Symbolic Capital," https://dx.doi.org/10.4135/9781412994248.n532

51 In writing this paragraph, I have benefited from the metaphors and phrases that Derrida has used in his seminal book *Archive Fever: A Freudian Impression*, trans. Eric Prenowitz (Chicago: University of Chicago Press, 2008).

52 "Who Is Keivan Emamverdi, and What Allegations Are Made against Him by Female Students?" YouTube, August 21, 2020, https://www.youtube.com/watch?v=UR5SEYh9iGs

53 Bourdieu, "The Forms of Capital," 249.

7 Whose Voice Is Missing? MeToo Digital Storytelling on Instagram and the Politics of Inclusion

Sincere thanks to my supervisors, Prof. Susanna Paasonen and Dr. Kata Kyrölä, as well as to the participants at the media studies research seminar at the University of Turku for their valuable suggestions and feedback.

1. Sara Ahmed, *Living a Feminist Life* (Durham, NC: Duke University Press, 2017), 200.
2. See K. Soraya Batmanghelichi and Leila Mouri, "Cyberfeminism, Iranian Style: Online Feminism in Post-2009 Iran," *Feminist Media Histories* 3, no. 1 (2017): 50–80; and Meaghan Smead Samuels, "Upgrading the Women's Movement in Iran: Through Cultural Activism, Creative Resistance, and Adaptability" master's thesis, University of Washington, 2018.
3. See Batmanghelichi and Mouri, "Cyberfeminism, Iranian Style."
4. Sima Shakhsari, *Politics of Rightful Killing: Civil Society, Gender, and Sexuality in Weblogistan* (Durham, NC: Duke University Press, 2020).
5. Ladan Rahbari, Susan Dierickx, Gily Coene, and Chia Longman, "Transnational Solidarity with Which Muslim Women? The Case of the My Stealthy Freedom and World Hijab Day Campaigns," *Politics and Gender* 17, no. 1 (2019): 1–24.
6. Sara Tafakori, "Digital Feminism beyond Nativism and Empire: Affective of Recognition and Competing Claims to Suffering in Iranian Women's Campaigns," *Journal of Women in Culture and Society* 47, no. 1 (2021): 47–80.
7. Nick Couldry, "Mediatization or Mediation? Alternative Understandings of the Emergent Space of Digital Storytelling," *New Media and Society* 10, no. 3 (2008): 374.
8. See Sonja Vivienne, *Digital Identity and Everyday Activism Sharing Private Stories with Networked Publics* (Basingstoke: Palgrave Macmillan, 2016).
9. See Nomy Bitman, "'Which Part of My Group Do I Represent?': Disability Activism and Social Media Users with Concealable Communicative Disabilities." *Information Communication and Society* 26, no. 3 (2021): 619–36; and Veronica Barassi, "Social Media Activism, Self-Representation and the Construction of Political Biographies," in *Routledge Companion to Media and Activism*, ed. Graham Meikle, 1st ed. (London: Routledge, 2018), 148–57.
10. See Asef Bayat, *Life as Politics: How Ordinary People Change the Middle East*, 2nd ed. (Stanford, CA: Stanford University Press, 2013); and Vivienne, *Digital Identity and Everyday Activism*.
11. See Sarah Banet-Weiser, *Empowered: Popular Feminism and Popular Misogyny* (Durham, NC: Duke University Press, 2018).
12. This leftist group started its work in the winter of 2010 as a Tehran-based women's rights collective. In spring 2014, the group expanded its scope and changed its name from Ta khanevadeh-ye Barabar (to an equal family) to Bidarzani (women's awakening). They announced the latter one represents the major aim of the group, which is consciousness-raising; see Batmanghelichi and Mouri, "Cyberfeminism, Iranian Style."
13. The Harasswatch group was established and inspired by campaigns and civil movements in other parts of the world, such as HarassMap in Egypt. The fieldwork

of this group began on March 8, 2018, with the design and distribution bundle of anti-harassment posters. Since 2019, their web-based platforms have been the space to discuss different types of sexual harassments, particularly in public places.

14 The history of #MeTooIran goes back a few months before the #MeToo spread rapidly in Iran, and it mainly focused on sharing others' sexual violence experiences. At the beginning, this page was initiated with the name @me_too_iran by a diaspora actress and feminist activist. She unfolded her experience of sexual harassment behind the scenes of Iranian serials and asked other women to send their stories. As the page was blocked in September 2020, group members created a new page with a new name.

15 See Aline Shakti Franzke, Anja Bechmann, Michael Zimmer, and Charles M. Ess and the Association of Internet Researchers, Internet Research: Ethical Guidelines 3.0, 2019, https://aoir.org/reports/ethics3.pdf (accessed October 18, 2021)

16 Sarah Banet-Weiser, Rosalind Gill, and Catherine Rottenberg, "Postfeminism, Popular Feminism and Neoliberal Feminism? Sarah Banet-Weiser, Rosalind Gill and Catherine Rottenberg in Conversation," *Feminist Theory* 21, no. 1 (2020): 9.

17 See Rosa Crepax, "The Aestheticisation of Feminism: A Case Study of Feminist Instagram Aesthetics," *ZoneModa Journal* 10, no. 1S (2020): 71–81.

18 See Laura Savolainen, Justus Uitermark, and John D. Boy, "Filtering Feminisms: Emergent Feminist Visibilities on Instagram," *New Media and Society* 24, no. 3 (2022): 557–79.

19 Harasswatch, me_too_movement_iran and Bidarzani had 46.5K, 22.9K, and 21.9K followers, respectively, when the study was conducted.

20 See Tama Leaver, Tim Highfield, and Crystal Abidin, *Instagram: Visual Social Media Cultures* (Newark: Polity, 2020).

21 See Matthew Salzano, "Technoliberal Participation: Black Lives Matter and Instagram Slideshows," Paper presented at AoIR 2021: The 22nd Annual Conference of the Association of Internet Researchers," 2021.

22 A trigger warning is a written or oral statement given directly before presenting material commonly known to cause trauma, which discloses that the content covered might be triggering for trauma survivors.

23 See Martin Gibbs, James Meese, Michael Arnold, Bjorn Nansen, and Marcus Carter, "Funeral and Instagram: Death, Social Media, and Platform Vernacular," *Information, Communication & Society* 18, no. 3 (2015): 255–68.

24 Leaver et al., *Instagram*.

25 See Diana Zulli, "Evaluating Hashtag Activism: Examining the Theoretical Challenges and Opportunities of #BlackLivesMatter," *Participation* 17, no. 1 (2020): 197–216.

26 Leaver et al., *Instagram*.

27 Leaver et al., *Instagram*, 215.

28 Vivienne, *Digital Identity and Everyday Activism*.
29 Anabel Quan-Haase, Kaitlynn Mendes, Dennis Ho, Olivia Lake, Charlotte Nau, and Darryl Pieber, "Mapping #MeToo: A Synthesis Review of Digital Feminist Research across Social Media Platforms," *New Media & Society* 23, no. 6 (2021): 1708.
30 See Naeemul Hassan, Manash Kumar Mandal, Mansurul Bhuiyan, Aparna Moitra, and Syed Ishtiaque Ahmed, "Nonparticipation of Bangladeshi Women in #MeToo Movement," *ACM International Conference Proceeding Series*, Association for Computing Machinery (2019).
31 See Michel Foucault, *Fearless Speech*, ed. Joseph Pearson (Los Angeles: Semiotext(e), 2001).
32 See Caroline Dadas, "Making Sense of #MeToo: Intersectionality and Contemporary Feminism," *Peitho* 22, no. 3 (2020), https://cfshrc.org/article/making-sense-of-metoo-intersectionality-and-contemporary-feminism/
33 See Foucault, *Fearless Speech*, 19.
34 See Tanya Serisier, *Speaking Out: Feminism, Rape and Narrative Politics* (London: Palgrave Macmillan, 2018).
35 Ruth Page, *Narratives Online Stories in Social Media* (Cambridge: Cambridge University Press, 2018), 197.
36 See Page, *Narratives Online Stories*.
37 See Zizi Papacharissi, *Affective Publics: Sentiment, Technology and Politics* (New York: Oxford University Press, 2015).
38 See Paul Dawson, "Hashtag Narrative: Emergent Storytelling and Affective Publics in the Digital Age," *International Journal of Cultural Studies* 23, no. 6 (2020): 968–83.
39 See Faiza Hirji, "Claiming Our Space: Muslim Women, Activism, and Social Media," *Islamophobia Studies Journal* 6, no. 1 (2021): 78–92.
40 See Nadia Aghtaie, "Rape within Heterosexual Intimate Relationships in Iran: Legal Frameworks, Culture and Structural Violence," *Families, Relationships and Societies* 6, no. 2 (2017): 167–83.
41 See Jessalynn Keller, Kaitlynn Mendes, and Jessica Ringrose, "Speaking 'Unspeakable Things': Documenting Digital Feminist Responses to Rape Culture," *Journal of Gender Studies* 27, no. 1 (2018): 22–36; and Kaitlynn Mendes, Jessalynn Keller, and Jessica Ringrose, "Digitized Narratives of Sexual Violence: Making Sexual Violence Felt and Known through Digital Disclosures," *New Media and Society* 21, no. 6 (2019): 1290–310.
42 See Gayatri Chakravorty Spivak, "Can the Subaltern Speak?," in *Can the Subaltern Speak: Reflections on The History of An Idea*, ed. Rosalind C. Morris (New York: Columbia University Press, 2010), 21–78.
43 Malin Holm, "The Rise of Online Counterpublics? The Limits of Inclusion in a Digital Age," doctoral dissertation, Uppsala University, 2019.

44 Kimberle Crenshaw, "Postscript," in *Framing Intersectionality Debates on a Multi-Faceted Concept in Gender Studies*, ed. Helma Lutz, Maria Teresa Herrera Vivar, and Linda Supik (Farnham: Ashgate, 2011), 221–33.
45 See Neha Kagal, Leah Cowan, and Huda Jawad, "Beyond the Bright Lights: Are Minoritized Women Outside the Spotlight Able to Say #MeToo?," in *#MeToo and the Politics of Social Change*, ed. Bianca Fileborn and Rachel Loney-Howes (Cham: Palgrave, 2019), 133–49.
46 See Arezoo Yari, Hosein Zahednezhad, Reza Ghanei Gheshlagh, and Amanj Kurdi, "Frequency and Determinants of Domestic Violence against Iranian Women during the Covid-19 Pandemic: A National Cross-Sectional Survey," *BMC Public Health* 21, no. 1727 (2021): 1–10.
47 See Verity Trott, "Networked Feminism: Counterpublics and the Intersectional Issues of #MeToo," *Feminist Media Studies* 21, no. 7 (2021): 1125–42.
48 See Anna Mollow, "Unvictimizable: Toward a Fat Black Disability Studies," *African American Review* 50, no. 2 (2017): 105–21.
49 Kagal et al. "Beyond the Bright Lights."
50 *Karkhaneh*, an online leftist magazine.
51 See Sara Ahmed, *The Cultural Politics of Emotion*, 2nd ed. (Edinburgh: Edinburgh University Press, 2014).
52 Naomi Barnes, "Trace Publics as a Qualitative Critical Network Tool: Exploring the Dark Matter in the #MeToo Movement," *New Media and Society* 22, no. 7 (2020): 1308.
53 See Leaver et al. *Instagram*.

8 Sexual Violence, MeToo, and Iranian Lesbians' Censored Voices

1 Asef Bayat, *Life as Politics: How Ordinary People Change the Middle East* (Stanford: Stanford University Press, 2013).
2 I prefer to use the words woman/women with an asterisk at the top to address all the current and historic discussions about them and to acknowledge all the differences in their use for different groups of people—simply to avoid reproducing them as gender or sex categories, biologic or not.
3 Howard S. Becker, *Outsiders: Études de sociologie de la deviance* (Paris: Éditions Métailié, [1985] 2020).
4 I borrow the title "sister ousider" from the well-known *Sister Outsider: Essays and Speeches*, a collection written by Audre Lorde. See: Audre Lorde, *Sister Outsider: Essays and Speeches* (Trumansburg, NY: Crossing, 1984).

5 « Au carrefour de multiples sites d'oppressions liées », Nassira Hedjerassi, Audre Lorde, l'outsider. Une poétesse et intellectuelle féministe africaine-américaine. Travail, genre et sociétés. 37, 2017, 125.
6 Natacha Chetuti-Osorovitz, "Reflections on Historic Lesbian Feminisms," in *Lesbian Feminism: Essays Opposing Global Heteropatriarchies*, ed. Niharika Banerjea, Kath Browne, Eduarda Ferreira, Marta Olasik, and Julie Podmore (Londres: Zed, 2019), 230.
7 Which is differentiated here from the sexist violence: by sexist violence, I mean the "acts of discrimination perpetrated because of the (considered) biological sex of the person, in this case the female sex," while the sexual violence is about the "assaults related to sexuality of the aggressor and the aggressed. About women, those assaults can be sexist or/and homophobe when they are committed for stigmatizing a homosexual woman." See Myaryse Jaspard, *Les violences contre les femmes* (Paris: La Découverte, 2005), 62.
8 I borrow this term from Betty Friedan for now and will explain it shortly.
9 Corina Schulze, Sarah Koon-Maganin, and Valerie L. Bryan, *Gender Identity, Sexual Orientation & Sexual Aggression: Challenging the Myths* (London: Lynne Rienner, 2019), xii.
10 It should be noted that in describing this case during the heyday of the Iranian MeToo movement, none of the names raised are mentioned in this text, to respect their willingness to be named or not, of which I am not aware as the author. The name of the accused person is also deliberately omitted in this text to avoid recounting charges that may or may not be subject to judicial review.
11 This video was first posted on his Instagram account. It is no longer accessible but can be watched here: https://www.youtube.com/watch?v=YZU7jJKvBH4 (last visited on November 2, 2022).
12 This audio can be listened here too: https://www.youtube.com/watch?v=oSUj9pb4eT0 (accessed October 31, 2022).
13 Jane Czyzselska, "Lesbophobia Is Homophobia with a Side-Order of Sexism," *Guardian*, Opinion, July 9, 2013.
14 See Natacha Chetcuti-Osorovitz, "De 'On ne naît pas femme' à 'On n'est pas femme': De Simone de Beauvoir à Monique Wittig," *Genre, sexualité & société*, no. 1, "Lesbiennes" (Printemps 2009), https://journals.openedition.org/gss/477 (accessed January 16, 2022).
15 The term "lavender menace" was used by Betty Friedan, the president of the National Organization for Women (NOW), in 1969, to describe associations with lesbianism as a "threat" to the feminist movement. As a result of this description, many lesbians, already active in NOW, decided to leave the organization in protest of its exclusion of lesbians.

16 Elise Chenier, "Lesbian Feminism," 2015, GLBTQ Encyclopedia: http://www.glbtqarchive.com/sshindex.html (last visited on January 14, 2022).
17 I do not include the letter "T" here, because trans people can have their activities in Iran, legally, even if it is also too difficult.
18 Monique Wittig, "On ne naît pas femme," *Questions féministes*, no. 8 (1980): 75–84.
19 Becker, *Outsiders*.
20 I should note again that the purpose here is not to assign a specific gender category to a particular group, or even to define a specific biological sex belonging to a specific sexual orientation. What is important here is the explanation of the rejection of those who, like others, are considered in society with administrative and nonadministrative, selective, or nonselective identities as women* but are marginalized and excluded from any discussion related to sexual violence by a group of these women*.
21 Preferably, the term "minorized groups" is used for what is normally called "minority groups"; the main reason, among others, is to draw attention to the active side of "building minorities" by dominant groups, instead of putting the "old-fashioned" emphasis on the passive side of "being a minority" inherently, whatever that means: based on quantitative discussions, or based on the discrimination and exclusion this "minority" suffers.
22 It should be noted that the identity of these people has been anonymized for their safety, they all identify as "lesbians," and my conversations with them outside the frame of the interview, but within a methodological frame of the storytelling, have informed my analysis. Our conversations were in Farsi, the first language of all of us, and all translations are mine, checked by all of them at the end. All respondents' identities are and remain anonymous. The pronouns used are nicknames.
23 Scholars have discussed this kind of improper use of the body, gender, and sexuality for nationalist purposes extensively. For instance, see Sara R. Farris's *In the Name of Women's Rights: The Rise of Femonationalism* (Durham, NC: Duke University Press, 2017), where the author shows how immigrant women's bodies have been (mis)used for the nationalist purposes of Western states, particularly in Europe, to give birth to next generations of these families, to be(come) the "good" citizens for their (grand)parents' destination countries, as the first generation does not belong to this category of good citizen because of all those supposed cultural differences. Azadeh Kian's "La fabrique du genre, des corps et des sexualités en Iran: entre nationalisme et islamisme," in *État-nation et fabrique du genre, des corps et des sexualités: Iran, Turquie et Afghanistan*, ed. Lucia Direnberger and Azadeh Kian (Aix-en-Provence: Presses universitaires de Provence, 2019), 21–47, also explains the use of the bodies of urban Shiite women speaking Persian as the women of

center, who have not been excluded in the process of building nation-states like *Other*(ed) women (nonurban, non-Shiite and non-Persian speaking), to reproduce the great guardians (nation) (and rather the sons) of the great mother (homeland), ruled by the great father (the state). Jasbir K. Puar coined the well-known term "Homonationalism," in *Terrorist Assemblages: Homonationalism in Queer Times* (Durham, NC: Duke University Press, 2007), to refer to homosexual bodies being (mis)used by nation-states for different political purposes, such as justifying wars, sanctions, and other kinds of interventions. Finally, Jules Falquet's "Lesbiennes migrantes, entre hétéro-circulation et recompositions néolibérales du nationalism," in *Le genre au cœur des migrations*, ed. Claire Cossée, Adelina Miranda, Nouria Oualin, and Djaouida Séhili (Paris: Édition Pétra, 2012), 123–48, shows how lesbian immigrant bodies and identities have always been used by French nationalists and neoliberal states.

24 I borrow this title from the well-known *Sister Outsider: Essays and Speeches*, a collection written by Audre Lorde.
25 Bayat, *Life as Politics*.
26 Simone De Beauvoir, *Le deuxième sexe* (Paris: Gallimard, 1949).
27 Becker, *Outsiders*, 38.
28 Nicholas Journet, "Outsiders: études de sociologie de la deviance," in *La Sociologie*, ed. Xavier Molénat (Auxerre: Éditions Sciences Humaines, 2009), 93–4.
29 Jess Ison, "'It's Not Just Men and Women': LGBTQIA People and #MeToo," in *#MeToo and the Politics of Social Change*, ed. Bianca Fileborn and Rachel Loney-Howes (London: Palgrave Macmillan, 2019), 151.
30 Silvia Federici, *Par-delà les frontières du corps* (Paris: Divergence, 2020), 72–3.
31 Shane Phelan, *Identity Politics: Lesbian Feminism and the Limits of Community* (Philadelphia: Temple University Press, 1989).
32 Elizabeth Spelman, *Inessential Woman: Problems of Exclusion in Feminist Thought* (Boston: Beacon, 1988).
33 Joshua Gamson, "Messages of Exclusion: Gender, Movements, and Symbolic Boundaries," *Gender and Society* 11, no. 2 (April 1997): 181.
34 Diana Fuss, ed., *Inside/Out: Lesbian Theories, Gay Theories* (New York: Routledge, 1991), 1.
35 Falquet, J. (2020). « De la lutte contre le racisme au soutien aux demandeuses d'asile lesbiennes : expériences lesbiennes féministes en France depuis la fin des années 90 », Recherches féministes, 33, 2, pp. 129–148.
36 Radicalesbians, "The Woman-Identified Woman," in *Radical Feminism*, ed. Anne Koedt, Ellen Levine, and Anita Rapone (New York: Quadrangle, 1973), 235, 240–5.

9 The White-Collars' New Masculinities in #MeToo: How to Maintain Gendered Privileges?

1. By "violence against women" in this study, I mean physical persecutions, rape, sexual coercion, sexual harassment, sexual blackmail, or similar forms of threats, unwanted sexual intercourse or sexual attention, sexual use or manipulation and abuse, unwelcome touching, and asking sexual favors in hierarchical formal relation. The list is obviously not exhaustive.
2. See Raewyn W. Connell, *Masculinities*, 2nd ed. (Berkeley: University of California Press, 2005); and *Gender and Power: Society, the Person and Sexual Politics* (New York: John Wiley, 2013).
3. Due to the fact that this is a sensitive issue with regard to the security of this group and these activists, to avoid any risks they may face by uncovering this information, I préférée not to mention their names.
4. See Robert W. Connell, "The Role of Men and Boys in Achieving Gender Equality," Group Meeting, organized by DAW in collaboration with iLO and uNAiDs, Brasilia, Brazil (2003); William J. Goode, "Why Men Resist," in *Rethinking the Family*, ed. Barrie Thorne and Marilyn Yalom (New York: Longman, 1982); Michael A. Messner and Nancy M. Solomon, "Social Justice and Men's Interests: The Case of Title IX," *Journal of Sport and Social Issues* 31, no. 2 (2007): 162–78; Bob Pease, *Undoing Privilege: Unearned Advantage in a Divided World* (Bloomsbury, 2010); and Sharon Rogers, "What Men Think about Gender Equality: Lessons from Oxfam GB Staff in Delhi and Dhaka," in *Gender Equality and Men: Learning from Practice* (Oxford: Oxfam GB, 2004).
5. Harry Ferguson, Jeff Hearn, Keith Pringle, Ursula Muller, Elzbieta Oleksy, Emmi Lattu, Teemu Tallberg, Voldemar Kolga, Irina Novikova, Alex Raynor, and Øystein Gullvåg Holter, "Critical Studies on Men in Ten European Countries: (4) Newspaper and Media Representations," *Men and Masculinities* 6, no. 2 (2003): 173–201. See Benno De Keijzer, "Masculinities: Resistance and Change," in *Gender Equality and Men: Learning from Practice*, ed. Sandy Ruxton (Oxfam GB, 2004), 28–49.
6. See Connell, *Masculinities*; Bob Connell, Tim Carrigan, and Lee John, *Toward a New Sociology of Masculinity* (Routledge, 2018); and Ronald F. Levant, "Toward the Reconstruction of Masculinity," *Journal of Family Psychology* 5, nos. 3–4 (1992): 379.
7. Raewyn W. Connell, and James W. Messerschmidt, "Faut-il repenser le concept de masculinité hégémonique?," *Terrains travaux* 2 (2015): 155.
8. Connell, *Masculinities*, 260.
9. Deniz Kandiyoti, *The Paradoxes of Masculinity: Some Thoughts on Segregated Societies* (Routledge, 2016), 196–212; Hossein Adibi, "Sociology of Masculinity in the Middle East," in *Social Change in the 21st Century*, 2006 Conference Proceedings (Queensland University of Technology, 2006), 1–10; and Marcia C.

Inhorn, *The New Arab Man: Emergent Masculinities, Technologies, and Islam in the Middle East* (Princeton, NJ: Princeton University Press, 2013), 900–1.
10 See Fataneh Farahani, "Diasporic Masculinities," *Nordic Journal of Migration Research* 2, no. 2 (2012): 159; Zara Saeidzadeh, "Are Trans Men the Manliest of Men?" Gender Practices, Trans Masculinity and Mardānegī in Contemporary Iran," *Journal of Gender Studies* 29, no. 3 (2020): 295–309; Minoo Moallem, "Staging Masculinity in Iran–Iraq War Movies," in *The Palgrave Handbook of Asian Cinema* (London: Palgrave Macmillan, 2018), 489–506; Shahin Gerami, "Islamist Masculinity and Muslim Masculinities," *Handbook of Studies on Men and Masculinities* 448 (2005); Mehri Honarbin-Holliday, "Emerging Forms of Masculinity in the Islamic Republic of Iran," *Cultural Revolution in Iran: Contemporary Popular Culture in the Islamic Republic* 41 (2013): 59; and Robert Joseph Bell, *Lūtī Masculinity in Iranian Modernity, 1785–1941: Marginalization and the Anxieties of Proper Masculine Comportment* (City University of New York, 2015).
11 Sivan Balslev, "Dressed for Success: Hegemonic Masculinity, Elite Men and Westernisation in Iran, c. 1900–40," *Gender & History* 26, no. 3 (2014): 545–64.
12 Shahin Gerami, "Mullahs, Martyrs, and Men: Conceptualizing Masculinity in the Islamic Republic of Iran," *Men and Masculinities* 5, no. 3 (2003): 257–74.
13 Alison Bailey, "Privilege: Expanding on Marilyn Frye's Oppression," *Journal of Social Philosophy* 29, no. 3 (1998): 109.
14 Goode, "Why Men Resist," 294.
15 Pease, *Undoing Privilege*, 2010.
16 Connell, *Masculinities*, 246; and Robert W. Connell, "Scrambling in the Ruins of Patriarchy: Neo-liberalism and Men's Divided Interests in Gender Change," in *Gender: From Costs to Benefits* (VS Verlag für Sozialwissenschaften, 2003), 58–69.
17 "Let us know that, like many other men, I am, in part, a victim of a patriarchal culture," one of the male accused wrote during #MeToo in Iran.
18 https://www.youtube.com/watch?v=xlfGWpbPJj8
19 Léo Thiers-Vidal, "De «L'Ennemi principal» aux principaux ennemis," *Position vécue, subjectivité et consciences masculines de domination* (Paris: L'Harmattan, coll. Savoir et formation, série Genre et éducation, 2010), 40; Colette Guillaumin, *Racism, Sexism, Power and Ideology* (Routledge, 2002); Christine Delphy, *L'ennemi principal-tome 1: Économie politique du patriarcat*, vol. 1 (Syllepse, 2013); and Dani Cavallaro, *French Feminist Theory: An Introduction* (A&C Black, 2003).
20 Alberto Godenzi, "Determinants of Culture: Men and Economic Power," ed. Ingeborg Breines, Robert Connell, and Ingrid Eide (Paris: UNESCO, 2000), 35–51.
21 Goode, "Why Men Resist," 295.

22. Morgan E. PettyJohn Morgan, Finneran K. Muzzey, Megan K. Maas, and Heather L. McCauley, "# HowIWillChange: Engaging Men and Boys in the# MeToo Movement," *Psychology of Men & Masculinities* 20, no. 4 (2019): 612.
23. Peter G. Jaffe, Janet R. Johnston, Claire V. Crooks, and Nicholas Bala, "Custody Disputes Involving Allegations of Domestic Violence: Toward a Differentiated Approach to Parenting Plans," *Family Court Review* 46, no. 3 (2008): 500–22.
24. About this exception case, see: https://www.bbc.com/persian/iran-53902802
25. https://www.youtube.com/watch?v=xlfGWpbPJj8
26. https://www.nytimes.com/2021/01/05/world/middleeast/iran-sexual-violence-metoo-women.html
27. https://twitter.com/SOmatali/status/1297060455249313793.
28. Heidi Hartmann, "The Unhappy Marriage of Marxism and Feminism," *Capital and Class*, March 4, 2015, 11, https://web.ics.purdue.edu/~hoganr/SOC%20602/Hartmann_1979
29. Messner and Solomon, "Social Justice and Men's Interests."
30. Charles Wright Mills, *White Collars: The American Middle Classes* (Oxford: Oxford University Press, 1951).
31. Edwin H. Sutherland, *White Collar Crime* (Yale University Press, 1983).
32. Sumita Kunashakaran, "Un (Wo)manned Aerial Vehicles: An Assessment of How Unmanned Aerial Vehicles Influence Masculinity in the Conflict Arena," *Contemporary Security Policy* 37, no. 1 (2016): 43.
33. Scott John, Kerry Carrington, and Alison McIntosh, "Globalization, Frontier Masculinities and Violence: Booze, Blokes and Brawls," *British Journal of Criminology* 50, no. 3 (2010): 393–413.
34. Michael Flood, "Men's Collective Struggles for Gender Justice," in *Handbook of Studies on Men and Masculinities*, ed. Michael Kimmel, Jeff Hearn, and R. W. Connell (Thousand Oaks, CA: Sage, 2005), 459.
35. https://www.youtube.com/watch?v=LK2SqZp9Xn0
36. https://www.radiofarda.com/a/31211636.html; https://www.youtube.com/watch?v=xlfGWpbPJj8
37. The stories published in the Persian websites of Bidarzani and Harassment Watch provide similar examples in this regard. Likewise, an activist-journalist in exile, who was accused by three women, expressed similar characteristics. For further details of these women's stories, see the statement released in 2017 by a group of women activists in Iran: https://www.facebook.com/notes/367637097759251/
38. Given that most of white-collar men in Iran have already had sufficient access to sexual relationships, their motivation for exercising violence goes beyond the satisfaction of their "sexual needs." The predominant driving force behind the harassment of this particular social layer is to prove their masculine power—to themselves as much as to others—and to gain control over the female body.

Internalizing the capitalist logic of competition (Robert W. Connell, *The Men and the Boys* [Cambridge: Polity, 2000], 52), the hyper-competitive characteristics of their male subjectivity led them to compete with other men over women's sexuality. Far from being a traditional or precapitalist form of patriarchy, this type of masculinity is specific to the "entrepreneurial culture" of the present time, but the further elaboration of this issue goes beyond the boundaries of this research. For more information, see: Connell, "Scrambling in the Ruins of Patriarchy," 58–69.

39 Noushin Ahmadi Khorasani, *Iranian Women's One Million Signatures Campaign for Equality: The Inside Story*, English ed. (Women's Learning Partnership, 2009); Haideh Moghissi, *Populism and Feminism in Iran: Women's Struggle in a Male-Defined Revolutionary Movement* (Springer, 2016); Afsaneh Najmabadi, "Feminism in an Islamic Republic," in *Islam, Gender and Social Change*, ed. Yvonne Haddad and John Esposito (1998), 59–84; Asef Bayat, "A Women's Non-movement: What It Means to Be a Woman Activist in an Islamic State," *Comparative Studies of South Asia, Africa and the Middle East* 27, no. 1 (2007): 160–72.

40 https://www.instagram.com/p/CEoHTFUHzv5/?utm_source=ig_web_copy_link

41 Godenzi, "Determinants of Culture."

42 Ellen Willis, "How Now, Iron Johns?," *Nation* 269, no. 20 (1999): 18–21.

43 https://www.ifop.com/publication/les-hommes-et-la-masculinite-a-lere-post-metoo/ (accessed November 2021).

44 Marc Bloch, *Apologie pour l'histoire* (A. Colin, 1949), 41.

45 https://www.instagram.com/p/CEoHTFUHzv5/?utm_source=ig_web_copy_link

46 Balslev, "Dressed for Success," 546.

47 These demarcations are performed in the name of gendered egalitarian values and with the gesture of "neutrality," but they are, in fact, for the benefit of men who defend their threatened masculinity. This complex process clearly demonstrates the need to break the male monopoly on the production and distribution of knowledge by which he also enjoys framing sexual harassment and its boundaries in favor of his social sex interest.

48 https://www.youtube.com/watch?v=xlfGWpbPJj8

49 https://www.instagram.com/p/CEoHTFUHzv5/?utm_source=ig_web_copy_link

50 See more than a dozen stories published by the @bidarzani platform in Telegram and Twitter.

51 https://www.instagram.com/p/CEoHTFUHzv5/?utm_source=ig_web_copy_link

52 Godenzi, "Determinants of Culture."

53 Connell and Messerschmidt, "Faut-il repenser," 185.

54 Bob Pease, "(Re)constructing Men's Interests," *Men and Masculinities* 5, no. 2 (2002): 173.

55 Connell, *Masculinities*; Goode, "Why Men Resist."

56 William J. Goode, "Why Men Resist," in *Rethinking the Family*, ed. Barrie Thorne and Marilyn Yalom (New York: Longman, 1982), 287–310; Flood, "Men's Collective Struggles"; Michael Flood and Kim Webster, "Preventing Violence before It Occurs: A Framework and Background Paper to Guide the Primary Prevention of Violence against Women in Victoria" (2007); James Lang, "Men, Masculinities and Violence," in International Conference on Eradicating Violence against Women & Girls: Strengthening Human Rights (Berlin, Germany, 2002); and VicHealth 2007.

57 Bob Pease, "Engaging Men in Men's Violence Prevention: Exploring the Tensions, Dilemmas and Possibilities," *Australian Domestic & Family Violence Clearinghouse*, no. 17 (2008): 1–20.

58 Michael Flood, "Men and #Metoo: Mapping Men's Responses to Anti-violence Advocacy," in *#MeToo and the Politics of Social Change* (Cham: Palgrave Macmillan, Cham, 2019), 285, 285–300.

59 Matt Englar-Carlson and Mark S. Kiselica, "Affirming the Strengths in Men: A Positive Masculinity Approach to Assisting Male Clients," *Journal of Counseling & Development* 91, no. 4 (2013): 399–409; Andrew King, "The 'Quiet Revolution' amongst Men: Developing the Practice of Working with Men in Family Relationships," *Children Australia* 30, no. 2 (2005), 33–7; Mark S. Kiselica, S. Benton-Wright, and Matt Englar-Carlson, "Accentuating Positive Masculinity: A New Foundation for the Psychology of Boys, Men, and Masculinity," in *APA Handbook of Men and Masculinities*, ed. Y. J. Wong and S. R. Wester (American Psychological Association, 2016), 123–43; and Limor Goldner and Yehuda Ruderman, "Toward Creating Positive Masculinity? Art Therapy as Seen by Male Art Therapists and Male Adolescent Clients," *Arts in Psychotherapy* 68 (2020): 101613.

60 Flood, "Men and #Metoo," 294.

61 Flood, "Men and #Metoo," 285.

62 https://twitter.com/Saheregan/status/1371902960373014528?s=20&t=3_y8DsEMEM-SZe8q7r4WVQ

10 *Hush! Girls Don't Scream* (2013) by Puran Derakhshandeh and the #MeToo Movement in Iran

1 "Decapitated Child Bride Highlights Iran's Lack of Protections for Girls and Women," *Center for Human Rights in Iran*, February 10, 2022, http://www.iranhumanrights.org/2022/02/decapitated-child-bride-highlights-irans-lack-of-protections-for-girls-and-women/

2. Rumina Ashrafi (fourteen) ran away with her boyfriend and was decapitated by her father in her sleep after she was returned to him by the police in 2020.
3. Shakiba Bakhtiar (sixteen) was stabbed to death by her father because she returned home late from the market in 2021.
4. Mubina Suri (sixteen) died at the hands of her husband because it was rumored that she was in an extramarital relationship in 2021.
5. See Claudia Yaghoobi, *Temporary Marriage in Iran: Gender and Body Politics in Modern Iranian Film and Literature* (Cambridge: Cambridge University Press, 2020) for a comprehensive theory of embodiment that speaks to the particular case of Iranian women to lay bare the politicization of their personal life, the state-sponsored corporealization of their bodies, the state-endorsed gender inequality, objectification, and violence.
6. Qur'an, Al-Saffat (37:106).
7. Feast of the Sacrifice.
8. Under Article 302 of Iran's penal code, perpetrators who can prove that their victim was guilty of a crime that is punishable by death (such as adultery) will not be subject to proportionate punishment such as retribution-in-kind and paying blood money.
9. In an interview, Muhamad Riza Ziba'i Nizhad, the head of the Family and Women's Research Center, mentioned that if "we prepare women to accept men's authority, violence against them will not happen."
"لایحه حمایت از زنان در برابر خشونت؛ شیر بی یال و دم و اشکم" [Bill for the Protection of Women against Violence: A Lion without Mane, Tail and Stomach]," *DW*, November 25, 2021, https://amp.dw.com/fa-ir/لایحه-حمایت-از-زنان-در-برابر-خشونت-شیر-بی-یال-و-دم-و-اشکم/a-59931740
10. Mala Htun and Francesca R. Jensenius, "Fighting Violence against Women: Laws, Norms & Challenges Ahead," *Daedalus* 149, no. 1 (2020), 153, https://www.jstor.org/stable/48563038 (accessed December 4, 2022).
11. Tara Sepehri Far, "Iran Is Having Its #MeToo Moment," September 9, 2020, https://www.hrw.org/news/2020/09/09/iran-having-its-metoo-moment
12. Simin Daneshvar (1921–2012) was a short-story writer, translator, and the first Iranian woman novelist.
13. Qtd in Farzaneh Milani, "Women's Autobiographies in Iran," in *Women's Autobiographies in Contemporary Iran*, ed. Afsaneh Najmabadi (Cambridge: Harvard University Press, 1990), 10.
14. Farzaneh Milani, *Veils and Words* (Syracuse: Syracuse University Press, 1992), 6.
15. Milani, *Veils and Words*, 203.
16. Milani, *Veils and Words*, 6.
17. A case in point is Sara Umatali, a journalist, who alleged that one of Iran's most prominent painters, Aydin Aghdashloo, assaulted her as she was interviewing him.

Following her allegations, a multitude of women came forward with similar stories about him and other influential men.

18 Jessica Bennett, "The #MeToo Moment: When the Blinders Come Off," *New York Times*, November 30, 2017, https://www.nytimes.com/2017/11/30/us/the-metoo-moment.html

19 "Get to Know Us: Our Vision & Theory of Change," *Me Too Movement*, n.d., https://metoomvmt.org/get-to-know-us/vision-theory-of-change/ (accessed February 28, 2022).

20 Alyssa Milano (@Alyssa_Milano), "If You've Been Sexually Harassed or Assaulted Write 'Me Too' as a Reply to This Tweet," *Twitter*, October 15, 2017, https://twitter.com/alyssa_milano/status/919659438700670976

21 Anna North, "#MeToo Movement: These 7 Facts Show Its Impact," October 4, 2019, https://www.vox.com/identities/2019/10/4/20852639/me-too-movement-sexual-harassment-law-2019

22 Tara Sepehri Far, "Iran Is Having Its #MeToo Moment."

23 Maziar Motamedi, "Iranians Break Taboos with Their Own Version of #MeToo," September 22, 2020, https://www.aljazeera.com/news/2020/9/22/iranians-break-taboos-with-their-own-version-of-metoo

24 Motamedi, "Iranians Break Taboos."

25 Sara Tafakori, "Iran's #MeToo Movement Challenges Patriarchy and Western Stereotypes," September 1, 2020, https://www.opendemocracy.net/en/north-africa-west-asia/irans-metoo-movement-challenges-patriarchy-and-western-stereotypes/

26 Amina Maher, interview by Fardad Farahzad, *The Lead*, Iran International, August 25, 2020.

Afterword: Patriarchalism, Male Abuse, and the Sources of the #MeToo Movement in the Muslim Middle East

We are grateful for the financial support, suggestions, and criticism we have received from our institutions, our friends, and our colleagues. Research funding came from NYU-Abu Dhabi, and Duncan and Suzanne Mellichamp Funds at the University of California, Santa Barbara. Maria Charles, Paolo Gardinali, Rujun Yang, Mohammadreza Mirzaei, Leila Zonouzi, Sarp Kurgan, and Mesadet Maria Sozmen provided us with advice and research assistance. Special thanks to Lui Cordero and Nicholas Murray for their editorial assistance. And finally, we thank Frieda Afary for sharing her reports on Middle East women.

1 In Iran, governmental restraints forced us to rely on the blogosphere and to use our own banner ads on private Iranian Azad university Facebook sites.

2 Tarana Burke, *Unbound: My Story of Liberation and the Birth of the Me Too Movement* (New York: Flatiron, 2021).
3 Becket Adams, "The Les Moonves and Mel Watt Misconduct Allegations Suggest That #MeToo Falls Disproportionately on Democratic Politicians and Left-Wing Luminaries," *New York Times*, 2018, https://www.washingtonexaminer.com/opinion/les-moonves-mel-watt-misconduct-allegations-metoo-falls-hard-democratic-politicians-left-wing-luminaries (retrieved on March 24, 2022). Among the luminaries accused were Mel Watt (former Democratic congressman), Les Moones (chief executive of CBS Corp.), Matt Lauer (top news anchor for NBC News), Morgan Freeman (Academy Award winner), Tom Brokaw (NBC news anchor), John Bailey (president of the Academy of Motion Pictures), Charlie Rose (television journalist), Michael Douglas (award-winning actor), Israel Horovitz (playwright), Garrison Keillor (journalist, Minnesota Public Radio), John Conyers (Democratic representative, US Congress), Al Franken (Minnesota senator), Dustin Hoffman (Academy Award winner), Oliver Stone (filmmaker), Andrew Cuomo (New York governor), and countless others.
4 For a partial list of powerful men accused, see https://www.glamour.com/gallery/post-weinstein-these-are-the-powerful-men-facing-sexual-harassment-allegations (retrieved on January 29, 2022).
5 Lisa Hajjar, "Religion, State Power, and Domestic Violence in Muslim Societies: A Framework for Comparative Analysis," *Law and Social Inquiry* 29, no. 1 (2004): 1–38. Lisa Hajjar, Eduardo de Leon Buendia, Patrick Fairbanks, Emma Kuskey, Sasha Misco, and Ada Quevedo, "Cultures and Resistance: The Struggle against Domestic Violence in Arab Societies," in Handbook of Healthcare in the Arab World (Cham: Springer, 2020), 6, https://doi.org10.1007/978-3-319-74365-3_201-1
6 N. J. Dawood, trans., *The Koran* (London: Penguin, 1996), 370.
7 Hajjar, et al. "Cultures and Resistance."
8 Cited in Denise Kindschi Gosselin, *Heavy Hands: An Introduction to the Crime of Intimate and Family Violence*, 4th ed. (London: Pearson, 2009), 13.
9 "Honour Based Violence Awareness Network," *Honour Based Violence Awareness Network*, 2022, http://hbv-awareness.com (retrieved on March 24, 2022).
10 "2020 Report on International Religious Freedom," US Department of State, May 12, 2021, https://www.state.gov/reports/2020-report-on-international-religious-freedom/pakistan/ (retrieved on March 24, 2022).
11 Hannah Ellis-Petersen, "Pakistan's #MeToo Movement Hangs in the Balance over Celebrity Case," *Guardian*, January 1, 2021.
12 Bina Shah, "The Real Enemy of Pakistani Women Is Not Men," *New York Times*, April 14, 2019, https://www.nytimes.com/2019/04/14/opinion/pakistan-womens-march.html (retrieved on March 24, 2022).

13 Erin Clare Brown, "MP Jailed for Sexual Harassment over Incident That Sparked 'Tunisia's #MeToo Movement,'" *National*, November 12, 2021.
14 "Tunisia's #MeToo: Landmark Sexual Harassment Case Kicks Off," *Aljazeera*, October 29, 2021; "Tunisia MP Jailed for Sexual Harassment in Landmark Case," *Aljazeera*, November 12, 2021.
15 "Turkish Writer Accused of Sexual Harassment Commits Suicide," *DuvaR.english*, December 11, 2020, https://www.duvarenglish.com/turkish-writer-accused-of-sexual-harassment-commits-suicide-news-55436
16 Unker Pelin, "#MeToo Movement Arrives in Turkey," Deutsche Welle (DW), December 17, 2020, https://www.dw.com/en/metoo-movement-arrives-in-turkey/a-55976425 (retrieved on March 24, 2022).
17 Marc Santora, "Turkey Considers Leaving Domestic Violence Treaty Even as Abuse Surges," *New York Times*, August 25, 2020.
18 Pelin, "#MeToo Movement Arrives in Turkey."
19 Santora, "Turkey Considers Leaving Domestic Violence Treaty."
20 Hajjar et al., "Cultures and Resistance," 17.
21 Alaa Alaswany, *Republic of False Truths* (New York: Alfred A. Knopf, 2021).
22 Hajjar et al., "Cultures and Resistance," 17.
23 "Rebelling against Rape: Egyptian Women Speak Up about Sex Crimes," *Economist*, November 14, 2020. See also Dara Elasfar, "Amid Pandemic, 'MeToo' Comes to Egypt," WJBDRadio.com, 2021, https://southernillinoisnow.com/2021/06/14/amid-pandemic-me-too-comes-to-egypt/; Declan Walsh, "The 22-Year-Old Force behind Egypt's Growing #MeToo Movement," *New York Times*, October 2, 2020.
24 Mona Eltahawy, "Why Do They Hate Us: The Real War on Women Is in the Middle East," *Foreign Policy*, April 23, 2012.
25 Yann Bouchez, "Tariq Ramadan Visé Par Une Cinquième Mise En Examen Pour Viol," *Le Monde*, October 23, 2020.
26 Mona Eltahawy, "Muslim Women, Caught between Islamophobes and 'Our Men,'" *New York Times* (Opinion), 2017, https://www.nytimes.com/2017/11/19/opinion/muslim-women-sexism-violence.html (retrieved on March 24, 2022).
27 Dina Alghoul, "Stop Protecting Sexual Abusers' Demand Algerian Women." *New Arab*, June 4, 2018.
28 Akram Belkaïd, "The Arab World Says #MeToo," *Le Monde diplomatique*, August 2021.
29 Anna Lekas Miller, "She Started #NotYourHabibti to Shine a Light on Sexual Harassment in the Palestinian Territories," *World* (Public Radio), 2018, https://theworld.org/stories/2018-02-02/she-started-notyourhabibti-shine-light-sexual-harassment-palestinian-territories
30 Miller, "She Started #NotYourHabibti."

31 Joseph Daher, "Palestine: 'No Liberation without Free Women,'" *International Viewpoint*, October 20, 2019.
32 Ayaan Hirsi Ali, *Prey: Immigration, Islam, and the Erosion of Women's Rights* (New York: Harper, 2021).
33 Banner advertisement for Iranian Facebook page, 2018, designed by Jade Borgeson.
34 We were able to code if our respondents were born in and/or lived in the country of their Facebook affiliation.
35 Comparing these rates to those of women's public and private abuse globally, we see that the rate of domestic violence among our female respondents is close to the global rate of domestic violence (30 percent) (Hajjar, "Religion, State Power, and Domestic Violence").
36 These three countries also have the lowest level of legal protection for women. Our criteria for the legal status of women included the following six items, measured in 2018: Whether polygamy was permitted; whether *talaq* (husband's unilateral right to revocation of marriage) is in force; whether laws gave a husband the right to control their wife's behavior (through a duty to obey, permission required to work or travel); whether laws gave lower punishment to men for domestic violence than for other types of violence; whether laws were more lenient in the case of honor killings of wives by husbands; whether abortion was illegal during the first ten weeks of gestation. For more on this, see Maria Charles, Roger Friedland, Janet Afary, and Rujun Yang, "Complicating Patriarchy: Gender Beliefs of Muslim Facebook Users in the Middle East, North Africa, and South Asia," *Gender and Society* 37, no. 1 (February 2023): 91–123; doi: 10.1177/08912432221137909.
37 We used eleven occupational categories in our logistic regressions where domestic workers were the left-out comparison category.
38 Mona Eltahawy, *Headscarves and Hymens: Why the Middle East Needs a Sexual Revolution* (New York: Farrar, Straus and Giroux, 2015), 82.
39 Fatma El-Zanaty, Enas M. Hussein Hussein, Gihan A. Shawky, Ann A. Way, and Sunita Kishor, "Egypt Demographic and Health Survey 1995" (Cairo: National Population Council, 1996), 208.
40 See Janet Afary, *Sexual Politics in Modern Iran* (Cambridge: Cambridge University Press, 2009); Roger Friedland, "Money, Sex, and God: The Erotic Logic of Religious Nationalism," *Sociological Theory* 20, no. 3 (2002): 381–425; and Sami Zubaida, "Women, Democracy and Dictatorship in the Context of the Arab Uprisings," in *The New Middle East: Protest and Revolution in the Arab World*, ed. F. Gerges (Cambridge: Cambridge University Press, 2013), 209–25.
41 We are not here including temporary marriage (*mut'a*) under polygamy, a specifically Shi'i practice, which was far cheaper and more a form of legal concubinage.

42 Fatima Mernissi, *Beyond the Veil: Male-Female Dynamics in Modern Muslim Society* (Bloomington: Indiana University Press, 1987), 114–16.
43 W. Robertson Smith and Stanley A. Cook, *Kinship and Marriage in Early Arabia* (Whitefish, MT: Kressinger, 1907).
44 Leila Ahmed, *Women and Gender in Islam: Historical Roots of a Modern Debate* (New Haven, CT: Yale University Press, 2021).
45 Labor Force Participation Rate, Female (% of Female Population Ages 15+) (Modeled ILO Estimate)—Middle East & North Africa, the World Bank, February 8, 2022, https://data.worldbank.org/indicator/SL.TLF.CACT.FE.ZS?locations=ZQ (retrieved on March 24 2022).
46 Sabha Mahmood, *The Politics of Piety: The Islamic Revival and the Feminist Subject* (Princeton, NJ: Princeton University Press, 2005).
47 Leila Ahmed, *A Quiet Revolution: The Veil's Resurgence from the Middle East to America* (New Haven, CT: Yale University Press, 2012).
48 Mounira Charrad, *States and Women's Rights: The Makings of Postcolonial Tunisia, Algeria, and Morocco* (Berkeley: University of California Press, 2011); Fatima Mernissi, *Beyond the Veil: Male, Female Dynamics in Muslim Societies*, rev. ed (Bloomington: Indiana University Press, 1987).
49 We explored the possibility that opposition to *talaq* found among both Islamist women and men might have something to do with the rise of romantic love as a basis of mate choice, which we have found in our previous work. Love, we reasoned, requires mutual consent, a reciprocal liberty to say yes and no to marriage for both men and women. *Talaq*, in contrast, is an extreme form of asymmetry, a singular male prerogative, built into marital law. In fact, we found absolutely no relationship between the importance of love as a basis of mate choice and opposition to *talaq* either among women or men, including Islamist women and men.
50 Hisham Sharabi, *Neopatriarchy: A Theory of Distorted Change in Arab Society* (Oxford: Oxford University Press, 1992).
51 Ali Rahnema, *An Islamic Utopian: A Political Biography of Ali Shariati* (London: I.B. Tauris, 1998); Meryem F. Zaman, "The Problem of the Rebellious Religious Women: Pakistan, Gender, and the Islamic Revival," *Social Politics: International Studies in Gender, State & Society* 27, no. 2 (2020): 212–33, https://doi.org/10.1093/sp/jxz001
52 Ervand Abrahamian, *Iran between Two Revolutions* (Princeton, NJ: Princeton University Press, 1982); Rami Ginat, *Egypt's Incomplete Revolution: Lutfi Al-Khuli and Nasser's Socialism in the 1960s* (London: Frank Cass, 1997).
53 Vivian Gornick, *The Romance of American Communism* (London: Verso, 2020).
54 Burke, *Unbound*.
55 Maxime Rodinson, *Islam and Capitalism* (Austin: University of Texas Press, 1978).

56 Gilles Kepel, *Jihad: The Trail of Political Islam*, trans. Anthony F. Roberts (Cambridge: Belknap, 2003).
57 Sayyid Qutb, *Milestones* (Indianapolis: American Trust Publications, 1990), 91.
58 Afshin Matin-Asgari, *Both Eastern and Western: An Intellectual History of Iranian Modernity* (Cambridge: Cambridge University Press, 2018). The enormous support of socialism among Islamists suggests that, just as the Islamists support a different financial order for capitalist finance, and thus a kind of Islamic capitalism, they also support a particular kind of socialism, one based primarily on issues of anti-Western imperialism, economic exploitation, redistribution, and the importance of human needs, as opposed to one that would extend women's rights, including the right to work. This is only a hypothesis, but the empirical result requires further investigation and intimates those different kinds of ideological formations and alignments are possible in these countries.
59 Matin-Asgari, *Both Eastern and Western*, chapter 6.
60 Kepel, *Jihad*; Richard P. Mitchell, *The Society of the Muslim Brothers* (Oxford: Oxford University Press, 1993).
61 Kevan Harris, *A Social Revolution: Politics and the Welfare State in Iran* (Oakland: University of California Press, 2017).
62 Mehrangiz Kar, *Pajuheshi dar Bareh-ye Khoshunat Aleyhe Zanan dar Iran* (Tehran: Entesharat Rowshangaran va Motale'at-e Zanan, 2000).
63 Our Palestinian respondents are drawn from residents of both Gaza, which is more Islamist, and the West Bank, which is less so.
64 This possibly requires further research. As we pointed out, human rights attorney Mehrangiz Kar, who used hospital and court records, showed that rates of domestic violence in Iran dramatically increased after 1979. Thus, in uncovering information about domestic violence in Islamist societies researchers must rely on similar sources of information such as police and hospital records.
65 Caitlin Moscatello, "Does Porn Damage Men? A Look at the Lasting, Unspoken Effects," *Glamour*, 2015, https://www.glamour.com/story/does-porn-damage-men (retrieved on March 24, 2022).
66 Because of the multiple ways in which internet use is part of obtaining sexual partners—prostitution, arranging casual sex, men who are unable to move easily to find mates, including men with disabilities—we do not have a discrete interpretation of this finding.
67 Afary, *Sexual Politics*, 293–303.
68 Norris and Inglehart, 2019.
69 See P. Norris and R. Inglehart (2019) *Cultural Backlash. Trump, Brexit, and Authoritarian Populism* (Cambridge: Cambridge University Press).

Bibliography

"2020 Report on International Religious Freedom." US Department of State, May 12, 2021. https://www.state.gov/reports/2020-report-on-international-religious-freedom/pakistan/ (retrieved March 24, 2022).

Abrahamian, Ervand. *Iran between Two Revolutions*. Princeton, NJ: Princeton University Press, 1982.

Abu-Lughod, Leila. *Do Muslim Women Need Saving*. Boston, MA: Harvard University Press, 2015.

Adams, Becket. "The Les Moonves and Mel Watt Misconduct Allegations Suggest That #MeToo Falls Disproportionately on Democratic Politicians and Left-Wing Luminaries." *New York Times*, 2018. https://www.washingtonexaminer.com/opinion/les-moonves-mel-watt-misconduct-allegations-metoo-falls-hard-democratic-politicians-left-wing-luminaries (retrieved March 24, 2022).

Adams, Carol J. *The Sexual Politics of Meat: A Feminist-Vegetarian Critical Theory*. New York: Continuum, 2010.

Adams, Carol J. "Woman-Battering and Harm to Animals." In *Animals and Women: Feminist Theoretical Explorations*, edited by Carol Adams and Josephine Donovan, 55–84. Durham, NC: Duke University Press, 1995.

Adibi, Hossein. "Sociology of Masculinity in the Middle East." In *Social Change in the 21st Century: 2006 Conference Proceedings*, 1–10. Queensland University of Technology, 2006.

Afary, Janet. "The Sexual Economy of the Islamic Republic." *Iranian Studies* 42, no. 1 (2009): 5–26.

Afary, Janet. *Sexual Politics in Modern Iran*. Cambridge: Cambridge University Press, 2009.

Afkhami, Mahnaz. "A Future in the Past: The 'Prerevolutionary' Women's Movement." In *Sisterhood Is Global*, edited by Robin Morgan, 330–7. New York: Anchor, 1984.

Afshar, Haleh. *Islam and Feminisms: An Iranian Case-Study*. New York: St. Martin's, 1998.

Afshar, Haleh. "Khomeini's Teachings and Their Implications for Women." *Feminist Review* 12, no. 1 (1982): 59–72. https://doi.org/10.2307/1394882.

Nadia Aghtaie, "Rape within Heterosexual Intimate Relationships in Iran: Legal Frameworks, Culture and Structural Violence," *Families, Relationships and Societies* 6, no. 2 (2017): 167–83.

Ahmed, Leila. *Women and Gender in Islam: Historical Roots of a Modern Debate*. New Haven, CT: Yale University Press, 2021.

Ahmed, Sara. *The Cultural Politics of Emotion*, 2nd ed. Edinburgh: Edinburgh University Press, 2014.

Ahmed, Sara. *Living a Feminist Life*. Durham, NC: Duke University Press, 2017.

Al-Ali, N. "Reconstructing Gender: Iraqi Women between Dictatorship, War, Sanctions and Occupation." *Third World Quarterly* 26, no. 4/5 (2005): 739–58.

Alaswany, Alaa. *Republic of False Truths*. New York: Alfred A. Knopf, 2021.

Alghoul, Diana. "Stop Protecting Sexual Abusers' Demand Algerian Women." *New Arab*, June 4, 2018.

Ali, Ayaan Hirsi. *Prey: Immigration, Islam, and the Erosion of Women's Rights*. New York: Harper, 2021.

Ali, Kecia Ali. *Marriage and Slavery in Early Islam*. Cambridge: Harvard University Press, 2010.

Ali, Kecia. "Muslims and Meat-Eating: Vegetarianism, Gender, and Identity." *Journal of Religious Ethics* 43, no. 2 (2015): 268–88.

Ali Kecia. *Sexual Ethics and Islam: Feminist Reflections on Quran, Hadith, and Jurisprudence*. London: One World, 2016.

Alinejad, Masih (@AlinejadMasih). "1—In response to my @washingtonpost op-ed on how @IlhanMN's proposed legislation against Islamophobia could silence legitimate concerns about Islamist extremism, her husband defamed me." Twitter, January 29, 2020. https://twitter.com/AlinejadMasih/status/1487446697915650057.

Alinejad, Masih. "Why I Am Opposed to Ilhan Omar's Bill against Islamophobia." *Washington Post*, January 25, 2022. https://www.washingtonpost.com/opinions/2022/01/25/why-im-opposed-ilhan-omars-bill-against-islamophobia/.

Alinejad, Masih, and Roya Hakakian. "Iranian Women Are Staging Offensive against Sexual Abuse. It's Long Overdue." *Washington Post*, August 26, 2020. https://www.washingtonpost.com/opinions/2020/08/26/iranian-women-are-staging-an-offensive-against-sexual-abuse-its-long-overdue/.

Althusser, Louis. *For Marx*. London: Verso, 2005.

Althusser, Louis, and Étienne Balibar. *Reading Capital: The Complete Edition*. London: Verso, 2016.

Amidi, Faranak. "100 Women: Muslim Women Rally Round #Mosquemetoo." BBC News, BBC, February 9, 2018. https://www.bbc.com/news/world-43006952.

Amin, Camron Michael. "Globalizing Iranian Feminism, 1910–1950." *Journal of Middle East Women's Studies* 4, no. 1 (2008): 6–30. https://doi.org/10.2979/mew.2008.4.1.6.

Amir-Ebrahimi, Masserat. "Transgression in Narration: The Lives of Iranian Women in Cyberspace." *Journal of Middle East Women's Studies* 4, no. 3, Special Issue: Innovative Women: Unsung Pioneers of Social Change, 2008, 89–118.

Anzaldúa, Gloria. *Borderlands/La Frontera: The New Mestiza*. San Francisco: Aunt Lute, 2012.

"Apostolic Letter *Ordinatio Sacerdotalis* of John Paul II to the Bishops of the Catholic Church on Reserving Priestly Ordination to Men Alone." 1994. https://www.vatican.

va/content/john-paul-ii/en/apost_letters/1994/documents/hf_jp-ii_apl_1994052 2_ordinatio-sacerdotalis.html.

"As a Serial Rapist Is Sentenced to Death, Victims Slam Lack of Justice." *IranWire*, July 11, 2022. https://iranwire.com/en/women/105617-as-serial-rapist-is-senten ced-to-death-victims-slam-lack-of-justice/.

Association of Internet Researchers (AoIR). "Ethical Decision-Making and Internet Research 3.0: Recommendations from the AoIR Ethics Working Committee." 2019. Retrieved from the AoIR website: https://aoir.org/reports/ethics3.pdf.

Atwood, Margaret. *The Handmaid's Tale*. Boston: Houghton Mifflin, 1986.

Awasthi, Bhuvanesh. "From Attire to Assault: Clothing, Objectification, and De-humanization: A Possible Prelude to Sexual Violence?" *Frontiers in Psychology* 8 (2017): 338.

"Ayatollah Bayat Zanjani: The Stoning Ruling Is Not in the Quran." Radio Farda, July 12, 2010. https://www.radiofarda.com/a/F11_Iran_adultery_stoning_ Ayatollah_Bayat_statement/2096964.html

Ayatollahi, Zahra. "Security of Women Against Violence Bill or the Implementation of Fifth Goal of the 2030 Document" *Keyhan Newspaper*, January 20, 2018, https://kayhan. ir/fa/news/121939/لایحه-امنیت-زنان-در-برابر-خشونت-یا-اجرای-هدف-5-سند-2030یادداشت-میهمان

"Aydin Aghdashloo." Wikipedia. Wikimedia Foundation, November 15, 2022. https:// en.wikipedia.org/wiki/Aydin_Aghdashloo

Azam, Hina. *Sexual Violation in Islamic Law: Substance, Evidence, and Procedure*. Cambridge: Cambridge University Press, 2015.

Bacchetta, Paola, Tina Campt, Inderpal Grewal, Caren Kaplan, Minoo Moallem, and Jennifer Terry. "Transnational Feminist: Practices against War." *Meridians: Feminism, Race, Transnationalism* 19, no. 3 (2020): 131–8.

Bahramitash, Roksana. "Iranian Women during the Reform Era (1994–2004): A Focus on Employment." *Journal of Middle East Women's Studies* 3, no. 2 (2007): 86–109. https://doi.org/10.2979/mew.2007.3.2.86.

Bahramitash, Roksana. "Islamic Fundamentalism and Women's Economic Role: The Case of Iran." *International Journal of Politics, Culture, and Society* 16, no. 4 (2003): 551–68.

Bahramitash, Roksana. "Islamic Fundamentalism and Women's Employment in Indonesia." *International Journal of Politics, Culture, and Society* 16, no. 2 (2002): 255–72.

Bahramitash, Roksana. "Myths and Realities of the Impact of Political Islam on Women: Female Employment in Indonesia and Iran." *Development in Practice* 14, no. 4 (2004): 508–20.

Bailey, Alison. "Privilege: Expanding on Marilyn Frye's 'Oppression.'" *Journal of Social Philosophy* 29, no. 3 (1998): 104–19.

Bakht, Natasha. "The Incorporation of Shari'a in North America: Enforcing the *Mahr* to Combat Women's Poverty Post-relationship Dissolution." In *The Oxford Handbook of Islamic Law*, edited by Anver M. Emon and Rumee Ahmed, 1–30. Oxford: Oxford University Press, 2015.

Balslev, Sivan. "Dressed for Success: Hegemonic Masculinity, Elite Men and Westernisation in Iran, c. 1900–40." *Gender & History* 26, no. 3 (2014): 545–64.

Banet-Weiser, Sarah. *Empowered: Popular Feminism and Popular Misogyny*. Durham, NC: Duke University Press, 2018.

Banet-Weiser, Sarah, Rosalind Gill, and Catherine Rottenberg. "Postfeminism, Popular Feminism and Neoliberal Feminism? Sarah Banet-Weiser, Rosalind Gill and Catherine Rottenberg in Conversation." *Feminist Theory* 21, no. 1 (2020): 3–24.

Bāqirī, Nafīsih. "Sīyāsat-i Kaifarī-i Īrān dar Rābiṭih bā Āzār-i Jinsī." *Faṣlnāmih-i ʿIlmī-Huqūqi-i Qānūnyār* 2, no. 6 ([1397] 2019): 419–33.

Barassi, Veronica. "Social Media Activism, Self-Representation and the Construction of Political Biographies." In *Routledge Companion to Media and Activism*, 1st ed., edited by Graham Meikle, 148–57. London: Routledge, 2018.

Barnes, Naomi. "Trace Publics as a Qualitative Critical Network Tool: Exploring the Dark Matter in the #MeToo Movement." *New Media and Society* 22, no. 7 (2020): 1305–19.

Bartky, Sandra L. "Foucault, Femininity, and the Modernization of Patriarchal Power." In *Writing on the Body: Female Embodiment and Feminist Theory*, edited by K. Conboy, N. Medina, and S. Stanbury, 129–54. New York: Columbia University Press, 1997.

Bassiri, Kaveh. "Masculinity in Iranian Cinema." Global Encyclopedia of Lesbian, Gay, Bisexual, Transgender, and Queer (LGBTQ) History, 2019.

Bates, Laura. *Men Who Hate Women: From Incels to Pickup Artists—The Truth about Extreme Misogyny and How It Affects Us All*. Naperville, IL: Sourcebooks, 2021.

Batmanghelichi, K. Soraya. *Revolutionary Bodies: Technologies of Gender, Sex, and Self in Contemporary Iran*. London: Bloomsbury Press, 2020.

Batmanghelichi, K. Soraya, and Leila Mouri. "Cyberfeminism, Iranian Style." *Feminist Media Histories* 3, no. 1 (2017): 50–80.

Bayat, Asef. *Life as Politics: How Ordinary People Change the Middle East*, 2nd ed. Stanford, CA: Stanford University Press, 2013.

Bayat, Asef. "A Women's Non-movement: What It Means to Be a Woman Activist in an Islamic State." *Comparative Studies of South Asia, Africa and the Middle East* 27, no. 1 (2007): 160–72.

Becker, Howard S. *Outsiders: Études de sociologie de la deviance*. Paris: Éditions Métailié, 1985.

Behdad, Ali. *Camera Orientalis: Reflections on Photography of the Middle East*. Chicago: University of Chicago Press, 2016.

Belkaïd, Akram. "The Arab World Says #MeToo." *Le Monde diplomatique*, August 2021.

Bell, Robert Joseph. *Luti Masculinity in Iranian Modernity, 1785–1941: Marginalization and the Anxieties of Proper Masculine Comportment*. Master's thesis, City University of New York Graduate Center, 2015.

Bennett, Jessica. "The #MeToo Moment: When the Blinders Come Off." *New York Times*, November 30, 2017. https://www.nytimes.com/2017/11/30/us/the-metoo-moment.html.

Berg. "Left of #Metoo." *Feminist Studies* 46, no. 2 (2020): 259–84. https://doi.org/10.15767/feministstudies.46.2.0259.

"The Bill on Dignity and Protection of Women against Violence." January 16, 2021. https://www.ekhtebar.com/?p=55043.

Bitman, Nomy. "'Which Part of My Group Do I Represent?': Disability Activism and Social Media Users with Concealable Communicative Disabilities." *Information Communication and Society* 26. 3 (2021): 619–36.

Bloch, Marc. *Apologie pour l'histoire ou métier d'historien*. Armand Colin, Cahier des Annales no. 3 (1949) (première édition, plusieurs fois rééditée).

Borgatti, Stephen P., Frans Stokman, Alvin Wolfe, George Barnett, Michael Link, David Kenny, Phillip Bonacich, Scott Feld, and Joel Levine. "Editorial Board," n.d.

Bouchez, Yann. "Tariq Ramadan Visé Par Une Cinquième Mise En Examen Pour Viol." Le *Monde*, October 23, 2020.

Bourdieu, Pierre. *Distinction: A Social Critique of the Judgement of Taste*. London: Routledge, 1984.

Bourdieu, Pierre. "The Forms of Capital." In *Handbook of Theory and Research for the Sociology of Education*, edited by John Richardson, 241–58. Westport, CT: Greenwood, 1986.

Bourdieu, Pierre. *Outline of a Theory of Practice*. Cambridge: Cambridge University Press, 2013.

Brenkert, George G. "Freedom and Private Property in Marx." *Philosophy and Public Affairs* 8 (1979): 122–47.

Brown, Erin Clare. "MP Jailed for Sexual Harassment over Incident That Sparked "Tunisia's #MeToo Movement." *National*, November 12, 2021.

Burelomova, Anastasia S., Marina A. Gulina, and Olga A. Tikhomandritskya. "Intimate Partner Violence: An Overview of the Existing Theories, Conceptual Frameworks, and Definitions." *Psychology in Russia: State of the Art* 11, no. 3 (2018): 128–44.

Burke, Tarana. *Unbound: My Story of Liberation and the Birth of the Me Too Movement*. New York: Flatiron, 2021.

Burke, Tarana, and Elizabeth Adetiba. "Tarana Burke Says #MeToo Should Center Marginalized Communities." In *Where Freedom Starts: Sex Power Violence #MeToo*, 28–38. Brooklyn: Verso, 2018.

Cahill, Ann J. *Rethinking Rape*. Ithaca, NY: Cornell University Press, 2001.

Cameron, Deborah. *Feminism: A Brief Introduction to the Ideas, Debates and Politics of the Movement*. Chicago: University of Chicago Press, 2019.

Cavallaro, Dani. *French Feminist Theory: An Introduction*. London: A&C Black, 2003.

Chehabi, Houchang E. "Staging the Emperor's New Clothes: Dress Codes and Nation-Building under Reza Shah." *Iranian Studies* 26, nos. 3–4 (1993): 209–33.

Chenier, Elise. "Lesbian feminism," 2015, glbtq, Inc.

Chetcuti-Osorovitz, Natacha. "De « On ne naît pas femme » à « On n'est pas femme »: De Simone de Beauvoir à Monique Wittig." *Genre, sexualité & société*, no. 1, "Lesbiennes" (Printemps 2009). https://journals.openedition.org/gss/477.

Chetcuti-Osorovitz, Natacha. "Reflections on Historic Lesbian Feminisms." In *Lesbian Feminism: Essays Opposing Global Heteropatriarchies*, edited by Niharika Banerjea, Kath Browne, Eduarda Ferreira, Marta Olasik, and Julie Podmore, 230–49. Londres: Zed, 2019.

"Child Sexual Abuse Case Against Quran Reciter In Iran Remains Closed." Farda, Radio. RFE/RL. https://en.radiofarda.com/a/child-sexual-abuse-case-agai nst-quran-reciter-in-iran-remains-closed/30021144.html (accessed February 17, 2022).

Christ, Carol P. "A New Definition of Patriarchy: Control of Women's Sexuality, Private Property, and War." *Feminist Theology* 24, no. 3 (2016): 214–25.

Chubin, Fae. "You May Smother My Voice, but You Will Hear My Silence: An Autoethnography on Street Sexual Harassment, the Discourse of Shame and Women's Resistance in Iran." *Sexualities* 17, no. 1/2 (2014): 176–93.

Cixous, Hélène. "The Laugh of the Medusa." *Signs* 1, no. 4 (1976): 875–93. https://doi.org/https://www.jstor.org/stable/3173239.

Connell, Bob, Tim Carrigan, and Lee John. *Toward a New Sociology of Masculinity*. Milton Park: Routledge, 2018.

Connell, Raewyn W. *Gender and Power: Society, the Person and Sexual Politics*. New York: John Wiley, 2013.

Connell, Raewyn W. *Masculinities*, 2nd ed. Berkeley: University of California Press 2005.

Connell, Raewyn W. *Masculinities*. Cambridge: Polity, 2005.

Connell, Raewyn W., and James W. Messerschmidt. "Faut-il repenser le concept de masculinité hégémonique? » *Terrains travaux* 2 (2015): 151–92.

Connell, Robert W. *The Men and the Boys*. Cambridge: Polity, 2000.

Connell, Robert W. "The Role of Men and Boys in Achieving Gender Equality." Group Meeting, organised by DAW in collaboration with iLO and uNAiDs. Brasilia, Brazil, 2003.

Connell, Robert W. "Scrambling in the Ruins of Patriarchy: Neo-liberalism and Men's Divided Interests in Gender Change." In *Gender: From Costs to Benefits*, edited by Ursula Pasero, 58–69. VS Verlag für Sozialwissenschaften, 2003.

Connell, Robert W., and James W. Messerschmidt. "Hegemonic Masculinity: Rethinking the Concept." *Gender & Society* 19, no. 6 (2005): 829–59.

Couldry, Nick. 2008. "Mediatization or Mediation? Alternative Understandings of the Emergent Space of Digital Storytelling." *New Media and Society* 10, no. 3: 373–91.

Crenshaw, Kimberle. "Mapping the Margins: Intersectionality, Identity Politics, and Violence against Women of Color." *Stanford Law Review* 43, no. 6 (1991): 1241–99.

Crenshaw, Kimberle. "Postscript." In *Framing Intersectionality Debates on a Multi- Faceted Concept in Gender Studies*, edited by Helma Lutz, Maria Teresa HerreraVivar, and Linda Supik, 221–33. Farnham: Ashgate, 2011.

Crepax, Rosa. "The Aestheticisation of Feminism: A Case Study of Feminist Instagram Aesthetics." *ZoneModa Journal* 10, no. 15 (2020): 71–81.

"The Criminal Justice System: Statistics." *Rape, Abuse and Incest National Network*, n.d. https://www.rainn.org/statistics/criminal-justice-system.

Dadas, Caroline. "Making Sense of #MeToo: Intersectionality and Contemporary Feminism." *Pith: The Journal of the Coalition of Feminist Scholars in the History of Rhetoric and Composition* 22, no. 3 (2020). https://cfshrc.org/article/making-sense-of-metoo-intersectionality-and-contemporary-feminism/.

Daher, Joseph. "Palestine: 'No Liberation without Free Women.'" *International Viewpoint*, October 20, 2019.

Dairiam, Mary Shanti. "CEDAW, Gender, and Culture." In *The Oxford Handbook of Transnational Feminist Movements*, 1st ed., 367–93. Oxford: Oxford University Press, 2015.

Danowski, James A. "Network Analysis of Message Content." *Progress in Communication Sciences* 12 (1993): 198–221.

Davis, Kathy, and Dubravka Zarkov. "Ambiguities and Dilemmas around #MeToo: #ForHow Long and #WhereTo?" *European Journal of Women's Studies* 25, no. 1 (2018): 3–9.

Dawood, Nessim Joseph, trans. *The Koran*. London: Penguin, 1996.

Dawson, Paul. "Hashtag Narrative: Emergent Storytelling and Affective Publics in the Digital Age." *International Journal of Cultural Studies* 23, no. 6 (2020): 968–83.

De Beauvoir, Simone. *Le deuxième sexe*. Paris: Gallimard, 1949.

De Beauvoir, Simone. *The Second Sex*. Translated and edited by H. M. Parshley. London: Jonathan Cape, 1956.

De Keijzer, Benno. "Masculinities: Resistance and Change." In *Gender Equality and Men: Learning from Practice*, edited by Sandy Ruxton, 28–49. Oxfam GB, 2004.

"Decapitated Child Bride Highlights Iran's Lack of Protections for Girls and Women." *Center for Human Rights in Iran*. February 10, 2022. http://www.iranhumanrights.org/2022/02/decapitated-child-bride-highlights-irans-lack-of-protections-for-girls-and-women/.

Dehghan, Saeed Kamali. "Mohsen Namjoo: Why the Iranian Bob Dylan Wants to Be Music's Banksy." *Guardian*, January 27, 2017, sec. Music. https://www.theguardian.com/music/musicblog/2017/jan/27/mohsen-namjoo-iranian-bob-dylan-interview.

Delphy, Christine. *L'ennemi principal-tome 1: Économie politique du patriarcat*. Vol. 1. Paris: Syllepse, 2013.

Derrida, Jacques. "Letter to a Japanese Friend." In *Derrida and Différance*, edited by David O. Wood and Robert Bernasconi, 1–6. Evanston, IL: Northwestern University Press, 1988.

Derrida, Jacques. *Archive Fever: A Freudian Impression*. Translated by Eric Prenowitz. Chicago: University of Chicago Press, 2008.

DeSouza, Wendy. *Unveiling Men: Modern Masculinities in Twentieth-Century Iran*. Syracuse, NY: Syracuse University Press, 2019.

Dingo, Rebecca. "Linking Transnational Logics: A Feminist Rhetorical Analysis of Public Policy Networks." *College English* 70, no. 5 (2008): 490–505. https://doi.org/10.2307/25472285.

Dingo, Rebecca. *Networking Arguments: Rhetoric, Transnational Feminism, and Public Policy Writing*, 1st ed. Pittsburgh, PA: University of Pittsburgh Press, 2012.

Dingo, Rebecca. "Networking the Macro and Micro: Toward Transnational Literacy Practices." *JAC* 33, no. 3/4 (2013): 529–52.

Doerfel, Marya L. "What Constitutes Semantic Network Analysis? A Comparison of Research and Methodologies." *Connections* 21, no. 2 (1998): 16–26. http://citeseerx.ist.psu.edu/viewdoc/download?doi=10.1.1.211.9021&rep=rep1&type=pdf#page=18.

Doerfel, Marya L., and George A. Barnett. "A Semantic Network Analysis of the International Communication Association." *Human Communication Research* 25, no. 4 (June 1, 1999): 589–603. https://doi.org/10.1111/j.1468-2958.1999.tb00463.x.

Drezner, Daniel W. "#MeToo and the Trouble with New Norms." *Washington Post*, February 14, 2018.

Eder, Maciej, Jan Rybicki, and Mike Kestemont. 2016. "Stylometry with R: A Package for Computational Text Analysis." *R Journal* 8, no. 1: 107–21. https://ruj.uj.edu.pl/xmlui/handle/item/35829.

Editorial. "12 Billion Sales Logic." Artmag, January 31, 2021. https://artmag.ir/en/painting/281-12-billion-sales-logic.

Egbert, C. K. "Why Consent Is Not Enough." *Feminist Current*, June 25, 2014. https://www.feministcurrent.com/2014/06/25/why-consent-is-not-enough/.

Eisenstein, Zillah. "Developing a Theory of Capitalist Patriarchy: and Socialist Feminism." In *Capitalist Patriarchy and the Case for Socialist Feminism*, edited by Zillah Eisenstein, 5–40. New York: Monthly Review, 1979.

El Saadawi, Nawal. *The Hidden Face of Eve: Women in the Arab World*. Translated by Sherif Hetata. London: Zed, 2007.

Elasfar, Dara. "Amid Pandemic, 'MeToo' Comes to Egypt." WJBDRadio.com, 2021. https://southernillinoisnow.com/2021/06/14/amid-pandemic-me-too-comes-to-egypt/.

Elliott, Gregory. "Symptomatic Reading." In *A Dictionary of Cultural and Critical Theory*, edited by Michael Payne and Jessica Rae Barbera, 583–679. Malden, MA: Wiley-Blackwell, 2013.

Ellis-Petersen, Hannah. "Pakistan's #MeToo Movement Hangs in the Balance over Celebrity Case." *Guardian*, January 1, 2021.

Eltahawy, Mona. *Headscarves and Hymens: Why the Middle East Needs a Sexual Revolution*. New York: Farrar, Straus and Giroux, 2015.

Eltahawy, Mona. "Muslim Women, Caught between Islamophobes and 'Our Men.'" *New York Times* (Opinion), 2017. https://www.nytimes.com/2017/11/19/opinion/muslim-women-sexism-violence.html (retrieved March 24, 2022).

Eltahawy, Mona. "Why Do They Hate Us: The Real War on Women Is in the Middle East." *Foreign Policy*, April 23, 2012.

El-Zanaty, Fatma, Enas M. Hussein Hussein, Gihan A. Shawky, Ann A. Way, and Sunita Kishor. *Egypt Demographic and Health Survey 1995*. Calverton, MD: National Population Council and Macro International, 1996.

Englar-Carlson, Matt, and Mark S. Kiselica. "Affirming the Strengths in Men: A Positive Masculinity Approach to Assisting Male Clients." *Journal of Counseling & Development* 91, no. 4 (2013): 399–409.

Ennaji, Moha, and Fatima Sadiqi. "Introduction: Contextualizing Gender and Violence in the Middle East." In *Gender and Violence in the Middle East*, edited by Moha Ennaji and Fatima Sadiqi, 1–10. London: Routledge, 2011.

Falquet, Jules. "Lesbiennes migrantes, entre hétéro-circulation et recompositions néolibérales du nationalisme." In *Le genre au cœur des migrations*, edited by Claire Cossée, Adelina Miranda, Nouria Oualin and Djaouida Séhili, 123–48. Paris: Édition Pétra, 2012.

Farahani, Fataneh. "Diasporic Masculinities." *Nordic Journal of Migration Research* 2, no. 2 (2012): 159.

Farris, Sara R. *In the Name of Women's Rights: The Rise of Femonationalism*. Durham, NC: Duke University Press, 2017.

Fassihi, Farnaz. "Iran Moves to Outlaw Sexual Violence and Harassment of Women." *New York Times*, January 5, 2021. https://www.nytimes.com/2021/01/05/world/middleeast/iran-sexual-violence-metoo-women.html.

Fassihi, Farnaz. "A #MeToo Awakening Stirs in Iran." *New York Times*, October 22, 2020, sec. World. https://www.nytimes.com/2020/10/22/world/middleeast/iran-metoo-aydin-aghdashloo.html.

Fazeli, Yaghoub. "Iranian Journalist Masih Alinejad's Brother Sentenced to 8 Years in Prison." *Al Arabiya English*, July 16, 2020. https://english.alarabiya.net/News/middle-east/2020/07/16/Iranian-journalist-Masih-Alinejad-s-brother-sentenced-to-8-years-in-prison-Lawyer.

Federici, Silvia. "Marx and Feminism." *tripleC* 16, no. 2 (2018): 468–75.

Ferguson, Harry, Jeff Hearn, Keith Pringle, Ursula Muller, Elzbieta Oleksy, Emmi Lattu, Teemu Tallberg, Voldemar Kolga, Irina Novikova, Alex Raynor, Øystein Gullvåg Holter. "Critical Studies on Men in Ten European Countries: (4) Newspaper and Media Representations." *Men and Masculinities* 6, no. 2 (2003): 173–201.

Fisher, Mark. *Capitalist Realism: Is There No Alternative*. Hants: Zero, 2009.

Flood, Michael. "Men and #Metoo: Mapping Men's Responses to Anti-violence Advocacy." In *#MeToo and the Politics of Social Change*, edited by B. Fileborn and R. Loney-Howes, 285–300. Cham: Palgrave Macmillan, 2019. https://doi.org/10.1007/978-3-030-15213-0_18.

Flood, Michael. "Men's Collective Struggles for Gender Justice." In *Handbook of Studies on Men and Masculinities*, edited by Michael Kimmel, Jeff Hearn, R. W. Connell, 458–65. Thousand Oaks, CA: SAGE, 2005.

Flood, Michael, and Kim Webster. *Preventing Violence before It Occurs: A Framework and Background Paper to Guide the Primary Prevention of Violence against Women in Victoria*. VicHealth, Australia, 2007.

Foucault, Michel. *Discipline and Punish: The Birth of the Prison*. New York: Vintage, 1977.

Foucault, Michel. *Fearless Speech*. Edited by Joseph Pearson. Los Angeles: Semiotext(e), 2001.

Fowler, Bridget. "Pierre Bourdieu: Unorthodox Marxist?" In *The Legacy of Pierre Bourdieu: Critical Essays*, edited by Simon Susen and Bryan S. Turner, 33–58. London: Anthem, 2011.

Freyer Stowasser, Barbara. *Women in the Qur'an, Traditions, and Interpretation*. Oxford: Oxford University Press, 1994.

Friedland, Roger. "Money, Sex, and God: The Erotic Logic of Religious Nationalism." *Sociological Theory* 20, no. 3 (2002): 381–425.

Fūminī, Maryam. "*Mushkilāt-i Shekāyat az Tajāvuz-i Jinsī dar Dastgāh-i Qaḍāei Irān*." [The difficulties of rape complaints in Iran's judicial system] [1399] 2020. https://www.aasoo.org/fa/articles/3224 (accessed March 31, 2023).

Fuss, Diana, ed. *Inside/Out: Lesbian Theories, Gay Theories*. New York: Routledge, 1991.

Gamson, Joshua. "Messages of Exclusion: Gender, Movements, and Symbolic Boundaries." *Gender and Society* 11, no. 2 (April 1997): 178–99.

Gerami, Shahin. "Islamist Masculinity and Muslim Masculinities." *Handbook of Studies on Men and Masculinities* 448 (2005).

Gerami, Shahin. "Mullahs, Martyrs, and Men: Conceptualizing Masculinity in the Islamic Republic of Iran." *Men and Masculinities* 5, no. 3 (2003): 257–74.

"Get to Know Us: Our Vision & Theory of Change." *Me Too Movement*. https://metoomvmt.org/get-to-know-us/vision-theory-of-change/ (accessed February 28, 2022).

Gholami, Shahin. "Analysis of the Neglected Dimensions of #MeToo in Iran." 2021. https://harasswatch.com/news/1706/هم%E8%80%2Cس-علیه-وتصدایی (accessed November 11, 2021).

Gibbs, Martin, James Meese, Michael Arnold, Bjorn Nansen and Marcus Carter "Funeral and Instagram: death, social media, and platform vernacular," *Information, communication & society* 18, no. 3 (2015): 255–68.

Gill, Rosalind, and Shani Orgad. "The Shifting Terrain of Sex and Power: From the 'Sexualization of Culture' to #Metoo." *Sexualities* 21, no. 8 (2018): 1313–24. https://doi.org/10.1177/1363460718794647.

Ginat, Rami. *Egypt's Incomplete Revolution: Lutfi Al-Khuli and Nasser's Socialism in the 1960s*. London: Frank Cass, 1997.

Godenzi, Alberto. "Determinants of Culture: Men and Economic Power." Edited by Ingeborg Breines, Robert Connell, and Ingrid Eide, 35–51. Paris: UNESCO, 2000.

Goldner, Limor, and Yehuda Ruderman. "Toward Creating Positive Masculinity? Art Therapy as Seen by Male Art Therapists and Male Adolescent Clients." *Arts in Psychotherapy* 68 (2020): 101613.

Golkar, Saeid. *Captive Society: The Basij Militia and Social Control in Iran.* New York: Columbia University Press, 2015.

Goode, William J. "Why Men Resist." In *Rethinking the Family*, edited by Barrie Thorne and Marilyn Yalom, 287–310. New York: Longman, 1982.

Goodmark, Leigh. *Decriminalizing Domestic Violence: A Balanced Policy Approach to Intimate Partner Violence.* Oakland: University of California Press, 2018.

Gornick, Vivian. *The Romance of American Communism.* London: Verso, 2020.

Grewal, Inderpal. *Transnational America feminisms, diasporas, neoliberalisms.* Durham, North Carolina: Duke University Press, 2005.

Guillaumin, Colette. *Racism, Sexism, Power and Ideology.* New York: Routledge, 2002.

"Gurbih." Farhang-i Fārsi-i Muʿīn, n.d. https://www.vajehyab.com/moein/%DA%AF%D 8%B1%D8%A8%D9%87.

Hadadi, Fazel. "Unconscious Sexual Assault; Criticism of Article 224 of the Islamic Penal Code 2013," *Rasail Journal* 2 (2016): 78.

Hajjar, Lisa. "Religion, State Power, and Domestic Violence in Muslim Societies: A Framework for Comparative Analysis." *Law and Social Inquiry* 29, no. 1 (2004): 1–38.

Hajjar, Lisa, Eduardo de Leon Buendia, Patrick Fairbanks, Emma Kuskey, Sasha Misco, and Ada Quevedo. "Cultures and Resistance: The Struggle against Domestic Violence in Arab Societies." In *Handbook of Healthcare in the Arab World*. Cham: Springer, 2020. https://doi.org/10.1007/978-3-319-74365-3_201-1.

Hakakian, Roya. "The Flame of Feminism Is Alive in Iran: While Western Activists Defend the Right of Muslim Women to Wear the Veil, Iranian Women Are Fighting for a Bigger Cause: Choice." *Foreign Policy*, March 7, 2019. https://foreignpol icy.com/2019/03/07/the-flame-of-feminism-is-alive-in-iran-international-wom ens-day/.

Hakakian, Roya. *Journey from the Land of No: A Girlhood Caught in Revolutionary Iran.* New York: Random House, 2005.

Hakakian, Roya. "A UN Farce Has Tragic Implications for Feminist Activists in Islam." *Washington Post*, April 27, 2021. https://www.washingtonpost.com/opini ons/2021/04/27/un-farce-has-tragic-implications-feminist-activists-iran/.

Hakakian, Roya. "Unveiling Iran." *New York Review of Books*, March 8, 2021. https:// www.nybooks.com/daily/2021/03/08/unveiling-iran/.

Hakakian, Roya, and Masih Alinejad. "There Are Two Types of Hijabs: The Difference Is Huge." *Washington Post*, August 4, 2019. https://www.washingtonp ost.com/opinions/global-opinions/there-are-two-types-of-hijabs-the-differe nce-is-huge/2019/04/07/50a44574-57f0-11e9-814f-e2f46684196e_story.html.

Hall, Rebecca Jane. "Feminist Strategies to End Violence against Women." In *Oxford Handbook of Transnational Feminist Movements*, 1st ed., 652–67. Cary: Oxford University Press, 2015.

Hamad, Ruby. *White Tears/Brown Scars: How White Feminism Betrays Women of Color*. New York: Catapult, 2020.

Harris, Kevan. *A Social Revolution: Politics and the Welfare State in Iran*. Oakland: University of California Press, 2017.

Hartmann, Heidi. "The Unhappy Marriage of Marxism and Feminism." *Capital and Class*, 2015. https://web.ics.purdue.edu/~hoganr/SOC%20602/Hartmann_1979 (accessed March 4, 2020).

"Harvey Weinstein Timeline: How the Scandal Unfolded," BBC News. April 7, 2021, sec.

"Harvey Weinstein Timeline: How the Scandal Has Unfolded." BBC News. February 24, 2023.

Hasham, Alysha. "Jian Ghomeshi Acquitted on Basis of 'Insistencies' and 'Deception.'" *Toronto Star*, March 24, 2016. https://www.thestar.com/news/jian-ghome shi/2016/03/24/jian-ghomeshi-verdict.html.

Hassan, Naeemul, Manash Kumar Mandal, Mansurul Bhuiyan, Aparna Moitra, and Syed Ishtiaque Ahmed. "Nonparticipation of Bangladeshi Women in #MeToo Movement." In *ACM International Conference Proceeding Series*. Association for Computing Machinery, 2019.

Hassan, Riaz. *Attitudes toward Veiling and Patriarchy in Four Muslim Societies: An Exploratory Study*. GE von Grunebaum Center for Near Eastern Studies, California: University of California, 2000.

Hedjerassi, Nassira, and Audre Lorde, "Au carrefour de multiples sites d'oppressions liées. l'outsider. Une poétesse et intellectuelle féministe africaine-américaine." *Travail, genre et sociétés* 37 (2017): 111–27.

Heidegger, Martin. *Being and Time: A Translation of Sein Und Zeit*. Translated by Joan Stambaugh. Albany: State University of New York Press, 2010.

Heller, Chaia. "Take Back the Earth." In *Earth Ethics: Environmental Ethics, Animal Rights, and Practical Applications*, edited by James P. Sterba. Englewood Cliffs, NJ: Prentice Hall, 1995.

Hemmati, Shahrzad. "Missing Criteria in the Iranian #MeToo Movement." *Iranian Women Association*, November 27, 2020. https://ir-women.com/17293.

Hemmati, Shahrzad. "Verification Methods of Harassment Narratives in Conversation with Samaneh Savadi, a Women Activist." *Iranian Women Association*, November 27, 2020. https://ir-women.com/17254.

Hesova, Zora. "Secular, Islamic or Muslim Feminism?" *Gender and Research* 20, no. 2 (2019): 26–46.

Hirji, Faiza. "Claiming Our Space: Muslim Women, Activism, and Social Media." *Islamophobia Studies Journal* 6, no. 1 (2021): 78–92.

Hochberg, Gil Z. *Visual Occupations*. Durham, NC: Duke University Press, 2015.

Holm, Malin. "The Rise of Online Counterpublics? The Limits of Inclusion in a Digital Age." Uppsala University, Department of Government, 2019.

Honarbin-Holliday, Mehri. "Emerging Forms of Masculinity in the Islamic Republic of Iran." *Cultural Revolution in Iran: Contemporary Popular Culture in the Islamic Republic* 41 (2013): 59.

Honour Based Violence Awareness Network. 2022. http://hbv-awareness.com (retrieved 24 March 2022).

Hoodfar, Homa. *The Women's Movement in Iran: Women at the Crossroad of Secularization and Islamization*. Montpellier: Women Living Under Muslim Laws, 1999.

hooks, bell. *The Will to Change: Men, Masculinity, and Love*. New York: Atria, 2004.

Htun, Mala, and Francesca R. Jensenius. "Fighting Violence against Women: Laws, Norms & Challenges Ahead." *Daedalus* 149, no. 1 (2020): 144–59.

Inhorn, Marcia C., and Ramy Aly. "The New Arab Man: Emergent Masculinities, Technologies, and Islam in the Middle East." xxii, 404 pp., tables, illus., bibliogr. (Princeton, NJ: Princeton University Press, 2013), 900–1.

"Iranian Artworks Go Under Hammer at Tehran Auction." Kayhan International, August 15, 2021. https://kayhan.ir/files/en/publication/pages/1400/5/23/2078_16577.pdf.

"The Iranian Government Passed a Bill Banning Violence against Women after a Decade of Controversy." euronews, January 4, 2021. https://per.euronews.com/2021/01/04/the-iranian-government-passed-a-bill-banning-violence-against-women-after-a-decade-of-cont.

"Iranians Speak Out over Sexual Harassment Scandal." BBC News. February 11, 2016, sec. Trending. https://www.bbc.com/news/blogs-trending-35535269.

Ison, Jess. "'It's Not Just Men and Women': LGBTQIA People and #MeToo." In *#MeToo and the Politics of Social Change*, edited by Bianca Fileborn and Rachel Loney-Howes, 151–67. London: Palgrave Macmillan, 2019.

Jaffe, Peter G., Janet R. Johnston, Claire V. Crooks, and Nicholas Bala. "Custody Disputes Involving Allegations of Domestic Violence: Toward a Differentiated Approach to Parenting Plans." *Family Court Review* 46, no. 3 (2008): 500–22.

Jaffe, Sarah. "The Collective Power of #MeToo." *Dissent* 65, no. 2 (2018): 80–7.

Jaspard, Maryse. *Les violences contre les femmes*. Paris: La Découverte, 2005.

Jayanetti, Chaminda. "New Equalities Commissioner Attacked 'Modern Feminism' and #Metoo." *Guardian*, Guardian News and Media, November 22, 2020. https://www.theguardian.com/society/2020/nov/22/new-equalities-commissioner-attacked-modern-feminism-and-metoo.

Jayawardena, Kumari. *Feminism and Nationalism in the Third World*. London: Zed, 1985.

Journet, Nicolas. "Outsiders: études de sociologie de la deviance." In *La Sociologie*, edited by Xavier Molénat, 93–4. Auxerre: Éditions Sciences Humaines, 2009.

Kagal, Neha, Leah Cowan, and Huda Jawad. "Beyond the Bright Lights: Are Minoritized Women Outside the Spotlight Able to Say #MeToo?" In *#MeToo and the Politics of Social Change*, edited by Bianca Fileborn and Rachel Loney-Howes, 133–50. Cham: Palgrave, 2019.

Kamel, Atena. "Can the Victim Speak?" *Zanan Emrooz*, issue 41 (2021): 8–14.

Kāmvarī, Nāzlī. "Kunish-i Guftār-i Ta'ṣīrguẕār bar Kampainhāy-i Ānlīn va Āflīn 'Alayh-i Qatl-i Nāmūsī, Tajāvuz-i Jinsī va Ḥijāb-i Ijbārī." In *Dar Mīyānih—Dar Ḥāshīyih: Dar Bāreh-i Lāyihay-i Faqr-i Ṭabaqih-i Mīyānī dar Iran*, edited by Nāzlī Kāmvarī, 235–80. Zamānih Media, 1400/2022.

Kandiyoti, Deniz. *The Paradoxes of Masculinity: Some Thoughts on Segregated Societies*. New York: Routledge, 2016.

Kar, Mehrangiz. *Pajuheshi dar Bareh-ye Khoshunat Aleyhe Zanan dar Iran*. Tehran: Entesharat Rowshangaran va Motale'at-e Zanan, 2000.

Kar, Mehrangiz, and Azadeh Pourzand. "Iranian Women in the Year 1400: The Struggle for Equal Rights Continues." *Atlantic Council*, April 2021. https://www.atlanticcouncil.org/wp-content/uploads/2021/04/Iranian_Women_in_the_Year_1400-The_Struggle_for_Equal_Rights_Continues.pdf.

Kashani-Sabet, Firoozeh. "Patriotic Womanhood: The Culture of Feminism in Modern Iran, 1900–1941." *British Journal of Middle Eastern Studies* 32, no. 1 (2005): 29–46.

Kassam, Ashifa. "Margaret Atwood Faces Feminist Backlash on Social Media over #Metoo." *Guardian*, Guardian News and Media, January 15, 2018. https://www.theguardian.com/books/2018/jan/15/margaret-atwood-feminist-backlash-metoo.

Keller, Jessalynn, Kaitlynn Mendes, and Jessica Ringrose. "Speaking 'Unspeakable Things': Documenting Digital Feminist Responses to Rape Culture." *Journal of Gender Studies* 27, no. 1 (2018): 22–36.

Kemmerer, Lisa. "Introduction." In *Sister Species: Women, Animals, and Social Justice*, edited by Lisa Kemmer, 1–44. Urbana: University of Illinois Press, 2011.

Kepel, Gilles. *Jihad: The Trail of Political Islam*. Translated by Anthony F. Roberts. Cambridge: Belknap, 2003.

Kermani, Hossein, and Marzieh Adham. "Mapping Persian Twitter: Networks and Mechanism of Political Communication in Iranian 2017 Presidential Election." *Big Data & Society* 8, no. 1 (2021): 20539517211025568.

"Keyvan Emamverdi Was Accused of Corruption on Earth." *Independent Persian*, January 4, 2021. https://www.independentpersian.com/node/111381#.YV-qtmgS_rc.telegram.

"Keyvan Emamverdi Was Arrested." *Iran International*, August 25, 2020. https://b2n.ir/u35897.

Khader, Serene J. *Adaptive Performances*. Oxford: Oxford University Press, 2011.

Khamenei.ir. "The Disaster of Countless Sexual Assaults on Western Women—Including Incidents Leading to #Metoo Campaign—and Islam's Proposal to Resolve It Http://English.Khamenei.Ir/News/5986/10-Facts-by-Ayatollah-Khamenei-Can-Hijab-Save-Western-Women Https://T.Co/TV1TzFcra4." Tweet. @khamenei_ir (blog), October 3, 2018. https://twitter.com/khamenei_ir/status/1047540289265647616.

Khorasani, Noushin Ahmadi. *Iranian Women's One Million Signatures Campaign for Equality: The Inside Story*, English ed. Women's Learning Partnership, 2009.

Kian, Azadeh. "La fabrique de genre, des corps et des sexualités en Iran: entre nationalism et islamisme." In *État-nation et fabrique du genre, des corps et des sexualités: Iran, Turquie et Afghanistan*, edited by Lucia Direnberger and Azadeh Kian, 21–47. Aix-en-Provence: Presses universitaires de Provence, 2019.

Kiarostami, Abbas. *Dah* [Ten]. 2002.

Kim, Mimi E. "From Carceral Feminism to Transformative Justice: Women-of-Color Feminism and Alternatives to Incarceration." *Journal of Ethnic and Cultural Diversity in Social Work* 27, no. 3 (2018): 219–33.

King, Andrew. "The 'Quiet Revolution' amongst Men: Developing the Practice of Working with Men in Family Relationships." *Children Australia* 30, no. 2 (2005): 33–7.

Kingsley, Patrick. "80 Sexual Assaults in One Day: The Other Story of Tahrir Square." *Guardian*, July 5, 2013. http://www.theguardian.com/world/2013/jul/05/egypt-women-rape-sexual-assault-tahrir-square.

Kirby, Stuart, Brian Francis, and Rosaline O'Flaherty. "Can the FIFA World Cup Football (Soccer) Tournament Be Associated with an Increase in Domestic Abuse?" *Journal of Research in Crime and Delinquency* 51, no. 3 (2014): 259–76.

Kiselica, Mark S., S. Benton-Wright, and M. Englar-Carlson. "Accentuating Positive Masculinity: A New Foundation for the Psychology of Boys, Men, and Masculinity." In *APA Handbook of Men and Masculinities*, edited by Y. J. Wong and S. R. Wester, 123–43. American Psychological Association, 2016. https://doi.org/10.1037/14594-006.

Kitzinger, Celia. "Heteronormativity in Action: Reproducing the Heterosexual Nuclear Family in After-Hours Medical Calls." *Social Problems* 52, no. 4 (2005): 477–98.

Kosofsky Sedgwisk, Eve. *Epistemology of the Closet*. Berkeley: University of California Press, 1990.

Kunashakaran, Sumita. "Un (Wo)manned Aerial Vehicles: An Assessment of How Unmanned Aerial Vehicles Influence Masculinity in the Conflict Arena." *Contemporary Security Policy* 37, no. 1 (2016): 31–61.

Labor Force Participation Rate, Female (% of Female Population Ages 15+) (Modeled ILO Estimate)—Middle East & North Africa. The World Bank. February 8, 2022. https://data.worldbank.org/indicator/SL.TLF.CACT.FE.ZS?locations=ZQ (retrieved March 24 2022).

Lang, Heather. "#MeToo: A Case Study in Re-embodying Information." *Computers and Composition*, Digital Technologies, Bodies, and Embodiments, 53 (September 1, 2019): 9–20. https://doi.org/10.1016/j.compcom.2019.05.001.

Lang, James. "Men, Masculinities and Violence." In *International Conference on Eradicating Violence against Women & Girls: Strengthening Human Rights*, Berlin, Germany. 2002.

Leaver, Tama, Tim Highfield, and Abidin Crystal. *Instagram: Visual Social Media Cultures*. Newark: Polity, 2020.

Lees, Sue. "Judicial Rape." *Women's Studies International Forum* 16, no. 1 (1993): 11–36.

"Lesbian Feminism," GLBTQ Encyclopedia: http://www.glbtqarchive.com/sshindex.html (last visited on January 14, 2022).

Levant, Ronald F. "Toward the Reconstruction of Masculinity." *Journal of Family Psychology* 5, nos. 3–4 (1992): 379.

"LGBTQ+ 'Panic' Defense." n.d. https://lgbtbar.org/programs/advocacy/gay-trans-panic-defense/.

Liao, Sara. "'#IAmGay# What About You?': Storytelling, Discursive Politics, and the Affective Dimension of Social Media Activism against Censorship in China." *International Journal of Communication* 13 (2019): 2314–333.

Lingis, Alphonso. "The Subjectification of the Body." In *The Body: Classic and Contemporary Readings*, edited by Donn Welton, 286–305. Oxford: Blackwell, 1999.

Lomax, Tamura A. "Occupy Rape Culture." *Feminist Wire*, November 5, 2011. http://thefeministwire.com/2011/11/occupy-rape-culture/.

Lorde, Audre. *Sister Outsider: Essays and Speeches*. Trumansburg, NY: Crossing Press, 1984.

MacKinnon, Catharine A. *Toward a Feminist Theory of the State*. Cambridge, MA: Harvard University Press, 1989.

Maclean, Mairi, Charles Harvey, and Gerhard Kling. "Pathways to Power: Class, Hyper-Agency and the French Corporate Elite." *Organization Studies* 35, no. 6 (2014): 825–55. https://doi.org/10.1177/0170840613509919.

Maghbouleh, Neda. *The Limits of Whiteness: Iranian Americans and the Everyday Politics of Race*, 1st ed. Stanford, CA: Stanford University Press, 2017.

Mahar, Cheleen, Richard K. Harker, and Chris Wilkes. "The Basic Theoretical Position." In *An Introduction to the Work of Pierre Bourdieu: The Practice of Theory*, edited by Richard K. Harker, Cheleen Mahar, and Chris Wilkes, 1–25. Palgrave Macmillan, 2003.

Maher, Amina. Interview. *The Lead*. By Fardad Farahzad. Iran International. August 25, 2020.

Mahmood, Saba. "Secularism, Hermeneutics and Empire: The Politics of Islamic Reformation." *Public Culture* 18, no. 6 (2006): 323–47.

Manikonda, Lydia, Ghazaleh Beigi, Huan Liu, and Subbarao Kambhampati. "Twitter for Sparking a Movement, Reddit for Sharing the Moment: #metoo through the Lens of Social Media." *ArXiv:1803.08022 [Cs]*, March 21, 2018. http://arxiv.org/abs/1803.08022.

Maranloo, Sahar. "Legal Reflections of the Women's Campaigns against Sexual Harassment." *Zanan Emrooz*, no. 41 (2021): 36–41.

Mardorossian, Carine M. "Toward a New Feminist Theory of Rape." *Signs* 27, no. 3 (2002): 743–75.

Markowitz, Sara. "The Price of Alcohol, Wife Abuse, and Husband Abuse." *Southern Economic Journal* 67, no. 2 (2000): 279–303.

Marx, Karl. *Capital: A Critique of Political Economy*, vol. 1. Translated by Ben Fowkes. New York: Vintage, 1976.

"Marxism, Feminism and #Metoo." 1917: Journal of the International Bolshevik Tendency. No. 41—Marxism, Feminism and #MeToo, 2019. http://www.bolshevik.org/1917/no41/ibt_1917_41_08_me_too.html.

"Masih Alinejad and Roya Hakakian on Feminism and Freedom in Iran." *Yale Law School*, February 8, 2019. https://law.yale.edu/yls-today/news/masih-alinejad-and-roya-hakakian-feminism-and-freedom-iran.

Matin-Asgari, Afshin. *Both Eastern and Western: An Intellectual History of Iranian Modernity*. Cambridge: Cambridge University Press, 2018.

Maton, Karl. "Habitus." In *Pierre Bourdieu: Key Concepts*, edited by Michael James Grenfell, 49–66. London: Taylor and Francis, 2008.

McDowell, Linda. *Gender, Identity and Place: Understanding Feminist Geographies*. Minneapolis: University of Minnesota Press, 1999.

McKenna, Mary, and Myles Baker. "Silvia Federici Challenges #MeToo Movement to Look at the Systemic, Economic Causes of Sexual Violence." Works in Progress, March 31, 2018. https://olywip.org/silvia-federici-challenges-metoo-movement-look-systemic-economic-causes-sexual-violence/.

McLaren, Leah. "The Cult of Jian: His Life as an Outcast, Who's Standing by Him, and Why He's Sure He'll Walk." *Toronto Life*, June 17, 2015. https://torontolife.com/city/cult-of-jian-ghomeshi-leah-mclaren/3/.

"Me Too: I Was Sexually Harassed at 11." BBC News. October 28, 2017, sec. Middle East. https://www.bbc.com/news/world-middle-east-41764156.

"Me Too Movement (Pakistan)." Wikipedia, 2022. https://en.wikipedia.org/wiki/Me_Too_movement_(Pakistan).

"MeToo Movement in Iran." Wikipedia, February 22, 2023. https://fa.wikipedia.org/wiki/جنبش_من_هم_در_ایران.

Medvetz, Thomas, Jeffrey J. Sallaz, and Erik Neveu. "Bourdieu's Capital(s): Sociologizing an Economic Concept." In *The Oxford Handbook of Pierre Bourdieu*, edited by Thomas Medvetz and Jeffrey J. Sallaz. Oxford: Oxford University Press, 2018.

Mendes, Kaitlynn, Jessalynn Keller, and Jessica Ringrose. "Digitized Narratives of Sexual Violence: Making Sexual Violence Felt and Known through Digital Disclosures." *New Media and Society* 21, no. 6 (2019): 1290–310.

Mendes, Kaitlynn, Jessica Ringrose, and Jessalynn Keller. "#MeToo and the Promise and Pitfalls of Challenging Rape Culture through Digital Feminist Activism." *European Journal of Women's Studies* 25, no. 2 (May 1, 2018): 236–46. https://doi.org/10.1177/1350506818765318.

Mernissi, Fatima. *Beyond the Veil: Male-Female Dynamics in Modern Muslim Society*. Bloomington: Indiana University Press, 1987.

Messner, Michael A., and Nancy M. Solomon. "Social Justice and Men's Interests: The Case of Title IX." *Journal of Sport and Social Issues* 31, no. 2 (2007): 162–78.

"#MeToo in Iran: Lessons & Questions across Platforms." https://scholar.google.com/citations?view_op=view_citation&hl=en&user=LRcf2hcAAAAJ&citation_for_view=LRcf2hcAAAAJ:9yKSN-GCB0IC (accessed February 17, 2022).

"Middle East Matters—'No Doesn't Mean No': Iran's 'Namjoo Scandal' Triggers Debate on Sexual Abuse," France 24, April 21, 2021. https://www.france24.com/en/tv-shows/middle-east-matters/20210421-no-doesn-t-mean-no-iran-s-namjoo-scandal-triggers-debate-on-sexual-abuse.

Middlemiss, Jim. "Navigating Sexual Harassment in a #Metoo World." Canadian Lawyer, September 21, 2018. https://www.canadianlawyermag.com/news/opinion/navigating-sexual-harassment-in-a-metoo-world/275467

Milani, Farzaneh. *Veils and Words*. Syracuse: Syracuse University Press, 1992.

Milani, Farzaneh. "Women's Autobiographies in Iran." In *Women's Autobiographies in Contemporary Iran*, edited by Afsaneh Najmabadi, 1–16. Cambridge, MA: Harvard University Press, 1990.

Milano, Alyssa (@Alyssa_Milano). "If You've Been Sexually Harassed or Assaulted Write 'Me Too' as a Reply to This Tweet: T.Co/K2oeCiUf9n." Twitter, October 15, 2017. https://twitter.com/alyssa_milano/status/919659438700670976.

Miller, Anna Lekas. "She Started #NotYourHabibti to Shine a Light on Sexual Harassment in the Palestinian Territories." *World* (Public Radio), 2018. https://theworld.org/stories/2018-02-02/she-started-notyourhabibti-shine-light-sexual-harassment-palestinian-territories.

Mills Wright, Charles. *White Collars: The American Middle Classes*. Oxford: Oxford University Press, 1951.

Milner, Jean-Claude. "Reflections on the Me Too Movement and Its Philosophy." *Problemi International* 3, no. 3 (2019): 65–89.

Mincheva, Dilyana. "#DearSister and #MosqueMeToo: Adversarial Islamic Feminism within the Western-Islamic Public Sphere." *Feminist Media Studies*. doi: 10.1080/14680777.2021.1984273 (online).

Mir Hosseini, Ziba. "Beyond Islam versus Feminism." *IDS Bulletin* 42, no. 1 (2011): 67–77.

Mir-Hosseini, Ziba. "The Conservative: Reformist Conflict over Women's Rights in Iran." *International Journal of Politics, Culture, and Society* 16, no. 1 (2002): 37–53.

Mir Hosseini, Ziba. "Feminist Voices in Islam: Promise and Potential." *Open Democracy*, November 19, 2012. https://www.opendemocracy.net/en/5050/feminist-voices-in-islam-promise-and-potential/.

Mir-Hosseini, Ziba. *Islam and Gender: The Religious Debate in Contemporary Iran*, vol. 7. Princeton, NJ: Princeton University Press, 1999.

Mir Hosseini, Ziba. "Muslim Women's Quest for Equality: Between Islamic Law and Feminism." *Critical Inquiry* 32, no. 4 (2006): 629–45.

Mir-Hosseini, Ziba. "The Politics and Hermeneutics of Hijab in Iran: From Confinement to Choice." *Muslim World Journal of Human Rights* 4, no. 1 (2007).

Mir Hosseini, Ziba. "What Is Islamic Feminism." *CILE Seminar on Ethics and Gender at the University of Oxford*. June 17, 2015. https://www.youtube.com/watch?v=Fzf2D43wcTc.

Mir-Hosseini, Ziba, Mulki Al-Sharmani, and Jana Rumminger. *Men in Charge? Rethinking Authority in Muslim Legal Tradition*. London: One World, 2015.

Mirsepassi, Ali. *Intellectual Discourse and the Politics of Modernization: Negotiating Modernity in Iran*. Cambridge: Cambridge University Press, 2000.

Mitchell, Richard P. *The Society of the Muslim Brothers*. Oxford: Oxford University Press, 1993.

Moallem, Minoo. *Between Warrior Brother and Veiled Sister: Islamic Fundamentalism and the Politics of Patriarchy in Iran*. California: University of California Press, 2005.

Moallem, Minoo. "'Foreignness' and Be/Longing: Transnationalism and Immigrant Entrepreneurial Spaces." *Comparative Studies of South Asia, Africa and the Middle East* 20, no. 1 (2000): 200–10.

Moallem, Minoo. "Iranian Immigrants, Exiles and Refugees: From National to Transnational Contexts." *Comparative Studies of South Asia, Africa and the Middle East* 20, no. 1 (2000): 161–4.

Moallem, Minoo. "Staging Masculinity in Iran–Iraq War Movies." In *The Palgrave Handbook of Asian Cinema*, edited by Aaron Han Joon Magnan-Park, Gina Marchetti, and See Kam Tan, 489–506. London: Palgrave Macmillan, 2018.

Moallem, Minoo. "The Texualization of Violence in a Global World: Gendered Citizenship and Discourses of Protection." *Review of Japanese Culture and Society* 11/12 (1999): 9–17.

Moallem, Minoo. "Universalization of Particulars: The Civic Body and Gendered Citizenship in Iran." *Citizenship Studies* 3, no. 3 (November 1, 1999): 319–35. https://doi.org/10.1080/13621029908420718.

Moallem, Minoo. "Whose Fundamentalism?" *Meridians* 2, no. 2 (2002): 298–301.

Modrek, Sepideh, and Bozhidar Chakalov. "The# MeToo Movement in the United States: Text Analysis of Early Twitter Conversations." *Journal of Medical Internet Research* 21, no. 9 (2019): e13837. https://www.jmir.org/2019/9/e13837/.

Moghadam, Valentine M. "Gender and Revolutionary Transformation: Iran 1979 and East Central Europe 1989." *Gender and Society* 9, no. 3 (1995): 328–58.

Moghadam, Valentine M. "Hidden from History? Women Workers in Modern Iran." *Iranian Studies* 33, no. 3/4 (2000): 377–401.

Moghadam, Valentine M. "Islamic Feminism and Its Discontents: Toward a Resolution of the Debate." *Signs* 27, no. 4 (2002): 1135–71. https://doi.org/10.1086/339639.

Moghadam, Valentine M. "Patriarchy in Transition: Women and the Changing Family in the Middle East." *Journal of Comparative Family Studies* 35, no. 2 (2004): 137–62.

Moghadam, Valentine M. "Transnational Feminist Activism and Movement Building." In *Oxford Handbook of Transnational Feminist Movements*, 1st ed., 53–81. Cary: Oxford University Press, 2015.

Moghadam, Valentine M. "Women's Economic Participation in the Middle East: What Difference Has the Neoliberal Policy Turn Made?" *Journal of Middle East Women's Studies* 1, no. 1 (2005): 110–46.

Moghissi, Haideh. "Islamic Feminism Revisited." *Comparative Studies of South Asia, Africa and the Middle East* 31, no. 1 (2011): 76–84.

Moghissi, Haideh. *Populism and Feminism in Iran: Women's Struggle in a Male-Defined Revolutionary Movement*. New York: Springer, 2016.

Moghissi, H. Islamic Cultural Nationalism and Gender Politics in Iran. *Third World Quarterly*, 29. 3 (2008), 541–554. http://www.jstor.org/stable/20455056

"Mohsen Namjoo Etteham "Tajavoz va Ta'roz-i Jinsi" ra "Qaviyyan" Takzib Kard. *Kayhan London*. Shahrivar 1399/29 August 2020. https://kayhan.london/fa/1399/06/08/%d9%85%d8%ad%d8%b3%d9%86-%d9%86%d8%a7%d9%85%d8%ac%d9%88-%d8%a7%d8%aa%d9%87%d8%a7%d9%85-%d8%aa%d8%ac%d8%a7%d9%88%d8%b2-%d9%88-%d8%aa%d8%b9%d8%b1%d8%b6-%d8%ac%d9%86%d8%b3%db%8c-%d8%b1%d8%a7.

Mollow, Anna. "Unvictimizable: Toward a Fat Black Disability Studies." *African American Review* 50, no. 2 (2017): 105–21.

Moore, Robert. "Capital." In *Pierre Bourdieu: Key Concepts*, edited by Michael Grenfell, 101–18. Stocksfield: Acumen, 2012.

Moore, Rob. *Education and Society: Issues and Explanations in the Sociology of Education*. Cambridge: Polity, 2004.

Moscatello, Caitlin. "Does Porn Damage Men? A Look at the Lasting, Unspoken Effects." *Glamour*, 2015. https://www.glamour.com/story/does-porn-damage-men (retrieved March 24, 2022).

Motamedi, Maziar. "Iranians Break Taboos with Their Own Version of #MeToo." September 22, 2020. https://www.aljazeera.com/news/2020/9/22/iranians-break-taboos-with-their-own-version-of-metoo.

Motamedi, Maziar. "Protecting Dignity: Iran's Push to Fight Violence against Women." *Al Jazeera English*, February 28, 2021. https://www.aljazeera.com/features/2021/2/28/protecting-dignity-irans-push-to-fight-violence-against-women.

Mouri, Leila, and Kristin Soraya Batmanghelichi. "Can the Secular Iranian Women's Activists Speak? Caught between the Political Power and the Islamic Feminist." In *Gender and Sexuality in Muslim Countries*, edited by Gul Ozyegin, 331–54. Farnham: Ashgate, 2015.

"Mowj-i Gostardeh-i Enteqadha 'Alayh-i Mohsen Namjoo: As Etteham-i Azar va Aziyyat ta Khod-Bozorgbini va Sokhanan-i Jinsiyyat Zadeh." *Kayhan London*, 29 Farvardin, 1400/ April 18, 2021. https://kayhan.london/fa/1400/01/29/%d9%85%d9%88%d8%ac-%da%af%d8%b3%d8%aa%d8%b1%d8%af%d9%87%e2%80%8c%db%8c-%d8%a7%d9%86%d8%aa%d9%8

2%d8%a7%d8%af%d9%87%d8%a7-%d8%b9%d9%84%db%8c%d9%87-%d9%85%d8%ad%d8%b3%d9%86-%d9%86%d8%a7%d9%85%d8%ac%d9%88.

Mulvey, Laura. *Visual and Other Pleasures*. New York: Springer, 1989.

Murphy, Meghan. "Jian Ghomeshi's 'Consent' Defence Shows Why 'Consent' Isn't Good Enough." *Feminist Current*, October 27, 2014. https://www.feministcurrent.com/2014/10/27/jian-ghomeshis-consent-defence-shows-why-consent-isnt-good-enough/.

Mynett, Tim. (@TimMynett). "So This lady Doesn't Want to Combat Islamophobia Because She Doesn't Like Muslims. Understood!." Twitter, January 26, 2022. https://twitter.com/TimMynett/status/1486354013612302338.

Najmabadi, Afsaneh. "The Erotic Vaṭan [Homeland] as Beloved and Mother: To Love, to Possess, and to Protect." *Comparative Studies in Society and History* 39, no. 3 (1997): 442–67.

Najmabadi, Afsaneh. "Feminism in an Islamic Republic: Years of Hardship, Years of Growth." In *Islam, Gender, and Social Change*, edited by Yvonne Yazbeck Haddad and John L. Esposito, 59–84. New York: Oxford University Press, 1998.

Najmabadi, Afsaneh. "Genus of Sex or the Sexing of 'Jins.'" *International Journal of Middle East Studies* 45, no. 2 (2013): 211–31.

Najmabadi, Afsaneh. "Mapping Transformations of Sex, Gender, and Sexuality in Modern Iran." *Social Analysis: The International Journal of Social and Cultural Practice* 49, no. 2 (2005): 54–77.

Najmabadi, Afsaneh. *Professing Selves: Transsexuality and Same-Sex Desire in Contemporary Iran*. Durham, NC: Duke University Press, 2013.

Najmabadi, Afsaneh. "Transing and Transpassing across Sex-Gender Walls in Iran." *Women's Studies Quarterly* 36, no. 3/4 (2008): 23–42.

Najmabadi, Afsaneh. "Verdicts of Science, Rulings of Faith: Transgender/Sexuality in Contemporary Iran." *Social Research* 78, no. 2 (2011): 533–56.

Najmabadi, Afsaneh. *Women with Moustaches and Men without Beards: Gender and Sexual Anxieties of Iranian Modernity*. Berkeley: University of California Press, 2005.

North, Anna. "#MeToo Movement: These 7 Facts Show Its Impact." October 4, 2019. https://www.vox.com/identities/2019/10/4/20852639/me-too-movement-sexual-harassment-law-2019.

Nussbaum, Martha C. *Citadels of Pride: Sexual Assault, Accountability, and Reconciliation*. New York: Norton, 2021.

Nussbaum, Martha C. "Objectification." *Philosophy and Public Affairs* 24, no. 4 (1995): 249–91.

Nussbaum, Martha C. "'Whether from Reason or Prejudice': Taking Money for Bodily Services." *Journal of Legal Studies* 27, no. 2 (1998): 693–734.

Ohlheiser, Abby. "The Woman behind 'Me Too' Knew the Power of the Phrase When She Created IT—10 Years Ago." *Washington Post*, WP Company, October 26, 2021.

https://www.washingtonpost.com/news/the-intersect/wp/2017/10/19/the-woman-behind-me-too-knew-the-power-of-the-phrase-when-she-created-it-10-years-ago/.

Olwan, Dana M. "Pinkwashing the 'Honor Crime': Murdered Muslim Women and the Politics of Posthumous Solidarities." *Signs: Journal of Women in Culture and Society* 44, no. 4 (June 1, 2019): 905–30. https://doi.org/10.1086/702311.

Olwan, Dana. "Gendered Violence, Cultural Otherness, and Honour Crimes in Canadian National Logics," *Canadian Journal of Sociology*, 38. 4 (2013): 533–56. https://doi.org/10.29173/cjs21196

Osanloo, Arzoo. *Forgiveness Work*. Princeton, NJ: Princeton University Press, 2020.

Paasonen, Susanna, Feona Attwood, Alan McKee, John Mercer, and Clarissa Smith. *Objectification: On the Difference between Sex and Sexism*. London: Routledge, 2021.

Page, Ruth. *Narratives Online Stories in Social Media*. Cambridge: Cambridge University Press, 2018.

Paidar, Parvin. *Women and the Political Process in Twentieth-Century Iran*, vol. 1. Cambridge: Cambridge University Press, 1997.

Papacharissi, Zizi. *Affective Publics: Sentiment, Technology and Politics*. New York: Oxford University Press, 2015.

Pearce, Ruth, Sonja Erikainen, and Ben Vincent. "TERF Wars: An Introduction." *Sociological Review Monographs* 68, no. 4 (2020): 3–24.

Pease, Bob. "Engaging Men in Men's Violence Prevention: Exploring the Tensions, Dilemmas and Possibilities." *Australian Domestic & Family Violence Clearinghouse*, no. 17 (2008): 1–20.

Pease, Bob. "(Re)constructing Men's Interests." *Men and Masculinities* 5, no. 2 (2002): 165–77.

Pease, Bob. *Undoing Privilege: Unearned Advantage in a Divided World*. London: Bloomsbury, 2010.

Pegu, Sanjana. "MeToo in India: Building Revolutions from Solidarities." *DECISION* 46, no. 2 (2019): 151–68.

PettyJohn, Morgan, Finneran K. Muzzey, Megan K. Maas, and Heather L. McCauley. "# HowIWillChange: Engaging Men and Boys in the# MeToo Movement." *Psychology of Men & Masculinities* 20, no. 4 (2019): 612.

Phelan, Shane. *Identity Politics: Lesbian Feminism and the Limits of Community*. Philadelphia: Temple University Press, 1989.

Philips, Abu Ameenah Bilal, and Jameelah Jones. *Polygamy in Islam*. Riyadh, Saudi Arabia: International Islamic Publishing House, 2005.

Pipyrou, Stavroula. "#MeToo Is Little More Than Mob Rule // Vs // #MeToo Is a Legitimate Form of Social Justice." *HAU: Journal of Ethnographic Theory* 8, no. 3 (2018): 415–19.

Popova, Milena. *Sexual Consent*. Cambridge, MA: MIT Press. 2019.

Powell, Anastasia. *Review of Bystander Approaches in Support of Preventing Violence against Women*. Australia: RMIT University, 2011.

Puar, Jasbir K. *Terrorist Assemblages: Homonationalism in Queer Times*. Durham, NC: Duke University Press, 2007.

Qajar, Aida. "An Iranian Star Who Doesn't Understand No Means No." *IranWire*, April 21, 2021. https://iranwire.com/en/features/69391/.

Quan-Haase, Anabel, Kaitlynn Mendes, Dennis Ho, Olivia Lake, Charlotte Nau, and Darryl Pieber. "Mapping #MeToo: A Synthesis Review of Digital Feminist Research across Social Media Platforms." *New Media & Society* 23, no. 6 (June 1, 2021): 1700–20. https://doi.org/10.1177/1461444820984457.

The Qur'an. Translated by Saheeh International. Riyadh: Al-Muntada Al-Islami, 2011.

Qutb, Sayyid. *Milestones*. Indianapolis: American Trust, 1990.

Radicalesbians. "The Woman-Identified Woman." In *Radical Feminism*, edited by Anne Koedt, Ellen Levine, and Anita Rapone, 240–5. New York: Quadrangle, 1973.

Rahbari, Ladan, Susan Dierickx, Gily Coene, and Chia Longman. "Transnational Solidarity with Which Muslim Women? The Case of the My Stealthy Freedom and World Hijab Day Campaigns." *Politics and Gender* 17, no. 1 (2019): 1–24.

Rahim, Ghomeishi. "Captivity in Captivity." @ghomeishi3—All Telegram Channel Posts, telemetr.io. https://telemetr.io/en/channels/1115454551-ghomeishi3/posts (accessed March 12, 2022).

Rahimi, Paria. "The Study of Cyber Activity Patterns of Women's Rights Activists and Their Relation to Activism in the Real Space." MA dissertation, University of Tehran, Tehran, 2018.

Rahnema, Ali. *An Islamic Utopian: A Political Biography of Ali Shariati*. London: I.B. Tauris, 1998.

Rastegar, Sarvenaz. "10 Years of Waiting for Nothing: Take a look at the Protection, Dignity, and Security of Women Against Violence Bill." *Iran Human Rights*, February 7, 2021. https://iranhr.net/fa/articles/4613/.

Ratcliffe, Krista. *Rhetorical Listening: Identification, Gender, Whiteness*. Carbondale: Southern Illinois University Press, 2005.

"Rebelling against Rape: Egyptian Women Speak Up about Sex Crimes." *Economist*, November 14, 2020.

Resch, Robert Paul. *Althusser and the Renewal of Marxist Social Theory*. Berkeley: University of California Press, 1992.

Rezaei, Roghayeh. "#MeToo Branded a Zionist Movement in High-Profile Tehran Rape Trial," *IranWire*, January 4, 2022. https://iranwire.com/en/features/11035.

Rezai, Yasamin. "#MeToo in Iran: Lessons & Questions Across Platforms." Instasociety, 2021. https://instasociety.org/issues/issue-ii/metoo-iran/ https://scholar.google.com/citations?view_op=view_citation&hl=en&user=LRcf2hcAAAAJ&citation_for_view=LRcf2hcAAAAJ:9yKSN-GCB0IC (accessed November 11 2022).

Rezai, Yasamin. *Performing# MeToo: How Not to Look Away*. Edited by Judith D. Rudakoff. United Kingdom: Intellect, 2021.

Riahi, Mohammad Esmaeil, and Tahereh Lotfi Khachaki. "Social Analysis of the Influencing Factors on the Experiencing Street Harassment by Female Students of

University of Mazandaran." *Strategic Research on Social Problems in Iran University of Isfahan* 5, no. 2 (2016): 69–88.

Riaz, Hassan. *Attitudes toward Veiling and Patriarchy in Four Muslim Societies: An Exploratory Study*. GE von Grunebaum Center for Near Eastern Studies, University of California, 2000.

Ricoeur, Paul. "The Model of the Text: Meaningful Action Considered as a Text." *New Literary History* 5, no. 1 (1973): 91–117. https://doi.org/10.2307/468410.

Rodinson, Maxime. *Islam and Capitalism*. Austin: University of Texas Press, 1978.

Rogers, Sharon. "What Men Think about Gender Equality: Lessons from Oxfam GB Staff in Delhi and Dhaka." In *Gender Equality and Men: Learning from Practice*, edited by Sandy Ruxton, 177–93. Oxford: Oxfam GB, 2004.

Rothblum, Esther D. "Transforming Lesbian Sexuality." *Psychology of Women Quarterly*, no. 18 (1994): 627–41.

Rudakoff, Judith. *Performing #MeToo: How Not to Look Away*. United Kingdom: Intellect, 2021.

Sadeghipouya, Mahdis. "'Sister Outsider': l'engagement politique des lesbiennes de descendance musulmane en France: entre objectivation intersectionnelle et subjectivation militante." PhD dissertation, Paris 8 Vincennes Saint Denis University, France (in progress since 2018).

Saeidzadeh, Zara. "'Are Trans Men the Manliest of Men?' Gender Practices, Trans Masculinity and Mardānegī in Contemporary Iran." *Journal of Gender Studies* 29, no. 3 (2020): 295–309.

Salime, Zakia. *Between Feminism and Islam: Human Rights and Sharia Law in Morocco*, 1st ed. Minneapolis: University of Minnesota Press, 2011.

Salzano, Matthew. "Technoliberal Participation: Black Lives Matter and Instagram Slideshows." Paper Presented at AoIR 2021: The 22nd Annual Conference of the Association of Internet Researchers, 2021.

Samuels, Meaghan Smead. "Upgrading the Women's Movement in Iran: Through Cultural Activism, Creative Resistance, and Adaptability." MA thesis (submitted), University of Washington, 2018.

Sanij, Neda. "زنان ایرانی که فریاد زدند: آن مرد به ما تجاوز کرد" BBC News فارسی. BBC, 2020. https://www.bbc.com/persian/iran-features-53873273.

Santora, Marc. "Turkey Considers Leaving Domestic Violence Treaty Even as Abuse Surges." *New York Times*, August 25, 2020.

Sarbar, Elnaz. "Caught in Identity Politics, I Will Not Be Silenced." MyStealthyFreedom.Org, January 23, 2022. https://www.mystealthyfreedom.org/caught-in-identity-politics-i-will-not-be-silenced/.

Savolainen, Laura, Justus Uitermark, and John D. Boy. "Filtering Feminisms: Emergent Feminist Visibilities on Instagram." *New Media and Society* 24, no. 3 (2020): 557–79.

Sayej, Nadja. "Alyssa Milano on the #MeToo Movement: 'We're Not Going to Stand for It Any More.'" *Guardian*, Guardian News and Media, December 1, 2017. https://

www.theguardian.com/culture/2017/dec/01/alyssa-milano-mee-too-sexual-harassment-abuse.

Schulze, Corina, Sarah Koon-Maganin, and Valerie Brayan. *Gender Identity, Sexual Orientation & Sexual Aggression: Challenging the Myths*. London: Lynne Rienner, 2019.

Scott, John, Kerry Carrington, and Alison McIntosh. "Globalization, Frontier Masculinities and Violence: Booze, Blokes and Brawls." *British Journal of Criminology* 50, no. 3 (2010): 393–413.

Screpanti, Ernesto. *Labour Value: Rethinking Marx's Theory of Exploitation*. Cambridge, UK: Open Book, 2019.

Seedat, Fatima. "Sexual Economies of War and Sexual Technologies of the Body: Militarised Muslim Masculinity and the Islamist Production of Concubines for the Caliphate." *Agenda: Empowering Women for Gender Equity: Women, Religion and* 30, no. 3 (2017): 1–14.

"Semantic Network Analysis of the International Communication Association | Human Communication Research | Oxford Academic." https://academic.oup.com/hcr/article-abstract/25/4/589/4554809?redirectedFrom=fulltext (accessed February 21, 2022).

Sen, Puran. "'Crimes of Honour', Value and Meaning." In *Hornour: Crimes, Paradigms, and Violence against Women*, edited by Lynn Welchman and Sara Hossain, 42–63. London: Zed, 2005.

SepanoData.Ir. "The Conditions of Domestic Violence in Iran in Two National Researches." Moavenat-e Zanan, 2015. https://women.gov.ir/fa/news/4755/.

Sepehri Far, Tara. "Iran Is Having Its #MeToo Moment," September 9, 2020. https://www.hrw.org/news/2020/09/09/iran-having-its-metoo-moment.

Serisier, Tanya. *Speaking Out: Feminism, Rape and Narrative Politics*. New York: Springer International, 2018.

Shah, Bina. "The Real Enemy of Pakistani Women Is Not Men." *New York Times*, April 14, 2019. https://www.nytimes.com/2019/04/14/opinion/pakistan-womens-march.html (retrieved March 24, 2022).

Shakhsari, Sima. "From Homoerotics of Exile to Homopolitics of Diaspora: Cyberspace, the War on Terror, and the Hypervisible Iranian Queer." *Journal of Middle East Women's Studies* 8, no. 3 (2012): 14–40. https://doi.org/10.2979/jmiddeastwomstud.8.3.14.

Shakhsari, Sima. *Politics of Rightful Killing: Civil Society, Gender, and Sexuality in Weblogistan*. Durham, NC: Duke University Press, 2020.

Shakhsari, Sima. "The Queer Time of Death: Temporality, Geopolitics, and Refugee Rights." *Sexualities* 17, no. 8 (December 1, 2014): 998–1015. https://doi.org/10.1177/1363460714552261.

Shakhsari, Sima. "Transnational Governmentality and the Politics of Life and Death." *International Journal of Middle East Studies* 45, no. 2 (2013): 340–42.

Shakhsari, Sima. "Weblogistan Goes to War: Representational Practices, Gendered Soldiers and Neoliberal Entrepreneurship in Diaspora." *Feminist Review*, no. 99 (2011): 6–24.

Sharabi, Hisham. *Neopatriarchy: A Theory of Distorted Change in Arab Society*. Oxford: Oxford University Press, 1992.

Shirazi-Mahajan, Faegheh. "The Politics of Clothing in the Middle East: The Case of Hijab in Post-Revolution Iran." *Critique: Journal of Critical Studies of Iran & the Middle East* 2, no. 2 (1993): 54–63.

Shoayb, Mohamad Mehdi. "Jurisprudential Analysis of Article 102 of the Criminal Procedure Code with Emphasis on the Concepts and Examples of Private Plaintiff." *Rasail journal* 8 (2017): 69.

"The Shocking Words of Mohsen Namjoo among His Friends and Fans." *Feminism Everyday*, April 17, 2021. https://facebook.com/100048665487265/videos/283104060106230/?refsrc=deprecated&_rdr.

Shojaee, Mitra. "Womesn's Protection against Violence Bill: The Lion without Mane, Tail and Belly," *Deutsche Welle*, November 25, 2021, https://www.dw.com/fa-ir/a-59931740/م•لایحه-حمایت-از-زنان-در-برابر-خشونت-شیر-بی-یال-و-دم-و-اش

Smith, Neil. "Homeless/Global: Scaling Places." In *Mapping the Futures: Local Cultures, Global Change*, edited by J. Bird, B. Curtis, T. Putnam, G. Robertson, and L. Tickner, 87–119. London: Routledge, 1993.

Snyder, Chris, and Linette Lopez. "Tarana Burke on Why She Created the #MeToo Movement—and Where It's Headed." *Business Insider*, December 13, 2017. https://www.businessinsider.com/how-the-metoo-movement-started-where-its-headed-tarana-burke-time-person-of-year-women-2017-12.

Southerton, Dale. "Symbolic Capital." In *Encyclopedia of Consumer Culture*, edited by Dale Southerton, 1418–20. Thousand Oaks, CA: SAGE, 2011. https://dx.doi.org/10.4135/9781412994248.n532.

Spelman, Elizabeth. *Inessential Woman: Problems of Exclusion in Feminist Thought*. Boston: Beacon, 1988.

Spivak, Gayatri Chakravorty. "Can the Subaltern Speak?" In *Can The Subaltern Speak: Reflections on the History of an Idea*, edited by Rosalind C. Morris, 237–84. New York: Columbia University Press, 2010.

"The Statement of Iranian Women in Cinema in Protest to Violence against Women in Cinema," Akhbar Rooz, April 1, 2022. https://www.akhbar-rooz.com/148050/1401/01/12/

Sutherland, Edwin H. *White Collar Crime*. Connecticut: Yale University Press, 1983.

Tadros, Mariz. "From Secular Reductionism to Religious Essentialism: Implications for the Gender Agenda." In *Oxford Handbook of Transnational Feminist Movements*, 1st ed., edited by Rawwida Baksh and Wendy Harcourt, 652–67. Cary: Oxford University Press, 2015.

Tafakori, Sara. "Digital Feminism beyond Nativism and Empire: Affective of Recognition and Competing Claims to Suffering in Iranian Women's Campaigns." *Journal of Women in Culture and Society* 47, no. 1 (2021): 47–80.

Tafakori, Sara. "Iran's #MeToo Movement Challenges Patriarchy and Western Stereotypes." September 1, 2020. https://www.opendemocracy.net/en/north-afr ica-west-asia/irans-metoo-movement-challenges-patriarchy-and-western-ster eotypes/.

Taj, Shadi (@Shadishaaaaad). "(8) تو فکر فرو رفته بودم که مسعود کاظمی از صندلی رو به روی من بلند شد و اومد کنار من روی مبل دونفره نشست. چرخید سمتم و بازوم رو گرفت" Twitter, December 18, 2020. https://twitter.com/Shadishaaaaad/status/1339814458395402241.

Tarighi, L. ed. "Annual Report on the Death Penalty in Iran 2020." *Iran Human Rights*, 2020. https://iranhr.net/media/files/Rapport_iran_2021-gb-290321-BD.pdf.

Tavakoli-Targhi, Mohamad. *Refashioning Iran*. Basingstoke: Palgrave, 2001.

Thiers-Vidal, Léo. "De «L'Ennemi principal» aux principaux ennemis." *Position vécue, subjectivité et consciences masculines de domination*. Paris: L'Harmattan, coll. Savoir et formation, série Genre et éducation (2010).

Tizro, Zahra. *Domestic Violence in Iran: Women, Marriage and Islam*. London: Routledge, 2012.

Tomaselli, Sylvana, and Roy Porter. *Rape: An Historical and Cultural Enquiry*. Oxford: Blackwell, 1986.

Tong, Rosemarie. *Feminist Thought: A More Comprehensive Introduction*. Boulder, CO: Westview, 2009.

Torabi, Maryamossadat. "Sexual Harassment and Iranian Law's Coverage." In *The Global #MeToo Movement: How Social Media Propelled a Historic Movement and the Law Responded*, edited by Ann M. Noel and David B. Oppenheimer, 255–260. Fastcase: A Full Court Press, 2020.

Tourage, Mahdi. "Affective Entanglements with the Sexual Imagery of Paradise in the Qur'an." *Body and Religion* 3, no. 1 (2019): 52–70.

"The Trial of Keyvan Emamverdi, Accused of Dozens of Rapes, Has Been Postponed." Radio Farda, September 26, 2021. https://www.radiofarda.com/a/31478617.html.

Trott, Verity. "Networked Feminism: Counterpublics and the Intersectional Issues of #MeToo." *Feminist Media Studies* 21, no. 7 (2021): 1125–42.

Truth, Soujourner. *Et ne suis-je pas une femme?* traduit de l'anglais (États-Unis) par Françoise Bouillot. Paris: Payot, 2021.

Truth, Soujourner. *L'histoire de ma vie*. traduit de l'anglais (États-Unis) par Françoise Bouillot. Paris: Éditions Payot & Rivages, 2022.

Tuerkheimer, Deborah. "Beyond #MeToo." *New York University Law Review* 94, no. 1146 (2019): 1147–208.

"Tunisia MP Jailed for Sexual Harassment in Landmark Case." *Aljazeera*, November 12, 2021.

"Tunisia's #MeToo: Landmark Sexual Harassment Case Kicks Off." *Aljazeera*, October 29, 2021.

"Turkish Writer Accused of Sexual Harassment Commits Suicide." *DuvarR.english* December 11, 2020. https://www.duvarenglish.com/turkish-writer-accused-of-sexual-harassment-commits-suicide-news-55436 (retrieved March 24, 2022).

Unker, Pelin. "#MeToo Movement Arrives in Turkey." Deutsche Welle (DW). December 17, 2020. https://www.dw.com/en/metoo-movement-arrives-in-turkey/a-55976425 (retrieved March 24, 2022).

"*Vakoneshha-i Gostardeh beh Inteshar-i Video va File-i Soti Mohsen Namjoo dar Bareh-i Azar Jinsi.*" BBC Farsi. 28 Farvardin 1400/April 17, 2021. https://www.bbc.com/persian/iran-56787193.

"The Victims' Lawyer: Keyvan Emamverdi Has Not Confessed to Raping 300 Women." Iran International, October 14, 2020. https://b2n.ir/p33599.

"The Violence against Women Campaign." https://pdvc.bidarzani.com/ (accessed October 1, 2021).

Vivienne, Sonja. *Digital Identity and Everyday Activism Sharing Private Stories with Networked Publics*. Basingstoke: Palgrave Macmillan, 2016.

Walsh, Declan. "The 22-Year-Old Force behind Egypt's Growing #MeToo Movement." *New York Times*, October 2, 2020.

Weeks, Kathi. *The Problem with Work: Feminism, Marxism, Antiwork Politics, and Postwork Imaginaries*. Durham, NC: Duke University Press, 2011.

"Who Is Keyvan Emamverdi and … Youtube.com." YouTube, August 21, 2020. https://www.youtube.com/watch?v=UR5SEYh9iGs.

"Who Is Keyvan Emamverdi? The Details of His Case." Vana News. https://b2n.ir/y70143 (accessed October 1, 2021).

"Who Is the Buyer of the 12 Billion Toman Painting?" Tabnak Javan. tabnakjavan, January 17, 2021. https://tabnakjavan.com/fa/news/33521/-یست‌خریدار-تابلوی-۱۲-میلیارد-تومانی

"Why Is the Judiciary Stalling on the Trial of Alleged Rapist Keyvan Emamverdi?" *IranWire*, June 3, 2022. https://iranwire.com/en/society/104816-why-is-the-judiciary-stalling-the-trial-of-alleged-serial-rapist-keyvan-emamverdi/.

Willis, Ellen. "How Now, Iron Johns?" *Nation* 269, no. 20 (1999): 18–21.

Wittig, Monique. "On ne naît pas femme." *Questions féministes*, no. 8 (1980): 75–84.

Wolff, Janet. "Reinstating Corporeality: Feminism and Body Politics." In *Feminine Sentences: Essays on Women and Culture*, edited by Janet Wolff, 120–40. Berkeley: University of California Press, 1990.

Wright, Robyn. "Iran's Kidnapping Plot Exposes Its Paranoia." *New Yorker*, July 19, 2021. https://www.newyorker.com/news/daily-comment/irans-kidnapping-plot-exposes-its-paranoia.

Xiong, Ying, Moonhee Cho, and Brandon Boatwright. "Hashtag Activism and Message Frames among Social Movement Organizations: Semantic Network Analysis and Thematic Analysis of Twitter during the #MeToo Movement." *Public Relations Review* 45, no. 1 (2019): 10–23. https://doi.org/10.1016/j.pubrev.2018.10.014.

Yaghoobi, Claudia. "Iranian Women and Shifting Sexual Ideologies, 1850–2010." In *Sexuality in Muslim Contexts: Restrictions and Resistance*, 52–79. London: Zed, 2012.

Yaghoobi, Claudia. "Mapping Out Socio-Cultural Decadence on the Female Body: Sadeq Chubak's Gowhar in Sange-e Sabur." *Frontiers: A Journal of Women Studies* 39, no. 2 (2018): 206–32.

Yaghoobi, Claudia. "Over 40 Years of Resisting the Compulsory Veiling: Relating Literary Narratives to Text-Based Protests to Cyberactivism." *Journal of Middle East Women's Studies* 17, no. 2 (2021): 220–39.

Yaghoobi, Claudia. *The Poetics and Politics of the Veil in Iran: An Archival and Photographic Adventure, Fatehrad Azadeh*. Bristol: Intellect, 2019.

Yaghoobi, Claudia. "Socially Peripheral, Symbolically Central: Sima in Behrouz Afkhami's Shokaran." *Asian Cinema* 27, no. 2 (2016): 151–63.

Yaghoobi, Claudia. *Temporary Marriage in Iran: Gender and Body Politics in Modern Iranian Film and Literature*. Cambridge: Cambridge University Press, 2020.

Yaghoobi, Claudia. "Yusuf's 'Queer' Beauty in Persian Cultural Productions." *Comparatist* 40 (2016): 245–66.

Yang, Aimei, and Shari R. Veil. "Nationalism versus Animal Rights: A Semantic Network Analysis of Value Advocacy in Corporate Crisis." *International Journal of Business Communication* 54, no. 4 (October 1, 2017): 408–30. https://doi.org/10.1177/2329488415572781.

Yari, Arezoo, Hosein Zahednezhad, Reza Ghanei Gheshlagh, and Amanj Kurdi. "Frequency and Determinants of Domestic Violence against Iranian Women during the COVID-19 Pandemic: A National Cross-Sectional Survey." *BMC Public Health* 21, no. 1 (2021): 1727.

Yazicioglu, Alara Efsun. *Pink Tax and the Law: Discriminating against Women Consumers*. London: Routledge, 2018.

Yeganeh, Nahid. "Women, Nationalism and Islam in Contemporary Political Discourse in Iran." *Feminist Review*, no. 44 (1993): 3–18. https://doi.org/10.2307/1395192.

Young, Robert J. C. "Rereading the Symptomatic Reading." In *The Concept in Crisis Reading Capital Today*, edited by Nick Nesbitt, 35–48. Durham, NC: Duke University Press, 2017.

Zahra Ayatollahi, "Security of Women Against Violence Bill or the Implementation of Fifth Goal of the 2030 Document" *Keyhan Newspaper*, January 20, 2018, https://kayhan.ir/fa/news/121939/
لایحه-امنیت-زنان-در-برابر-خشونت-یا-اجرای-هدف-5-سند-2030یادداشت-میهمان

Zaman, Meryem F. "The Problem of the Rebellious Religious Women: Pakistan, Gender, and the Islamic Revival." *Social Politics: International Studies in Gender, State & Society* 27, no. 2 (2020): 212–33. https://doi.org/10.1093/sp/jxz001.

Zarkov, Dubravka, and Kathy Davis Davis. "Ambiguities and Dilemmas around #MeToo: #ForHowLong and #WhereTo?" *European Journal of Women's Studies* 25, no. 1 (2018): 3–9.

Zavattaro, Staci M., P. Edward French, and Somya D. Mohanty. "A Sentiment Analysis of U.S. Local Government Tweets: The Connection between Tone and Citizen Involvement." *Government Information Quarterly* 32, no. 3 (July 1, 2015): 333–41. https://doi.org/10.1016/j.giq.2015.03.003.

Zine, Jasmin. "Between Orientalism and Fundamentalism: The Politics of Muslim Women's Feminist Engagement." *Muslim World Journal of Human Rights* 3, no. 5 (2006): 1–24.

Žižek, Slavoj. "On #MeToo Movement." Russia Today. YouTube, January 17, 2019. https://www.youtube.com/watch?v=ai_UAPaoEW4.

Zubaida, Sami. "Women, Democracy and Dictatorship in the Context of the Arab Uprisings." In *The New Middle East: Protest and Revolution in the Arab World*, edited by F. Gerges, 209–25. Cambridge: Cambridge University Press, 2013.

Zulli, Diana. "Evaluating Hashtag Activism: Examining the Theoretical Challenges and Opportunities of #BlackLivesMatter." *Participations: Journal of Audience and Reception Studies* 17, no. 1 (2020): 197–216.

"100 Women: Muslim Women Rally Round #MosqueMeToo—BBC News." 2020. https://www.bbc.com/news/world-43006952 (accessed February 17, 2022).

Contributors

Janet Afary is Mellichamp Professor of Religious Studies at the University of California, Santa Barbara. Her books include: *Sexual Politics in Modern Iran* (2009), *Foucault and the Iranian Revolution: Gender and the Seductions of Islamism* (2005; with Kevin B. Anderson), and *Iranian Romance in the Digital Age: From Arrange Marriage to White Marriage* (2021; with Jesilyn Faust).

Roger Friedland is Emeritus Professor of Religious Studies and Sociology at the University of California, Santa Barbara. He seeks a religious sociology of institutional order equally applicable to market value, love, and salvation. He is also working with Janet Afary and Maria Charles on the relationship between gender, love, religion, and intimate life among tens of thousands of respondents in seven Muslim-majority countries. The first paper from that project, "Love in the Middle East: The Contradictions of Romance in the Facebook World," was published in 2016, by *Critical Research on Religion*, with Cambria Nasland and Paolo Gardinali. Friedland is also analyzing constellations of practice to uncover the institutional logics of intimate life in an American university campus with Henk Roose and John Mohr.

Golnar Gishnizjani is a PhD researcher at the Department of Media Studies, University of Turku. Her project is focused on the digital feminism activism of women in Iran and the diaspora that received a personal grant from the Kone Foundation. The study critically analyzes ways of disclosing invisible layers of struggles and reclaiming bodily autonomy on social media. In her research, alongside specific hashtags as case studies, glimpses of daily life shared by Iranian women on different digital platforms, especially amid crisis and upheaval, are considered activism practices. Her areas of interest include digital activism, digital storytelling, affect, feminist praxis, autoethnography, and thinking with our own bodies as a research resource. Gishnizjani received her master's degree in media education from the University of Lapland. She also holds a master's degree in social communication sciences from the University of Tehran and a bachelor's in public relations from Allameh Tabataba'i University.

Yalda N. Hamidi (She/Her/Hers) is Assistant Professor of Gender and Women's Studies, faculty fellow for "Teaching toward Social Justice" at Minnesota State University (MNSU) Mankato, and a member of Ms. Committee of Scholars. In her research, Yalda adopts an anti-racist and transnational feminist lens. Yalda's recent article, "Politics of Location in *Persepolis*: The Social and Literary Construction of the Place, Space, and Belonging for Iranian Women in Persepolis versus Iran," published in the *Journal of Middle East Women's Studies*, relies on a transnational and anti-racist feminist literary analysis to emphasize the necessity of politics of location in criticizing the histories of the nation, highlight the role of trauma in the formation of Iranian feminism/s, and challenge the cultural and literary representation of Iran for the voices the graphic novel leaves behind. In her subsequent work, *Cartography of Transnational Iranian Feminist Struggles*, Yalda argues that the scene of the transnational Iranian feminism/s has at least four distinctive voices of multicultural, postcolonialist, queer and ethnic, and white feminism/s. This research provides decolonial methodologies for rhetorical listening to these voices. It strongly advocates for an anti-racist and social justice–oriented lens to address the gaps, retrieve the ghostly voices, and bring the margins of Iranian feminism/s into its center. At MNSU Mankato, Yalda teaches transnational, postcolonial, Islamic feminism/s, feminist pedagogy, and queer of color critique courses. She collaborates with women's centers and nonprofits to share stories of Iranian feminism/s and literature with the public. Yalda's Islamic Feminism Book Club has received Feminist Change Agent Award from the National Women's Studies Association. Additionally, she has received multiple other awards for her work on social justice, advocacy, and mentoring students from underrepresented communities.

Niloofar Hooman is a PhD candidate in the Department of Communication Studies and Media Arts at McMaster University, Canada. She is also completing a joint graduate diploma (PhD) in gender and social justice. Niloofar holds a PhD in communication (2019), an MA in cultural studies and the media (2010), and a BA in social communications (2007) from the University of Tehran. Her research encompasses theories of new media, digital culture, digital activism, feminism, and gender, as well as critical studies of marginalized bodies. Niloofar's doctoral dissertation concentrates on the embodiment, performances of nudity, and unveiling as political actions in Iran. Her work has been published in *New Media & Society*, the *International Journal of the Image*, *LGBTQ Digital Cultures: A Global Perspective*, and in a popular media outlet, the *Conversation*. Niloofar is also a graduate resident with the Sherman Center for Digital Scholarship, where she conducts a critical qualitative project to provide a nuanced account of nude activism in the Iranian context.

Charlotte Hoppen is a PhD student in sociology at the University of California, Santa Barbara. Her research areas are inequalities related to gender, education, organizations, labor, and the family. She is a graduate associate of the Broom Center for Demography and uses quantitative and qualitative methods. She received her MA in sociology from the University of California, Santa Barbara, in 2022 and her BA in sociology and organizational studies from the University of Michigan, Ann Arbor, in 2020.

Ziba Jalali Naini is the founder and owner of Shirazeh Publishing House with more than 450 books published on human sciences. She has worked as publisher, editor, and translator since 1994. She received the best book award for 2004 from Women's Cultural Association. Her studies and career include the three different fields of business management (BA École Supérieure de Commerce de Paris (ESCP)), French literature (DEA Sorbonne Paris), and women's studies (UCLA). She has twenty years of experience in the field of research journalism and has written various articles and essays in different magazines. She has also established different NGOs on human rights support for women and youth, such as Vistamehr in 2003. Since 2000, she has been a member of IRWI, a national NGO of independent women researchers, for which she has researched and written the report titled "Analysis of Girl child and Youth Conditions in Iran" in Non-Governmental Report for Beijing +10.

Dilyana Mincheva is an assistant professor in critical media in the Department of Communication Studies and Media Arts at McMaster University, Canada. She is the bearer of two international awards for research excellence (2012 and 2015) granted by the *Journal of Religion and Spirituality in Society* and the author of the monograph *The Politics of Western Muslim Intellectual Discourse in the West: The Emergence of a Western-Islamic Public Sphere* (2016). Mincheva has published extensively on topics such as religion, feminism, and representation and is currently at work on a second monograph focused on socially and cinematically mediated forms of Islamic feminism.

Esha Momeni lectures in gender studies at the University of California, Los Angeles. Her research focuses on the production, embodiment, and comprehension of masculine identities in discursive practices in dialogue with global contemporary gender ideologies. Her work deals with modern Iran and the Middle East.

Paria Rahimi is a PhD student in theory and criticism at Western University. Before proceeding to a master's degree in gender studies at McMaster University, Paria obtained her MA in communication studies from the University of Tehran, completing her thesis on the study of digital activism in the Iranian feminist movement. She has a diploma in cinema and took courses in creative writing with the prominent Iranian novelist Shahrnush Parsipur. She has hosted podcasts, written short stories, and made several experimental movies. Her areas of study primarily focus on resistance studies, autonomist Marxism, and

Lacanian psychoanalysis. Paria is an academic activist who extensively writes and translates texts on anti-capitalist feminism and voluntarily serves anti-oppressive organizations and collectives.

Yasamin Rezai (she/they/او) is a PhD candidate at the Department of Modern Languages and Literatures (MLL) at the University of Miami, where she has taught French, Persian, and Italian. Her academic work is focused on the intersection of critical data feminist studies, new media, and performance studies by employing digital humanities tools and data-driven approaches. Her research is focused on instapoetry, data culture, and online activism. She is the cofounder of Instasociety.org, an open-access research resource exploring how social media changes popular culture. Yasamin's works have appeared in academic journals such as *Digital Humanities Quarterly* and *Critical Studies in Media Communication*, and her research was presented at conferences by Cultural Studies Association and Modern Languages Association.

Somayeh Rostampour is a lecturer in sociology at the University of Reims in France. She is a feminist researcher and activist in the field of political sociology and gender studies. She holds a PhD in sociology from the University of Paris 8. Her thesis focuses on the practices of women fighters in the Kurdistan Workers' Party (PKK) in Turkey from 1978 to the present, together with the construction of the Jineolojî as a local knowledge rooted in the production and circulation of feminist knowledge in the Global South. At the moment, Rostampour is working on the intersection of gender, ethnicity, and class in Kurdistan, Turkey, and Iran as part of larger process of social movements and alternative feminisms in the Middle East.

Mahdis Sadeghipouya is a doctoral researcher in gender and sexuality studies—sociology at Paris 8 Vincennes Saint-Denis University, affiliated to Laboratoire d'Études de genre et de sexualité (LEGS—UMR 8238 CNRS), and Lecturer in Western Brittany University. She is working on her PhD thesis "with" activist lesbians of color and of Muslim origin in France. She has been a women's and LGBTIQ+ activist in Iran since 2012, and today she works on subjects such as femonationalism in the context of Iranian politics and the Iranian feminist movement, Western Asian feminisms, political lesbianism, migration, and exile. Her translation in Farsi of Sara R. Farris's *In the Name of Women's Rights: The Rise of Femonationalism*, the book in which Farris has theorized the term "femonationalism," will be published shortly in Iran.

Mehdy Sedaghat Payam received his PhD in English from Victoria University of Wellington in New Zealand. Currently, he is doing his second PhD, on comparative literature, at the University of Maryland. His academic work focuses on how technology and literature have influenced each other. This influence can come in various shapes and forms, which can either be literature oriented (electronic literature) or literary criticism oriented (digital humanities). Mehdy's work has appeared in *Digital Studies*, the *Bloomsbury Handbook of Electronic Literature*, and *Advances in Digital Scholarly Editing*. Since the past two years, he has also been working on a Mellon-awarded project to develop an OCR engine for Persian and Arabic scripts. He is also a published novelist, and his first novel, *Secret of Silence*, was published in Persian in 2009.

Mahdi Tourage is associate professor of religious studies and social justice and peace studies at King's University College, London, Ontario. He is the author of *Rumi and the Hermeneutics of Eroticism* (2007) and the edited volume *Esoteric Lacan* (2019; with Philipp Valentini). His publications have appeared in *Iranian Studies*, the *International Journal of Zizek Studies*, and the journal *Body and Religion*. His areas of interest are Islamic religious thought, Sufism, and postmodern theories of gender and sexuality.

Claudia Yaghoobi is a Roshan Institute Professor and the director of the Center for the Middle East and Islamic Studies at the University of North Carolina, Chapel Hill. She is a scholar of Iranian cultural studies, and gender and sexuality studies with a focus on the members of sexual, ethnic, and religious minoritized populations. She is the author of *Transnational Culture in the Iranian Armenian Diaspora* (2023), *Temporary Marriage in Iran: Gender and Body Politics in Modern Persian Literature and Film* (2020), and *Subjectivity in 'Attar, Persian Sufism, and European Mysticism* (2017).

Maryam Zehtabi is an assistant professor and general faculty at the University of Virginia teaching women, gender and sexuality studies, and Middle Eastern and South Asian languages and cultures. Her recent projects have focused on child marriage, the #MeToo Movement in Iran, and the ramifications of sex work in the country from the Constitutional Revolution of early twentieth century to the present day through the lens of Persian literature and film. Her works have appeared in the *International Journal of Persian Literature*, the *Guardian*, and the *Journal of Middle East Women's Studies*.

Index

9/11 attack 44
1979 Revolution xvii, 6, 16, 19, 41, 42, 46, 47, 51, 137, 151, 155, 157, 194–5, 199, 200

abusers 1, 28, 29, 31, 74, 102, 115, 116, 141, 146, 157
accumulation 7, 67, 96, 99, 107
"achieving modernity" 14
Adham, Marzieh 78, 227 n.22
adultery 27, 29, 153, 184, 191, 206 n.13, 243 n.8
  definition 212 n.11
  forced xiv
  vicarious 187
Afary, Janet 9, 211 n.48, 218 n.32, 247 n.36
  Sexual Politics in Modern Iran 2, 47, 206 n.2, 208 n.14, 218 n.31, 247 n.40
Afkhami, Mahnaz 2, 210 n.42
  Sisterhood Is Global 2, 206 n.2
Afshar, Haleh 46, 217 n.26, 217 n.27
agency 3, 16, 21, 25, 26, 31, 56, 68, 113, 149, 156, 157, 208 n.2, 229 n.26
aggressor xiii, xviii, 146, 235 n.7
Aghdashloo, Aydin 75, 94, 96–7, 139, 142, 148, 212 n.10, 229 n.35, 243 n.17
Ahmed, Sara 107, 231 n.1, 234 n.51
Ailes, Roger 162
Alaswany, Alaa 168, 246 n.21
Algeria 9, 161, 163, 169–70, 171, 175
Alinejad, Masih 26, 32–4, 211 n.3, 212 n.3, 213 n.17, 214 n.20, 214 n.23, 214 n.25, 214 n.26, 214 n.27
Alphan, Melis 167
Althusser, Louis 91, 92, 228 n.15
Amidi, Faranak 74, 226 n.4
Amin, Shadi 75
Amini, Zhina 12, 21
Amir-Ebrahimi, Masserat 6, 207 n.17
anti-capitalist activist 102, 104, 284

anti-fundamentalist Iranian transnational feminism 45–8
anti-imperialism 24
anti-imperialist Iranian transnational feminism 48–50
anti-Iranian campaign 28
anti-Muslim 28, 34
anti-neoliberalist Iranian transnational feminism 50
apparatus 18, 99, 105
Article 286 of Islamic Law 98
Ayatollahi, Zahra 35, 36, 215 n.29

backwardness 18
bad-hijab woman (improperly veiled woman) 18, 19, 20
Baha'i women 28
Bahrami, Mitra 155
Bahramitash, Roksana 50, 219 n.50
Bailey, Alison 137, 239 n.13
Balassanian, Sonia 1
Balslev, Sivan 144, 239 n.11, 241 n.46
Banu Gökarıksel 6, 207 n.16
Barnes, Naomi 120, 234 n.52
Batmanghelichi, Kristin Soraya 37, 212 n.7, 215 n.34, 216 n.1, 231 n.2, 231 n.3, 231 n.12
  Revolutionary Bodies: Technologies of Gender, Sex, and Self in Contemporary Iran 2, 206 n.2
"battered women's movement" 40
Bayat, Asef 131, 231 n.10, 234 n.1, 241 n.39
been fighters everywhere 134
Behdad, Ali 15, 208 n.17, 208 n.18
Bennett, Jessica 152, 243 n.18
Bidarzani 26, 30, 109, 110, 115, 139, 231 n.12, 232 n.19, 240 n.37, 241 n.50
Black Lives Matter movement 112
Bloch, Marc 144, 241 n.44

Borna News Agency 26
Bourdieu, Pierre 5, 94–7, 99, 101, 102, 104, 207 n.12, 229 n.23, 229 n.24, 229 n.25, 229 n.27, 229 n.28, 229 n.29, 229 n.31, 229 n.32, 229 n.33, 229 n.37, 229 n.39, 230 n.41, 230 n.48, 230 n.49, 230 n.53
bourgeois woman 89, 104
Bueno-Hansen, Pascha 43
Burke, Tarana xii, 51, 89, 90, 128, 152, 161, 205 n.1, 206 n.1, 220 n.54, 227 n.3, 228 n.6, 244 n.2, 248 n.53, 248 n.54

capital
  cultural 95, 96, 99, 100–2, 118, 141
  economic 7, 95, 96, 97, 99, 100, 102, 105, 118
  ownership 93
  punishment 23, 29, 55, 62
  social xiii, 2, 95, 99, 100, 101, 102
  symbolic 93–100, 102–5, 140, 229 n.38, 229 n.40, 230 n.50
capitalism 57, 58, 62, 68, 90, 91, 104, 105, 248 n.58
capitalist society 7, 9, 57, 90
Capital (Marx) 58, 92, 95, 221 n.32, 223 n.71, 228 n.15, 228 n.17
CEDAW *see* Convention on the Elimination of All Forms of Discrimination against Women
Chakalov, Bozhidar 78, 81, 86, 227 n.21, 227 n.24
chastity 18, 61, 114, 181
Chehabi, Houchang E. 14, 208 n.12, 208 n.13, 208 n.15
Chetcuti-Osorovitz, Natacha 126, 235 n.6, 235 n.14
class
  lower class, society xvi, 16, 104
  middle-class 2, 9, 16, 20, 40, 41, 99, 128, 135, 136, 139–43, 148, 162, 171
  status and marginalization 118
  upper class, society 7, 40
class-based movement xvi, 6, 7, 10
class-blind 104
Clubhouse 72, 75
Code Pink 48
Colak, Ibrahim 167

conflict theory 94
Connell, Raewyn W. 16, 136–8, 209 n.23, 225 n.105, 238 n.2, 238 n.4, 238 n.7, 238 n.8
consent 2, 7, 8, 22 n.27, 43, 53, 54, 55–7, 58–60, 62, 63, 66, 67, 68, 69, 83, 84, 87, 114, 141, 145, 146, 221 n.14, 221 n.15, 221 n.16, 221 n.17, 221 n.18, 221 n.20, 221 n.21, 221 n.22, 221 n.26, 221 n.29, 222 n.44, 222 n.45, 223 n.66, 223 n.74, 224 n.85, 225 n.99, 225 n.112, 248 n.49
Constitutional Revolution of 1906 41
contract 8, 20, 53, 61, 62, 64, 66–9
  labor, Marxist analysis 57–60
Convention on the Elimination of All Forms of Discrimination against Women (CEDAW) 43, 150, 217 n.12
"corruptor upon the earth" (*mufsid-i fil 'arz*) 28, 29, 98
Cosby, Bill 162
Couldry, Nick 108, 231 n.7
Council of Professional Ethics in Cinema xix
counter-value 100
Covid-19 pandemic 107, 118, 168, 234 n.46
Crenshaw, Kimberlé 117, 234 n.44
CSW *see* UN Commission on the Status of Women
cultural appropriation 44
cultural capital 96, 99, 100–2, 118, 141
  acquisition of 95
  conversion 95
  forms 95

Daneshvar, Simin 151, 243 n.12
de Beauvoir, Simone 59, 127, 222 n.43, 235 n.14, 237 n.26
deconstruction 43, 92, 93, 128, 228 n.19
"defending" Islamism 34, 35
Derakhshandeh, Puran 9, 149–59, 242
Derrida, Jacques 92, 228 n.19, 230 n.51
DeSouza, Wendy 16, 208 n.19, 209 n.24
deviance 18, 130, 131, 132, 234 n.3, 237 n.28

diaspora 8, 26, 33, 39–52, 74–6, 108, 214 n.21, 216 n.1, 217 n.15, 217 n.19, 219 n.47, 219 n.48, 232 n.14
   dilemmas and positionalities, Iranian #MeToo 32–5
   Islamic feminism 37
digital media
   activism 3, 108
   Instagram 110–13
   protest 4
   storytelling 107–22, 231 n.7
   anonymous shared stories 113–17
   campaigns 108
   definition 108
   Instagram 110–13
   methods and study cases 109–10
   subalterns 117–20
   women's engagement 107–8
Dingo, Rebecca 52, 220 n.58
discourses, Iranian nationalism 46–7
disinterestedness 95, 99, 146
domestic abuse 12, 25, 39, 174, 175, 178, 216 n.3, 224 n.89
domestic violence xvii, 2–4, 10, 40, 45–7, 66, 91, 118, 161, 163–8, 170, 171, 175, 176, 178, 195–6, 199, 200, 201, 202, 208 n.4, 221 n.7, 228 n.10, 234 n.46, 239 n.23, 245 n.5, 245 n.7, 246 n.17, 246 n.19, 246 n.35, 247 n.36
   global average 163
   in Iran 12
   prevention of 28
   subalterns 118
   against women's bodies 47
double exclusion 124–5

economic capital 7, 95, 96, 97, 99, 100, 102, 105, 118
Eder, Maciej 84, 227 n.25
Egypt 9, 65, 161, 163, 168–9, 171, 175, 192, 195, 231 n.13, 246 n.23
Eltahawy, Mona 168, 169, 246 n.24, 246 n.26, 247 n.38
Emamverdi, Keyvan 27–9, 74, 75, 91, 97–104, 212 n.7, 230 n.44, 230 n.45, 230 n.52
emotional and verbal abuse 12
enforced sexuality 4
Enghelab Square 98

equal in dignity 36
Erdoğan, Recep Tayyip 167
Etemad 26
Europeanization of Iranians 13–14
event 30, 31, 63, 64, 93, 117, 155, 172, 178, 182, 183, 200
"ex-Muslim" 26

Facebook banner ads 10, 161, 171–2
Faravaz 93
Farhadi, Asghar 154
Federici, Silvia 90, 222 n.42, 228 n.7, 237 n.30
female body
   boundaries and ownership of 24
   criminalization of 45
   heterosexual man, viewpoint of 15
   hijab, enforcement of 8
   lesbian bodies 128, 130
   and male proletarian 90
   and modern nation-state image, Iran 14
   objectification 14–17
   ownership 24, 61
   and sexuality 66
   sex worker 67–8
   shielding 18
   subordination 3, 5
   unrestricted access to 13
   untrammeled power, men 164
feminism
   border 35–7
   digital 110, 231 n.6
   human rights-based 43, 45
   indigenous form of 36
   religion-based 36, 37
   transnational 39
   see also Iranian feminism
feminism on the border 35–7
feminist activism 3, 24, 25, 26, 28, 42, 76, 117, 120, 121, 131
feminist humanitarianism 42
Feminist Strategies to End Violence against Women 40, 216 n.4
field 13–14, 17, 39, 49, 71, 94, 97, 99, 100, 102, 136, 140, 142, 162
Flood, Michael 147, 240 n.34, 241 n.56, 242 n.58, 242 n.60, 242 n.61
Foreign Policy 32

Forms of Capital, The 95, 229 n.28, 229 n.29, 229 n.30, 230 n.53
Foucault, Michel 114, 207 n.14, 233 n.31, 233 n.33
Freidan, Betty 133
Freudian dream interpretation 92
Friedland, Roger 9, 247 n.36, 247 n.40
fundamentalism 42, 49, 209 n.21, 212 n.4, 219 n.50
Fuss, Diana 134, 237 n.34

Gamson, Joshua 132, 237 n.33
gay community 50
gender
  categorization 126–7
  equality 44, 137, 140, 146, 159, 163, 238 n.4, 238 n.5
  hierarchy 15, 136, 137, 143, 146
  impunity 139
  inequality 27, 44, 63, 147, 243 n.5
  injustice 24
  justice 9, 28, 37, 64, 135, 148, 240 n.34
  privilege 9, 135–48
  segregation xi, 3, 17
gender-based violence 4, 19, 21, 39, 40, 45, 139, 216 n.3
  criminalization 59
  definition 4
  interpersonal 12, 40, 51
  Iran 10, 12, 13, 52
  Iranian feminism 40–2, 45, 46
gendered inequalities 44
gendered privilege 9, 135–48
gendered servitude 5
gendered violence 2, 8, 44, 49, 136, 142, 147, 217 n.17
  in Iranian feminism 40–2
  legal code 142
  and masculinity 137–8
  see also gender-based violence
Gerami, Shahin 16, 209 n.25, 209 n.27, 209 n.28, 239 n.10, 239 n.12
Ghassempour, Fatemeh 12
gheirat xii, 61
Gholami, Shahin 26, 28, 29, 212 n.9
Ghooshe, Shima 25, 27–31, 35, 98, 211 n.2, 212 n.11
Gill, Rosalind 90, 228 n.9, 232 n.16, 248 n.56

Girl's House, The (Shah Hosseini) 154
Gishnizjani, Golnar 9
global culture 6
Gökarıksel, Banu 6, 207 n.16
Green Movement, the 23
Grewal, Inderpal 44, 217 n.15, 219 n.46
Guardian 145

habitus 94, 99, 102
Hajjar, Lisa 163, 245 n.5, 245 n.7, 246 n.20, 246 n.22, 249 n.64
Hakakian, Roya 26, 32–4, 213 n.17, 213 n.18, 214 n.19, 214 n.20, 214 n.23, 215 n.27
Hall, Rebecca Jane 40, 44, 216 n.4, 217 n.16
Hamad, Ruby 40, 216 n.6
Hamedi, Niloofar 26, 30
Hamidi, Yalda Nafiseh 8
Handmaid's Tale 40, 216 n.5
Harasswath 109
hate crimes 33, 212 n.3
hegemonic masculinity 14–17, 19, 20, 21, 136, 137, 140, 142, 143, 209 n.23
Heidegger, Martin 92, 228 n.16
Heideggerian phenomenology 92
hermeneutical method 91, 92
heteronormativity, Iran 13–14
heterosexual male domination 4, 5
"hexis" 5
Heydari, Muna 149
Heydari Kaydan, Minoo 26, 30
hijab
  compulsory 12, 17, 18, 33, 73
  discourse, Islamic Republic 17–18
  enforcement of 8
  Islamic Republic's advertisement 11, 12, 13
  safety in public 11, 12
  as security measure 11, 12
  sexual assault prevention 72
  state propaganda 13, 17
Hochberg, Gil Z. 13, 208 n.9
homoerotic desire 14
homoeroticism 13
honor-based violence 33, 35
honor killings xii, 4, 21, 39, 43, 45, 62, 165, 170, 180, 181, 185–7, 189, 190, 191, 198, 199, 200, 202, 247 n.36
honor *(nāmūs)* xii, 15, 156

honour crime 44, 217 n.17
Hoodfar, Homa
  Women's Movement in Iran, The 2, 206 n.2
Hooman, Niloofar 8
Hoppen, Charlotte 9
Hosseinifar, Maryam Sadat 26
hostile masculinity 8, 21
Htun, Mala 150, 151, 243 n.10
human rights-based Iranian transnational feminism 43-5
"*Hush! Girls Don't Scream* (Derakhshandeh) 9, 149-59
hypermasculinity 16, 17, 63, 141

ICPD *see* UN International Conference on Population and Development
IMNA News Agency 26
imperialism 17, 37, 50, 164, 248 n.58
included nowhere 134
indignant resistance, men 137-40
industrialization 16
inferior bodies 5
infrastructure 94, 100, 104
innocence *(ismat)* xii, xiii, xiv, 82, 92, 158
Instagram 9, 27, 31, 33, 72, 74, 75, 78, 81, 91, 93, 94, 107-22, 126, 139, 144, 168, 169, 232 n.17, 232 n.18, 232 n.20, 232 n.21, 232 n.23, 234 n.53, 235 n.11
  aesthetics 110-13
  anonymity 113-17
  feminism 110
  hashtagging 112
  slideshows 112
  Stories 112, 115
  templatability 113
  visibility and connectivity 111-13
interest xiv, 10, 31, 32, 47, 56, 64-8, 73, 79, 89, 95, 97, 98, 99, 102, 104, 109, 113, 117, 118, 136, 138, 140, 141, 142, 146, 150, 170, 171, 179, 185, 191, 196, 199, 238 n.4, 239 n.16, 240 n.29, 241 n.47, 241 n.54
international human rights 44
international solidarity 42
intersectional lens 90
intersectional struggles 9
intimate partner violence (IPV) xvii, 59, 66, 206 n.11, 222 n.37

Iranian art 15
Iranian cinema xix, xviii, 157, 202, 209 n.26
Iranian Cinema Actors Association, The xix
Iranian feminism
  diasporic developments of 26
  gendered and sexual violence 40-2
  transnational
  anti-fundamentalist 45-8
  anti-imperialist 48-50
  anti-neoliberalist 50
  human rights-based 43-5
Iranian #MeToo movement 7
  activists 30, 31, 33
  Aghdashloo's case 96-7
  barriers, participation 27
  capital ownership 93-5
  definition 29
  Emamverdi's case 28, 29, 74, 97-104
  familiarity and locality 23-4
  feminism on the border 35-7
  feminist movement 32
  history of 91
  Instagram 110-17
  methodology and sources 24-6
  mobilization, Iran 125-6
  Namjoo's case 75-6, 93-5
  native informant 32-5
  outset 72-5
  particularities 23
  polemic 33
  power relations 93, 94, 99, 102, 104
  privileged class 27
  public conversation 28
  public denunciations 34
  subalterns 117-20
  symptomatic reading 91-3
  Twitter data analysis 77-9
    categories 81-4
    frequent terms 84-6
    scraping 79-81
  see also Iranian feminism
Iranian Student News Agency (ISNA) 26, 208 n.3
Iranian Women's Association 26, 30, 31
Islamic feminism 23, 26, 32, 33, 42, 212 n.7, 215 n.30, 215 n.31, 215 n.33, 215 n.34, 215 n.35, 218 n.38
  advocates and enemies of 48

critical issues 42
  as diasporic phenomenon 37
  resistance 36, 37
Islamic feminists 33, 36, 42, 212 n.7, 215 n.30, 215 n.34
Islamic law 6, 29, 60, 98, 142, 178–88, 190, 191, 194, 202, 215 n.30, 223 n.52, 223 n.54, 223 n.55, 223 n.61, 223 n.62
Islamic Penal Code, the xiv, xv, xvii, 27, 127, 205 n.7
Islamic Republic
  hegemonic masculinity 14–17
  hijab discourse 17–18
  modernization 13–14
  rejecting Western style 17
  revolutionary man's masculinity 19–20
  sex-segregation policies 17
Islamic Revolution of 1979 6, 46, 151
Islamic specificity 23
Islamism
  patriarchal and sexist practices 179–86
  and socialism 178–9
  state ideology 199–201
Islamophobia 26, 33–5, 44, 169, 211 n.3, 212 n.3, 214 n.24, 214 n.25, 233 n.39
Islamophobia bill 33
Ison, Jess 132, 237 n.29
Ivy League campus, America 32, 33

Jafari, Reza 12
Jalali Naini, Ziba 7
Jayawardena, Kumari 41, 216 n.7
Jensenius, Francesca R. 150, 151, 243 n.10
"justice by the citizens" xiv

Kamel, Atena 26, 27, 212 n.5
Kar, Mehrangiz 199, 214 n.21, 249 n.62
Kashani-Sabet, Firoozeh 41, 216 n.8
Kavanaugh, Brett 162
Kermani, Hossein 78, 227 n.22
Khamenei, Ali 72, 73
Khani, Mina 75
Khodir, Sabah 168
Khomeini, Ayatollah 18, 46, 60
Kiarostami, Abbas 67, 225 n.107

lavender menace 126–7
Leaver, Tama 113, 232 n.20, 232 n.24, 232 n.26, 232 n.27, 234 n.53
lesbian 7, 9, 10, 123–34, 235 n.15
  exclusion from debates 124–5, 127, 131, 133, 134
  feminists 131–3
  lavender menace 126–7
  "non-movement" 131, 241 n.39, 253
  sexual violence, experience of 127–31
  violence and exclusion 124–5, 127, 133–4
lesbianism 129, 134, 235 n.15
lesbophobia 124, 126, 128, 130–3, 235 n.13
Letter to My Mother, A (Maher) 154
#LetUsTalk 33
liberal feminism 8, 23–37
liberal feminists 8, 23–37, 104
Loesch, Dana 113
lower-class manhood 16
lūtī 16

Maher, Amina 154, 155, 244 n.26
Mahi 93
Makhlouf, Zouhair 166
male gaze 14–17, 21
male gaze theory 15
male libido 8, 13
male sexual aggressiveness 13, 18, 179
male sexual violence 63
  blaming women 8, 13
Maranloo, Sahar 26, 27, 212 n.6
Mardorossian, Carine M. 3, 206 n.3
Marx, Karl 57–9, 63, 70, 92, 94, 95, 221 n.32, 222 n.41, 222 n.42, 223 n.71
Marxists 16, 53, 57–60, 63, 68, 89, 91, 94, 95, 102, 104, 228 n.14, 229 n.32, 229 n.37
Marxist theory of labor 53
masculinity
  hegemonic 14–17, 19, 20, 21, 136, 137, 140, 142, 143, 209 n.23
  legitimized 143–6
  as male privilege 137
  patriarchy and 143–6
  revolutionary 18–20
  theological 137
  and violence against women 13
material conditions of the workplace 59, 90
maximization of profit 100
McDowell, Linda 5, 207 n.15
men as protectors 15, 16
meta-field 97, 100

#MeToo movement xi–xii, xiv–xviii, 1, 7, 8, 9, 57, 80, 109, 111, 112, 114, 232 n.19, 243 n.19
  Algeria 169–70
  criticisms 89, 90
  and digital feminist research 76–7
  Egypt 168–9
  international scene 162
  Iranian social media platforms 11
  outset, Iran 72–5
  Pakistan 165–6
  Palestine 170–1
  Tunisia 166
  Turkey 167
  United States, origin of 161–2
  see also Iranian #MeToo movement
middle class 2, 9, 16, 20, 41, 99, 118, 128, 135, 136, 139–43, 148, 162, 163, 171
  Iran 20
  modern women 20
  "Tehrani woman" 16
Middle East 4, 7, 9, 50, 162–5, 174, 176, 200
Middle East, North Africa, and South Asia (MENASA) countries 164, 177
Milano, Alyssa xii, 113, 115, 153, 205 n.2, 244 n.20
militarism 49
Mills, Charles Wright 140, 240 n.30
Mincheva, Dilyana 8, 37, 215 n.35
Mir-Hosseini, Ziba 33, 36, 37, 48, 209 n.32, 210 n.33, 214 n.22, 215 n.30, 215 n.31, 215 n.32, 218 n.37, 222 n.46
  Islam and Gender: The Religious Debate in Contemporary Iran 48, 210 n.35, 218 n.36
misogynistic system 90
misogynist relations 103
misogyny 24, 27, 30, 32, 35, 126, 128, 132, 150, 158, 161, 170
  systemic 33
Mjalli, Yasmeen 170
Moallem, Minoo 15, 21, 218 n.43, 219 n.44, 219 n.45, 219 n.46, 238 n.10
  Between Warrior Brother and Veiled Sister: Islamic Fundamentalism and Politics of Patriarchy in Iran 49, 209 n.21, 209 n.22, 211 n.47

mobility, public spaces 6
modernization process
  Iran 13–14
  and Islamic fundamentalism 49
Modrek, Sepideh 78, 81, 86, 227 n.21
Moghadam, Valentine 39, 42, 43, 46, 48, 50, 216 n.2, 216 n.10, 216 n.11, 217 n.14, 217 n.25, 218 n.38, 218 n.39, 219 n.51, 220 n.52, 220 n.53
Moghissi, Haideh 46, 48, 212 n.7, 215 n.33, 218 n.28, 241 n.39, 249 n.67
Momeni, Esha 8
monetary profit 94, 95, 100
Moore, Roy 162
Morad, Vali 26
#MosqueMeToo 73, 74, 169, 215 n.35, 226 n.4
Motahari, Ayatollah 18
Mouri, Leila 37, 212 n.7, 215 n.34, 216 n.1, 231 n.2, 231 n.3, 231 n.12
Muhebi, Marziyih 153, 154
Mulvey, Laura 15, 208 n.16
"Muslim woman with false consciousness" 26
Mynett, Tim 33, 211 n.3, 214 n.24
Myspace 89
#MyStealthyFreedom 33

Najmabadi, Afsaneh 2, 13, 47–9
  Women with Moustaches and Men without Beards 2, 206 n.2, 208 n.7
nā-mahram (unrelated) males 20
Namjoo, Mohsen 75–6, 93–6, 229 n.22
nationalism 41, 46, 218 n.28, 218 n.30, 226 n.14, 237 n.23, 247 n.40
native informant 26, 32–5, 212 n.3
Nazar Ahari, Shiva 26, 30
neoliberalism 37, 49
New York Review of Books 32
New York Times 75, 139, 152, 168
non-binary and queer folks 10
"non-legitimate" women 124
Norouzi, Kambiz 26, 30, 31
Norouzi, Shaghayegh 75, 80, 87
noumenon 92

Occupy Movement, the 64
Olwan, Dana M. 44, 217 n.17, 217 n.18

Omar, Ilhan 33, 211 n.3, 214 n.25, 214 n.26
O'Reilly, Bill 162
Orgad, Shani 90, 228 n.9
outsider 123, 128, 131–3, 235 n.5

Page, Ruth 115, 233 n.35, 233 n.36
Pahlavi, Reza Shah 14, 16, 41
Pahlavi decadence 16, 18
Pahlavi era 47
Pahlavi reign, second (1941–79) 16
Paidar, Parvin 46, 47, 218 n.30
Pakistan 9, 44, 161, 163, 165–6, 175, 200, 245 n.11
Palestine 9, 161, 163, 170–1
Panida 93, 94
parrhesia 114, 121
patriarchalism 171
  and Islamism 179–86, 190, 191
  sexual molestation 198
  socialists 193
patriarchy 4, 27, 30
  and capitalism 104
  destruction of 36
  gendered sociocultural 30
  and masculinity 143–6
  patriarchal societies 4, 5, 144, 147
  retrograde religious 36
patriotic womanhood 41
Pease, Bob 146, 238 n.4, 239 n.15, 241 n.54, 242 n.57
Pedarian, Morteza 26
perpetrators xii, xiii, xiv, 4, 21, 28–31, 51, 54, 55, 58, 63, 89, 99, 102, 104, 125, 130, 131, 135, 136, 138–48, 150, 152, 165, 167, 176, 177, 199, 243 n.8
petit-bourgeois 99
PettyJohn, Morgan E. 138, 239 n.22
Phelan, Shane 132, 237 n.31
phenomenology 92
phenomenon xvii, 37, 44, 92, 111, 117, 121, 122, 145, 181, 188
physical abuse 12, 201
Pinkwashing the Honour Crime 44
polemic 33
political correctness 90
political economy 7, 9, 50, 89–105, 192–5, 201, 221 n.32

pornography 181, 186–9, 191, 193, 196, 200–2
positive masculinity study 147
post-structure 93
Preservation of Dignity and Protection of Women against Violence xv
Prohibition of Domestic Violence Campaign 91, 228 n.10
proletarian 90
protective masculinity 16
protector/guardianship 15, 16, 35
psychoanalytical term 92

Qajar era (late nineteenth century) 15
Qajar paintings 13
Quan-Haase, Anabel 76, 77, 226 n.8, 226 n.11, 233 n.29
Qur'an 36, 46, 61, 65, 66, 73, 150, 163, 181–5, 196, 206 n.13, 223 n.58, 223 n.59, 243 n.6

Rahimi, Hourieh 91
Rahimi, Hussein 98
Rahimi, Paria 9, 228 n.11
rape
  capital punishment for 23, 29
  as 'corruption on Earth' 28, 29
  criminalization 32
  Emamverdi's case 74, 97–104
  marital 25, 84, 118, 119
  military 75
  public conversation 28
  punishment 29
rape culture 31, 32, 55, 63, 64, 69, 75, 80, 84, 116, 138, 233 n.41
Ratcliffe, Krista 51, 52, 220 n.55, 220 n.56
re-Islamization policies 46
religious exclusivism 23
Research Center for Women and Family in Tehran 12
revolutionary masculinity 18–20
Rezai, Yasamin 8, 226 n.3
rhetorical listening
  definition 51
  gendered and sexual violence, Iranian feminism 40–2
  steps 52
  transnational feminism, Iranian

anti-fundamentalist 45–8
anti-imperialist 48–50
anti-neoliberalist 50
human rights–based 43–5
Ricoeur, Paul 92, 228 n.13
Rostampour, Somayeh 9
Rudakoff, Judith 73, 225 n.2, 226 n.5, 226 n.6

Sadeghipouya, Mahdis 9
sadistic personality disorder 98
Sadr, Shadi 45
Salesman, The (Farhadi) 154
sameness 43
same-sex
  desires 49
  practices 13
  relationships 131
Sami Azar, Alireza 97
Sanij, Neda 11, 208 n.1
Savadi, Samaneh 26, 31, 32, 213 n.14
scholastic field 99
Sedaghat Payam, Mehdy 8
"self-hating Muslim" 26
semantic network analysis 77
Sepehri Far, Tara 151, 153, 243 n.11, 244 n.22
sexism 162, 163, 171, 179, 181, 186–92, 200–3
sex-segregation policies 17
sexual assault xi, 2, 3, 7, 9, 10, 27
  awareness 74
  child 73
  Emamverdi's case 28, 29, 97–104
  force in 104
  Islamic solutions, prevention 72
  Latin America 43
  testifies 45
  unequal power relations 104
  women journalists 74
sexual desire 13, 18, 20
Sexual Economy of the Islamic Republic, The 47
sexual harassment 2, 4, 5, 6, 8, 162
  Afghan women, Iran 119
  anonymity of accusers 30, 31
  awareness campaigns 29
  criminalization 25, 32
  digital campaign 91

disclosing stories 114, 115
Iran 13
Iranian white-collar men 141–2
justice 27
of low-paid women 89
middle-class women 162–3
Namjoo's case 93–5
normalization of 11–21
public conversation 28
social marginalization and ostracization 27
Tehran's public spaces 11
Twitter 30
workplace 89, 90, 118
sexual violence xii, xix, 1, 3, 4, 8
  as inadvertent offences 145–6
  lesbians
    exclusion from debates 124–5, 127, 131, 133, 134
    experience of 124, 127–31
    as lesbophobic punishment 130
    male impunity 135
    myths 128
Shad, Luna 93
Shafi, Meeshah 165
Shahidian, Hamed 48
Shakhsari, Sima 44, 49, 50, 217 n.19, 219 n.47, 219 n.48, 219 n.49, 231 n.4
sharia-derived legal system 25
Shia Islam 23, 32, 35, 36, 45
Showkaran (Hemlock 1998) 19, 20
sigheh marriages (temporary marriages) 19, 20, 67
sin 20
Sisyphean circulation 96
SMOs *see* Social Movement Organizations
Sobhani, Arash 75
social and moral order 18
social capital xiii, 2, 95, 99, 100, 101, 102
social class 91, 141, 146–8
social formation 94
socialism 192–5
social justice 36, 51
  divine-oriented 30
social media xii, xiii, 1, 2, 4, 6, 8, 9, 11, 23, 24, 39, 51, 54, 71–9, 83, 86, 88, 97, 103, 107–9, 111, 118, 124, 125, 135, 136, 138, 139, 141, 149, 153, 161, 164, 166, 168, 170, 187, 205 n.4, 211 n.2,

217 n.20, 226 n.8, 231 n.9, 232 n.20, 232 n.23, 233 n.29, 233 n.35, 233 n.39
anonymity of 30, 34, 64, 73–5, 82, 91, 97, 98, 113–17, 164, 167, 211 n.2
hashtag activism 76, 77, 226 n.9, 226 n.12, 226 n.16, 227 n.2, 227 n.18, 227 n.19, 227 n.20, 232 n.25
LGBTQ community 76
Toussi's case 73, 74
victim blaming 75, 80–4, 87, 114
see also Instagram; Twitter
Social Movement Organizations (SMOs) 77, 78, 79, 88
social network 77, 95, 101, 102, 120, 139, 141, 152, 154
societal hierarchy 4, 94, 99, 102
speaking out 74, 82, 114, 115, 123, 125, 169, 233 n.34
Spelman, Elizabeth 132, 237 n.32
Spotify 94
state brutality 12
state feminism 41
street harassment, female students 12–13
structuralist 92, 94
structures of power 53, 62, 65, 68, 69
subaltern population 117–20
subordinated masculinity 16
subordination, female body 3, 5
Sunna, the 36
superstructure 94
Sutherland, Edwin H. 140, 240 n.31
Swartz, David 96, 97
symbolic, the 94, 95, 99, 100, 102, 103, 104
symbolic capital 93–100, 102–5, 140, 229 n.38, 229 n.40, 230 n.50
symbol of defiance 18
symptomatic reading 9, 89–105, 228 n.17, 228 n.18, 228 n.20
 Capital 95
 deconstruction 92–3
 latent meanings 92
 and Marxism 92
 social order 91

taboo-breaking, the xiii, xvi, 159
Taliaat 170
Tavakoli-Targhi, Mohamad 14
Tehrani woman, prototype of 16

Tehran University 27, 74, 98, 99
theory of capital 94
theory of practice 97, 102
Tizro, Zahra 45, 60, 61
 Domestic Violence in Iran: Women, Marriage and Islam 2, 4, 206 n.2, 207 n.7, 207 n.11, 216 n.3, 218 n.29, 220 n.5, 221 n.7, 222 n.37, 222 n.47, 222 n.48, 222 n.49, 222 n.50, 222 n.51, 223 n.56, 223 n.57, 223 n.61, 223 n.65
Tohidi, Nayereh 48
Toptas, Hasan Ali 167
Torabi, Maryamossadat 45
tough guy *(lūtī)* 16
Tourage, Mahdi 8, 223 n.58
Toussi, Saeed 73–5
trace xii, 26, 71, 92, 93, 100, 103, 120, 161, 234 n.52
trace publics 120, 234 n.52
transnational feminism
 anti-fundamentalist 45–8
 anti-imperialist 48–50
 anti-neoliberalist 50
 human rights–based 43–5
Transnational Feminist Network (TFN) 49
transsexualities 49
Trump, Donald 162
Truth, Sojourner 128
Tunisia 9, 161, 163, 166, 171, 175, 181, 245 n.14
Turkey 6, 9, 161, 167, 171, 175
Twitter 8, 24, 25, 33
 confirmation, sexual crime 30
 data analysis, #MeTooIran
 categories 81–4
 content words 86
 educational 82
 frequent terms 84–6
 methodologies 77–8
 Namjoo's case 75–6
 narrative 82
 scraping 79–81
 semantic network analysis 77
 support 81–2
 uncategorized 82, 83
 victim blaming 82, 83, 87
#MosqueMeToo 73, 74, 169, 215 n.35, 226 n.4

political and social atmosphere,
  Iran 78–9
public testimonies 26, 30

UDHR *see* Universal Declaration of
  Human Rights
ultraconservatism 36
Ummah (society/community) 18
UN Commission on the Status of Women
  (CSW) 43
Unequal power relationships 4
UN Fourth World Conference on Women
  45
UN International Conference on
  Population and Development (ICPD)
  45
United States xii, xvi, 1, 32, 34, 55, 57, 72,
  78, 128, 153, 161, 162, 192, 202, 211
  n.3, 227 n.21
Universal Declaration of Human Rights
  (UDHR) 43
universal human values 23
University of Mazandaran 12, 208 n.5
University of Tehran 27, 74, 98, 99,
  228 n.11
urban-driven elitism 28
urbanization 16
urban women 16, 117, 162

victim blaming xiii, 11, 30, 39, 75, 80–4,
  87, 114, 205 n.3
violence
  bad-hijab woman 19
  colonial/imperial 40
  gendered and domestic, Iranian
    feminism 40–2
  historical justification 162–4
  see also gender-based violence
visuality 13–14
visual power relation 15
Vivienne, Sonja 108, 113, 231 n.8, 231
  n.10, 233 n.28

Wacquant, Loïc 96
Washington Examiner 162
Washington Post 32, 33
Webber, Max 94

Weblogistan 49, 107
Weinstein, Harvey xii, 57, 74, 90, 96, 162
Westernization 16
Western male gaze 14
white-collar
  male violence 140–2
  masculinities 9, 135–48, 240 n.38
Wittig, Monique 127, 235 n.14, 236 n.18
women
  ban from stadium 19
  de-stigmatization of 31
  disempowerment of 190
  employment status 47
  men's abuse 174–8
  oppression on 24, 46, 73, 118, 120
  as the protected 15
  public molestation 10, 161, 168, 175–8,
    195–8, 200–2
  and religion 48
  rights, protection of 29
  rights and well-being 33
  sigheh 19
  violence against 39
  vulnerability to sexual exploitation 118
  see also lesbian
Women, State, and Ideology in Iran 46
Women's Awakening 14, 41
Women's Socio-cultural Council 35

xenophobia 33
Xiong, Ying 76–8

Yaghoobi, Claudia 19, 20, 47, 66, 67, 207
  n.4, 207 n.10, 210 n.40, 210 n.41, 210
  n.42, 210 n.43, 210 n.44, 210 n.45,
  216 n.3, 218 n.33, 223 n.72, 224 n.95,
  225 n.100, 225 n.102, 242 n.5
YouTube 33

Zafar, Ali 165, 166
Zaki, Bassam 168
Zanan Emrooz 26, 27
Zehtabi, Maryam 9
Zendegi-ye Khosusi (Private Life 2011)
  19, 20
Žižek, Slavoj xvi, 90, 205 n.9,
  228 n.8

www.ingramcontent.com/pod-product-compliance
Lightning Source LLC
Chambersburg PA
CBHW070749020526
44115CB00032B/1600